ANCIENT GREEK AND ROMAN BRONZES

BY

WINIFRED LAMB, M.A.

KEEPER OF THE GREEK AND ROMAN DEPARTMENT, FITZWILLIAM MUSEUM
CAMBRIDGE

Enlarged Edition with a Foreword and Reference Bibliography

by

LENORE KEENE CONGDON

WITH 96 PLATES AND 37 ILLUSTRATIONS IN THE TEXT

ARGONAUT, INC., PUBLISHERS
CHICAGO   MCMLXIX

Library of Congress Catalogue Card No. 67-17575

First Printing: May, 1969

FOREWORD

Some of the most beautiful objects in museums are the smaller sculptures and utensils which were closely associated with the daily life of the Greek and Roman people. The spectator who discovers these frequently overlooked articles soon finds himself admiring the taste and fine craftsmanship evinced in many of them. Through study of the minor objects one can achieve a better understanding f the artists or craftsmen of their time than is often possible with the more famous major works of art. One reason for this is that the large sculptures were often melted down, broken or burned either accidentally or purposely for their metallic or lime content. The smaller, usually less important, items have been considerably more fortunate, partly because of their greater numbers and partly because many of them were placed in tombs and thus were preserved. It is rare for even the better museums to have any major original Greek sculpture; however in many secondary collections at least a few of the lesser objects occur. These smaller sculptures and implements were crafted in various materials, bronze being one of the more common. Miss Lamb's book deals exclusively with the small bronzes.

These Greek and Roman bronzes, so attractive to the eye of the ordinary beholder, are of very great value to the art historian since the designs and figures utilized were often based on or copied from now missing works of art. Through such objects it is possible to understand and often illustrate the artistic trends and metal working techniques of a particular period far more completely than from the large sculptures. which too often suffered destruction to the point where complete sequences of originals are very rare. Further, the small bronzes permit one to trace the development of a particular motif (i.e. the Gorgon head) or object (such as hand mirrors) or to observe the growth and influence of particular artists or artistic schools (for example, the followers of Polykleitos; the development of the Pergamene school).

Winifred Lamb's opus is one of the most extensive works on small sculptural and decorative bronzes written to date. The book was published originally in 1929, at the end of an era of meticulously detailed studies of various historical problems of art; the great majority of her statements remain valid today. Her coverage, which includes the general development of bronzes from pre-Hellenic to Roman times and studies of individual object groupings or types, is still unsurpassed in thoroughness by the handful of more recent writers who have undertaken the problem.

Two important additions appear in this reissue.First. a bibliography has been compiled from Miss Lamb's wealth of copious but often incomplete or now obscure footnotes. This material has been arranged by chapters, identifying and completing most of her references to assist those wishing to work with her source material. Secondly, a select bibliography on small bronzes has been developed, organized into seven categories such as general publications, technical reports, bronze types and chronological groupings. This covers much of what has been written in this field from 1929 to 1966, as well as some supplementary general references prior to 1929. With these additions, it is hoped that the reissue of Winifred Lamb's *Greek and Roman Bronzes* will be useful not only as a re-presentation of an outstanding text, but also as a source of reasonably complete bibliographical reference material for scholars working in the field of ancient bronze.

LENORE O. KEENE CONGDON

Pittsfield, Mass. 1969

PREFACE

THIS book is intended both for those who want an account of the general development of Greek and Roman bronzes, and for those who seek information on some particular group. The former will find what they need at the beginning of each chapter; the latter can look up the group that concerns them under its own heading. Those who are sufficiently interested in the subject to read the whole book may complain that the treatment is inconsistent : such inconsistency is, however, inevitable, for what is important in one period is not necessarily so in the next.

The bronzes that have been chosen for discussion fall into two classes, figures on the one hand, decorative bronzes on the other. Only the smaller figures are included : life-sized bronzes are omitted, as well as bronzes over one metre high. The sections on decorative bronzes deal with reliefs, engravings, and such objects as are not purely utilitarian : bronze vases are given a place, since their shapes are not only beautiful in themselves, but also reflect the taste of the periods to which they belong.

Besides expressing my own views, I have endeavoured to put students in touch with what has been already written by other scholars, and, especially, to point out any object or group of objects that has received particular attention. Unfortunately, this involves the risk of spoiling the proportions of the book, for my predecessors have not been impartial : while certain aspects of the subject have been discussed again and again, by different archæologists, with different results, others have been almost completely ignored. For instance, countless pages have been written about the Argivo-Corinthian reliefs, whereas hardly anything is known about the dating of Roman statuettes.

The footnotes will show that most of the literature on both figures and decorative bronzes is contained in learned periodicals or accounts of excavated sites. Three books are, however, invaluable : Neugebauer's *Antike Bronzestatuetten*, Langlotz' *Frühgriechische Bildhauerschulen*, and G. M. Richter's *Catalogue of Bronzes in the Metropolitan Museum*. An excellent summary of the literary evidence will be found in the introduction to Walters' *Catalogue of Bronzes in the British Museum*, while technical questions (which, in the following pages are not treated separately, but in connection with particular objects) can be studied at length in Vol. I of Lehmann-Hartleben and Klüge's *Die antiken Grossbronzen*.

It is a pleasure to acknowledge the help this book has received from others.

I should like, in the first place, to thank Mr. Walters and Mr. Forsdyke for facilities for studying the bronzes at the British Museum : I am especially indebted to Mr. Walters for allowing me to publish the hydria on Plate LVIII and to Mr. Forsdyke for valuable advice and criticism.

I am, moreover, under a particular debt to Dr. Kastriotis for permission to illustrate certain unpublished bronzes at Athens, particularly those on Plates XLVI *a* and LX *b*, as well as for affording me every opportunity of examining the collection: also to Mlle. Pappaspiridou for her unfailing courtesy in giving me access to and information about the bronzes.

I am also deeply indebted to Professor Dr. Neugebauer for help in connection with the bronzes at Berlin.

I should like to add my thanks to M. Michon at the Louvre, to M. Babelon at the Bibliothèque Nationale, to Professor Dr. Sieveking at Munich, to Hofrat Dr. Bankö at Vienna, to Dr. Doro Levi at Florence, to Dr. Mingazzini at Naples, to Dr. Xanthoudides at Candia, and to Miss Richter at New York for the kindness received at their hands.

Permission to reproduce illustrations has been given by Sir Arthur Evans, Geheimrat Professor Dr. Pernice, M. Salomon Reinach, Professor Dr. Sieveking : also by the British School at Athens (for the *Annual of the British School*), the Hellenic Society (for the *Journal of Hellenic Studies*), the Académie des Inscriptions et Belles Lettres (for the two works published by Leroux : see below), the Deutsches Archaeologisches Institut (for *Athenische Mitteilungen*), the Bibliothèque d'Art et d'Archéologie (for Perdrizet, *Bronzes . . . de la Collection Fouquet*), and the Reale Accademia dei Lincei (for *Notizie degli Scavi*).

The following publishers have sanctioned reproductions from the works specified, for further acknowledgments of which, see list of illustrations :—

Beck (Furtwängler, *Kleine Schriften*).
Bestetti & Tumminelli (*Bolletino d'Arte*).
Boccard (*Fouilles de Delphes*).
Cambridge University Press (Cook, *Zeus*, I).
de Gruyter (Gerhard, *Etruskische Spiegel* and Pernice, *Hellenistische Kunst in Pompei*).
Hoepli (*Monumenti dei Lincei*).
Leroux (de Ridder, *Catalogue de la Collection de Clercq* and *Monuments Piot*).
Macmillan & Co. (*Annual of the British School at Athens ; Journal of Hellenic Studies ;* Evans, *Palace of Minos;* Bosanquet and Dawkins, *Palaikastro*).

Oxford University Press (Stuart-Jones and others,
Catalogue of the Conservatori Museum).
Quaritch (Evans, *Prehistoric Tombs of Knossos*).
Springer (Furtwängler, *Olympia IV*).

Professor Dr. Karo, Dr. Langlotz, Mr. Charles Seltman, and the Hellenic Society have generously lent me
photographs and drawings.   Miss Mary MacNeill has
helped me with the indexing.   My warmest thanks
are   due   to   those   who   have   read   my   manuscript :
Mr. G. M. Young, Prof. Bernard Ashmole, and Dr. A. B.
Cook.
                                                            W. L.

April, 1929

NOTE ON THE SPELLING OF GREEK WORDS
AND PLACE-NAMES

INCONSISTENCY is inevitable, for in some cases
an English version is offensive, while in others a
Greek version is pedantic.   My system is to adopt
the Greek version where possible, and the English
where imposed by long use.   Therefore, *Menelaion*
and *Argive Heraeum* may occur on the same page.
    Another inconsistency is occasioned by the itali-
cising of foreign words.   I have used Roman letters
for those which, like " chiton " and " Kouros," have
been adopted by archæologists into their vocabulary.

CONTENTS

CHAPTER I

THE PREHISTORIC PERIOD

PAGE

A. Utensils and Decorative Work 1
B. Statuettes 18

CHAPTER II

THE SUB-MYCENEAN, TRANSITIONAL AND GEOMETRIC PERIODS

A. Sub-Mycenean and Transitional Period 31
B. Geometric Period 36

CHAPTER III

THE EARLY ARCHAIC (ORIENTALISING) PERIOD, *c.* 700-575 B.C.

A. Early Decorative Work, Vases, etc. 53
B. Statuettes 73

CHAPTER IV

THE SIXTH CENTURY: STATUETTES

. . 81

CHAPTER V

THE SIXTH CENTURY: DECORATIVE WORK AND UTENSILS IN BRONZES

A. Reliefs 113
B. Figures cut out from a Sheet of Bronze 124
C. Greek and Etruscan Mirrors 125
D. Paterae 131
E. Tripods 131
F. Bronze Vases 133
G. Candelabra 140

CHAPTER VI

THE EARLIER FIFTH CENTURY

PAGE

A. Statuettes 141
B. Decorative Work, Vases, etc. 158

CHAPTER VII

THE LATER FIFTH AND THE FOURTH CENTURY

A. Statuettes 167
B. Decorative Work, Vases, etc. · 174

CHAPTER VIII

THE HELLENISTIC PERIOD, OR THE HELLENISTIC TRADITION

A. Statuettes 195
B. Decorative Work, Vases, etc. 210

CHAPTER IX

ROMAN BRONZES

A. Statuettes 216
B. Decorative Work, Vases, etc. 233

SUBJECT INDEX 247
MUSEUM INDEX 257

LIST OF ILLUSTRATIONS
IN THE TEXT

CHAPTER I

FIG.   PAGE
1. Sword from Tomb 44, Knossos. (From Evans, *Prehistoric Tombs of Knossos*, p. 62, Fig. 66) 11
2. Bronze ewers. (From drawings by Piet de Jong and C. Waterhouse.) (*a*) *Palaikastro*, I, Pl. XXVI. (*b*) From Evans, *Prehistroic Tombs*, p. 40, Fig. 36. (*c*) From Mycenae. (*d*) From *B.S.A.*, 1903, p. 122, Fig. 76 *a* . 13
3. (*a*) Lamp from tomb at Knossos. (From Evans, *Prehistoric Tombs*, p. 39, Fig. 35 *a* and *b*.) (*b*) Tripod from tomb at Knossos. (From Evans, *Prehistoric Tombs*, p. 42, Fig. 38.) (*c*) Basin from Tylissos. (From 'Εφ. 'Αρχ., 1912, p. 221, Fig. 30.) (*d*) Bowl from Knossos. (From *B.S.A.*, 1903, p. 128, Figs. 82 and 83.) (*e*) Clay tablet from Knossos. (From *B.S.A.*, 1903, p. 128, Fig. 84) . 14
4. Bowl with leaf ornament from Knossos. (From *Prehistoric Tombs*, p. 122, Fig. 116) 15
5. Bronzes from Palaikastro. (From *Palaikastro*, p. 122, Figs. 101, 102 and 103). 17

CHAPTER II

1. Animal shapes cut out of a sheet of bronze. (From *Olympia*, IV, Pl. X, Nos. 90, 91) 39
2. Animals made out of a folded sheet of bronze. (From *Olympia*, IV, Pl. X, Nos. 96, 97) 39
3. Dappled horse from Olympia. (From *Olympia*, IV, Pl. XII, No. 200 *a*) 40
4. Bull from Olympia. (From *Olympia*, IV, Pl. XII, No. 187) . 40
5. Geometric tripods. (From *Olympia*, IV, Pl. XXXIV) . . 45
6. Fibula, in Munich. (From *Jahrbuch*, 1916, p. 297, Fig. 3) . 48
7. Fibulae, in Munich. (From *Jahrbuch*, 1916, Pls. 17 and 18) . 51

CHAPTER III

1. Early engraving from the Acropolis. (From *J.H.S.*, XIII, p. 245, Fig. 17) 58
2. Early relief from Olympia. (From *Olympia*, IV, Pl. XXXVII, No. 694) 59
3. Mitra from Rethymno. (From *Ath. Mit.*, 1906, Pl. 23) . 61
4. Breastplate from the River Alpheois. (From *Olympia*, IV, Pl. LIX) 63

PAGE

FIG.
5. Fragment from the Acropolis. (From *J.H.S.*, XIII, p. 259,
   Fig. 26).   65
6. Fragment from the Acropolis. (From *J.H.S.*, XIII, p. 268,
   Fig. 32).   66
7. Phialae from Olympia. (From *Olympia*, IV, Pl. LII) .   .   69
8. The La Garenne tripod. (From *Olympia*, IV, p. 115) .   .   72

CHAPTER IV

1. Calf from Olympia. (From *Olympia*, IV, Pl. LVI, No. 961)   105

CHAPTER V

1. Bronze of Argivo-Corinthian type from the Acropolis, Athens.
   (From a drawing by C. Waterhouse).   .   .   .   113
2. Argivo-Corinthian relief. (From *Olympia*, IV, Pl. XXXIX,
   No. 699 a)   115
3. Argivo-Corinthian relief. (From *Ath. Mit.*, 1895, Pl. XIV)   117
4. Etruscan mirror in the British Museum. (From Gerhard,
   Klügmann and Körte, *Etruskische Spiegel*, V, Pl. 14) .   130
5. Italian amphora from Cumae. (From a drawing by Piet de
   Jong after *M.d.L.*, XXII, Pl. LXXVI)   .   .   .   138

CHAPTER VI

1. Mirror from Locri Epizephyrii. (From *Notizie degli Scavi*,
   1914, Supp., p. 18, Fig. 18)   159
2. Mirror of Peloponnesian type from Sparta. (From *B.S.A.*,
   XXVI, p. 272, Fig. 6)   160

CHAPTER VII

1. Engraved mirror in the Louvre. (From Pfuhl, *Malerei und
   Zeichnung der Griechen*, III, p. 252, Fig. 624)   .   179
2. Kylix of " Galaxidhi Type." (From a drawing by C. Waterhouse)   186
3. Typical Etruscan cista. (From a drawing by Piet de Jong) .   189
4. Engraving from the Ficoroni cista. (From Pfuhl, *op. cit.*,
   p. 253, 4, Fig. 628)   190
5. (a) Etruscan mirror in New York. (From Gerhard, Klügmann
   and Körte, *Etruskische Spiegel*, V, Pl. 107.) (b) Praenestine mirror in London. (From Gerhard, *Etruskische
   Spiegel*, Pl. 399)   192
6. Typical Etruscan pointed situla. (From a drawing by Piet
   de Jong)   193

CHAPTER IX

1. Dispater and wheel. (From A. B. Cook, *Zeus*, I, Fig. 208)   .   231
2. Heads by Gaulish artists at St. Germain-en-Laye. (From
   Reinach, *Antiquités Nationales*, Nos. 217, 219) .   .   232
3. Saucepans from the workshop of C. Cipius Polybius. (From
   Willers, *Neue Untersuchungen*, Fig. 44, p. 77) .   .   243

LIST OF PLATES
AT THE END OF THE BOOK

PLATE

I. Inlaid dagger from Mycenae. (From *Drawings by M. Emile Gilliéron*.)

II. Daggers from Mycenae. (From Ἀθηναῖον, X.)

III. Dagger from Crete. (From Evans, *Palace of Minos*, I, p. 718, Fig. 541.) Swords from Mycenae. (From Ἀθηναῖον, X.)

IV. (a) and (b) Primitive figures from Phylakopi and Troy II. (c) and (d) Cretan worshippers, at Vienna and Cambridge.

V. (a) and (b) Worshipper from Anatoli, in British Museum. (c) and (d) Worshipper from Tylissos, at Candia.

VI. Bull and acrobat in the Spencer-Churchill Collection. (*Photo, Hellenic Society*.)

VII. Women worshippers: (a) At Berlin. (b) and (c) From Hagia Triadha, at Candia.

VIII. Worshippers: (a) From Tylissos, at Candia. (b) From the Harbour Town, at Candia. (c) At Leyden.

IX. Worshippers: (a) From Gournia, at Candia. (b) and (c) At Berlin. (d) At Vienna.

X. (a) Sub-Mycenaean bowl from Cyprus, in the Cyprus Museum. (From *B.S.A.*, XVIII, Pl. VIII.) (b) Tripod from Cyprus, at New York.

XI. Proto-Geometric tripods from Athens: (a) From grave on Pnyx. (b) From Tiryns.

XII. (a) Stand from Larnaka, at Berlin. (b) Stand from Enkomi, in the British Museum.

XIII. Geometric objects, at Cambridge. (a) Ducklings. (b) Ring, birds, pendants, and bead. (c) Animals on stands.

XIV. (a) Mare and a foal from Olympia, at Athens. (b) Deer and fawn from Olympia, at Athens.

XV. Geometric warriors. (a) From Athens. (b) and (c) From Olympia. (d) From Delphi. (From *Fouilles de Delphes*, V, Pl. I, 7.)

XVI. (a) Charioteer from Olympia, at Athens. (b) Women dancing from Olympia, at Athens.

XVII. Bronzes in the North Greek style: (a) From Thermon. (b) From Kardhitza. (c) From Delphi.

XVIII. (a) Cretan shield in Candia. (b) Tyszkiewicz Plate. (From Fröhner, *Collection Tyszkiewicz*, Pl. XV.)

b

PLATE
XIX. Figures of huntsmen from Crete, in the Louvre. (*Photo,*
    Giraudon.)
XX. Early male figures: (*a*) and (*b*) From Athens. (*c*) From
    Boeotia. (From Fröhner, *Collection Tyszkiewicz*, Pl.
    XLV.)
XXI. Early Kouroi: (*a*) From Crete. (*b*) From Delphi. (*c*)
    At Stockholm.
XXII. Early Korai: (*a*) From Sparta. (From *B.S.A.*, XV, Pl. X.
    Photo, Hellenic Society.) (*b*) From Boeotia. (From
    Sale Catalogue of the Tyszkiewicz Collection, Pl. XIII.)
    (*c*) From Ephesus.
XXIII. (*a*) Bronzes from Sparta. (From *B.S.A.*, XV, Pl. IX.)
    (*b*) Protome from the Acropolis, Athens.
XXIV. (*a*) and (*b*) Early Etruscan figures from Brolio. (*Photos,*
    Brogi.) (*c*) and (*d*) Candelabrum from Vetulonia, at
    Florence.
XXV. Cretan bronzes: (*a*) and (*c*) In the Louvre. (*Photos,*
    Giraudon.) (*b*) At Berlin.
XXVI. (*a*) and (*b*) Herakles, at Cassel. (*c*) Zeus Lykaios, at Athens.
XXVII. Spartan bronzes: (*a*) At Vienna. (*b*) At Athens. (*c*) At
    Sparta.
XXVIII. (*a*) Soldier from Lakonia, at Athens. (*b*) Soldier from
    Messenia, at Athens. (*c*) Zeus from Olympia, at Athens.
    (*d*) Artemis from Olympia, at Athens.
XXIX. Arcadian bronzes: (*a*) Hermes, at Athens. (*b*) Shepherd,
    at Berlin. (*c*) and (*d*) Man with fox, at Berlin.
XXX. Arcadian bronzes: (*a*) Goddess from Tegea, at Athens.
    (*b*) and (*c*) Artemis from Lousoi, at Frankfurt-am-
    Main.
XXXI. Arcadian bronzes: (*a*) Shepherd, at Athens. (*b*) Peasant,
    at Berlin. (*c*) Peasant, at Athens. (*d*) Dead fox, at
    Athens.
XXXII. (*a*) Statuette by Hybrisstas, in the Dutuit Collection.
    (*Photo, Giraudon.*) (*b*) Rider from Dodona, at Athens.
    (*c*) Flute player from Dodona, at Athens.
XXXIII. Girl athletes: (*a*) From Albania. (*Photo, Mansell.*) (*b*)
    From Dodona.
XXXIV. Kouroi: (*a*) From Longa, at Athens. (*b*) From the Ptoön,
    at Athens. (*c*) From Naxos, at Berlin. (*d*) From
    Dodona, in the Louvre. (*Photo, Giraudon.*)
XXXV. (*a*) and (*b*) Goddess, in the Fitzwilliam Museum. (*c*) Female
    figure from the Ptoön, at Athens. (*d*) Artemis Daida-
    leia, at Boston.
XXXVI. Ionian bronzes: (*a*) Kouros, at Delphi. (From *Fouilles de*
    Delphes, V, Pl. I, 6.) (*b*) Kore from the Acropolis, at
    Athens. (*c*) Female figure from Olympia, at Athens.
XXXVII. Athenian bronzes: (*a*) Athena. (*b*) Kore. (*c*) Kouros.
XXXVIII. (*a*) Pegasus from the Acropolis, at Athens. (*b*) Horse from
    Dodona, in the Louvre.
XXXIX. (*a*) Centaur from the Acropolis, in the Bibliothèque Nation-
    ale. (*Photo, Giraudon.*) (*b*) Horseman from Grumen-
    tum, in the British Museum. (*Photo, British Museum.*)

PLATE

XL. Etruscan bronzes : (a) Priest (?), at Florence. (b) Youth, in the British Museum. (*Photo, Mansell.*) (c) Herakles, at Este. (From *Bolletino d'Arte, Anno* III, *Serie* II, p. 454, Fig. 4.)

XLI. Etruscan bronzes : (a) Female figure, in the Bibliothèque Nationale. (*Photo, Giraudon.*) (b) Ajax stabbing himself, at Florence. (c) Female figure from Perugia, in the British Museum. (*Photo, Mansell.*)

XLII. (a) Helmet from Axos, at Candia. (*Photo, Maraghiannis.*) (b) Relief from the Acropolis. (*Photo, Hellenic Society,* from *J.H.S.*, XIII, Pl. VIII.)

XLIII. (a) Archer from Olympia, at Athens. (b) Detail of hydria, at Munich.

XLIV. (a) Mirror handle, in the Louvre. (b) Athena from the Acropolis, at Athens. (c) Mirror handle, at Berlin. (d) Patera handle, at Cambridge.

XLV. (a) Tripod from Metaponto, at Berlin. (b) Tripod from Vulci, in the British Museum. (*Photo, Mansell.*)

XLVI. (a) Jug from Corinth, at Athens. (b) Hydria from Randazzo, at Berlin.

XLVII. (a) Crater, at Munich. (b) Plate, at Berlin.

XLVIII. (a) Vase from Capua, in the British Museum. (*Photo, Mansell.*) (b) The Grächwyl hydria, at Berne.

XLIX. (a) The Monteleone Chariot, at New York. (b) Vase from Capodimonte, at Florence. (c) Relief, at Munich.

L. Relief from tripod, in the Loeb Collection. (From *A.J.A.*, 1908, Pl. XV.)

LI. (a) Apollo, at Delphi. (From *Fouilles de Delphes*, V, Pl. V.) (b) Kanephoros from Paestum, at Berlin. (c) Armed runner, at Tübingen.

LII. (a) Youth from Ligourio, at Berlin. (b) Youth from Corfu, in the British Museum. (*Photo, Mansell.*) (c) Dionysos, in the Louvre. (*Photo, Giraudon.*) (d) Discobolos, at New York.

LIII. Athenian bronzes : (a) Woman dancing from the Acropolis. (b) Athlete, in the Louvre. (*Photo, Giraudon.*) (c) Discobolos from the Acropolis.

LIV. (a) Zeus from Dodona, at Berlin. (b) Pan from Arcadia, at Berlin.

LV. (a) Girl with dove from Thessaly. (b) Girl spinning.

LVI. South Italy and Sparta : (a) Athlete from Aderno. (b) Athlete, at New York. (c) Trumpeter from Sparta.

LVII. Arcadia : (a) Artemis, at Berlin. (b) Hermes, at Athens. (c) Artemis, at Athens.

LVIII. Hydria, in the British Museum.

LIX. (a) Jug with Argive inscription, at New York. (b) Amphora, in the Vatican. (*Photo, Alinari.*)

LX. (a) Mirror, in the Louvre. (*Photo, Giraudon.*) (b) Mirror, at Athens. (c) Mirror and scent bottle, in the Louvre. (*Photo, Giraudon.*)

LXI. Bronzes after Polykleitos : (a) and (b) In the Louvre. (*Photos, Giraudon.*) (c) In the Bibliothèque Nationale. (*Photo, Giraudon.*)

PLATE
LXII. (*a*) Polykleitan Athlete, at Athens. (*b*) and (*c*) Bathing girl, at Munich. (*d*) Aphrodite, in the British Museum.

LXIII. (*a*) Zeus from Paramythia, in the British Museum. (*b*) Herakles, at Berlin. (*c*) Poseidon from Dodona, at Berlin.

LXIV. (*a*) Resting Maenad, at Berlin. (*b*) Relief from Lake Bracciano, in the British Museum.

LXV. Etruscan bronzes : (*a*) Fourth century Mars, in the British Museum. (*Photo, British Museum.*) (*b*) Fifth century Mars, at Florence. (*Photo, Alinari.*) (*c*) Minerva from Apiro, at Berlin.

LXVI. (*a*) Figures from lid of Ficoroni Cista. (*Photo, Alinari.*) (*b*) Etruscan woman, in the British Museum. (*Photo, Mansell.*)

LXVII. (*a*) Relief from Palestrina, in the Villa Guilia. (*Photo, Alinari.*) (*b*) One of the Siris bronzes, in the British Museum.

LXVIII. Mirrors from Vonitza, at New York.

LXIX. (*a*) Mirror with Pans quarrelling, at New York. (*b*) Engraved mirror-cover, in the British Museum. (*Photo, Mansell.*)

LXX. (*a*) South Italian mirror. (*b*) Medallions from harness.

LXXI. Hydriae, at Athens.

LXXII. Reliefs from the Perseus Pail, at Berlin.

LXXIII. (*a*) Pail, at Berlin. (*b*) Italian hydria, at Naples. (*Photo, Anderson.*)

LXXIV. (*a*) Negro minstrel, in the Bibliothèque Nationale. (*Photo, Giraudon.*) (*b*) Satyr from Pergamon, at Berlin. (*c*) Dancer, at Munich.

LXXV. (*a*) Gaulish slinger, at Berlin. (*b*) Gaul from Talamone, at Florence.

LXXVI. (*a*) Little girl with puppy, at New York. (*b*) Barbarian, in the Louvre. (*c*) Etruscan child, in the Vatican. (*Photo, Alinari.*)

LXXVII. (*a*) Sick man from the Wyndham Cook Collection. (From *Wyndham Cook Sale Catalogue*, Pl. XXX.) (*b*) Grotesque, at New York. (*c*) Beggar, at Berlin.

LXXVIII. (*a*) Old woman, at Vienna. (*b*) Philosopher, at New York. (*c*) Hellenistic ruler, at Naples. (*Photo, Alinari.*)

LXXIX. Bronzes from ship wrecked off Mahedia. (From *Monuments Piot*, 1910, Pls. I, II, III.)

LXXX. (*a*) Egyptian priest. (From Perdrizet, *Bronzes Grecs de la Collection Fouquet*, Pl. XXII.) (*b*) Minerva from Orte, in the Vatican. (*Photo, Alinari.*) (*c*) Poseidon, in Loeb Collection.

LXXXI. Vessels and tripod from Pompeii. (*Photos, Brogi.*)

LXXXII. Craters, at Naples. (*a*) (*Photo, Brogi.*) (*b*) (From Pernice, *Hellenistische Kunst in Pompei*, Pl. XI.)

LXXXIII. Etruscan Candelabra. (*a*) In the British Museum. (*b*) At Florence. (*Photo, Alinari.*) (*c*) In the Vatican.

LXXXIV. Hellenistic and Roman Candelabra, at Naples. (*a*) From Pernice, *op. cit.*, p. 43, Fig. 53. (*b*) and (*c*) *Photos, Brogi.* (*d*) From Pernice, *op. cit.*, p. 55, Fig. 73.

PLATE

LXXXV. Roman bronzes : (*a*) and (*c*) Lares, in the Louvre. (*Photos, Giraudon.*) (*b*) Roman sacrificing, in the British Museum.

LXXXVI. Roman bronzes: (*a*) Gaulish prisoner, in the British Museum. (*Photo, Hellenic Society.*) (*b*) Handle with barbarian woman, in the Louvre. (*Photo, Giraudon.*) (*c*) Roman priestess, in the British Museum. (*Photo, Hellenic Society.*)

LXXXVII. Bronzes after Polykleitos : (*a*) In the British Museum. (*b*) In the Bibliothèque Nationale. (*Photo, Giraudon.*)

LXXXVIII Archaistic bronzes : (*a*) Kore, in the British Museum. (*Photo, Mansell.*) (*b*) Hermes, at Boston. (*c*) Payne Knight Apollo, in the British Museum. (*Photo, Mansell.*)

LXXXIX. (*a*) Venus from Nocera. (*Photo, Alinari.*) (*b*) Venus of Syrian type. (From de Ridder, *Catalogue de la Collection de Clercq*, III, Pl. XXI.) (*c*) Cupid from Herculaneum. (From Comparetti and de Petra, *La Villa Hercolanese dei Pisoni*, Pl. XVI, 4.)

XC. (*a*) Archer from London, in the British Museum. (*b*) Jupiter Dolichenus from Lichtenberg, at Berlin.

XCI. Provincial bronzes : (*a*) Diana from Scheibbs, at Vienna. (*b*) Dispater from Gaul, in the British Museum. (*Photo, Mansell.*)

XCII. The Goddess Artio and Bear, at Berne.

XCIII. Inlaid couch, in the Conservatori. (From Stuart-Jones and Others, *Catalogue of the Conservatori Museum*, Pl. 63.)

XCIV. Handle with captive barbarians, in the Louvre. (*Photo, Giraudon.*)

XCV. (*a*) Crater from Boscoreale, at Berlin. (*b*) Pail from Pompeii, at Naples. (*Photo, Anderson.*)

XCVI. (*a*) Jug from Pompeii. (*Photo, Brogi.*) (*b*) Pail from Germany. (From Willers, *Neue Untersuchungen*, Pl. I, 2.) (*c*) Crater from Pompeii. (*Photo, Brogi.*) (*d*) Jug, in the Bibliothèque Nationale. (*Photo, Giraudon.*)

ABBREVIATIONS

Ann. d. I.	= Annali dell' Instituto.
Anz.	= Archäologischer Anzeiger (Beiblatt zum Jahrbuch).
Arch. Zeit.	= Archäologische Zeitung.
Ath. Mit.	= Mitteilungen des Deutschen Archäologischen Instituts, Athenische Abteilung.
B.C.H.	= Bulletin de Correspondance Hellénique.
B.S.A.	= Annual of the British School at Athens.
C.A.H.	= Cambridge Ancient History.
C.I.G.	= Corpus Inscriptionum Graecarum.
C.I.L.	= Corpus Inscriptionum Latinarum.
Comptes Rendus	= Comptes Rendus de l'Académie des Inscriptions.
Daremberg & Saglio	= Daremberg & Saglio, Dictionnaire des Antiquités.
Δελτίον	= Ἀρχαιολογικὸν Δελτίον. (1915 ff.)
Ducati, *E.A.*	= Ducati, *Etruria Antica.*
Ducati, *Storia*	= Ducati, *Storia del' Arte Etrusca.*
Ἐφ. Ἀρχ.	= Ἐφημερὶς Ἀρχαιολογική.
Führer	= Berlin, Führer durch das Antiquarium I (Bronzen).
I.G.	= Inscriptiones Graecae.
Jahrb.	= Jahrbuch des Deutschen Archäologischen Instituts.
Jahreshefte	= Jahreshefte des Oesterreichischen Archäologischen Institutes in Wien.
J.H.S.	= Journal of Hellenic Studies.
Mon. d. I. or *M. d. I.*	= Monumenti dell' Instituto di Corrispondenza Archeologica.
Naples, Guida	= Bassi, Gabrici and others, *Guida . . . del Museo Nazionale di Napoli.*
Neugebauer	= Neugebauer, *Antike Bronzestatuetten.*

P. of M.	= Evans, *Palace of Minos.*
Palaikastro	= Bosanquet and Dawkins, *The Unpublished Objects from the Palaikastro Excavations,* I
P.T.K.	= Evans, *Prehistoric Tombs of Knossos.*
Phylakopi	= Hellenic Society, Supplementary Papers 4. Excavations at Phylakopi in Melos.
Reinach, *Rép.*	= Reinach, *Répertoire de la Statuaire.*
Rev. Arch.	= Revue Archéologique.
Rev. Et. Gr.	= Revue des Études Grecques.
de Ridder	= (In the case of bronzes from the Acropolis)— Bronzes trouvés sur l'Acropole d'Athènes. (In the case of other bronzes at Athens)— Bronzes de la Societé Archéologique d'Athènes.
Röm. Mit.	= Mitteilungen des Deutschen Archäologischen Instituts, Römische Abteilung.
Staïs	= Staïs, *Marbres et Bronzes du Musée National.*

NOTE

References to Schliemann's *Tiryns & Mycenae* are to the pages of the English edition.

References to Bossert's *Alt Kreta* are to the edition of 1923.

" Catalogue " with the author's name, refers to the catalogue of bronzes in the museum in question.

Measurements of the objects illustrated on the plates and in the text are given in the footnotes : they are omitted only in the few cases where they cannot be ascertained.

Museum inventory numbers are given if they appear in an official published catalogue.

BIBLIOGRAPHY

The bibliographies added to this 1969 edition form a completely new section of the book. To facilitate research and documentation, the lists of books and articles used by the author have been classified in Section A (*Bibliography of the First Edition*) and those selected by the editor for further reference are in Section B. (*A New Select Bibliography*). The bibliography of section B covers works through 1967. Unfortunately, due to various circumstances which have been unavoidable, there are some lacunae in Section A where complete references have not been discovered. The subdivisions of the two sections are listed below:

A. BIBLIOGRAPHY OF THE FIRST EDITION: 1929
I. General Works
II. Chapter I - The Prehistoric Period
III. Chapter 2 - The Sub-Mycenaean, Transitional and Geometric Periods
IV. Chapter 3 - The Early Archaic (Orientalizing) period ca. 700-575 B.C.
V. Chapter 4 - The Sixth Century: Statuettes
VI. Chapter 5 - The Sixth Century: Decorative Work and Utensils in Bronze
VII. Chapter 6 - The Earlier Fifth Century
VIII. Chapter 7 - The Late Fifth and Fourth Century
IX. Chapter 8 - The Hellenistic Period, or the Hellenistic Tradition
X. Chapter 9 - Roman Bronzes

B. A NEW SELECT BIBLIOGRAPHY
XI. General Works
XII. Catalogues of Museums and Major Collections
XIII. Catalogues of Major Bronze Exhibitions
XIV. Excavation Reports
XV. Bronze and Bronze Working
XVI. Vessels and Implements
    1. Armor
    2. Bronze Vessels
    3. Bronze Reliefs
    4. Mirrors and Paterae
    5. Miscellaneous Implements, Furnishings
XVII. Addenda to Sections II to X.
    1. Prehistoric Period
    2. Geometric and Archaic
    3. Classical and Hellenistic
    4. Etruscan and Roman

ABBREVIATIONS

[Abbreviations of periodicals used in the bibliographies, cited according to present standard usage, followed, in parentheses, by Miss Lamb's occasional alternate ver—sions.]

AA (Anz) – Archäologischer Anzeiger
ActaA - Acta Archaeologica
AJA (A.J.A.) – American Journal of Archaeology
ArtB – Art Bulletin
AthMitt (Ath. Mit.) – Mitteilungen des deutschen Archäologischen Instituts, Athenische Abteilung
AZ (Arch. Zeit.) - Archäologische Zeitung
BCH (B. C. H.) – Bulletin de correspondance hellénique
BSA (B. S. A.) –British School at Athens Annual
Deltion, Δελτίον – Archaiologikon deltion. Ἀρχαιολογικὸν Δελτίον
EphArch, Arch Eph, Ἐφ Αρχ – Ephemeris Archaiologike; Archaiologike Ephemeris. Ἐφημερίσ Ἀρχαιολογική
JdI (Jahrbuch) – Jahrbuch des k. deutschen archaeologischen Instituts
JHS (J. H. S.) – Journal of Hellenic Studies
JOAI (Jahreshefte) – Jahreshefte des oesterreichischen archäologischen Instituts
MAAR – Memoirs of the American Academy in Rome
Mond. dei L. (M. de L.) – Monumenti Antichi pubblicati per cura della R. Accademia Nazionale dei Lincei
MonPiot (Mon. Piot) – Monuments et mémoires publ. par l'Académie des inscriptions et belles lettres, Fondation Piot
RömMitt (Röm. Mit) – Mitteilungen des deutschen archäologischen Instituts, Römische Abteilung

A. BIBLIOGRAPHY OF THE FIRST EDITION: 1929

I. GENERAL WORKS

[Comprising books appearing in 3 or more chapters. Full data and titles will be quoted only here, along with indications as to which chapters the books are used for; further reference in the body of the bibliography will be by Miss Lamb's abbreviations only.]

Beazley, J.D. "Early Greek Art." *CAH IV. The Persian Empire and the West.* Cambridge, 1926. 579-610. (Lamb, chapters 2-5)

Bossert, T.H. *Alt Kreta.* Berlin, 1923. (Lamb, chapters 1-3).

Casson, S. "Bronze Work of the Geometric Period and its Relation to Later Art." *JHS* 42 (1922) 207-219. (Lamb, chapters 2-4).

Cook, A.B. *Zeus: A Study in Ancient Religion.* Vol. 1. *Zeus God of the Bright Sky.* Vol. 2. *Zeus God of the Dark Sky.* Cambridge, 1914, 1925. (Lamb, chapters 2-4, 7, 9).

De Ridder, A. *Catalogue des bronzes de la Société Archéologique d'Athènes.* Paris, 1894. (Lamb, chapters 2-5, 7).

——, *Les Bronzes Antiques du Louvre.* Vol. 2. *Les Instruments.* Paris, 1915. (Lamb, chapters 1, 3-8).

Ducati, P. *Etruria Antica.* II. Paravia, 1927. (Lamb, chapters 2-4, 8).

——, *Storia dell'arte etrusca.* Vols. 1, 2. Florence, 1927. (Lamb, chapters 3-8).

Fölzer, E. *Die Hydria.* Leipzig, 1906. (Lamb, chapters 5-7).

Furtwangler, A. *Die Bronzen.* Vol. IV of *Olympia: Die Ergebnisse der von dem deutschen Reich veranstalteten Ausgrabung.* Berlin, 1890. [Rp. 1967] (Lamb chapters 2-6).

——, *Kleine Schriften.* Munich, 1912 (Vol. 1), 1913 (Vol. 2). (Lamb, chapters 1, 2, 4-6, 8).

——, *Masterpieces of Greek Sculpture.* London, 1903. [Rp., Chicago 1964] (Lamb, chapters 6, 7, 9).

Langlotz, E. *Fruehgriechische Bildhauerschulen.* Nürnberg, 1927. (Lamb, chapters 4-6,9).

Neugebauer, K.A. *Antike Bronzestatuetten.* (Abbreviated *A.B.* in main bibliography). Berlin, 1921. (Lamb, chapters 1-9).

——, "Erwerbungen der Antikensammlungen in Deutschland. Berlin. Antiquarium." *AA* 37 (1922) 59-119. (Lamb, chapters 1, 3, 4, 6-9).

——, *Führer durch den Antiquarium.* Vol. 1. *Bronzen.* Berlin, 1924. (Lamb, chapters 4, 5, 7-9).

Perdrizet, P. *Fouilles de Delphes.* Athens 1901; Paris, 1908. (Lamb, chapters 2-6)

Pernice, E. *Hellenistische Kunst in Pompeji.* Vol.4.*Gefasse und Gerate.* Berlin, 1925. (Lamb. chapters 7-9).

Praschniker, G., "Bronzene Spiegelstutze in Wiener Hofmuseum." *Jahreshefte* 15 (1912) 219-252 (Lamb, chapters 5, 6, 9)

Richter, G.M.A. *Catalog of Greek, Etruscan and Roman Bronzes.* New York, 1915. (Lamb, chapters 2, 4-9).

Roscher, W. *Ausführliches Lexikon der griechischen und römischen Mythologie.* Leipzig, 1884 - 1937. Vol. 2. 1183, 1892. (Lamb, chapters 4, 6, 9).

Schwendemann, K. "Der Dreifuss." *JdI* 36 (1921) 98-185. (Lamb, chapters 1-3, 5, 9).

Stäis, V. *Marbres et bronzes du Musée National.* Athens, 1910. (Lamb, chapters 2, 3, 5-7).

Strong, E. *Exhibition of Ancient Greek Art.* (Burlington Fine Arts Club.) London, 1904. (Lamb, chapters 4, 5, 8).

Waldstein, C. *The Argive Heraeum.* (Volume unspecified, although probably Vol. 2) Boston, 1905. (Lamb chapters 2,3,5,6).

Walters, H.B. *Catalogue of the Bronzes, Greek, Roman and Etruscan . . . in the British Museum.* London, 1899. (Lamb, chapters 4-7,9).

II. CHAPTER 1–THE PREHISTORIC PERIOD

Bassi, D., Gabrici and others. *Guida illustrata del Museo Nazionale di Napoli.* Naples, 1911.

Bosanquet and Dawkins. *The Unpublished Objects from the Palaikastro Excavations.* Vol. 1 London 1923.

Bossert, T.H. *Alt Kreta* (see general bibliography)

Boyd-Hawes, H. *Gournia.* Philadelphia, 1908.

Chatzidakis, J. "Τρία Μωαϊκα εἰδωλια" ("Three Small Idols from Mycenae.") *Deltion.* 2 (1916) 164-170.

Déchelette, J. *Manuale d'archéologie prehistorique celtique et gallo-romaine.* Paris, 1908.

De Ridder. *Catalogue.* (Louvre.) (See general bibliography.)

Dörpfeld, W. *Troja und Ilion I.* Berlin, 1902.

Evans, Sir A.J. *Cretan Pictographs and Pre-Phoenician Script.* London 1895.

——, "Mycenean Tree and Pillar Cult and its Mediterranean Relations." *JHS* 21 (1901) 99-204.

——, "The Palace of Knossos." *BSA* 9 (1902 - 1903). 1-153.

——, *The Palace of Minos.* " 7 vols. (Unspecified as to which used.) London, 1921 - 1936.

——, "Prehistoric Tombs of Knossos," *Archaeologia* 59 (1906) 391-562.

Forsdyke, J. . "Prehistoric Aegean Pottery." *Catalogue of Greek and Etruscan Vases in the British Museum.* Vol. 1, part 1. London, 1912.

Furtwängler, A. *Die antike Gemmen.* Vols. 1-3. Leipzig & Berlin, 1900.

——, *Kleine Schriften.* (See general bibliography)

"Gillierons Nachbildungen Mykenischer Altertumer." *AA* 18 (1903) 157-162.

Hellenic Society. *Excavations at Phylakopi in Melos.* (Supplementary Papers 4) *JHS* (no further information available)

Hogarth, D.G. "The Dictaean Cave." *BSA* 6 (1899 - 1900) 64-116.

M. de L. 6 (1897) incl. 176-179. (No further information available.)

Mosso, A. *Dawn of Mediterranean Civililization.* London, 1910.

Müller, W.A. *Nacktheit und Entblössung in der altorientalischen und älteren griechischen Kunst.* Leipzig. 1906.

Myres, J.L. "Neolithic and Bronze Age Cultures." *CAH* I - *Egypt and Babylonia to 1580 B.C.* Cambridge, 1923.57-111.

Neugebauer, K.A. *AB* (See general bibliography.)

——, *Berlin Antiquarium.* (See general bibliography.)

Peet, T.E., T. Ashby, E.T. Leeds. "The Western Mediterranean." *CAH* II - *The Egyptian and Hittite Empires to c. 1000 B.C.* Cambridge, 1924.563-601.

Pernice, E. "Untersuchungen zur antiken Toreutik." *Jahreshefte* / (1904) 154-197.

Perrot, G., C. Chipiez. *Histoire de l'art dans l'antiquitie.* Vol. 6. Paris, 1882.

Pryce, F.N. "A Minoan Bronze Statuette in the British Museum." *JHS* 41 (1921) part 1. 86-90.

Ridgeway, W. *Early Age of Greece.* Cambridge, 1901.

Rodenwaldt, G. and K. Müller. *Tiryns.* Vol. 2. Athens & Munich, 1912.

Savignoni, L. "Scavi e Scoperte nella Necropoli di Phaestos." *M. de L.* 14 (1904) 501-676.

Schliemann, H. *Mycenae. (Mykenae.)* New York & Leipzig, 1878.

——, *Tiryns.* New York, 1885.

Schneider, R.V. "Neuere Erwerbungen der Antikensammlung des Österreich-ischen Kaiserhauses in Wein 1880 - 1891. Forsetzung und Schlufs." *AA* 7 (1892) 48-56.

Schwendemann, K. *Jahrbuch 1921.* (See general bibliography.)

Smith, C. "Excavations in Melos, 1897." *BSA* 3 (1896 - 1897) 1-30.

Spratt, T.A.B. *Travels and Researches in Crete.* London, 1865.

Tsountas, C. "Finds From Mycenae." (In Greek) *EphArch* (1891) 1-44.

——, "Investigations in Laconia and the grave of Vaphio." (In Greek) *EphArch* (1889) 129-172.

Tsountas, C. and J. Manatt. *The Mycenaean Age.* 1897. [Rp. 1969]

Van Hoorn, G. "Eine minoische Bronze in Leiden." *JdI* 30 (1915) 65-73.

Wace, A.J.B. and M.S. Thompson. *Prehistoric Thessaly.* Cambridge, 1912.

Xanthoudides, S. *Vaulted Tombs of the Messara.* London, 1924.

III. CHAPTER 2—THE SUB-MYCENAEAN, TRANSITIONAL AND GEOMETRIC PERIODS

Bates, W.N. "Two Labors of Hercules on a Geometric Fibula." *AJA* 15 (1911) 1-17.

Beazley, J.D. *CAH* IV. (See general bibliography.)

Blinkenberg, C. *Fibules greques et orientales.* Copenhagen, 1926.

Bossert, H. *Alt Kreta.* (See general bibliography.)

Boyd, H.A. "American School of Classical Studies at Athens - Excavations at Kavousi, Crete, in 1900." *AJA* 5 (1901) second series. 132-137.

British Museum. *Catalogue* (No further information available)

Brueckner, A. "Ein athenischer Grabfund der geometrischen periode." *AthMitt* 18 (1893) 414-415.

Casson, S. "The Dorian Invasion reviewed in the Light of some New Evidence." *Antiquaries' Journal* (1921) 199-221.

——, "Excavations in Macedonia." *BSA* 24 (1919 - 1921) 1-33.

——, in *JHS* 1922. (See general bibliography.)

Cook, A.B. "Animal Worship in the Mycenaean Age." *JHS* 14 (1894) 81-169.

——, *Zeus II.* (See general bibliography.)

Dawkins, R.M. "Archaic Finds from the Artemesium." (Olympia.) *BSA* 12 (1905 - 1906) 318-330.

De Ridder, A. *Catalogue* (Athens). (See general bibliography.)

Dörpfeld, W. "Das altar des Heiligtums von Olympia." *AthMitt* 31 (1906) 205-218.

——, *Alt-Ithaka.* Munich, 1927. [Rp. 1966]

Droop, J.P. "The Early Bronzes." (One of several articles on "Laconia: Excavations at Sparta, 1907"). *BSA* 13 (1906 - 1907) 107-117.

Ducati, P. *Etruria Antica.* (See general bibliography.)

Evans, Sir A.J. *The Palace of Minos at Knossos.* 7 vols. London, 1921 - 1926.

Furtwängler, A. *Aegina: Das Heiligentum der Aphaia.* Munich, 1906.
——, "Bronzi arcaici provenienti della grecia." *Annali dell'Instituto* 52 (1880)
    118-135.
——, *Kleine Schriften.* (See general bibliography.)
——, *Olympia IV.* (See general bibliography.)
Gardner, E.A. and S. Casson. "Macedonia: Antiquities Found in the British Zone,
    1915 - 1919." *BSA* 23 (1918 - 1919) 10-40.
Hall, E.H. *Excavations in Eastern Crete. Vriokastro.* Philadelphia. 1909.
Hogarth, D.G. "Knossos: Early Town and Cemeteries." *BSA* 6 (1899-1900)
    70-85.
Lamb, W. "The Megaron." (from 'The Palace' at the "Excavations at
    Mycenae" series). *BSA* 25 (1921-1923) 232-256.
Markides, M. "A Mycenean Bronze in the Cyprus Museum." *BSA* 18 (1911 -
    1912) 95-97.
M. de L. 4 (1895) incl. p. 185. (No further information available.)
Mit. Anthrop. Gesellschaft Wein.   (article on northern fibulae. No further
    information available.)
Mosso, A. *The Palaces of Crete and their Builders.* London, 1907.
Murray, A.S. A. Smith and H.B. Walters. *Excavations in Cyprus.* London, 1900.
Museo Italiano Atlas 11 (1888). (Text p. 689), pls. 1-5, 9, 10. (No further
    information available.)
Neugebauer, K.A. *AB* (See general bibliography)
Perdrizet, P. *Fouilles de Delphes..* (See general bibliography.)
Pernice, E. "Erwerbungen der Antikensammlung in Deutschland. Berlin. Anti-
    quarium." *AA* 19 (1904) 17-46.
Philadelpheus, Alex. "Sixth Archaeological District. The Mycenean Treasure from
    Tirynth." (In Greek) *Deltion* 2 (1916) supplement 13-21.
Reichel, W. and A. Wilhem. "Das Heiligthum der Artemis zu Lusoi." *Jahreshefte* 4
    (1901) 1-89.
Reisinger, E. "Geometrische Fibeln in Munchen." *JdI*31 (1916) 288-305.
Richter, G.M.A. *Catalogue.* (See general bibliography.)
Romeos, K.A. "From the prehistoric Thermon." *Deltion* 1 (1915) 225-279.

Schliemann, H. *Mycenae.* New York & Leipzig, 1878.
Schwendemann, K. *Jahrbuch* 1921. (See general bibliography.)
Stäis, V. *Catalogue.* (See general bibliography.)
Thompson, M.S. "Some notes on Homeric Armour." *Liverpool Annals* 5 (1912)
    5-20.
Wade-Gery, H.T. "The Dorians." *CAH* II - *The Egyptian and Hittite Empires to c.
    1000 B.C.* Cambridge 1924. 518-541.
Waldstein, G. *Argive Heraeum* (See general bibliography)
Xanthoudidou, Et. A. "From Crete" (In Greek) *EphArch* (1904) 1-56.

IV. CHAPTER 3—THE EARLY ARCHAIC (ORIENTALIZING) PERIOD, c. 700–575 B.C.

"Archäologische Gesellschaft zu Berlin 1921: Januar-Sitzung." *AA* 36 (1921)
    231-237.
Bather, A.G. "The Bronze Fragments of the Acropolis: II." *JHS* 13 (1892 - 1893)
    232-271.
Beazley, J.D. *CAH* IV. (See general bibliography.)
Bosanquet, R.C. "Excavations at Palaikastro," *BSA* 11 (1904 - 1905) 298 - 308.
Bossert, H. Th. *Alt Kreta.* (See general bibliography.)
Carapanos, C. *Dodone et ses ruines.* Paris, 1878.
Casson, S. *JHS* 1922. (See general bibliography.)

Collignon, M. *Histoire de la sculpture grecque* I. Paris, 1892.

Cook, A.B. *Zeus I.* (See general bibliography.)

De Ridder, A. *Catalogue* (Athens). (See general bibliography)

——, *Catalogue* (Louvre). (See general bibliography.)

Ducati, P. *Etruria Antica.* (See general bibliography.)

——, *Storia.* (See general bibliography)

Frohner, W. *Apollon, bronze archaïque de la collection du compte Michel Tyszkiewicz.* Paris, 1894. Also in *Monuments Piot II* (1895) 137-143.

Frothingham, A.J., Jr. "Early Bronzes Recently Discovered on Mt. Ida in Krete." *The American Journal of Archaeology and of the History of the Fine Arts.* 4 (1888) 431-449.

Furtwängler, A. *Olympia IV.* (See general bibliography.)

Gardner, P. "Some Bronzes Recently Acquired for the Ashmolean Museum." *JHS* 30 (1910) 226-235.

Hogarth, D.G. *British Museum Excavations at Ephesus.* London. 1908.

Hopkinson, J.H. "Note on the Fragment of a Painted Pinax from Praesos." *BSA* 10 (1903 - 1904) 148-153.

Kourouniotis, K. "Excavations and researches at Chios." (In Greek)*Deltion* 1 (1915) 64-93.

Mackenzie, D. "Cretan Palaces and Aegean Civilisation." *BSA* 111 (1904-1905) 181-223.

Milani, L.A. *Monumenti Scelti.* Florence, 1905.

Minto, A. "Regione VII (Etruria), Vetulonia." *Notizie degli Scavi* (1913) 426-439.

Montelius, O. *La Civilisation primitive en Italie depuis l'Introduction des metaux.* Stockholm, 1895 - 1910. (Serie B)

Museo Italiano Atlas. 11 (1888) Text, p. 689; Pls. 1-5, 9-10.

Neugebauer, K.A. *Berlin Antiquarium.* (See general bibliography.)

Orsi, P. "Regione III . . . Rosarno Medina. Esplorazione di un grande deposito di terrecotte Ieratiche." *Notizie degli Scavi* (1913) 55-144.

Perdrizet, P. *Fouilles de Delphes..* V. (See general bibliography.)

Pfuhl, E. *Malerei und Zeichnung der Griechen.* Munich, 1923.

Poulsen, F. "Eine Kretische Mitra." *AthMitt* 31 (1906) 373-391

——, *Der Orient und die Frühgriechische Kunst.* Leipzig & Berlin, 1912.

Price, E.R. "Pottery of Naucratis." *JHS* 44 (1924) 180-222.

Randall-MacIver. *Villanovans and Etruscans.* Oxford, 1924.

Romeos, K.A. "Investigations at Kinouria." (In Greek) *Praktika* (1911) 253-279.

Schwendemann, K. *Jahrbuch* 1921 (See general bibliography.)

Stäis, V. *Catalogue.* (See general bibliography.)

Thiersch, H. "Altkretisches: Kuretengerät." *AA* 28 (1913) 47-53.

Thompson, M.S. "The Menelaion." (Part of several articles on "Laconia: Excavations at Sparta, 1909.") *BSA* 15(1908 - 1909) 108-157.

Von Bissing, Fr. W.F. "Untersuchungen über die 'phoinikischen' Metallschalen." *JdI* 38 - 39 (1923 - 1924) 180-241.

Wace, A.J.B. and W. Lamb. "The Pithos Area." (from "The Palace" in the "Excavations at Mycenae" series) *BSA* 25 (1921-1923) 160-178.

Waldstein, G. *Argive Heraeum.* (See general bibliography.)

V. CHAPTER 4—THE SIXTH CENTURY:STATUETTES

Anno III Serie II (April) p. 453. (No further information available.)

Babelon, E. and J.A. Blanchet. *Catalog des bronzes antiques de la Bibliothèque Nationale.* Paris, 1895.

Baur, P.V.C. *Centaurs in Greek Art.* Berlin, 1912.

Beazley, J.D. *CAH* IV. (See general bibliography.)
Bieber, M. *Die antiken sculpturen und bronzen des Königl. Museum Friedericianum in Cassel; im auftrage der museumsdirektion heransgeben von Margaret Bieber.* Marburg, 1915.
Casson, S. *JHS* 1922. (See general bibliography.)
Cook, A.B. *Zeus I.* (See general bibliography.)
De Ridder, A. *Catalogue* (Athens). (See general bibliography).
——, *Catalogue* (Louvre.) (See general bibliography.)
——, "Statuette de bronze de l'Acropole." *BCH* 18 (1894) 44-52.
Dickens, G. *Catalogue of the Acropolis Museum.* Cambridge, 1912 - 1921.
——, "Damophon of Messene . . .III." *BSA* 17 (1910 - 1911) 80-87.
——, "The Hieron of Athena Chalkiokos." (one of several articles on "Laconia: Excavations at Sparta 1907.") *BSA* (1906 - 1907) 137-154.
Ducati, P. *Etruria Antica.* 2. (See general bibliography.)
——, *Storia.* (See general bibliography.)
Filow, B. D. and K. Schkorpil. *Die archäische Nekropole von Trebenischte am Ochrida-See.* Berlin & Leipzig, 1927.
Furtwängler, A. "Eine Argivische Bronze." *50th Winckelmanns Programm.* Berlin, 1890. 125-153.
——, *Kleine Schriften II.* (See general bibliography.)
——, *Olympia IV.* (See general bibliography.)
Gardiner, E.N. "Notes on the Greek Foot Race." *JHS* 23 (1903) 261-291.
Gardner, P. *Catalogue of Greek Coins, Peloponnesus.* London, 1887. (Rp. 1963)
Holleaux, M. "Fouilles au Temple d'Apollon Ptoos." *BCH* 10 (1886) 190-199; 11 (1887) 354-363; 12 (1888) 280-404.
Jones, Stuart. *Ancient Writers on Greek Sculpture.* London, 1895. [Rp. Chicago, 1966.]
Knossos Catalogue. (No further information available.)
Körte, G. *Göttinger Bronzen.* Berlin, 1917.
Kourouniotis, K. "Excavation of Lykaion." (In Greek) *EphArch* (1904) 153-214.
——, "Excavation of the Shrine of Nomios Pan." (In Greek) *Praktika* (1902) 72-75.
Lamb, W. "Arcadian Bronze Statuettes." *BSA* 27 (1925 - 1926) 253-276.
Langlotz, E. (See general bibliography.)
Müller, V. "Gerwandschemata der archaischen Kunst." *AthMitt* 46 (1921) 36-69.
Neugebauer, K.A. *A.B.* (See general bibliography.)
——, *Berlin Antiquarium.* (See general bibliography.)
——, *Führer.* (See general bibliography.)
Pausanias. *Description of Greece.* 5:16, 8:8, 18, 38.
Perdrizet, P. *Bronzes grecs d'Egypte de la collection Fouquet.* Paris, 1911.
——, *Fouilles de Delphes IV..* (See general bibliography.)
——, "Hèrmes Criophoré." *BCH* 27 (1903) 301-313.
Pfuhl, E. *Malerei und Zeichnung der Griechen.* Munich, 1923.
Reichel, W. and A. Wilhem. "Das Heiligthum der Artemis zu Lusoi." *Jahreshefte* 4 (1901) 1-89.
Richter, G.M.A. *Catalogue.* (See general bibliography.)
Rodenwaldt, G. "Ein archaischer Torso in Athen." *AthMitt* 46 (1921) 27-35.
——, *Die Kunst der Antike.* Berlin, 1927.
Roscher, W. *Lexikon.* (See general bibliography.) 1 pt. 2 "Herakles" (A. Furtwängler) 2135-2252.
Rouse, W.H.D. *Greek Votive Offerings.* Cambridge, 1902.
Strong, E. *Burlington Fine Arts Catalogue.* (See general bibliography.)
Studniczka, F. "Des Arkaders Phauless Wiehbeschencken Pan." *AthMitt* 39 (1905) 65-72.

Tsountas, Chr. "From the Amyklaion." (In Greek) *EphArch* (1892) 1-26.

Versakis, F. "The Shrine of the Corinthian Apollo." (In Greek)*Deltion* 2 (1916) 65-118.

Von Stradonitz, Kekule. "Die Griechische Skulptur." (in *Handbucher der Koniglicher Museen zu Berlin*) Berlin 1907.

Walters, H.B. *Catalogue.* (See general bibliography.)

Wiegand, Th. "Archaische Statue in Samos." *AthMitt* 31 (1906) 87-88.

VI. CHAPTER 5—THE SIXTH CENTURY: DECORATIVE WORK AND UTENSILS IN BRONZE

"Archaologisches funde im Jahre 1903." *AA* 19 (1904) 97-152.

"Archäologische Gesellschaft zu Berlin 1924: März-Sitzung." *AA* 38-39. (1923 - 1924) 300-341.

"Archäologische Gesellschaft zu Berlin 1925: März-Sitzung." *AA* 40 (1925) 172-228.

Bather, A.G. "The Bronze Fragments of the Acropolis:II." *JHS* 13 (1892 - 1893) 232-271.

Baumeister, A.; et al. *Denkmäler des klassischen Altertums zur Erläuterung des Lebens des Griecher und Römer in Religion, Kunst, und Sitte.* Vol. 2. Munich & Leipzig 1885 - 1889 (3 vols.)

Beazley, J.D. *CAH IV.* (See general bibliography.)

British Museum. *Bronzes.* (no further information. Walters, *Catalogue?*)

Buschor, E. and W. von Massow. "Vom Amyklaion." *AthMitt* 52 (1927) 1-85.

Campanile, T. "Statuetta di Eracle in Bronzo d'arte Etrusca." *Bolletino d'Arte* second series vol. 3, X'Fascicolo (1924) 453-462.

Chase, G.H. "Three Bronze Tripods belonging to James Loeb, Esq." *AJA* 12 (1908) 287-323.

Déchelette, J. *Manuel d'archeologie préhistorique celtique et gallo-romaine II.* Paris, 1908.

De Ridder, A. *Catalogue* (Athens). (See general bibliography.)

——, *Catalogue* (Louvre). (See general bibliography.)

——, *De Ectypis quibusdam Aeneis quae falso vocantur Argivo-Corinthica.* Paris, 1896.

——, "Fouilles d'Orchomene." *BCH* 18 (1895) 137-224.

——, "Speculum." Daremberg and Saglio, *Dictionnaire des antiquites.* 4.1. 1873-1919 (Rp. 1965) 1422-1430.

Ducati, P. "Contributo allo studio degli Specchi etruschi figurati." *RömMitt* 27 (1912) 243-285.

——, *Storia.* (See general bibliography.)

Farrel, J. "The Archaic Terracottas from the sanctuary of Orthia." *BSA* 14 (1907-1908) 48-73.

Filow, B. D. and K. Schkorpil. *Die Archaische Nekropole von Trebenischte am Ochrida-See.* Berlin and Leipzig, 1927.

Fölzer, E. *Die Hydria.* (See general bibliography)

Furtwangler, A. *Aegina. Das Heiligentum der Aphaia.* Munich, 1906.

——, "Carri in bronzo di Monteleone e S. Mariano." Brunn-Bruckmann *Denkmäler griechischer und Römischer skulptur.* Monaco, 1885 - 1907. 586-589 (volume unspecified.)

——, "Erwerbungen der Antikensammlungen in Deutschland." *AA* 6 (1891) 115-127.

——, "Erwerbungen der Antikensammlungen in Deutschland." 1893. Berlin. *AA* 9 (1894) 115-122.

——, *Kleine Schriften.* (See general bibliography. Vols. 1, 2.)

——, *Olympia IV.* (See general bibliography.)

xxxii GREEK AND ROMAN BRONZES

Gerhard, E.; Klügmann, and G. Körte. *Etruskische Spiegel.* Vol. 5, Berlin, 1840 - 1897. (5 volumes total.)
Gervasio, M. *Bronzi Arcaici e ceramica geometrica nel Museo di Bari.* (Vol. 16 of Commisione Provinciale de Archeologia e storia patria.) Bari, 1921.
Holleaux, M. "Bronzes Trouvés à Ptoion." *BCH* 16 (1892) 348-369.
Körte, G. *Das Volumniergrab bei Perugia.* Berlin, 1909.
Kourouniotis, K. "Excavation of Kotilos." *Eph Arch* , (1903) 151-188.
Lefage, G. "Kottabos." Daremberg and Saglio - *Dictionnaire des Antiquités.* 3.1 (1900) 866-869.
Langlotz, E. (See general bibliography.)
Minns, E.H. *Scythians and Greeks.* Cambridge, 1913. [Rp. 1966]
M.de L. 22 (1913) incl. p. 561, pl. 76:3. (No further information.)
Neugebauer, K.A. *A.B.* (See general bibliography.)
— —, *Führer.* (See general bibliography.)
— —, "Reifarchaische Bronzevasen mit Zungenmuster." *RömMitt* 38 (1923 - 1924) 341-440.
Notizie degli Scavi (1894) incl. 137-139. (No further information available.)
Orsi, P. "Camarine, campagne archeologiche del 1899 e 1903." *M. de L.* 14 (1905) 757-952.
Patroni, G. "Regione III (Lucania et Bruttii). Lucania. Nuovo richerche de antichita nell Lucania. XII Sala consilina." *Notizie degli Scavi,* (1897) incl. p. 164.
Perdrizet, P. *Fouilles de Delphes.* (see general bibliography).
Pernice, E. "Glaukos von Chios." *JdI* 16 (1901) 107-111.
— — —, "Tarentiner Bronzegefässe." *JdI* 35 (1920) 83-96.
Petersen, E. "Bronzen von Perugia." *RömMitt* 9 (1894) 253-318.
Praschniker, C. "Bronzene Spiegelstütze im Berliner Antiquarium." *Jahreshefte* 18 (1915) 57-60.
— —, *Jahreshefte* 1912. (See general bibliography)
Richter, G.M.A. *Catalogue.* (See general bibliography.)
Savignoni, L. "Di un bronzetto archaico dell'Acropoli di Atene e di una classe di tripodi di tipo graeco-orientale." *M. de L.* 7 (1898) 177-376.
Schumacher, K.A. *Beschreibung der Sammlung antiker Bronzen.* Karlruhe, 1890.
Schwendemann, K. *Jahrbuch, 1921.* (See general bibliography.)
Sieveking, J. *Der Bronzen der Sammlung Loeb.* Munich. 1913.
Stais, V. *Catalogue.* (See general bibliography.)
Strong, E. *Burlington Fine Arts Catalogue.* (See general bibliography)
Thiersch, H.; and A. Furtwängler. *Aegina, das Heiligtum der Aphaia.* Munich, 1906.
Tsountas, Chr. "From the Amyklaion," *EphArch* (1892) 1-26.
Von Stradonitz, R. Kekule; and A. Furtwängler. "Erwerbungen der Antikensammlung in Deutschland. 1892. Berlin. *AA* 8 (1893) 72-102.
Waldstein, C. *Argive Heraeum.* (See general bibliography.)
Walters, H.B. *Catalogue.* (See general bibliography.)
Wolters, P. "Bronzereliefs von der Akropolis zu Athen." *AthMitt* 20 (1895) 473-482.
Woodward, A.M. "Archaeology in Greece, 1926-1927." *JHS* 47 (1927) 234-263. Excavations at Sparta. *BSA* 13 (1906-1907), ff. (No specifications given as to which year of the Woodward papers this is, or the pages.)

VII. CHAPTER 6—THE EARLIER FIFTH CENTURY

Annual Report of the Museum of Fine Arts. Boston, 1899. 139 ff.
BM Catalogue. (No indication as to whether this is Walter's catalogue or another.)
Bulle, H. *Der Schöne Mensch in Altertum.* Munich & Leipzig, 1912.

BIBLIOGRAPHY xxxiii

Bulletin of the Metropolitan Museum of Art. New York, 1926. 8.

Buschor, E.; and R. Hamman. *Die Skupturen des Zeustempel zu Olympia.* Marburg, 1924.

Collignon, M. *Histoire de la sculpture grecque.* Vol. 1. Paris 1892.

Cook, A.B. *Zeus II.* (See general bibliography.)

De Ridder, A. *Catalogue des bronzes trouvés sur l'Acropole d'Athènes.* Paris, 1896.

— —, *Catalogue* (Louvre). (See general bibliography.)

Dickens, G. "The Hieron of Athena Chalkiokos." (one of several articles on "Laconia: Excavations at Sparta 1907.") *BSA* 13 (1906 - 1907) 137-154.

Ducati, P. *Storia.* (See general bibliography.)

Duhn, F. V. "Funde und forschungen Italien 1914-1920." *AA* 36 (1921) 34-230

Friedrichs, K. *Berlins Antike Bildwerke.* Vol. 2. *Geräthe und Bronzen im Alten Museum.* Berlin, 1860. (Kleinere Kunst und Industrie im Alterthum . . .)

Fölzer, E. *Die Hydria.* (See general bibliography)

Furtwängler, A. "Eine Argivische Bronze." *50th Winckelmanns Programm.* Berlin, 1890. 125-153.

— —, "Herakles." In W. Roscher - *Lexikon.* (See general bibliography.) 1 pt. 2 (1886 - 1890) 2135-2252.

— —, *Kleine Schriften II.* (See general bibliography.)

— —, *Masterpieces.* (See general bibliography.)

— —, *Olympia IV.* (See general bibliography.)

— —, *Sammlung Sabouroff.* Berlin, 1897.

Gardiner, E.N. "Notes on the Greek Foot Race." *JHS* 23 (1903) 261-291.

— —, "Throwing the Diskos," *JHS* 17 (1908) 1-36.

Hauser, F. "Zur Tübinger Bronze." *JdI* (1887) 95-107.

— —, "Zur Tübinger Bronze." *JdI* 10 (1895) 183-203.

Hill, Sir G.F. *Select Greek Coins.* Paris, 1927.

Jones, S. *Ancient Greek Writers on Greek Sculpture.* London, 1895. [Rp. Chicago, 1966].

Kourovniotis, K. "Vases from Eretria," *EphArch* (1903) 1-38

Lamb, W. "Arcadian Bronze Statuettes." *BSA* 27 (1925 - 1926) 253-276.

Langlotz, E. (See general bibliography.)

Lechat, H. "Aphrodite." (a bronze from the Caraponos Collection.) *BCH* 15 (1891) 461-481.

Lohde, L. *Die Skene der Alten. 20th Winckelmannsprogramm.* Berlin, 1860.

Mahler, A. "Der Angebliche Herakles des Onatas." *Jahreshefte* 2 (1899) 77-80. •

Maiuri, R. (actually unsigned.) "Regione III (Lucanis et Bruttii). Brutti Scavi a Calabria nel 1913 (relazione preliminadre) Locri Epizepyrii." *Notizie degli Scavi.* (1913) 3-54.

Neugebauer, K.A. *A.B.* (See general bibliography.)

— —, *Berlin Antiquarium.* (See general bibliography.)

— —, "Reifarchaische Bronzevasen mit Zungenmuster." *RömMitt* 38 (1923 - 1924) 341-440.

Pappadakis, Nik G. "Second Archaeological District. Excavation of the Eschara on Oeta." *Deltion* (1919) supplement. 25-34.

Perdrizet, P.*Fouilles de Delphes V.* (see general bibliography.)

Pernice, E. "Erwerbungen der Antikensammlung in Deutschland. Berlin. Antiquarium." *AA* 19 (1904) 17-46.

Praschniker, C. *Jahreshefte* 1912. (See general bibliography.)

Richter, G.M.A. *Catalogue.* (See general bibliography.)

— —, *Festschrift für Amelung.* (No further information available.)

Schwabe, L. "Wagenlenker, Bronze in Tübingen." *JdI* I (1886) 163-175.

Stäis, V. *Catalogue.* (See general bibliography.)
Studniczka, F. *Kalamis: Ein Beitrag zur griechischen Kunstgeschichte.* Leipzig, 1905.
Waldstein, C. *Argive Heraeum.* (See general bibliography.)
Walters, H.B. *Catalogue.* (See general bibliography).
Weicker, G. *Die Seelenvogel in der alten litteratur und Kunst.* Leipzig, 1902.
White, H.G.E. "Two Athletic Bronzes at Athens." *JHS* 36 (1916) 16-24.
Wiegand, T. *Bronzefigure einer Spinnerin.. 73rd Berlin Winkelmannsprogramm.* Berlin, 1913.
Woodward, A.M. "The Acropolis." *BSA* 26 (1923 - 1924) 253-276.

VIII. CHAPTER 7—THE LATER FIFTH AND THE FOURTH CENTURY

Annual Report of the Museum of Fine Arts. Boston, 1903. 61.
Behn, F. *Die Ficoronische Ciste.* Leipzig. 1907.
Berl. Phi. Wochenschrift. 7 (1900) 628. (No further information available.)
B.M. 1904, 7-8; 1906, 4-5. (No further information available. Uncertain whether this refers to Walter's catalogue or some other of the London museum.)
Carapanos, C. *Dodone et ses ruines.* Paris, 1878.
Comptes Rendue de l'Academie des Inscriptions. 7 (1865) 164 ff. (No further information available.)
Cook, A.B. *Zeus I.* (See general bibliography.)
Delbrüeck, R. "Archäologische Funde im Jahre 1909: Italien." *AA* 25 (1910) 171-195.
Della Seta, A. *Museo di Villa Giulia.* Rome, 1918.
De Ridder, A. *Catalogue* (Athens.) (See general bibliography.)
——, *Catalogue.* (Louvre.)(See general bibliography.)
Ducati, P. *Storia.* (See general bibliography.)
Fölzer, E. *Die Hydria.* (See general bibliography.)
Frazer, J.G. (transl.). *Pausanias' Description of Greece.* Vol. 5. London, 1898. (Commentary on Paus. X: 38).
Furtwängler, A. *Meisterwerke der griechisches Plastik.* (Also referred to by Lamb as *Masterpieces.* See general bibliography.)
Furtwängler, A.; and K. Reichhold. *Griechischer Vasenmalerei.* 3 vols. Munich, 1900 - 1932. (vol. used unspecified.)
Gerhard, E.; K. Klügmann, G. Körte. *Etruskische Spiegel.* Berlin, 1840 - 1897. Vol. 5. (of 5 vol. series.)
Habich, G. "Erwerbungen der Antiken-Sammlungen Munchens 1909." *AA* 25 (1910) 480.
Hekler, A. "Beiträge zur Geschichte der antiken Panzerstatuen." *Jahreshefte* 19-20 (1919) 198-241.
Heydemann, H. "Mitteilungen aus den Antikensammlungen in Ober und Mittelitalien." *Drittes Hallisches Wincklemannsprogramm.* Halle, 1878.
Hill, Sir G.F. *Select Greek Coins.* Paris, 1927.
Kazarow, G. "Grabfund bei Mesambria." *AthMitt* 36 (1911) 308-316.
Klein, W. *Praxiteles.* Leipzig, 1898.
Marshall, F.H. "Some Recent Acquisitions of the British Museum." *JHS* 29 (1909) 151-167.
Matthies, G. *Die Pränestischer Spiegel: ein Beitrag zur italischen Kunst und Kulturgeschichte.* Strassbourg 1912.
Michaelis, A. *Ancient Marbles in Great Britain.* (C.A.M. Fennell, transl.) Cambridge, 1882.
Monumenti Inediti Pubblicati dall'Instituto di Corrispondenza Archaeologica. 6-7 (1857 - 1863) incl. 64.
Neugebauer, K.A. *A.B.* (See general bibliography).
——, *Berlin Antiquarium.* (See general bibliography.)
——, *Führer.* (See general bibliography.)

Paciaudi, P.M. *Monumenta Peloponnesia.* Rome, 1761.
Pernice, E. *Hellenistiiche Kunst in Pompeji.* (See general bibliography.)
Petersen, E. "Verschiedenes aus Suedi lien." *RömMitt* 12 (1897) 112-143
Pfuhl, E. *Malerei und Zeichnung der Griechen.* Munich 1923.
Pollack, L. "Griechischer Spiegel aus Cumae.'*Jahreshefte* 7 (1904) 203-208.
Puschi, A. "Silbernes Trinkhorn aus Tarent in Triest." *Jahreshefte* 5 (1902)
    112-123.
Reinach, S. *Antiquités de Bosphore Cimmérien.* Paris, 1892.
Richter, G.M.A. *Catalogue.* (See general bibliography.)
Rostovtzeff, M.I. *Iranians and Greeks in South Russia.* Oxford, 1922.
Rumpf, A. "Relief in Villa Borghese." *RömMitt* 38 (1923 - 1924) 446-478.
Schröder, B. *Griechische Bronzeeimer in Berlin Antiquariumm.* 74th
    Winckelmannsprogramm. Berlin, 1914.
Sieveking, J. *Der Bronzen der Sammlung Loeb.* Munich, 1913.
——, "Ein Grossgriechisches Tonmodell für Toreutische Arbeit." *Münchner
    Jahrbuch* 12 (1922-1923) 117-129.
Stäis, V. *Catalogue.* (See general bibliography.)
"Tumulus d'Alexandropol." *Recueil d'antiquités de la Scythie.* (1866) 1-25.
VonStackleberg, O.M. *Die Gräber der Hellenen.* Berline, 1837.
Von Stradonitz, Kekule. *Bronzen aus Dodona in den Koniglichen Museen zu
    Berlin.* Berlin 1909.
Walters, H. B. *Catalogue.* (see general bibliography.)
Zeitschrift d. Münch. Altertumsvereins. (1902) 1 ff. (No further information
    available).

IX. CHAPTER 8–THE HELLENISTIC PERIOD, OR THE HELLENISTIC TRADITION

Banko, J. "Bronzestatuette einer alten Frau im Wiener Hofmuseum." *Jahreshefte*
    19-20 (1919) 296-298.
Bienkoswki, P. *De speculis etruscia et cista in Museo principum Czartowski
    Cracoviae.* Krakow, 1912.
De Ridder, A. *Catalogue* (Louvre.) (See general bibliography.)
Dickins, G. *Hellenistic Sculpture.* Oxford, 1920.
Ducati, P. *Etruria Antica.* (See general bibliography.)
——, *Storia.* (See general bibliography.)
Furtwängler, A. *Kleine Schriften I.*(see general bibliography)
Hartwig, P. *Die Griechischen Meisterschalen der Bluthezeit des strengen roth
    figurigen Stiles.* Stuttgart & Berlin, 1893.
Merlin, A. "Statuettes de bronze trouvés en mer près de Mahdia (Tunisie.)"
    MonsPiot 18 (1910) 5-17.
Merlin, A.; and L. Poinssot. "Bronzes trouvés en mer près de Mahdia." *MonsPiot*
    17 (1909) 29-57.
Michaelis, A. "Der Schöpfer der Attalischen Kampfgruppen." *JdI* 8 (1893)
    119-134.
Neugebauer, K.A. *A.B.* (See general bibliography.)
——, *Berlin Antiquarium.* (See general bibliography)
———, *Führer.* (See general bibliography)
Perdrizet, P. *Bronzes grecs d'Égypte de la Coll. Fouquet.* Paris. 1911.
Pernice, E. *Hellenistische Kunst in Pompeji.* (See general bibliography.)
Pharmskoswky, B. "Archaeologische Funde im Jahre 1905. Südrussland." *AA* 21
    (1906) 34-230.
Puschi, A. "Silbernes Trinkhorn aus Tarent in Triest." *Jahreshefte* 5 (1902)
    112-123.
Reinach, A.J. "Les Galates dans l'art Alexandria." *MonsPiot* 18 (1910) 37-115.
Reinach, S. *Répertoire de la statuaire grecque et romaine.* Vol. 4. Paris, 1910.
Reisch, E. "Die Tempeldienerin des Nikomachos." *Jahreshefte* 19-20 (1919) 299

Richter, G.M.A. *Catalogue;* (see general bibliography).
Savignoni, L. "Minerva Vittoria." (Excursus II). *Ausonia* 5 (1910) 101-108.
Schulten, A. "Archäologische Funde in Jahre 1908. Nordafrika." *AA* 24 (1909) 189-228.
——, "Archaeologische Funde im Jahre 1909: Nordafrika." *AA* 25 (1910) 258-262.
——, "Archäologische Funde im Jahre 1911. Nordafrika." *AA* 27 (1912) 387-394.
Sieveking, J. *Der Bronzen der Sammlung Loeb.* Munich, 1913.
Strong, E. *Burlington Fine Arts Catalogue.* (See general bibliography.)
Von Stradonitz, R. Kekule. *Bronzestatuette eines kämpfenden Galliers in den Königlichen Museen . . . . . 69th Winckelmannsprogramm.* Berlin, 1909.
Wace, A.J.B. "Apollo Seated on the Omphalos." *BSA* (1902 - 1903) 211-242.
——, "Grotesques and the Evil Eye." *BSA* 10 (1903 - 1904) 103-113.
——, "Hellenistic Royal Portraits." *JHS* 25 (1905) 86-104.
Wolters, P. "Mitteilungen aus den British Museum. Part 4 - Zum Attalischen Weihgeschenk." *JdI* 1 (1886) 54-87.

X. CHAPTER 9–ROMAN BRONZES

Bachofen, J.J.*Der Bär in der Religionen der Alterthums.* Basel, 1863.
Bassi, D.; A. Ruesch, Gabrici, etc. *Guida illustrata del Museo Nazionale de Napoli.* Naples, 1911.
B.M. Catalogue. p. 53. (No further information available).
Chaffers, W.' "Bronze Figure of an Archer." *Archaeologia* 30 (1843 - 1844) 543-545.
Comparetti, D.P.A.; and G. de Petra. *La Villa Hercolanese dei Pisoni.* Torino, 1883.
Cook, A.B. *Zeus I.* (See general bibliography.)
Deonna, W. "Notes archéologiques. Au Musée d'Art et d'Histoire de Genève." *Revue archéologique* (1919) 98-142.
De Ridder, A. *Catalogue de la collection de Clerq III.* Paris, 1905.
——, "Speculum." Daremberg and Saglio. *Dictionnaire des Antiquités.* 4.2 (1422-)
Furtwangler, A. *Masterpieces.* (See general bibliography.)
Hekler, A. "Die hellenistischen Bronzegefässe von Egyed." *JdI* 24 (1909) 28-40.
Kenner, F. "Beiträge zu einer chronik der archäologischen Funde in der Österreichischen monarchie (1864 - 1866) von Dr. Friedrick Kenner. IX Fortsetzung." *Archiv für Künde Österreichischer Geschichtsquellen.* 38 (1867) 121-338.
Langlotz, E. (See general bibliography.)
Maiuri, A. "La raffigurazione del Placentarius in quattro bozzetti Pompeiani." *Bolletino d'Arte* Series 2 No. 5, Fascicolo 6. (1925) 268-274.
Mau, A. *Pompeji in Leben und Kunst.* New York, 1907.
Neugebauer, K.A. *A.B.* (See general bibliography.)
——, *Berlin Antiquarium.* (See general bibliography.)
——, *Führer.* (See general bibliography.)
Overbeck, J.; and A. Mau. *Pompeii in seinen Gebäuden, Alterthumer, und Kunstwerken.* Leipzig, 1884.
Pernice, E. "Bronzen aus Boscoreale." *AA* 15 (1900) 182.
——, "Der Dreifuss aus dem Isistemple in Pompeji." *JdI* 23 (1908) 106-111.
——, *Hellenistische Kunst in Pompeji.* (See general bibliography.)
Pliny. *Natural History.* 34:48.
Praschniker, G. *Jahreshefte 1912.* (See general bibliography.)
Reinach, S. *Antiquités Nationales.* 2 vols. Paris, 1889, 1894. Vol. 2.
Richter, G.M.A. *Catalogue.* (See general bibliography.)
Schroder, B. *Griechische Bronzeeimer in Berlin Antiquarium.* 74th *Winckelmannsprogramm.* Berlin, 1914.

Schwendemann, K. *Jahrbuch 1921*. (See general bibliography.)

Seure, G. "Un char Thraco-Macedonien." *BCH* 28 (1904) 210-237.

Strong, E. *Roman Sculpture from A ugustus to Constantine*. (Also called, by Lamb, *Sculture Romana*.) London, 1907.

Stuart-Jones, H. *Catalogue of the Conservatori Museum*. Oxford. (no date.)

Vallentin, F. "Monuments épigraphiques de la Creuse." *Bulletin épigraphique de la Gaule*. (1881) 129-138.

Walters, H.B. *Catalogue*. (See general bibliography.)

Willers, H. *Neue Untersuchungen uber die romische bronzeindustrie von Capua und Niedergermanien, besonders auf die funde aus Deutschland und dem Norden hin von Heinrich Willers*. Leipzig & Hannover, 1907.

− −, *Die römischen Bronzeimer von Hemmor*. Hannover & Leipzig, 1901.

Wissowa, G. "Larea." Roscher II (See general bibliography.) pt. 2. (1894 - 1897)

B. A NEW SELECT BIBLIOGRAPHY

[Includes material not utilized by Miss Lamb, as well as a selection of important works published after 1929 up to 1967.]

XI. GENERAL WORKS

Åberg, N. "Bronzeseitliche u. früheisenzeitliche chronologie." *Mnemosyne* 3 (1936) 181 ff.

Bieber, M. *Alexander the Great in Greek and Roman Art*. Chicago 1964. [includes the bronze statuettes of Alexander]

Boardman, J. *Greek Art* (The World of Art Series). London 1964

Charbonneaux, Jean. *Les bronzes grecs*. Paris 1958. transl. by Katherine Watson as *Greek Bronzes*, New York 1962.
Probably the most important volume on bronzes to appear since Miss Lamb's. Although not as extensive, it includes both types and chronology of small bronzes as well as sections on famous bronze collections, exhibitions and care of bronzes. Good bibliography.

Childe, Gordon V. *The Bronze Age*. London 1963. [References to bronze implements appear throughout the historical discussions]

− − −, *The Dawn of European Civilization*. New York 1957. 15-83, 229-251 deal with artifacts including bronzes.

Eggers, H. J. *Der Römische Import in freien Germanian*. Hamburg 1951.

Gjødesen, Mogens. "Greek Bronzes: A Review Article." *AJA* 67 (1963) 333-351 (Comprehensive review and criticism of Charbonneaux.)

Jantzen, Ulf. "Bronzewerkstätten in Grossgriechenland und Sizilien." *JdI* 13th Ergängungsheft (1937) 1-68.

Jex-Blake, K. and E. Sellers. *The Elder Pliny's Chapters on the History of Art*. Preface to the first American edition and Select Bibliography 1896-1968 by R. J. Schoder, S.J. Chicago 1968.

Lubke, W.; E. Pernice. *Die Kunst der Griechen*. Vienna 1948.

Mylonas, George E. (ed.))*Studies Presented to David Moore Robinson*. Vol. 1. St. Louis 1951. (Numerous essays on all aspects of Greek sculpture)

Neugebauer, Karl A. *Bronzegerät des Altertums*. (Abbreviated as *AB*) Berlin 1927.

Richter, G. M. A. *Animals in Greek Sculpture*. London and New York 1930.

− − −, *A Handbook of Greek Art*. London 1959, 1962. 173-192. (Chapter 4 on small bronzes) 193-215. (Chapter 5, decorative metalwork)

− − −. *The Sculpture and Sculptors of the Greeks*. 3rd ed. New Haven 1950. (Bronze figurines are included in the study of the development of Greek sculpture).

Seltman, Charles. *Approach to Greek Art.* New York 1960. (Much of his approach is based on small bronze works.)

Schoppa, H. *Die Kunst der Römerzeit in Gallien, Germanien und Brittanien.* Bonn 1957.

Schuchardt, W. H. *Antike Plastik.* Berlin 1962.

———, *Die Kunst der Griechen.* Berlin 1940.

Zervos, Christian. *L'Art en Grece.* Paris 1934.

XII. CATALOGUES OF MUSEUMS AND MAJOR COLLECTIONS

Arndt, Paul. *La Glyptotheque Ny Carlsberg, fondée par Carl Jacobsen. Les monuments antiques.* Munich 1912.

Beazley, J.D. and F. Magi. *La Raccolta Benedette Guglielmi nel Museo Gregoriano Etrusco.* Vatican 1939.

Charbonneaux, Jean. *La sculpture grecque au Musée du Louvre.* Paris 1936, New ed. 1965.

Chase, George H. and Cornelius C. Vermeule. *Greek, Etruscan and Roman Art.* (The classical collections of the Museum of Fine Arts, Boston) Meriden 1963.

Den Boersted, M. H. P. *The Bronze Vessels* (Description of the collections in the Rijksmuseum G. M. Kam at Nijmegen, Vol. V) Nijmegen 1956. [Extensive bibliography on bronzes found in Northern Europe].

Froehner, William. *Collection Julien Gréau. Bronzes antiques.* Paris 1885. (Hotel Drouot sale).

Herbert, Kevin. *Ancient Art in Bowdoin College.* Cambridge 1964. 116-127, small bronzes.

Hill, Dorothy Kent. *Catalogue of Classical Bronze Sculpture in the Walters Art Gallery.* Baltimore 1949.

Menzel, H. *Die Römischen Bronzen aus Deutschland.* I Speyer (1960), II Trier (1966)

Michaelowski, Kazimierz. *Sztuka Staroztyna.* Warsaw 1955. 33-48; 198-202.

Neugebauer, Karl A. *Katalog der statuarischen Bronzen im Antiquarium Staatliche Museen zu Berlin.* Vol. i. *Die minoischen und archaeischer griechischen Bronzen;* Vol. ii. *Die griechischen Bronzen des Klassischen Zeit und des Hellenismus.* Berlin. Vol. i, 1931; Vol. ii, 1951.

Nicholls, Richard. *A Catalogue of the Greek and Roman Bronzes in the Fitzwilliam Museum.* Cambridge [in preparation].

Richter, G. M. A. *Catalogue of Greek, Etruscan and Roman Bronzes.* New York, The Metropolitan Museum of Art. 1915.

———, *Handbook of the Classical Collection.* New York 1930.

———, *Handbook of the Etruscan Collection.* New York 1940.

———, *Handbook of the Greek Collection.* Cambridge 1965.

Rolland, H. *Bronzes antiques de Haute Provence.* Suppl. 18 of *Gallia* 1965.

Schumacher, Karl. *Beschreibung der Sammlung antiker Bronzen.* Karlsruhe 1890.

Simonett, Ch. *Die römischen Bronzestatuetten der Schweiz.* Basel 1929.

Walters, H. B. *Select Bronzes.* London 1915.

Zadoks-Jitta, A.N. and others. *Roman Bronze Statuettes from the Netherlands. I.* Groningen 1967.

XIII. CATALOGUE OF MAJOR BRONZE EXHIBITIONS

Albright Art Gallery. *Master Bronzes selected from Museums and Collections of America.* Buffalo 1937.

Braemer, F. *L'art dans l'occident Romain.* Paris 1963 [Exhibition in the Louvre].

Chase, George H. *Greek and Roman Sculpture in American Collections.* Cambridge 1924.

Del Chiaro, Mario A. *Etruscan Art from West Coast Collections* Univ. of California Art Gallery, Santa Barbara 1967.

Doppelfeld, O. (ed.) *Römer am Rhein.* Koln 1967. [Exhibition at Cologne. A major reference for bronzes found in northern Europe].

Hanfmann, George M. A. *Ancient Art in American Private Collections.* [Exhibition at Fogg Art Museum, Harvard University]. Lunenberg 1954.

———, and J. Coolidge. *The Beauty of Ancient Art.* [Exhibition of the Norman Schimmel Collection in the Fogg Museum, Harvard University] Mainz 1964. Part I - Classical Antiquity.

LaBaume, P. *Römische Kleinkunst.* Rheinische Kunststatten 1962.

Mitten, David G. and S. Doeringer. *Master Bronzes from the Classical World.* [Exhibition at the Fogg Museum, Harvard University; the City Art Museum, St. Louis, and the Los Angeles County Museum of Art. Dec. 1967-May 1968] Mainz 1967.

Robinson, Francis W. *Small Bronzes of the Ancient World.* Detroit Institute of Arts. Detroit 1947.

Schefold, Karl. *Meisterwerke griechischer Kunst.* Basel-Stuttgart 1960.

Von Bothmer, Dietrich. *Ancient Art from New York Private Collections.* [Exhibition at the Metropolitan Museum of Art] New York 1961.

———, *Greek, Etruscan and Roman Antiquities.* [Century Exhibition] New York 1950.

XIV. EXCAVATION REPORTS

Amandry, P. "Vases, bronzes et terres cuites de Delphes." ("Fouilles de 1938") *BCH* 62 (1938) 305-331.

Joffroy, R. *Le Trésor de Vix.* Paris 1955

Kunze, Emil, etc. *Bericht über die Ausgrabungen in Olympia.* Berlin 1961.

Lamb, Winifred. "Bronzes from the Acropolis, 1914-1927." [Excavations at Sparta 1927] *BSA* 28 (1926-27) 85-95.

Nennesy, J. B. *Stephania: A Middle and Late Bronze Age Cemetery in Cyprus.* London 1965.

Will, E. *"Groupe de bronze du V siècle trouvé à Delphes."* *BCH* 70 (1946) 639-648.

XV. BRONZE AND BRONZE-WORKING

Caley, Earle R. *Analysis of Ancient Metals.* New York 1964 [Includes valuable data on Greek bronze composition].

———, "Chemical CInvestigation of Two Ancient Bronze Statuettes Found in Greece." *The Ohio Journal of Science* 51 (1951) 12-14.

Casson, S. *The Techniques of Early Greek Sculpture.* 1933

Charbonneaux, Jean. *Greek Bronzes.* New York 1962. 19-40 [technique]

Charles, J. A. "Early Arsenical Bronzes-A Metallurgical View." *AJA* 71 (1967) 21-26 [Includes early Cycladic material]

Congdon, Lenore Keene, "Metallic Analyses of Three Caryatid Mirrors." *AJA* 71 (1967)

Forbes, R. J. *Studies in Ancient Technology.* Vols. 8-9. *Metallurgy in Antiquity* [Vol. 8 includes studies of tools and techniques; Vol. 9 includes bronze and bronze working]. Leiden 1964.

Hill, Dorothy Kent. *Catalogue of Classical Bronze Sculpture in the Walters Art Gallery.* Baltimore 1949. [The introduction is primarily on technique].

Kluge, K.; K. Lehmann-Hartleben. *Die antiken Grossbronzen.* Bd. II. *Die antike Erzgestaltung und ihre technischen Grundlagen.* Berlin 1927.

Maryon, Herbert. "Metal-Working in the Ancient World." *AJA* 53 (1949) 93.125

Panseri, G.; M. Leoni. "The Manufacturing Technique of Etruscan Mirrors." *Conservation* 3 (1957) 49-62.

Picard, Charles. *Manuel d'archéologie grecque, la Sculpture.* Vol. 1. Paris 1935. 174-187 [technique].

Renfrew, Colin. "Cycladic Metallurgy and the Aegean Early Age." *AJA* 71 (1967) 1-20.
Robinson, Francis W. *Small Bronzes of the Ancient World.* Detroit 1947. Introduction 3-5 [technique].

XVI. VESSELS AND IMPLEMENTS

1. ARMOR

Catling, H. W. "Bronze cut-and-thrust Swords in the East Mediterranean." *Proc. of the Prehistoric Society.* 1956.
Sanders, N. K. "The First Aegean Swords and their Ancestry." *AJA* 65 (1961) 17-29.
―――, "Later Aegean Bronze Swords." *AJA* 67 (1963) 117-153.
Snodgrass, A. *Early Greek Armour and Weapons from the End of the Bronze Age to 600 B. C.* Edinburgh 1964.

2. BRONZE VESSELS

Brendel, Otto J. "Three Archaic Bronze Dishes in Italy." *AJA* 47 (1943) 193-208.
Daux, G. "Chroniques des fouilles, 1962." *BCH* 87 (1963) 802 ff., pl. 16. [Krater of Derveni]
Diehl, Erika. *Die Hydria.* Mainz 1964.
Goldman, Bernard. "The Development of the Lion Griffin." *AJA* 64 (1960) 319-328. [Protome cauldrons].
Haynes, S. *Etrsucan Head Vases.* [no further information available]
Den Boersted, M. H. P. *The Bronze Vessels.* [Description of the Collections in the Rijksmuseum G. M. Kam at Nijmegen, Vol. V.] Nijmegen 1956. [Reference bibliography, x-xvii]
Hill, Dorothy Kent. "A Class of Bronze Handles of the Archaic and Classical Periods. " *AJA* 62 (1957) 193-195.
―――, "The Long-Beaked Bronze Jug in Greek Lands." *AJA* 66 (1962- 57-63.
―――, "Techniques of Greek Metal Vases and its bearing on Vase Forms in Metal and Pottery." *AJA* 51 (1947) 248-256.
Hood, M. S. F. "Archaeological Reports." *JHS* 84 (1961) 15 ff [Derveni Krater]
Jantzen, Ulf. "Griechische Bronzeteller." *AM* 63-64 (1938-1939) 140 ff.
―――, *Griechischen Griefenkessel.* Berlin 1955.
―――, *Griechische Griff-Phialen.* 114 *Winckelmannsprogramm der Archaeologischen Gesellschaft zu Berlin.* Berlin 1958.
Lehman, Karl. "Bronze Pail of Athena Alakoneia." *Hesperia.* 28 (1959) 153-161.
Ny Carlsberg Glyptotek. *From the Collections of Ny Carlsberg Glyptotek.* Vol. 2. Copenhagen 1938. 140-168. [Bronze export vessels in Denmark from Greece, Campania and Etruria].
Riis, P. J. "The Danish Bronze Vessels of Greek, Early Campanian and Etruscan, Manufacture." *Acta Archeologica* 30 (1959) 1-50.
Robinson, David Moore. "New Greek Bronze Vases-a Commentary on Pindar." *AJA* 46 (1942) 172-197.
Rumpf, A. "Krater Lakonikos." *Charites E. Langlotz: Studien für Altertumswissenschaft.* Bonn. 127- 135 [Shows that the Vix Krater is probably the Krater Lakonikos.]
Szilagyi, Janos Gyorgy. "Trouvailles grecques sur territoire de la Hongrie." *8mem Congres International d'archaeologie classique. La Rayonnement des civilisations grecque et romaine sur les cultures peripheriques.* Paris 1965. 386-390. [2 bronze Greek export vessels and possibility of a connection with the amber trade.]
Vanderpool, Emily. "Newsletter from Greece." *AJA* 66 (1962) 289-390. [Includes the Krater of Derveni].

3. BRONZE RELIEFS

Hanfmann, George M.A. "Etruscan Bronze Reliefs."*ARTB*19(1937) 463-484.

Hill, Dorothy Kent. "Ancient Metal Reliefs".*Hesperia*12(1944) 97-114.

————,"More about Ancient Metal Reliefs". *Hesperia* 13(1945) 87-89.

Kunze, Emil. *Kretische Bronzereliefs.* Berlin 1931.

Mitten, David G. "An Archaic Bronze Relief of a Hoplite in the McDaniel Collection." *Harvard Studies in Classical Philology.* 67 (1963) 303-306.

Roberts, Helle S. "Some Bronze Plaques with Repoussé Decoration in the Danish National Museum." *ActaA* 34 (1963) 135-184.

4. MIRRORS AND PATERAE

Amandry, P. "Manches de patere et miroir grecs." *Mon Piot* 47 (1953) 47-70

Beazley, Sir John D. "A Greek Mirror in Dublin." *Proc. Royal Irish Academy* 45 (1939) 31-39.

Congdon, Lenore O. K. "Two Bronze Mirror Caryatids in the National Museum of Warsaw." *AJA* 70 (1966) 161-164.

————, *Greek Caryatid Mirrors.* [in preparation. Includes a descriptive and photographic catalogue of all known Greek mainland mirrors of the caryatid variety].

Dumont, Charles; and J. C. Chaplain. *Les céramiques de la Grèce propre.* Vol. 2 *Mélanges archéologiques.* Paris 1890. (Excellent references to mirrors).

Gjødesen, Mogens. "Bronze Paterae with Anthropomorphic Handles." *AA* 15 fasc. 3 (1944)

Hoffman, Herbert. "Graeco-Scythian Mirrors." *AJA* 69 (1965) 65-66.

Karouzou, Semni P. "Attic Bronze Mirrors." *Studies Presented to David Moore Robinson.* Vol. 1 (G. E. Mylonas, ed.) St. Louis 1951. 565-586.

Michon, Etienne. "Mirors grecs a pied, bronzes du Musée du Louvre." *MonsGr* 2 nos. 19-20 (1891-92) 3-35.

Prachniker, Camillo. "Bronzene Spiegelstütze in Wiener Hofmuseum." *JOAI* 15 (1912) 219-252.

Zdojewska, Wanda. "Fragmenty Greckich Luster Stojacych W. Muzeum Narodowm w Warszawie." *Rocznik Museum Narodowego w Warszawie* 9 (1965) 52-84.

Zuchner, W. *Griechische Klappspiegel.* Jdi 14th Ergangungsheft. Berlin 1942.

5. MISCELLANEOUS IMPLEMENTS, FURNISHINGS

Benti, L. "I Tripodi Loeb." *Tyrrhenika: Saggi di Studi Etruschki.* Milan 1957.

Hill, Dorothy Kent. "To Perfume the Etruscans and the Latins." *Archaeology* 18 (1965) 187-190.

Hoffman, Herbert. "A Bronze Fulcrum in Providence." *AJA* 61 (1957) 167-168.

Jacobsthal, P. *Greek Pins and their Connexions with Europe and Asia.* New York 1956.

Richter, G. M. A. *Ancient Furniture: A History of Greek, Etruscan and Roman Furniture.* Oxford 1926.

Ternbach, Joseph. "The Restoration of an Etruscan Bronze Tripod." *Archaeology* 17 (1964) 18-25.

XVII. ADDENDA TO SECTIONS II–X

1. PRE-HELLENIC PERIOD

Catling, H. W. *Cypriot Bronzework in the Mycenaean World.* Oxford 1964.

————, *Mycenaean Bronzes.* (Studies in Mediterranean Art Series No. 10) [in preparation].

Charbonneaux, Jean. *L'art égéen.* Paris & Brussels 1929.

Hall, Harry R. H. *Aegean Archaeology.* London 1913.

Hutchinson, R. W. *Prehistoric Crete.* Middlesex & Baltimore 1962.

Matz, Friedrich. (A.E. Keep transl.) *The Art of Crete and Early Greece.* New York 1962. [Includes study of bronze artifacts].

Pendlebury, John D. *The Archaeology of Crete: An Introduction.* London 1939, New York 1965.

Vermeule, Emily. *Greece in the Bronze Age.* Chicago 1964. [Includes studies of relevant bronze artifacts. Noteworthy for a very extensive and thorough bibliography].

Zervos, Chr. *L'art des Cyclades, du début à la fin de l'age de Bronze.* Paris 1957.

2. GEOMETRIC AND ARCHAIC PERIODS

Amyx, D. A. "Geometric Platform Bronzes." *AJA* 53 (1949) 147-148.

Blumel, Karl. *Die archaisch Griechischen Skulpturen der Staatlichen Museen zu Berlin.* Berlin 1963.

Hafner, Ursula. *Das Kunstschaffen Lakoniens in archaischer Zeit.* Munich 1965. [An important dissertation, privately published, including a catalogue of many Laconian bronzes and artifacts].

Himmelmann-Wildschutz, Nikolaus. *Geometrische Plastik: Bemerkungen zur Geometrischen Plastik.* Berlin 1964.

Hoffman, Herbert. "Two Unknwon Greek Bronzes of the Archaic Period." *AJA* 68 (1964) 185-188.

Matz, Friedrich. *Geschichte der griechischen Kunst.* Vol. 1. *Die geometrische und die früharchaische Form.* Frankfurt 1950.

Payne, Humfrey. *Necrocorinthia.* Oxford 1931. [Includes many bronze objects of the late archaic to early classical period.] 210 ff.

Payne, Humfrey and others - *Perachora: The Sanctuaries of Hera Akraia and Lemenia.* Vol. 1: *Architecture, Bronzes, Terra cottas.* Oxford 1940. p. 123 ff. [late archaic, early classical bronzes. Especially important for its discussion of the Corinthian school of bronzeworking.]

Richter, Gisela M.A. *Kouroi.* London 1960. [Includes small male bronze figures in the study of the kouros type.]

3. CLASSICAL AND HELLENISTIC PERIODS

Bieber, Margaret. *Sculpture of the Hellenistic Age.* 2nd ed. New York, 1961.

Charbonneaux, Jean. *La sculpture grecque classique.* 2 vols. Paris, 1943, 1945.

Elderkin, G.W. "Bronze Statuettes of Zeus Keraimos." *AJA* 44 (1940) 225-233.

Fuchs, W. *Der Schiffsfund von Mahdia.* Tubingen, 1963. [Re-publication of the Hellenistic ship finds at Mahdia.]

Hanfmann, George M.A. "An Early Classical Aphrodite." *AJA* 66 (1962) 281-284.

Poulsen, Van Hager. "Der strenge Stil. Studien zur Geschichte der griechischen Plastik, 480-460." *ActaA* 8 (1937) 1-142.

Schwabacher, Willy. "The Olympian Zeus before Phidias." *Archaeology* 14 (1961) 104-109. [Bronze statuettes of Zeus for the basis of much of the discussion.]

Wiegand, Theodor. *Bronzefigur einer Spinnerin, im antiquarium der Koniglicher Museum.* (73 *Winckelmannsprogram . . .*)

4. ETRUSCAN AND ROMAN

Boschi, Luigi. *I Bronzetti Romani di Montorio Veronese.* Venice 1962.

Charbonneaux, Jean. *L'art au siècle d'Auguste.* Paris 1948.

Congdon, Lenore O. K. "The Mantua Apolla of the Fogg Art Museum" *AJA* 67 (1963) 7-13.

Cook, Brian F. "The Goddess Cybele: A Bronze in New York." *Archaeology* 19 (1966) 251-257.

Giglioli, E. Q. *L'arte etrusca*. Milan 1934. [Extremely comprehensive picture source on Etruscan mirrors].

Hamburg, P. G. *Studies in Roman Imperial Art.* Copenhagen 1945.
Hanfmann, George M. A. *Altetruskische Plastik I.* Würzburg 1936.
———, "A Bronze Portrait of Julia Domna." *Annual Report of the Fogg Art Museum* (1955-1956) 42-43.
———, "An Etruscan Goddess." *Archaeology* 9 (1956) 230-232. (Also *Annual Report of the Fogg Art Museum* (1955-1956) 44-45, 60).
———, *Etruskische Platik.* Stuttgart 1956.
Hill, Dorothy Kent. "A Cache of Bronze Portraits of the Julio-Claudians." *AJA* 43 (1939) 401-409.
Maxwell-Hyslop, R. R. "Urartian Bronzes in Etruscan Tombs." *Iraq* 17 ʼ(1956) 150 ff.
Menzel, Heinz. *Römische Bronzen in Speyer.* Mainz 1960 (Vol. 2 - book of pictures)
Richardson, Emeline H. "The Etruscan Origins of Early Roman Sculpture." *MAAR* 21 (1953) 77-124.
———, *The Etruscans, Their Art and Civlization.* Chicago 1964. [Includes an excellent bibliography].
———, "The Recurrent Geometric in the Sculpture of Central Italy." *MAAR* 27 (1962) 159-198.
Richter, G. M. A. *Handbook of the Etruscan Collection.* New York 1940.
Riis, Poul J. *Tyrrhenica.* Copenhagen 1941.
Rizzo, G. E. "Copie romane della statue di bronzo a Pompeioani." *Bullettino della Commissione Archeologia Comunate di Roma* 53 (1925) 13-24.
Strong, Eugenie S. *Art in Ancient Rome.* Vols. 1, 2. New York 1928. [Includes the minor arts].

GREEK AND ROMAN BRONZES

CHAPTER I

THE PREHISTORIC PERIOD

A. UTENSILS AND DECORATIVE WORK

BEFORE the Heroic Age, says Hesiod in the *Works and Days*, were the people who lived in the Age of Bronze : " of bronze were their weapons, and of bronze their houses, and they worked in bronze." [1] Though his description is fanciful, particularly in the matter of the houses, the tradition he followed commemorates an archæological fact. The Bronze Age is that phase of civilisation when men had first learned to make their implements of metal, and this metal was bronze or its main ingredient, copper : the uses of iron were not yet understood. In Greece, it succeeds the Neolithic Period and precedes the Heroic Age described by Homer, which is the transition from bronze to iron.

Therefore, the history of bronze in the Bronze Age is, in the first place, the history of common tools and weapons. It is intimately bound up with the history of the peoples who made them, their migrations and trade routes ; one cannot discuss the one without discussing the other.

In the second place, and later in the period, there is a decorative element. Men learned how to hammer and engrave and inlay patterns on the objects they used, and the history of bronze can then be connected with that of the arts, such as carving and painting.

Apart from the instruments, decorated or undecorated, of peace and war, there is a class of objects that have no practical

[1] ll. 150, 151.

value but a high religious and artistic importance—the small bronze figures, mostly of men and women, which are the most important of our few records of Cretan sculpture.

At some time in the twelfth century B.C. the transition from the Bronze to the Iron Age begins. Bronze was then sparingly used for weapons and tools, since iron had taken its place, but more widely employed in decorative work and for figures ; it is these, therefore, which form the basis of comparison between the work of the prehistoric and subsequent periods, and which are the subject of our book.

Very few words will suffice to introduce the peoples who, in the Bronze Age, inhabited Greece and the Greek islands, and who concern us as the makers and users of the bronze works of art described in this chapter.

The Cretans occupy the centre of the stage ; a race which rapidly advanced in culture and had a natural aptitude for art. Politically and artistically they dominated the Aegean. Their art is often called " Minoan," after their legendary King Minos, and the Bronze Age in Crete is divided into and measured by the nine Minoan Periods.[1]

The inhabitants of the Greek mainland also play an important part, which begins, for us, about the year 1600 B.C., after their dependence on Crete had produced what is usually termed the Mycenaean civilisation. The name " Mycenaean " was chosen because Mycenae was not only the richest of the mainland sites, but also the first important one to be explored. There has been much controversy as to the respective shares of the Cretans and the mainlanders in manufacturing the finer objects of art found at Mycenae and elsewhere. It will be sufficient for us to illustrate the objects, and to leave the judgment to others.

[1] The dating is as follows (see Forsdyke, *Catalogue of Vases in British Museum*, I, 1, p. xi, which is here followed except that I have substituted 1475 for 1450 as the end of the L.M. I) : Early Minoan I, 3400-2800 B.C. ; Early Minoan II, 2800-2400 B.C. ; Early Minoan III, 2400-2100 B.C. ; Middle Minoan I, 2100-1900 B.C. ; Middle Minoan II, 1900-1700 B.C. ; Middle Minoan III, 1700-1580, B.C. ; Late Minoan I, 1580-1475 B.C. ; Late Minoan II, 1475-1375 B.C. ; Late Minoan III, 1375-1100.

For objects from the Cyclades the term " Cycladic " is substituted for " Minoan " : for objects from the Mainland of Greece the term " Helladic " and, from 1580 onwards, Mycenaean.

The people of the Cyclades make a brief appearance as the owners of one bronze statuette.

The Cypriotes are most conspicuous at the beginning and at the end of the Bronze Age. At the beginning, their possession of copper mines and their proximity to Asia Minor enabled them to supply others with raw material, and to transmit knowledge from East to North and West. Towards the end of our period, they shared with Rhodes the distinction of being among the last places to preserve the traditions of Cretan art. They are associated, as will be seen, with bronze objects of a particular type (Chapter II).

Last comes Troy, representing one aspect of the culture and traditions of Asia Minor. It is to the second of its nine successive cities that the well-known primitive bronze statuette belongs (p. 18). At this period, which begins in the second half of the third millennium and ends early in the second millennium, Troy was still uninfluenced by the Cretan civilisation, though it had points of contact with Cyprus, and affinities with Thrace and Macedonia. The sixth city was the city of Priam, and the city whose fortunes were involved with those of Greece ; but it produced no ornamental bronze work and no bronze statuettes.[1]

The discovery of how to melt and cast metal, though it is one of the most important in the history of man, did not, at first, bring any marked change. Stone implements were only gradually replaced by copper, and stone was used side by side with copper in what is sometimes called the Chalcolithic Age, which preceded the full Age of Bronze. Even in the latter, certain kinds of stone implements survived, such as the flint and obsidian arrow-heads which occur in Mycenaean tombs.

Of the inhabitants of Greece and the Islands, the first to use copper were the Cypriotes and Cretans. The Cypriotes may have learned the art from Asia Minor, the Cretans from Egypt, Asia Minor or Cyprus, probably Cyprus. Critics have long disputed whether the working of this metal was first discovered in Egypt or Asia ;[2] the credit should probably be given to the latter.

[1] See Dörpfeld, *Troja und Ilion*, I, p. 393.
[2] For the claims of Egypt and Anau to priority in copper working, see *Cambridge Ancient History*, I, pp. 90, 91.

We know for certain that the knowledge was carried from South-East to North-West over Europe by more than one route. From Crete, it spread through the Cyclades to the Peloponnese and Central Greece, and, later, across the sea to Sicily and South Italy. From Cyprus and Asia Minor, it passed into South-Eastern Europe. An interesting point is that neither of these two currents touched Thessaly for a long time. Its backward people continued to use stone implements when their neighbours were using bronze.

The history of bronze will be best understood if we consider questions of material and technique before examining the objects themselves.

MATERIALS—Copper was easily obtained. Large supplies were found in Cyprus and exported thence to Egypt [1] and, no doubt, to Greece and the other Aegean islands. It could also be obtained, in smaller quantities, in some of the islands, e.g. Paros and Gaudos,[2] and in certain districts of Greece. These include Mount Othrys, Euboea (Chalkis and Aidepsos), Boeotia, and one or two places in the Peloponnese.

For a time copper implements were used, but the pure metal is not strong, and cannot be sharpened to a really good cutting edge : these defects could be improved by a proportion of copper oxide being left in the copper at the last stage of smelting, as was often done in Cyprus.

Some time in the third millennium B.C., it was discovered that the best results were obtained by an alloy of tin and copper, in other words, bronze.

The use of the tin raises an important question which must have been an anxious problem for primitive man. Where could tin be obtained ?

The tin mines of Khorassan were probably known very early to the people of Asia Minor.[3] More accessible to the Aegean are those of the Iberian peninsula : [4] it is of these that Ezekiel

---

[1] Mentioned in documents of the time of Thotmes III (1501-1447 B.C.).
[2] Xanthoudides, *Vaulted Tombs of the Messara*, p. 27.
[3] See Déchelette, *Manuel d'Archéologie Celtique et Gallo-Romaine*, Vol. II, I, p. 95.
[4] So Déchelette, *loc. cit.* Leeds is inclined to think there was little trade between Spain and the East before 1000 B.C., *Cambridge Ancient History*, II, p. 590. Mr. O. Davies, in a paper read before the British Association in 1928, publishes his discovery of a source of supply at Kirrha.

(*c.* 580 B.C.) speaks when he says that the Phoenicians of Tyre got their tin from Tarshish (Gades). Most productive of all were the mines of the British Isles, though they were possibly not known to the Aegean at the earliest period. But, from what we have learned concerning the enterprise of the early traders, we can well believe that they were soon discovered. Their identification with the Kassiterides of Herodotus is now widely accepted : [1] that Herodotus is so vague as to their whereabouts may be due to the route being kept a trade secret.

Tin must have been valuable, since it was so hard to procure. At first it was used too economically : a blade from the first palace at Phaestos contains only 3·146 per cent of tin.[2] On the other hand, an early dagger from the small tholos at Hagia Triadha has 14·22 per cent, an extravagant proportion. The proper ratio is 10 per cent : the Cretans and the other inhabitants of Greece and the islands attained this gradually ; the Cypriotes much more slowly, not, in fact, before the Mycenaean influence reached Cyprus towards the end of the Bronze Age.

TECHNIQUE—The metal was first smelted ; ancient slag-heaps have been found in several places in Greek lands, e.g. at Chrysokamina, near Hierapetra (Crete).[3] The final casting was usually done in a stone mould, and many of these moulds have survived. The type employed is apparently the simple as opposed to the bivalve mould : [4] i.e. the metal was poured into a hollow of appropriate shape which was covered with a stone. The moulds are usually brick-shaped blocks of stone with hollows on all faces shaped for various implements. They must have been valuable, for at Gournia,[5] a town in Crete, where more than one house belonged to a metal-worker, a cracked mould had been most elaborately repaired by a strip

[1] See Déchelette, *op. cit.*, p. 96.
[2] Mosso, *Dawn of Mediterranean Civilisation*, pp. 305, n. 2, and 306.
[3] Xanthoudides, *Vaulted Tombs of the Messara*, p. 27.
[4] Déchelette, *op. cit.*, pp. 181 ff. ; Pernice, *Jahreshefte*, VII, pp. 189 ff. Possible double or bivalve moulds, mentioned in Pernice's article, are regarded as moulds for waxen and other models which would require a further mould to be reproduced in metal (pp. 189, 191). Pernice discovered by experiment that not all the surviving moulds were used for the finished metal object : also (p. 187) that in some of the Trojan moulds, the hollow should only be partly filled with metal to obtain a good result.
[5] Boyd-Hawes, *Gournia*, Pl. III, 67, p. 32.

of bronze being passed round it and tightened with wedges. A number of moulds come from the second and the later cities of Troy, and there are examples from Palaikastro (Crete), Sesklo (Thessaly),[1] and other sites. It has been shown that wax models were used as early as the seventh, and perhaps also the second city of Troy.[2]

After being cast, the objects were often finished off with the hammer, particularly the axes and chisels, where a slightly spreading cutting edge was required. Holes for rivets in the tang of weapons were made by a piece of wood or other material being inserted into the mould, round which the molten metal would flow. Ornaments in relief were usually cast in the mould and retouched with the hammer or engraving tool. Incised ornaments could be made with a good bronze tool, as experiments have shown. Joins were almost always made by means of rivets, except for decorative non-structural details, such as the leaves on the rim of the bowl from Knossos (p. 12). The neck of the ewer (p. 12) is exceptional. Here, two bits of metal were welded together, but the soldering of important joins was the discovery of a later age. The artistic skill of the prehistoric people shows itself in the way they used the necessary rivet as a decorative feature : this will be particularly appreciated in the case of the vases described on page 12.

Of inlaying, as illustrated by the swords from the Shaft Graves of Mycenae, an account will be given in a later section.

BRONZE WEAPONS AND TOOLS—The earliest objects in metal are daggers that also might be used as spear-heads, and flat celts that developed on the one hand into axes, on the other into chisels. Both daggers and celts were indispensable, the one for warfare, the other both for war and carpentry. The drill, too, appears early, and, a little later, the spear-head as distinct from the dagger. With the earliest copper daggers in Crete and the Cyclades are found objects that are not necessities but luxuries, such as razors and tweezers for removing hairs : these, though they suggest a civilisation somewhat more advanced, can scarcely be later in date.

---

[1] Troy, see *Jahreshefte*, VII, p. 187 ; Palaikastro, see Bosanquet and Dawkins, *Palaikastro*, I, p. 124 ; Sesklo, see Wace and Thompson, *Prehistoric Thessaly*, p. 74.
[2] *Jahreshefte*, VII, p. 189.

As time went on, the shapes were improved by each succeeding generation. The short triangular daggers were lengthened, and strengthened by a midrib. The Cypriote daggers, with their midrib prolonged into a tang which could be inserted into the hilt, also became longer. Gradually, both forms grew into swords : some of the swords, in their turn, grew into the long, slender rapiers of the Second Late Minoan Period.

Other weapons, too, were developed : spear-heads, sword-heads and knives. Objects such as the axe and the ritual double axe play an important part. The different kinds of tools—chisels, borers, saws, sickles, etc.—were elaborated, in spite of the softness of the metal. Toilet accessories take their place among man's possessions at various times during the period ; mirrors not, apparently, earlier than the fifteenth century.[1] Metal vases were sometimes substituted for the more fragile vases in pottery.

But, since we are concerned only with such objects as have artistic significance, the purely useful tools and weapons have no claim to be discussed here. Certain of the weapons, however, and many of the vases were selected by the Minoan and Mycenaean artists as a suitable field for decoration, and these come within the compass of our book.

DECORATION OF SWORDS AND DAGGERS—An early example of a decorated dagger belongs to the Second Middle Minoan Period.[2] It comes from the Lasethi district of Crete, perhaps originally from the Psychro Cave itself. It is triangular in shape, and originally had a small tang (now broken away) to facilitate mounting. On both sides of the blade are incised pictures which may have been filled with gold wire : one picture shows two bulls charging, the other, a huntsman, perhaps the owner of the dagger himself, spearing a wild boar (Pl. 3).

A group of highly ornamented swords and daggers belongs to the end of the Middle Minoan Period and the First Late Minoan Period. The best-known examples are those which come from the Shaft Graves at Mycenae,[3] the burying place

[1] The mirrors were usually circular discs, often provided with handles of another material.

[2] In a private collection, *Palace of Minos*, pp. 718 ff., and Fig. 541. The man wears gaiters and an unusual arrangement of belt and loin-cloth.

[3] The Shaft Grave dynasty may be dated from shortly before 1600 B.C. to near the end of the sixteenth century, *B.S.A.*, XXV, p. 119.

of the ruling dynasty. The daggers are in one sense the discovery of Schliemann, since he excavated them and published them, as yet uncleaned, with the other objects from the Shaft Graves. In another sense they are the discovery of the Greek archæologist Koumanoudes, since it was he who first cleaned them and revealed the inlay that the incrustation of the bronze had hidden.

In shape they are nothing new : their form is developed from the tanged and triangular daggers of the earlier periods, and akin to that of the dagger with the man and boar described above (p. 7).

Their elaborate technique is, however, a startling advance on anything hitherto described, though to those who are acquainted with other achievements of Minoan artists, it takes its place as one among many manifestations of their skill. We cannot trace all the steps by which such perfection was reached, but we can infer some of them from examples of gold and silver work belonging to the period, from earlier examples of the inlaying of materials other than metal (shell, ivory, faience, etc.), and from analogous Egyptian metal-work. Much of the technique may have been learned from Egypt. On the other hand, the style and conventions of the scenes which decorate the daggers are best understood if they are compared with those of Cretan fresco painting with which they have much in common.

There are three main forms of decoration : relief, inlay, and inlay combined with relief.

The relief is produced by casting, outlines being subsequently sharpened by chasing, and interior details marked by incision.

The inlay [1] is the result of the juxtaposition of different kinds of metal. These were, in most cases, applied to a strip of oxidised silver [2] which, when finished, was slid into small grooves in the blade (Pl. 1) and made secure by overlapping edges of bronze hammered down upon it. The strip itself was

[1] For the following account, I am indebted to M. Emile Gilliéron, who generously allowed me to profit by his wide experience of Minoan technique. I have also examined all the daggers personally.

[2] See, however, *Anz.*, 1903, p. 159, No. 22, where the ground is said to contain silver and iron.

prepared in the following way : small cavities in its surface receive figures cut out from pieces of gold or silver : in the case of the stalks of flowers, or other slender lines, a piece of gold wire could be inserted into a groove. The gold and silver were then hammered into place. A final application of niello was often added, since its black colouring was an effective foil to the other metals. It was allowed to melt, in a suitable degree of heat, all over the surface of the blade, and thus it filled any cavities, such as the incised details on the bodies of the cats (No. I below) and the background behind the cats (also on No. I). Polishing then removed all the niello not wanted for the design ; that, for instance, which covered the gold and silver inlay. Rarely, a few details were picked out in copper. The combination of inlay and relief is used for No. III below.

The most important of the daggers are as follows :—[1]

I. Plate 1 [2]—On both sides, but with slight variations, are cats pursuing birds by a river full of fishes. Beside the river grow flowers, lotus or papyrus. The river was oxidised silver, and the background niello, but both materials have almost disappeared. All the cats save two are gold, with portions of the body in silver ; but on each side of the dagger one cat is distinguished by being mainly of oxidised silver. The ducks' bodies are gold, their wings silver. The flowers are silver with leaves, stalks and stamens in gold. One of the cats' ears and a stripe on one of the ducks are picked out in copper. It is interesting to compare this dagger with the cat chasing a bird in a landscape of rocks and flowers from the fresco at Hagia Triadha.[3] From the Fifth Shaft Grave.

II. Plate 2 [4]—On one side is a lion hunt. The men's bodies, the lions and the spears are gold, the shields, girdles and the stomachs of the lions silver. Niello is used for details. The perfection of some of the details and the absence of others, such

---

[1] Perrot and Chipiez, *Histoire de l'Art*, VI, pp. 779 ff.; see also Ἀθηναῖον, X, p. 309 ; *Anz.*, 1903, p. 159. The latter contains a reliable account, which differs in one or two details from the view of M. Emile Gilliéron, fils, especially concerning the use of electrum. M. Gilliéron thinks no electrum was used, and that there was no iron in the oxidised silver background of No. II.

[2] Athens, 765 ; length, ·19 m.

[3] See Bossert, *Alt Kreta*, Pls. 67, 68.   [4] Athens, 394 ; length, ·237 m.

as fingers and some of the features, recalls the miniature frescoes from Knossos, which cannot be far removed in date.[1]

On the other side is a lion pursuing deer (lion and deer in gold and silver as above). Here, however, the deer are drawn according to the same conventions as we see in a much later fresco from Tiryns [2] (the cross markings on the back, and the lighter colour of the stomach). From the Fourth Shaft Grave.

III. Plate 2 [3]—On both sides, running lions, with rocks as background. The lions are in relief with the inlay applied to the surface of the relief. The rocks are flat : they are drawn in bands of colour (gold, electrum and silver), as is always the case in Minoan painting. No niello used. From the Fourth Shaft Grave.

IV.[4]—On both sides, lilies. The petals are electrum, the stamens dark gold. The flowers are a slightly more formal version of the lilies on a M.M. III fresco painting from Knossos. The gold hilt, which has been preserved, is also decorated with lilies. From the Fifth Shaft Grave.

V. Plate 3 [5]—On both sides, galloping horses in relief in plain bronze. This is a good example of the characteristic Cretan " flying gallop." From the Fifth Shaft Grave.

VI. Plate 3 [6]—On both sides, griffins, in relief in plain bronze. From the Fifth Shaft Grave.

VII.[7]—Griffins in relief.

VIII.[8]—On both sides, a plate of gold ornamented with spirals and rosettes, picked out in niello, which, filling the engraved lines, outlines the design in black. The linked spirals are one of the favourite patterns of the Cretan and Mycenaean artists. Compare a fresco from Knossos,[9] and a less close parallel from Mycenae.[10] Fifth Shaft Grave.

The Shaft Graves of Mycenae are not the only tombs that have produced daggers of this kind. Other examples have

---

[1] See Evans, *P. of M.*, I, p. 527, and *J.H.S.*, XXI, Pl. V.
[2] Rodenwaldt, *Tiryns*, II, Pl. XV.
[3] Athens, 395 ; length, ·21 m. See *Anz.*, 1903, p. 159, No. 23, where the view is taken that the rocks are of electrum of different shades. M. Emile Gilliéron, fils, is, however, of opinion that only gold and silver are used.
[4] Athens, 764 ; length, ·115 m.
[5] Athens, 748 ; length, ·73 m.   [6] Athens, 747 ; length, ·43 m.
[7] Athens ? length, ·79 m.   [8] Athens, 744 ; length, ·225 m.
[9] Bossert, *Alt Kreta*, Pl. 50.   [10] *B.S.A.*, XXV, Pl. XXIX.

been found at Vapheio, the Argive Heraeum and Thera. From the tholos at Vapheio [1] come three fragments, the first with fishes and parts of swimming (?) figures, the second with a decorative design in black and gold, the third indeterminate.

From the Argive Heraeum comes a fragment with dolphins and another with silver doves.[2] On the latter, the details are of gold and the background of gold and (?) niello.

The fragment from Thera [3] is adorned with double axes.

The inlaid daggers are, from the artistic point of view, unsurpassed. They must, however, have been more for ornament than for use, and were probably worn on state occasions only.

It was in the next period (Late Minoan II) that the finest weapons were made, the long rapiers, of which the most perfect come from the cemetery of Zafer Papoura. These, too, are decorated : the rapier from the Tomb 44,[4] which measures 91·3 cm., is ornamented with delicate spirals in relief on the midrib and the sides of the hilt (Fig. 1). The spirals are a motive much used in weapons of the period, though rarely with more effect.

In the Third Late Minoan Period this high standard was not maintained : the blades become shorter and the quality poorer. It is not surprising that the men who wielded them were unable to defend themselves against the inroads of a newer and stronger race.

FIG. 1.—Sword from Tomb 44, Knossos.

BRONZE VASES—The importance of copper and bronze vessels in the Early Minoan and First and Second Middle Minoan Periods is proved by imitations belonging to the same

[1] Athens National Museum. See *Essays presented to Sir Arthur Evans*, p. 63, Pl. XI ; 'Εφ. 'Αρχ., 1889, Pl. 7, 1, and 7, 2.

[2] Athens National Museum ; *A.J.A.*, 1925, p. 425.

[3] At Copenhagen ; Tsoundas and Manatt, *Mycenaean Age*, pp. 200 and 235, Fig. 118.

[4] At Candia ; *Prehistoric Tombs of Knossos*, p. 62, Fig. 66. The drawing shews it freed from the incrustation which still covers it.

date in pottery.[1] Actual examples are rare : there exists, however, a fine M.M. II copper basin from Kalathiana, of which the bowl is hammered out of one sheet of metal.[2] The earlier strata of Troy (i.e. the second to fifth cities) produced pails, a saucer and a two-handled pan,[3] all of which must be dated before 1800.

The great age for the manufacture of bronze ware was that which covered the transition from the Middle Minoan to the Late Minoan Period (M.M. III (b) and L.M. I (a)). Here belong several deposits of bronze vases in private houses : [4] the finest of these deposits has been selected for description.

It was found in one of the small walled spaces in the North-West Treasure House at Knossos,[5] and consisted of five bronze vases, remarkable for the beauty of their workmanship. One is a ewer (Fig. 2 (d)) : its body is made of two pieces of metal riveted together, and adorned with a pattern which was current at the period. The neck is joined by welding. There are also four one-handled bowls, two of which deserve special mention. The bowl with the lily pattern, in repoussé work on the rim (Fig. 3 (d)), must have been one of the most exquisite pieces of metal-work the Cretan artists produced, while the bowl in Fig. 4 is interesting technically. Its rim is decorated in repoussé work with what looks like the tips of a spray of leaves ; another layer of metal, with a leaf ornament in high relief, is soldered or welded above it. The result suggests three sprays of leaves superposed.

To the same period we can attribute the basins from Tylissos,[6] which attract attention both by their size and by their workmanship. They were made of seven plates of copper,

[1] P. of M., I, Figs. 47 (note especially the imitation of metal rivets) nad 183.

[2] At Candia ; Xanthoudides, Vaulted Tombs, p. 87, No. 1491, Pl. XLV ; ht., ·085 m. ; diam., ·30 m. The handles are riveted to the rim. The date suggested on Pl. XLV is M.M. II.

[3] Dörpfeld, Troja und Ilion, I, pp. 348 ff.

[4] For their explanation and for further discussion see P. of M., II, pp. 623 ff.

[5] At Candia ; B.S.A., 1903, pp. 121 ff. ; P. of M., II, pp. 637 ff.

[6] At Candia ; Ἐφ. Ἀρχ., 1912, pp. 220, 221. Another view is implied in Jahrb., 1921, p. 120. The largest basin at Candia is bent, and the distortion widened it.

These basins were, presumably, used for heating water, but they are too heavy to have been suspended by the handles, as Hazzidakis has suggested.

exclusive of the handles, carefully riveted together (Fig. 3 (c)) :
the largest is 1·40 m. in diameter, ·44 m. deep, and is provided
with three handles.

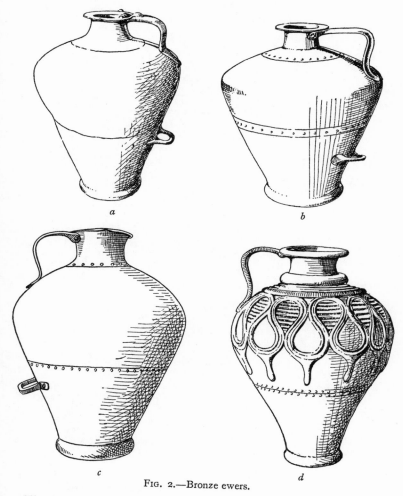

FIG. 2.—Bronze ewers.

The Fourth Shaft Grave at Mycenae,[1] which belongs to the
early part of the L.M. I, contained as many as thirty-two
bronze vessels, including those which were too fragmentary for

[1] Schliemann, *Mycenae*, pp. 273 ff.   Objects at Athens.

(*a*) Lamp from tomb at Knossos.

(*b*) Tripod from tomb at Knossos.

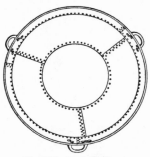

(*d*) Bowl from Knossos.

(*c*) Basin from Tylissos.

(*e*) Clay tablet from Knossos.

Fig. 3.

preservation. They were arranged at the sides of the grave. Besides a tripod, there were ewers, deep bowls, pails and wide basins with two or three handles. Some shewed traces of fire, having evidently been used for cooking.

The ewers, with their rounded shoulders and graceful curves, should be contrasted with the more angular ewers of the Second Late Minoan Period. The arrangement of the metal plates [1] which combine to form the body is shown in Fig. 2 (c).[2] The tripod, with two horizontal handles, one vertical handle and a lip, is important, since it is among the earliest tripods known to us.

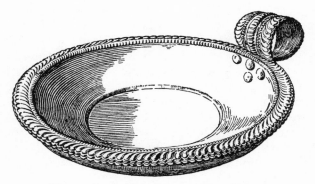

FIG. 4.—Bowl with leaf ornament from Knossos.

Passing to the Second Late Minoan Period, we find, among the objects from Palaikastro,[3] a ewer which already differs from those found at Mycenae by the sharper division between neck and shoulder, and the more abrupt transition from shoulder to body (Fig. 2 (a)). A quantity of L.M. II pottery, with which it was found, dates it between 1575 and 1475 B.C. The sheets of metal which compose it are fastened together by rivets : three sheets were used, of which the junctions can be seen just above the lower handle and just above the neck.

Bronze vessels have also been found among the contents of Cretan and Mycenaean tombs belonging to the Second Late

[1] All the ewers are made of riveted plates of metal in the usual manner, except the curious wide-mouthed one, No. 683, which has a join above, but not below, the shoulder.

[2] Athens, 604 ; ht., ·56 m.

[3] At Candia ; *Palaikastro*, p. 121, Pl. XXVI ; ht., ·55 m.

Minoan Period, though not in great numbers. Their comparative scarcity in this connection is not surprising.[1] They were objects of value, giving a certain status to their possessor, and it was a question whether the heir of the deceased could bring himself to part with them. Only a very pious man would put the family plate into the family vault.

The tombs at Phaestos [2] have, however, produced several vases ; so, too, have three of the tombs at Knossos. Two of the latter, the tomb of the Tripod Hearth, No. 14, and the Chieftain's Grave, No. 36, have made important contributions.

In the tomb of the Tripod Hearth was found [3] a large group of vases. One is a ewer, made of riveted sheets of bronze, and even more angular in outline than the ewer from Palaikastro (Fig. 2 (b)). An interesting lamp, with trimmers attached to a chain [4] (Fig. 3 (a)), and a one-handled bowl like those from the palace, must both have come from the same workshop, since they have the same criss-cross pattern on their rims. Very similar is the pattern on the neck of a third vase, a spouted ewer. None of these vases are as fine as those of the earlier group described on page 12. Certain vessels from this tomb have knobbed projections on the handles : it has been suggested that the knobs were used for winding cloth round when the handles were hot.[5]

A bronze tripod [6] should also be mentioned, since it stands even closer to the classical Greek type than the tripod from Mycenae. The handles are vertical, the legs slightly bent (Fig. 3 (b)) : unlike those of the corresponding Greek tripods (pp. 44 ff.), they join the body, not at the rim, but below the shoulder.

The other tomb, No. 36,[7] contained vases of which the

---

[1] See the discussion of this question by Evans in *P.T.K.*, p. 119. Good examples of bronze vessels from tombs on the mainland are at Nauplia, from Asine. The magnificent series of vases from the new Swedish excavations at Dendra were discovered too late to appear in this book.

[2] At Candia ; *M.d.L.*, XIV, p. 542.

[3] At Candia ; *P.T.K.*, pp. 34 ff., pp. 118 ff., and Pl. LXXXIX ; ht., ·35 m. ; *P. of M.*, II, p. 635.

[4] *P.T.K.*, pp. 39 and 40, Fig. 35. Inner diam. of bowl, ·19 m.

[5] *Op. cit.*, p. 119.

[6] *P.T.K.*, Fig. 38 ; ht. of bowl, ·155 m. ; diam., ·42 m. ; *Jahrb.*, 1921, p. 120. Another Cretan type of tripod has straight sides, to the base of which the legs are fixed.

[7] At Candia ; Evans, *P.T.K.*, pp. 51 ff.

best is a large ewer, very like the one from Palaikastro. Its vertical handle is finished above and below with cockle shells in relief : its body is composed of as many as three plates.

A few remarks on technique must be added. The construction of the vases depends on the riveting of sheets of metal : the inevitable rivets were, however, made the most of for decorative purposes, as we see in the basins from Tylissos and many of the ewers. They were even copied on clay imitations of metal vases, as on the well-known jug from Palaikastro.[1]

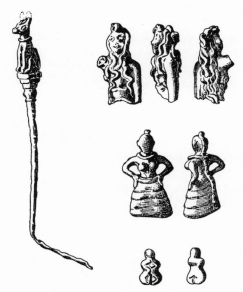

FIG. 5.—Bronzes from Palaikastro.

The rim of the one-handled bowl described on page 12 is, on the other hand, an interesting example of welding or soldering, so, too, the neck mentioned on the same page.

Fig. 3 (e) [2] shows an inscribed clay tablet from Knossos. It must be an inventory of bronze vases : the shapes it illustrates are already familiar to us from the finds at Knossos and elsewhere ; and we admire the precision of the Minoan clerk who drew them so faithfully.

[1] *Palaikastro*, Pl. 18 b, and see above, p. 15, n. 3.
[2] *B.S.A.*, IX, 1903, p. 128.

OBJECTS DECORATED WITH FIGURES—Certain objects which are, in a sense, intermediate between the decorated weapons, etc., and the human figures, should be described here.

The most important is a knife handle, finished off with a man's head, from the Psychro Cave.[1] The way the eyes protrude, like buttons, and the smiling lips, make it distinctive. The date is probably Middle Minoan III.

A similar motive occurs much earlier, in the second city of Troy,[2] where the hilt of a dagger of Cypriote type is adorned with a bull's head.

From near Palaikastro [3] comes a pin, tipped with a pert little dog wearing a collar (Fig. 5). The date is uncertain,[4] but probably within the late Minoan Period.

B. STATUETTES

STATUETTES FROM TROY AND MELOS—The earliest representation of the human form in bronze which has any claim to be mentioned here, comes from the second city of Troy (see p. 3). The figure is now at Berlin,[5] and is ·15 m. high (Pl. 4 b and c). Its relations are with Cyprus and Asia Minor rather than with Crete. The ears pierced for ear-rings, the nose, like an animal's muzzle, the arms, which were both originally bent inwards, these all recall Cypriote terra-cottas. Some scholars consider it to be Babylonian in origin.[6] Behind the feet is a kind of projection or stand, such as is sometimes found supporting primitive terra-cottas.[7] Behind the head are what may be the remains of a bronze tang or channel, not completely removed after casting, through which the metal entered the mould.

---

[1] At Candia; B.S.A., VI, p. III ; Bossert, op. cit., Pl. 129.

[2] Dörpfeld, Troja und Ilion, I, p. 345, Fig. 264.

[3] At Candia; Palaikastro, p. 122, Fig. 101.

[4] A remarkable pendant, ornamented with half a female figure, from near Sitanos, should have concluded our list, but we have no proof as to whether it is Minoan or not. Furtwängler, Kleine Schriften, II, p. 455 ; M.d.L., VI, p. 176, Fig. 6.

[5] In the Museum für Völkerkunde. Neugebauer, Pl. 4, p. 17, and p. 127 (which see for other references).

[6] Wace and Thompson, Prehistoric Thessaly, p. 259 ; Evans, Cretan Pictographs, pp. 132 ff.

[7] E.g. Neugebauer, Pl. 2.

From Phylakopi in Melos [1] comes the statuette illustrated on Pl. 4 a. It was found between the walls of a house, not, apparently, in any particular stratum. Therefore its date is uncertain, nor do we know whether it was of local manufacture or imported : the latter is more probable. The figure represents a man in a long garment : the curiously high crown of the head may be a fault of modelling, or represent a cap or deformed skull.

CRETAN STATUETTES—The people of prehistoric Crete were not sculptors, though they were skilful at carving stone vases with figures in relief, and at modelling plaster reliefs to vary the decoration of their walls. They have, however, left us a number of small statuettes in bronze and other materials, of which many are so good as to make the absence of full-sized statues surprising. This absence can scarcely be explained by their ignorance of the process of hollow casting, since they might have employed plates of beaten copper. We can only surmise that sculpture was a form of art that did not appeal to the Cretan temperament. Their artists were brilliant and rapid workers, but wherever they had to deal with anything on a large scale, whether the decoration of a wall or floor, or the building of a palace, they saw it as an aggregate of parts, not as a whole with the parts subordinate.

Be this as it may, the small bronze statuettes are attractive to the modern eye because of their realism and because of a certain roughness of surface, due to a peculiarity of their manufacture, which recalls the effect aimed at by modern impressionists.

They were cast solid, presumably from a wax or clay model, but the surface was not smoothed off when they were taken from the mould, though details were sometimes added with a graving tool. The result is that the features were often blurred and small excrescences are left here and there.

This is one point wherein the Cretan artists differ from the Egyptian, whose bronzes were finished smoothly. Another has been indicated above : the inability or unwillingness of the Cretans to make life-sized statues. A third, less striking,

[1] Athens, 11,711 ; *Excavations at Phylakopi*, pp. 186, 189, Pl. XXXVII ; B.S.A., III, Pl. III ; Ridgeway, *Early Age of Greece*, p. 55.

perhaps, is that, whereas the Egyptian figures, like the archaic Greek, were always stiff and formal, the Cretan were sometimes comparatively free.   It is curious how little Egyptian influence can be traced in Cretan bronzes, considering the close trade relations of the two countries.

The subjects of the Cretan bronze statuettes give us a clue to their purpose.   Nearly all represent worshippers, men or women, in an attitude of adoration.   Evidently they were, like the other statuettes in terra-cotta, faience and ivory, intended for votive offerings, and dedicated to the mother goddess, or, perhaps, to her young consort.   Even the bull and acrobat, No. 18 below, an apparent exception, has a religious significance, since the games in which such acrobats took part were more ritual than secular.

The figures are, therefore, important not only as works of art but as records of Minoan religion.   Whenever the find-spot of a bronze is known, it proves to be a house or palace : probably the bronze worshipper adorned the household shrine.

Any one who studies Cretan and Mycenaean painting can get a general idea of its development, and a vivid idea of its decline : this is not so with the bronzes.   A few can be dated by the circumstances of their discovery, more by comparing their style with that of other works of art.   The result is that we can place a number of them in the Third Middle Minoan and First Late Minoan Periods (1700-1580 and 1580-1475 B.C.), when Cretan art was at its best, but we know little of the early stages, and any conclusions we draw about the later stages are only tentative.   A large proportion, for the most part of inferior quality, remain unassigned to any period, and until new discoveries give us fresh grounds for dating them, we must resist the temptation to use them for filling either of the gaps. The most useful evidence for classifying these undated bronzes is provided by the terra-cotta figurines that have been found in deposits of most periods from the Neolithic to the very late Bronze Age.   It is to them that we should look for the origin of Cretan bronze statuettes, since an unbaked clay figure may have produced the mould for the first bronze ; and among them, perhaps, that parallels for some of the undated bronzes may be found.

Their evidence is particularly helpful for the earlier part of the Middle Minoan Period, and has suggested the attribution of our No. 1 to a date not too far removed from that of the Petsofa terra-cottas.[1]

An account of the surviving Cretan bronzes is given in the following pages. A classification according to subject has been combined, as closely as possible, with a chronological arrangement. The latter is controversial, the former is not : it has, therefore, been given the chief place, contrary to the plan adopted in the earlier part of this book. Certain bronzes stand out from the rest, and are described singly : many are second, or even third rate : these are grouped together, or mentioned in connection with one of the more important figures.

MALE FIGURES.

(1) *Male Worshipper* [2] (Pl. 4 *d*)—This statuette was purchased by the Vienna Museum in 1892, and was said to come from the finds of Halbherr and Fabricius, presumably, therefore, from Southern Crete. Besides a double belt, a long flap or apron is worn behind and in front. This flap is supposed to be a feature of the Third Middle Minoan Period.[3] There is a distinct resemblance to the male figure from Gournia (No. 9), and one important difference : whereas the Gournia bronze has the weight a little on the left leg and the body slightly turned, the Vienna bronze is completely frontal. The base is square with a tang below it. The tang is the remains of the channel through which the metal was poured into the mould, left to facilitate mounting.

(2) *Male Worshipper from the Psychro Cave* [4]—He comes from the same stratum of the Psychro Cave as that which yielded the inscribed Libation Table,[5] and is assigned by Evans to the Third Middle Minoan Period. The costume consists of a belt and " kilt " with a long apron in front : the right hand is raised in adoration. Base as in No. 1.

(3) *Youth, from the Harbour Town of Candia* [6] (Pl. 8 *b*)—The

---

[1] *P. of M.*, I, p. 151, Fig. 111.
[2] Vienna, 921 ; ht., ·094 m. ; Bossert, *Alt Kreta*, Pls. 141 *b*, 142 *b* (there dated L.M. III) ; and *Anz.*, 1892, p. 48.
[3] *P. of M.*, I, p. 681.
[4] At Oxford ; ht., ·078 m. ; *P. of M.*, I, pp. 681, 682, Fig. 501.
[5] *Ibid.*, I, p. 627.
[6] Candia ; ht., ·115 m. ; Neugebauer, Pl. 8 ; Δελτίον, II, 1916, pp. 168 ff. ; *P. of M.*, II, Part I, pp. 234, 235, Fig. 132.

young man has long curling hair. He wears boots, a belt, a loin-cloth, bracelets, and a gold ring round the neck. The boots (or puttees) are marked with engraved lines. The most interesting feature is the conical cap or helmet : its nearest parallel is on a sealing from the temple repositories, Knossos,[1] but it also recalls the head-dress of the female figure from Petsofa and the helmets of the bronzes from the Phoenician coast discussed below (p. 29). With these it shares another peculiarity, the stalk-like projections below the feet, representing the channel through which the bronze was poured. A lump of metal acts as a stand (cf. Pl. 25). The arms are held before the body in a position recalling that of the Petsofa figures, though they are here extended farther from the body. Evidently the attitude is one of adoration. The bronze is attributed by Evans to the Third Middle Minoan Period.

Nos. 4 and 5 are two portly middle-aged Cretan gentlemen.

(4) *Male Worshipper* [2] (Pl. 5 *a*, *b*)—This figure was recently discovered among the " unclassified and suspect bronzes " to which a previous generation had assigned it. It was originally found by Capt. Spratt at Anatoli, near Hierapetra. It represents a man standing at attention, with the right hand raised in the characteristic attitude of adoration. Unlike the typical Cretan of the time, he is rather stout. He wears the short boots that neither ancient nor modern Cretan can dispense with, a belt and a loin-cloth covered with a garment like a kilt. Above the belt is what may be the upper part of the kilt or an extra piece of cloth wrapped round the waist. There is a loop above it at the right-hand side. In front, the kilt falls in the long flap or apron, characteristic of the Third Minoan Period. The hair hangs in curls behind : above the right ear is an object that may be a curl or a snake, like that on the Snake Goddess from Knossos. Details are emphasised by incised lines, e.g. on the boots. The material is almost pure copper. The figure is finished off by a small stand with a tang below it (cf. Nos. 1 and 2).

(5) *Male Worshipper from Tylissos* [3] (Pl. 5 *c*, *d*)—A figure

[1] *P. of M.*, I, p. 680, Fig. 500 *a*.
[2] British Museum ; ht., ·195 m., or ·22 m. with base ; *J.H.S.*, XLI, p. 86, Pl. I ; Spratt, *Travels and Researches in Crete*, I, p. 290.
[3] At Candia ; ht., ·25 m. ; 'Εφ. 'Αρχ., 1912, Pl. 17.

similar to No. 4, shewing very clearly the way the body is thrown back, a pose common in Cretan art. The man's hair falls in thick strands : he wears a ring round his neck, a belt, boots, and the usual combination of kilt and loin-cloth, with a short flap in front and behind. Though the date is probably Late Minoan I, it cannot be far removed from that of the British Museum Worshipper. Base as last.

(6) *Male Worshipper from Tylissos* [1] (Pl. 8 a)—He is younger and slenderer than No. 4, but his attitude is that of No. 4 exaggerated, with the chest thrown out and the knees drawn back. He wears a necklace and bracelet, and a pair of anklets : his belt is knotted round his waist.

(7) *Male Worshipper.* [2] *Acquired at Athens* (Pl. 4 c)—The figure wears a loin-cloth, which has a flap, like an apron, falling down behind. There is no trace of hair on the back, but two small projections above the forehead in front may be remains of a head-dress. The surface is too poor to allow certainty. Costume and proportions suggest the First Late Minoan Period.

(8) *Male Worshipper, said to come from near Phaestos* [3] (Pl. 8 c)—The youth has long hair, which has been partly rubbed away behind. Both his hands are raised, his head is bent forward, and his body thrown back. It has been suggested that he was a flute player or that he carried an offering, but while the former alternative would be unusual, the latter does not seem appropriate to the position of the hands. More probably it is an attitude of prayer. The flat cap is paralleled by that worn by the attendant of the Snake Goddess from Knossos.[4] The arrangement of the kilt and loin-cloth is uncertain : a flap from the back may have been attached in front with the ends doubled up : another flap hangs down behind, and may be of leather, since it has a central seam which gives it much the appearance of a tail coat.

The style is that of the First Late Minoan Period.

(9) *Male Figure from Gournia* [5] (Pl. 9 a)—The man wears a belt and a loin-cloth and has long curling hair. The weight is

[1] At Candia ; ht., ·17 m.   [2] Cambridge ; ht., ·09 m.
[3] At Leyden ; ht., ·14 m. ; *Jahrb.*, 1915, Pl. I, p. 65, which see for detailed discussion of the costume ; Bossert, *Alt Kreta*, Pl. 133.
[4] *P. of M.*, I, p. 504.
[5] At Candia ; ht., ·135 m. ; Boyd-Hawes, *Gournia*, Pl. XI ; Neugebauer, Pl. 10.

more on the left foot than on the right : the position is, therefore, freer than in any of the preceding examples, though the execution is, otherwise, not first class. The rigidity of figures like Nos. 2, 4 and 5 is partly due to the fact that they are standing at attention : the woman at Berlin, on the other hand, prays with her head and body slightly inclined to one side.

The Gournia statuette is one of the few of which the find-spot and context are known : it was discovered in a building of the First Late Minoan Period. Base of usual type.

(10) *Male Worshipper*.[1] " *From Crete* " (Pl. 9 *b*)—Though poorer than No. 9, it resembles it sufficiently to be placed next it in the list.

(11) *Male Worshipper*.[2] *From the same source as No. 1* (Pl. 9 *d*)—A youth with spiral curls, for which there is no exact parallel, wearing a belt and a loin-cloth with a flap behind. The right arm raised, in adoration, recalls that of the warriors of the Geometric Period (Pl. 15) who brandish a spear. The figure is completely frontal and remarkably elongated. The eyes are rendered with unusual care and distinctness, both the lid and the pupil being marked. The modelling of the cheeks is so salient that it recalls the cheek pieces of a helmet. A late date (L.M. III—1400-1100) has been suggested for the figure,[3] on the grounds that the unnatural proportions, the formal arrangement of the hair, imply that art had become crystallised and degenerate. There is not yet enough evidence to confirm the date : no figures in the round belonging with certainty to the Third Late Minoan Period are as yet known, save Mycenaean terra-cottas of an entirely different type.

(12) *Male Figure*[4] (Pl. 9 *c*)—This bronze is remarkable, and in many ways different from other Cretan figures. No garment is worn save a belt round the waist : from the belt

---

[1] Berlin, 30,023 ; ht., ·075 m. ; *Anz.*, 1922, p. 60, Fig. 1.

[2] Vienna, 922 ; ht., ·115 m. ; Bossert, *op. cit.*, Pls. 141, 142 ; Neugebauer, *op. cit.*, Pl. II, p. 24 ; *Anz.*, 1892, p. 48.

[3] Bossert, *op. cit.*, *loc. cit.* ; Neugebauer, *op. cit.*, p. 25. It is possible that evidence may turn up to prove that figures with long legs and short body are as late as has hitherto been assumed : it must not, however, be forgotten that these proportions occur in a male figure from Petsofa (*P. of M.*, Fig. 111, i.). They also occur in a bronze statuette of comparatively early date from Knossos, at Candia.

[4] Berlin, 10,518 ; ht., ·235 m. ; Bossert, *op. cit.*, Pl. 139 ; Müller, *Nacktheit und Entblössung*, p. 65.

hangs a knife, unless it be the end of the belt itself. It was an unusual thing for Cretans to be completely naked : herein they differed from the classical Greeks. The width of the shoulders, too, is unusual, and the position of the arms is not that adopted by Cretan worshippers. The technique, on the other hand, shews all the peculiarities of Cretan bronze casting. The rough surface is unmistakable. Notice the rendering of the collar-bones and chest. It may be that the artist was trying to portray what were to him the eccentricities of a foreigner : hence the absence of clothes and unduly broad shoulders. If this view be accepted, there is no need to consider the statuette as a survival of Minoan art in the Geometric Age.[1]

Three fragmentary figures should be mentioned here :—
The first is the fragment of a young male worshipper,[2] said to come from near Smyrna. The figure is probably a boy, though at first sight it might be taken for a woman. He wears a fillet, a girdle, a bracelet on the left upper arm, and, round the neck, what might be a ring (cf. No. 5) : this, however, is doubtful. On the forehead are what appear from the drawing to be the remains of a hand, as in No. 5—the right hand raised in salute. A date in the First Late Minoan Period seems probable.
The second is the upper part of a young worshipper from Palaikastro[3] (Fig. 5). It should be compared with the bronze just described, though it has different features and a different arrangement of the hair. The date is uncertain.
The third figure was found among the bronzes in the Psychro Cave.[4]

Male figures of inferior style are numerous : several come from Hagia Triadha, one from Tylissos, three from the Psychro Cave.[5] Amongst these we can distinguish bronzes which resemble the Gournia figure in not having the weight evenly

[1] As Müller does, *op. cit.*, p. 65.
[2] At Frankfurt-am-Main ; ht., ·065 m. ; Furtwängler, *Kleine Schriften*, II, p. 453 ; Bossert, *Alt Kreta*, Pl. 138.
[3] At Candia ; ht., ·033 m. ; *Palaikastro*, p. 123, Fig. 102.
[4] At Oxford.
[5] The Tylissos figure will be published shortly. One of the Hagia Triadha bronzes is illustrated in Bossert's *Alt Kreta*, Fig. 136 a, and Maraghianni's *Antiquités Crétoises*, I, Pl. 26. All the bronzes are at Candia save one " from South Crete," in the Museo Kercheriano, Rome. For the Psychro Cave bronzes, now at Candia and Oxford, see *B.S.A.*, VI, p. 107, Pl. X.

distributed on both legs, and bronzes with the long legs and short body which recall terra-cottas, especially those of Pet- sofa. These figures are all worshippers, who salute the deity with one hand raised to their forehead. This salute is typically Minoan, though it may have survived among the rough figures of the transitional period which succeeded the Minoan.

FEMALE FIGURES.

(13) *Woman Worshipper*[1] (Pl. 7 *a*)—This statuette was for a long time supposed, on insufficient grounds, to come from Troy. The style is most typically Cretan. The woman's right hand is raised in adoration, her left hand half raised, perhaps to grasp one of the three snakes that are twined in a knot at the back of her neck : the head of one of these is seen crowning the hair. She may be regarded as an attendant of the Snake Goddess, like the faience votary from Knossos. Her costume is that of a Minoan lady of the time, a bodice open in front, a belt, and flounced skirt. The figure is partly hollow at the base, which would make it easier to fix in place. The period is Late Minoan I.

(14 and 15) *Two Women Worshippers, from Hagia Triadha*[2] (Pl. 7 *b* and *c*)—Figures similar to the last but more roughly finished. They are probably of the same date : unfortunately, no description is given by the excavators of how they were found. The smaller has both hands raised in an attitude similar to the Leyden figure, and had been repaired in several places : the larger, a stout, rather florid lady, raises one hand only.

To the same class belongs a female figure with over-developed breasts, from the Psychro Cave.[3] Another type is represented by No. 16, a *Woman Worshipper, from Palaikastro*[4] (Fig. 5). The figure is small and without much detail. Her hands are on her hips, recalling the ritual action of the goddess on the gold ring from Mycenae.[5] She wears a flounced skirt, a bodice open in front, and a collar. The object on her back is prob- ably a snake. The evidence for the date is considered by the

---

[1] Berlin ; ht., ·19 m. ; *P. of M.*, I, p. 507 ; Bossert, *Alt Kreta*, Pls. 131, 132.
[2] At Candia ; ht., ·15 m. and ·085 m. ; Bossert, *Alt Kreta*, Pls. 136*b* and 137.
[3] At Oxford.
[4] At Candia ; ht., *c.* ·07 m. ; Dawkins, *Palaikastro*, p. 122, Fig. 103, and p. 123.
[5] Bossert, *Alt Kreta*, Pl. 324 f.

excavator to be uncertain, but to point to the Third Late Minoan Period : he adds, however, that the style seems earlier.

Small, inferior female figures were found both at Hagia Triadha and in the Psychro Cave.[1] From the last-named site comes yet a third type of woman, with a plain, bell-shaped skirt, and both arms raised as far as the breast. The most we can say about these is that they are in a style appropriate to terra-cottas, which cannot be accurately dated.

(17) *A female figure from Crete*, now in the Louvre, has been attributed, with some probability, to the Third Late Minoan Period. She wears a polos, like the terra-cotta women from mainland graves (1380-1100), and has the same pinched, bird-like features as they.[2] The dress is unusual : the arms are held in one of the positions used by Cretans at prayer : the abnormal feature is the low-waisted skirt, for which I know of no parallel among Minoan figures.

(18) *Bull and Acrobat*[3] (Pl. 6)—Though bull-leaping scenes are common in painting and gem engraving, this is the only example hitherto found in bronze. Perhaps the artist who modelled it wished to try and adapt a popular subject to his own particular material : his main problem was the casting of the acrobat, who is in the middle of a somersault, having let go the horns in order to land with his feet on the bull's neck. The solution was to use the hair as a support for the acrobat's head : the arms, which would have stuck out inconveniently, were stumped off at the elbows. It appears that this bronze was not cast from a double mould : had it been, we should have found a ridge marking the join, for the Cretans did not eliminate such details. Beneath the bull's front feet is the usual attachment to facilitate mounting. Evans assigns the group to the First Late Minoan Period on the evidence of style. Since the bull-leaping scenes had probably a ritual significance, this, like the other bronze figures, may be considered as votive.

---

[1] See p. 25, n. 5.

[2] Louvre, No. 80 ; ht., ·098 m. ; *Catalogue*, Pl. 10 ; Neugebauer, Pl. 5, p. 25 ; Bossert, *op. cit.*, Pl. 140 ; Furtwängler, *Kleine Schriften*, II, p. 455, " from a cave in Crete."

[3] Spencer-Churchill Collection, Northwick Park ; ht., ·114 m. ; length, ·156 m. ; *J.H.S.*, XLI, pp. 247 ff. ; *P. of M.*, II, p. 651.

Five roughly made figures differ, more or less, from the typical Cretan figures. Eventually they may become important for dating purposes. Two (*a* and *b*) recall the Neolithic clay figurines and may be early, or a survival of an early type : three have a disproportionately long body. Most Cretan bronzes are short in the body and long in the leg, but the bronze from Gournia has comparatively short legs ; and, curiously enough, two bronzes, apparently of the transitional period, also from East Crete (p. 35), are of the long-bodied type. Perhaps a local " peasant style " influenced the figure from Gournia.

The five figures in question are as follows :—

(*a*) Small, primitive "idol" found in a L.M. II house at Palaikastro [1] (Fig. 5).

(*b*) Small, primitive idol.[2] Of a different shape, but also recalls early figurines.

(*c*) Male figure " from Crete." [3] Very rough workmanship.

(*d*) Male (?) figure from near Malia.[4]

(*e*) Male figure from near Praesos. Right hand raised to forehead.[5]

A number of STATUETTES OF EXCEPTIONAL OR FOREIGN TYPE have been discovered at various sites in the area under discussion, and cannot be omitted.

The excavations at Tiryns [6] and Mycenae [7] yielded two : a silver figure of similar style comes from Thessaly,[8] another bronze one from the cave of Hermes Kranaios at Sybrita, in Crete,[9] and a whole series from the Phoenician coast.[10] They are characterised by their conical helmet : the raised right hand originally held a spear, the left a round shield. The

[1] At Candia ; ht., *c.* ·03 m. ; *Palaikastro*, Fig. 104, pp. 122, 123.
[2] At Oxford.
[3] Berlin, 10,825 ; ht., ·053 m. ; *Anz.*, 1922, p. 61.
[4] At Candia ; Δελτίον, 1916, pp. 161 ff., and Fig. 2, p. 167. I disagree with the attribution to L.M. I.
[5] At Candia ; *M.d.L.*, VI, p. 179, Fig. 15.
[6] Schliemann, *Tiryns*, p. 166, Fig. 97.
[7] Ἐφ. Ἀρχ., 1891, p. 21, Pl. II, 4. From a late house, north-east of the Lion Gate.
[8] At Oxford ; Evans, *J.H.S.*, XXI, p. 126, Fig. 16.
[9] At Oxford ; *J.H.S.*, XXI, p. 125, Fig. 15.
[10] Helbig, *Quaest. Myc.*, p. 18, and *Jahreshefte*, XII, 27.

examples found in Greek lands are usually regarded as imported from the east,[1] with the possible exception of one
from Thessaly, though it has been suggested that they form
a separate and superior group of local manufacture.[2] The
evidence, on the whole, seems overwhelmingly in favour of
their being imports : they are so close in style to the specimens
from the Phoenician coast that it seems impossible that they
should have been made by another race. They should, therefore, be regarded as an interesting proof of trade between
Greece and the Orient.

The Bronze Age of South-Eastern Europe came to an end
about the twelfth century B.C. This is a time of which we
know remarkably little : the two facts of importance are,
firstly, the replacing of bronze by iron for tools and weapons,
and secondly, the overthrow of the civilisation of Crete and
Mycenae by the migrations and invasions of more primitive
peoples. The art of the Bronze Age naturally disappeared
and remained forgotten, until recent excavations once more
brought it to light. There is, however, one link between the
old culture and that which was to follow : the pottery of
the Late Bronze Age develops almost imperceptibly into that
of the Early Iron Age. With metal-working, on the contrary,
there is a distinct break. The reasons for this, and the characteristics of the bronzes of the Early Iron Age will be discussed
in the following chapter.

[1] Helbig, *Jahreshefte*, XII, p. 29 ; Furtwängler, *Kleine Schriften*, II,
p. 457 ; *Antike Gemmen*, III, 18, n. 7. To Helbig's list, add No. 899 in the
Bibliothèque Nationale from Cyprus.
[2] Evans, *J.H.S.*, XXI, p. 125.

CHAPTER II

THE SUB-MYCENAEAN, TRANSITIONAL AND GEOMETRIC PERIODS

IN the Iron Age of Greece, art was forced to develop again from the beginning, while technical skill developed, not from the beginning, but from a less advanced stage than that to which the Cretans had brought it.

The centuries that follow the downfall of Cretan and Mycenaean culture are essentially a "dark age," for Greece became once more a primitive, instead of a highly civilised country. It is a time of upheavals and migrations, culminating in the traditional Dorian Invasion. When archæology shall have produced sufficient material to supplement tradition, we may be able to write its history : at present we can dogmatise to the extent of distinguishing two periods. The first, from about 1150 to 1000 B.C., may be called the Transitional Period, when the Sub-Mycenaean merges into the Proto-Geometric culture. The second, from about 1000 to 700 B.C., is the Geometric Period proper, during which the obscurity gradually becomes less dense, and historical Greece begins to take its familiar shape. The term Geometric applies to the decoration of objects by lines, circles, etc., which contrast with the naturalism of the Minoan Age.

It is during the Late Mycenaean and Transitional Periods that Cyprus comes to the fore. After the Mycenaean civilisation had made itself felt in the island, about 1400 B.C., works of art in the Mycenaean style were produced there : they continued to be made for some time after the destruction of the cities of Crete and the mainland. A distinct group of bronzes is associated with Cyprus during the period, and these date from some time in the thirteenth century to the ninth century B.C.

The bronzes of the true Geometric Period are, on the other hand, best represented on those sites that were to become the important art centres of classical Greece, sites like Sparta, Olympia and Athens.

A. SUB-MYCENAEAN AND TRANSITIONAL PERIODS

It would not come within the scope of this book to discuss the replacing of bronze by iron for tools and weapons. The earliest iron swords hitherto found in Greek soil are from East Crete,[1] and may belong to the twelfth century B.C.: from Enkomi in Cyprus come two iron knives which may be attributed to twelfth or eleventh centuries.[2] By the tenth century the use of iron was widespread. Hence it follows that we must exclude from Chapter II some of the objects treated of in Chapter I. The use of bronze was now confined to those things that had to be made of a malleable substance, such as ornaments, vessels (though here iron was sometimes used), figures, and surfaces destined for engraved or hammered decorations.

EARLY FIBULAE—One of the most significant signs of the passing of the Mycenaean civilisation is the use of brooches and safety-pins (fibulae). The Minoan close-fitting costume, as worn, for instance, by the Berlin worshipping woman (Pl. 7) did not need these: the dress of the classical Greeks, like that of their northern neighbours, depended on them. The fibula is, of course, a development of the pin, effected by bending a piece of bronze wire, giving it a spring to prevent breaking when it is bent, and some device by which the pointed end can be protected.[3] On the whole, evidence points to the fibula having been evolved north of Greece, though a good case has also been made out for its having reached Greece from Cyprus.[4]

The primitive fibulae of the Sub-Mycenaean and Proto-Geometric Periods were not meant for decoration: they concern us here because from them developed the types common in the true Geometric Age: it was on these that the early Greeks, with the naïve confidence of children, drew whatever men and beasts appealed to their fancy.

[1] *Liverpool Annals*, V, 1912, p. 5; *A.J.A.*, 1901, pp. 132-137.
[2] Murray, Smith and Walters, *Excavations in Cyprus*, Fig. 25, No. 1482, and Pl. II, 995. See also *Liverpool Annals, loc. cit.*
[3] For general discussion, see C. Blinkenberg, *Fibules Grecques et Orientales.*
[4] Thompson, *Liverpool Annals*, V, 1912, pp. 10-12.

SUB-MYCENAEAN TRIPODS AND BRONZES OF SIMILAR STYLE—
This is the place to describe a series of bronzes that extends
from the late Mycenaean into the full Geometric Period,[1] chief
of which are seven bronze tripods, and the fragments of two
bronze vessels.

The Mycenaean character of the decoration of the two
vessels and the first tripod is very arresting : readers may
possibly resent their inclusion in this chapter. Nevertheless,
all these objects are intimately bound up with the rest of the
group, the group survives into the Dipylon Period, and its
description must not be divided.

It is, of course, unusual to find a series of bronzes bridging
the gap between Mycenaean and Geometric art.[2] Such an
exception to the general rule would surprise us, were it not
that the objects in question are so intimately connected with
Cyprus that we may safely assume their origin to be Cypriote.[3]
In this island, as we have seen, Mycenaean culture survived
when it had died elsewhere.

Of the vessels, only the rim and handles survive : to these
the body must have been attached by rivets. The complete
bowl was probably intended to stand on a tripod.

One example is in the Cyprus Museum, and comes from
Kurion [4] (Pl. 10 *a*). On the rim are chiselled a row of jars,
between borders of rope pattern. On the handles are demons
or monsters in pairs. They are a familiar feature of Cretan
art, and may represent men wearing the skins of animals.[5]
Each of them raises one paw, as though in adoration. Where
the base of the handle widens to a disc are octopods and rocks,
a typical Cretan motive.

The other rim and handles are in New York, and come from
the Cesnola collection.[6] On the rims are galloping lions, bulls
and a boar : at the edge is a rope ornament. On the handles

[1] E. Hall, *Vrokastro*, pp. 132 ff., and Schwendemann, *Jahrbuch*, 1921,
pp. 103 ff.
[2] Cf., however, the type of geometric tripod described on pp. 44, 45.
[3] The home of this series is, presumably, Cyprus, though the tripods from
Vrokastro and Knossos may have been made in Crete.
[4] *B.S.A.*, XVIII, pp. 95 ff., Pl. VIII. See *P. of M.*, II, p. 652, where the
vessel, restored as a hydria, is attributed to L.M. I.
[5] *J.H.S.*, XIV, p. 154.
[6] No. 620, Richter, *Catalogue*, pp. 222 ff. See, however, *P. of M.*, II,
p. 652, where the vessel is attributed to L.M. I.

are demons in pairs with water jars : on the discs below the handles are bulls' heads.

The first of the tripods, also in New York,[1] has a frieze of galloping animals round the rim : it is the " flying gallop," beloved of the Cretan artist. The tripod displays the herring-bone pattern on the legs, the Ionic capitals above the legs, and the rope pattern edging, that are features of the group. Its shape is shewn on Pl. 10. Together with the two bowls, it should be assigned to a date between 1250 and 1100.

All the remaining tripods are like it in form but omit the animal friezes. All are cast.

A list is here given, in which the tripod with the galloping animals already described reappears, for the sake of completeness.

1. Tripod from Kurion, Cyprus [2] (Pl. 10 b). Frieze of animals on the ring which originally supported the bowl.

2. Tripod from Vrokastro, Crete.[3] No pattern on ring or legs, but legs finished off with Ionic volutes. Found with Sub-Mycenaean pottery.

3. Miniature Tripod. From Enkomi, Cyprus. On ring, spiral ornament ; on legs, herring-bone pattern ; above legs, Ionic volutes. From Grave 58. Suggested date, eleventh century.[4]

4. Tripod from Geometric Cemetery, Knossos.[5] Above legs, Ionic volutes.

The grave in which the tripod was found has been dated in the eleventh or tenth centuries.

5. Tripod from Geometric Grave near the Pnyx [6] (Pl. 11 a). Found with bowl and lid. On ring, interrupted spiral ornament and rope pattern ; on legs, herring-bone pattern. Ionic volutes.

The grave has been dated in the ninth century.

[1] See No. 1 below.
[2] New York, No. 1180 ; ht., ·374 m. ; Richter, *Catalogue*, pp. 345 ff. ; *Jahrb.*, 1921, p. 103.
[3] At Candia ; ht., ·374 m. ; E. Hall, *Vrokastro*, pp. 132 ff., Pl. XXXIV, 1.
[4] B.M. Inv. 97, 4-1, 1516 ; *Jahrb.*, 1921, p. 104 (which see for references) ; E. Hall, *op. cit., loc. cit.*, confuses it with No. 6 below.
[5] At Candia ; ht., ·18 m. ; *Jahrb.*, 1921, p. 104 ; *B.S.A.*, VI, p. 83 ; E. Hall, *op. cit.*, Pl. XXXIV, 2.
[6] Athens, 7940 ; ht., ·45 m. ; *Jahrb.*, 1921, p. 103 ; *Ath. Mit.*, 1893, 414, Pl. XIV.

6. Tripod from the "Foundry Site," Enkomi, Cyprus.[1] Bands of rope pattern on ring. Legs finished with Ionic volutes. Pendants hang from the ring, between the legs and the supports. Tenth century ?

7. Tripod from Tiryns [2] (Pl. 11 *b*). Rope pattern on ring and legs, pendants from rim, of which four represent fruits (?), four, geometric-looking birds. Ionic volutes crown the legs : part way up the legs are rams' heads (?) The tripod may be tenth century : it was part of a hoard of objects dating from the Mycenaean and the Geometric Periods. Fragments of similar tripods have been unearthed at Olympia.[3]

Closely associated with the tripods are some remarkable bronzes from Cyprus.

Two are stands for vases, mounted, like miniature waggons, on wheels. One is from Larnaka, now at Berlin [4] (Pl. 12 *a*) ; the other, of which but little remains, from Enkomi, now in the British Museum.[5] The former is remarkably well preserved, and has all the decorative motives used so often on the tripods : rope pattern, interrupted spirals, supports crowned by Ionic volutes. Even the manner in which the square stand is carried by the staves which rise above the wheels is reminiscent of the tripods. On the corners of the stand are perched birds, recalling the animals on the pendants of No. 7.

Another of the Cypriote bronzes is the stand illustrated on Pl. 12 *b*.[6] To the more usual motives it adds one that is new in this connection, though known from pottery and Mycenaean frescos,[7] the women who, framed in panels made by the interrupted spiral, appear to be looking from windows.

One scholar has pointed out the remarkable fact that the

---

[1] B.M. Inv. 97, 4-1, 1571 ; ht., ·43 m. The tripod was put together from fragments too late to be published with the other Enkomi finds. It is illustrated by E. Hall (*Vrokastro*, Pl. XXXIV, 3), who mistook it for the tripod from Grave 58 ; Inv. 97, 4-1, 1571.

[2] Athens, 6229 ; ht., ·35 m. ; *Jahrb.*, 1921, p. 104 ; Δελτίον, 1916, pp. 13 ff. (supplement), p. 16, Fig. 21.

[3] *Olympia*, IV, Nos. 823, 824. See pp. 130, 131.

[4] Furtwängler, *Kleine Schriften*, II, p. 298 ; *Anz.*, 1904, p. 31, No. 43.

[5] B.M. Inv. 97, 4-1, 1460 ; Murray, Smith and Walters, *Excavations in Cyprus*, p. 15, Figs. 24 *a*, 25.

[6] Furtwängler, *op. cit.*, p. 300 ; Murray, Smith and Walters, *op. cit.*, p. 10, Fig. 18. From Tomb 63, Enkomi.

[7] *B.S.A.*, XXV, p. 251.

bronze "waggons" tally with the description given of the *mekônôth* made by Hiram of Tyre for King Solomon's temple.[1] The temple belonged to the tenth century B.C.: the bronzes may be earlier.

It will be seen that the same motives are repeated in all the specimens in this group,[2] which is made easily recognisable by the smallness of the repertory.

THE TRANSITIONAL PERIOD IN CRETE—A number of bronze statuettes, some from the Psychro Cave,[3] some from the Cave of Hermes Kranaios at Sybrita,[4] one from Vrokastro,[5] appear to have been made during the centuries which succeeded the Minoan and preceded the Orientalising Period. Many of the oxen from the Psychro Cave recall the geometric oxen from Olympia (see pp. 39, 40), though the details differ, and they are of the long-horned, Cretan breed. An examination of the figures from the Psychro Cave suggests that the naked men with disproportionately long bodies are Proto-Geometric: if so, we should expect certain similar figures from Hagia Triadha to be contemporary,[6] but we cannot be sure till we know more about the circumstances of their finding.

From Eastern Crete come two female figures, long of body, with a curious hollow on the top of the head, and each wearing several tight necklaces, which may represent a local, transitional style, though there is some evidence for considering them Minoan.[7]

Unfortunately, most of the figures which can be claimed for this period are so poor and so isolated, that a description would be unprofitable until further researches have been made.

[1] Furtwängler, *op. cit.*, pp. 298 ff.   See 1 Kings vii. 27-37.
[2] The stand, B.M., 1920, 12-20, 1, with a figure and a conventionalised tree in each panel, is on the outskirts of this group, though it is distinctly more Oriental in character.   Panels are a feature of the Berlin stand from Larnaka, and the British Museum stand with women's heads.   The zigzag strip of bronze that decorates the ring in which the vase would sit occurs on a miniature tripod of another type from Enkomi, also in the British Museum.
[3] At Candia and Oxford; *B.S.A.*, VI, Pl. X.
[4] At Candia and Oxford; *Museo Italiano*, II.
[5] Hall, *Vrokastro*, p. 121, Fig. 71.
[6] Unpublished.
[7] One at Hierapetra; ht., ·085 m.; *M.d.L.*, IV, p. 185, Fig. 20.   One at Oxford "from East Crete."   The head recalls the group of figures discussed by Evans in *Palace of Minos*, II, Part I, pp. 255 ff.

B. THE GEOMETRIC PERIOD

Many sites in Greece have yielded bronze objects of a distinctive type which is now universally associated with the Geometric Period (Pl. 13).

The objects, in spite of their marked Geometric character, are of various kinds. There are beads and pendants, the latter often adorned with a bird. There are small birds on round, open-work stands : sometimes from the stand rises a stalk carrying two birds' heads, or the heads of two bulls, back to back. Horses and cows are found in numbers : the horses, especially, are often mounted on little stands, in this case oblong.

Pins, too, are characteristic of these deposits : they are usually finished with big flat heads, below which are knobs of equal size. Most typical are the fibulae, or safety-pins. Some have a corrugated bow, some are spiral or spectacle fibulae, some have a large catch-plate on which are incised drawings.

Of the sites where these objects have been found, the most important is Olympia.[1] Here, between the years 1875 and 1881, a large number of Geometric bronzes were unearthed, especially in the low strata. They included pins, pendants, bird-pendants, and statuettes of birds and animals. Brooches, particularly " spectacle-brooches," were also found, and varieties of the bow fibula with a large ornamented catch-plate or a decoration of knobs on the bow.

Similar objects were discovered during the excavations of the British School at Sparta between 1906 and 1910 [2] : here were spectacle-brooches, bronze pins with corrugations of equal size and statuettes of birds and horses. The animal statuettes were found among the upper layers of Geometric pottery, while a few come from among the pottery of a still later period.[3] They may, therefore, be assigned to the eighth century B.C. It is noticeable that the horses are all of the fully developed Geometric type (see below, p. 39) : the earlier horses are represented at Olympia.

Olympia and Sparta are, perhaps, the most important sites that have produced Geometric bronzes, but one can trace the

---

[1] *Olympia*, IV, p. 28.   [2] *B.S.A.*, XII-XVI.   [3] *Loc. cit.*, XIII, p. 111.

deposits in the Peloponnese, at Rhodes, and throughout Central and Northern Greece into Macedonia.[1] They are evidently of local workmanship.

In the Peloponnese, the bronzes from the Argive Heraeum,[2] Aegina [3] and Lousoi in Arcadia deserve mention. The last-named site produced an attractive pair of horses [4] fastened to an open-work stand : the Heraeum bronzes include brooches, pins, horses and some splendid peacocks, engraved with eyes, of which Hera might well be proud.

The series from Rhodes is interesting : [5] it consists of birds, and the heads of birds or bulls, back to back, on round stands. Rhodian Geometric fibulae, too, are often decorated with bronze birds.

Fine statuettes of horses and a few birds were discovered on the Acropolis at Athens. [6]   There are examples from Thebes, Elatea and the Ptoön in Boeotia,[7] and from Delphi in Phocis.[8] In the north-west they are represented at Leukas,[9] Thermon,[10] Agrinion [11] and Dodona.[12]

The bronzes from Volo (Iolkos) and Velestino (Pherae) in Thessaly are particularly choice.[13] The Thessalian artist appears to have specialised on birds. He made birds on pendants or beads, and birds on open-work stands, crested birds with two heads, and less fantastic birds with only one head but of various shapes, and birds which appear to be mounted on two little wheels. He also made horses on stands, knobbed brooches in great numbers, some spectacle brooches and some plain fibulae.

---

[1] For list of sites producing these objects, see Casson, *Antiquaries' Journal*, 1921, p. 204, to which I am much indebted.
[2] At Athens ; Waldstein, *Argive Heraeum*, Pl. 72 ff.
[3] Furtwängler, *Aegina*, Pl. 113 ff.
[4] At Athens, 14,839 ; *Jahreshefte*, 1901, p. 48, Fig. 63.
[5] *B.M. Catalogue*, p. 12 ; A. B. Cook, *Zeus*, I, p. 331. He points out the connection between the wheel, the stand and the solar disc.
[6] Staïs' *Catalogue*, p. 260 ; Athens, Nos. 6534-6555 (horses) ; Birds, Athens, 6508, 6679.
[7] *Antiquaries' Journal*, 1921, p. 207.
[8] *Fouilles de Delphes*, V, pp. 45 ff.
[9] Dörpfeld, *Ath. Mit.*, 1906, p. 208, and *Alt Ithaka*, I, pp. 169, 326.
[10] Excavated by Romaios, 1913-14 ; Ath. Nat. Mus., 14,563, 14,757.
[11] Berlin, No. 7342.
[12] Ath. Nat. Mus., 640, 645, 646, horses ; 223, 296, 308, spectacle fibulae.
[13] Unpublished. In the National Museum, Athens. The examples on Pl. 13 *b*, *c* were purchased at Athens and said to come from Velestino.

To pass further north : a characteristic set of objects, including spectacle brooches, a horse and bird-pendants has been found
at Chauchitza in Macedonia ;[1] spectacle brooches at Pateli on
Lake Ostrovo ;[2] typical beads, pendants and spectacle brooches
at Amphipolis.[3]

The Geometric spectacle brooches, pendants, beads and birds
are found on yet more northerly sites : good examples come from
Glasinaz (particularly Podlaze) in Bosnia.[4] These are the objects that mark the more primitive settlements and shew the
relationship between Greece and the north. The horses, cows
and some of the birds are later. We shall see the Greek version
in the bronzes described in this chapter, but among early
Italian examples there are birds and oxen that are remarkably
close in style to those made by the Greeks.

An attempt has been made to regard the Greek bronzes as
typical " Dorian " productions,[5] since they are found at the
pre-eminently Dorian site, Sparta, and at other sites which can
be connected with the main lines of the Dorian invasion. One
objection to this theory is that the animal statuettes have been
found at Athens, an essentially non-Dorian centre. Another is
that many of the sites, e.g. the Thessalian, that can be considered
as being on the Dorian line of march, are not Dorian in the
narrower sense of the word, as used by the Greeks themselves.[6]
A better case can be made out for the spectacle brooches, which
are not associated with Athens : their chief importance, however,
lies in their northern connection, for they have been found not
only at the same sites as the birds and pendants, but also in
large numbers on the Adriatic coast and in Central Europe,
particularly at Hallstatt.

It is interesting to note that the type of fibula with the large
catch-plate illustrated on Fig. 6 is more or less confined to
Greece. Its chief feature is the decoration on the plate, which
will be discussed in a later section.

---

[1] *B.S.A.*, XXIII, p. 32, Pl. VII, and XXIV, p. 15, Pl. I; *Antiquaries'*
Journal, 1921, Pls. VI, VII.
[2] At Constantinople; *Antiquaries' Journal*, 1921, p. 209.
[3] Vienna, Naturhistorisches Staatsmuseum.
[4] *Mit. Anthrop. Gesellschaft Wien*, XIX, pp. 24 ff. See especially, p. 43,
Fig. 79.
[5] *Antiquaries' Journal*, 1921, p. 199.
[6] See *Cambridge Ancient History*, II, p. 525.

ANIMAL STATUETTES—Though animal statuettes are represented at many sites, their development is best studied at Olympia.[1] Here, in contrast to Sparta, we have a complete series, from the most primitive to the most perfect. The earliest stage is the representation of an animal in two dimensions only : he is cut out of a sheet of copper or bronze as though seen from above (Fig. 1).[2] In some, at least, of these examples, the legs

FIG. 1.—Animal shapes cut out of a sheet of bronze.

might be bent so that the animal could stand. In the next stage, the animal is cut out of a sheet of metal and then bent double along the back, so that he is supported on his four legs, as though cut out of paper by a child (Fig. 2).[3] Finally, the bronze was not only bent, but also hammered, an important innovation.

Another method of producing these statuettes was to cast them : this resulted in two styles : (1) a copy in bronze of a

FIG. 2.—Animals made out of a folded sheet of bronze.

terra-cotta figurine ; (2) a copy of the cast and hammered type described in the last paragraph. It is from the second style that the most advanced Geometric animals are derived. They shew considerable skill, for the casting of the slender legs cannot have been easy. In appearance they are formal, like toys, with cylindrical heads, short round bodies, long straight legs, and, frequently, a long tail. Often they are mounted on stands, which are usually not solid, but shew an open-work pattern and a careful finish on the base. Sometimes the animal is marked

[1] See *Olympia*, IV, pp. 28 ff.
[2] *Ibid.*, Nos. 90 (length, ·058) and 91 (length, ·054).
[3] *Ibid.*, Nos. 96 (length, ·038), and 97 (length, ·043).

with lines drawn by a sharp point,[1] nor could anything be more delightful than the rocking-horse dapples incised on the fore and hind quarters of one small horse from Olympia (Fig. 3), or the wrinkles on the nose of the bull (Fig. 4).[2]

Nearly all the earlier animals were horses and cows, but in the latest class we find stags, hares, goats and a beetle.[3] Some of the birds from Olympia appear to belong to the late group, but the evidence from other sites proves that birds are among the earliest subjects attempted.

FIG. 3.—Dappled horse from Olympia.　　　FIG. 4.—Bull from Olympia.

The custom of supplying the animals with stands facilitated the making of groups. The most common and most pleasing of these are the groups of mares and foals, found on many sites (Pl. 14 a).[4] There is also a deer and fawn [5] (originally there were twins) (Pl. 14 b), a deer attacked by hounds,[6] very stiff and formal, and a centaur and man, of which more later.

HUMAN AND OTHER FIGURES—The earliest of the human figures must be distinctly later than the earliest of the cows and horses, and much later than the earliest pendants and

[1] This is also the case in some of the less finished examples. *Olympia*, IV, p. 38.

[2] *Ibid.*, No. 200 a, and No. 187; hts., ·055 m. and ·045 respectively.

[3] *Ibid.*, Pl. XIII.

[4] Athens, 6199; ht., 11 m.; *Olympia*, 217.

[5] Athens, 6193; ht., 105 m.; *Olympia*, 219 (where the fawn is interpreted as a hound).

[6] At Olympia; Neugebauer, p. 29, Fig. 1.

birds.[1] The development of the human figure follows almost the same lines as that of the animal type. Here, again, we have two methods : on the one hand, the influence of terra-cotta work, producing stumpy figures that may well have been cast from the same mould as the terra-cottas themselves ; on the other hand, cast bars of bronze hammered and welded into figures which are generally as thin and lanky as the early cast animals. The first method is responsible for certain objects like clothes-pegs from Olympia.[2] The second method admitted elaboration and improvement. The four figures on Pl. 15 shew clearly both the craftsman's limitations and his struggle to surmount them. Each represents a warrior who originally held a spear in his raised right hand. A is from the Acropolis : [3] the arms are merely hammered bars of appropriate shapes now bent out of their original position. The right hand must have once held a spear, thrust through the hole pierced in the palm : to the left hand, a shield may have been affixed. A short beard gives a formidable appearance to the chin, but the features are negligible. B is from Olympia,[4] long of limb like the horses, marked with a slit for mouth and holes for eyes. He is bearded, and wears a conical cap or a helmet, and a girdle (barely visible). There are two holes in the stand for attachment to some other base, and holes in the hands through which a pair of spears could be fastened. C, also from Olympia,[5] shews a distinct advance, both in the modelling of the face and bust, and in the casting of features and helmet. The truculent expression is a great, though no doubt unintentional, achievement. The right hand originally held a spear, the left, a shield. D, from Delphi,[6] foreshadows the work of the next period.

Of all the types favoured by Geometric art, that of the warrior was the most popular. Female figures are comparatively rare, and never became stylised. The woman from Delphi [7] is, however, of the same family as the older generation of warriors.

---

[1] The more primitive may belong to the late 9th century and the first half of the 8th : the more advanced to the second half of the 8th, overlapping, possibly, into the 7th.   [2] *Olympia*, IV, 233, 235.

[3] Athens, 6616 ; ht., ·21 m. ; de Ridder, *Catalogue*, 692.

[4] Athens, 6178 ; ht., ·15 m. ; *Olympia*, 244.

[5] At Athens, 6177 ; ht., ·245 m. ; *Olympia*, IV, No. 247.

[6] *Fouilles de Delphes*, V, Pl. I, 7 ; ht., ·22 m.

[7] *Ibid.*, Pl. I, 1. Other examples occur.

A few of the less common, more individual types must be mentioned. Riders, with or without their horses, have been found at Olympia.[1] They are an appropriate dedication on a site where horse racing was to be so prominent a feature.

Still more characteristic of the taste of the Greek sporting man were the chariots and their drivers. Some are thoroughly primitive,[2] others more developed. The best known of them is one of the very latest products of Geometric art [3] (Pl. 16 a). The limbs are not lanky, like those of many of the warriors, and the curves are not too strongly accentuated. Observe how he bends his knees, in order to retain his balance. The helmet, unfamiliar to us, is of a shape not unusual at the period ; the jagged crest occurs on other figures of charioteers from the same site.

The Centaur and Man in the Pierpont Morgan collection [4] form a group which is less advanced, and in all ways typically Geometric. They may be wrestling, but they are not in violent movement or close proximity : such things could not be achieved at so early a date, when " figures touched but gingerly." [5]   The equine part of the centaur is just like countless Geometric horses, but he is distinguished by the beautiful herring-bone pattern which marks the hairs on his back and tail. He is closely related to other primitive, less handsome centaurs from Olympia.[6]

Groups in the " terra-cotta style " from Olympia,[7] and elsewhere,[8] of women dancing in a ring (Pl. 16 b), are interesting because the subject occurs in Minoan times,[9] but was alien to later Greek art. Olympia also produced a number of uncouth figures reminiscent of Cyprus and the East.[10] A " minotaur," now in the Louvre,[11] seems unusual at first sight, but ceases to

---

[1] Olympia, IV, Nos. 255-258.   [2] Ibid., Nos. 248 and 250.
[3] Athens, 6190; Olympia, IV, 249 ; Neugebauer, Pl. 15; ht., ·103 m.
[4] Neugebauer, Pl. 16.
[5] Beazley, C.A.H., IV, p. 585.   [6] E.g. Olympia, 215.
[7] Athens, 6236 ; ht., ·08 m. ; Olympia, IV, 263 ; Berlin, Ol., 8702.   For the latter, see Neugebauer, Pl. 13 ; ht., ·047 m.
[8] Athens, 13,788, from Arcadia.
[9] Bossert, Alt Kreta, Fig. 113; Mosso, Palaces, p. 283, Fig. 136, from Palaikastro.
[10] Olympia, IV, Nos. 234, 240, 241.
[11] Louvre, I, No. 104, Pl. 12 ; Neugebauer, Pl. 14.

surprise us if we imagine him standing, as he originally stood, supporting one of the handles of a tripod.

LOCAL STYLES—Two groups of figures can be distinguished and associated with particular districts.

The first group is composed of men and women with remarkably long necks, disproportionately short legs, and, usually, accessories in bronze wire. They represent warriors or women. Of the examples that I would assign to the group, three come from Aetolia, one from Delphi, and one from Thessaly. They can, therefore, be assigned to *Northern Greece;* and were probably more at home in North-Western Greece than in Thessaly, since the Aetolian examples are both more numerous and more primitive.

They are as follows :—

1. From Thermon[1] (Pl. 17 *a*). The so-called Artemis : a female figure, with a wire necklace and a wire object in one hand.

2. From Thermon.[2] Male figure.

3. From Thermon.[3] Male figure, very poor quality.

4. From Delphi [4] (Pl. 17 *c*). Female figure bent out of its original position with a twisted wire necklace, and a belt.

5. From Kardhitza [5] (Pl. 17 *b*). A warrior who carries a shield ornamented with dots punctured from behind and tied on with bronze wire : the girdle, however, is cast with the figure.

The Kardhitza bronze is obviously the latest of the series ; whereas the other examples belong to the eighth century with the possible exception of No. 2, this one may well have been made in the early seventh. Thessaly and Aetolia were distinctly more backward than the rest of Greece, and it is not surprising that they should, at this period, produce something queer and barbaric.

The second group comes from *Cyprus*. Here, the bronzes are short and thick but full of life and movement. A man and his team ploughing, two pairs of wrestlers, contrast with the stiff figures made elsewhere.

[1] Athens, 14,494 ; Δελτίον, 1915, p. 271, Fig. 39 ; ht., ·22 m.
[2] Athens, 14,755 ; ht., ·20 m. ; Δελτίον, 1915, p. 273, Fig. 40.
[3] Athens, 14,756 ; ht., ·11 m ; Δελτίον, 1915, p. 273, 4, Fig. 41.
[4] At Delphi ; ht., ·10 m. ; *Fouilles de Delphes*, V, No. 35, Fig. 117, and Pl. II, 3.
[5] Athens, 12,831 ; ht., ·28 m. ; Staïs, p. 305 ; Neugebauer, Pl. 12.
[6] Examples in the British Museum.

In examining the men and animals made by the Geometric craftsman one can find practically no points of contact with Minoan art. It has been pointed out [1] that, whereas pottery remained in use throughout the periods as disturbed as the twelfth to tenth centuries in Greece, bronze figures, being a luxury, ceased to be made. Therefore, between Minoan and Geometric pottery there is a perceptible transition : between Minoan and Geometric bronze figures there is a distinct break.

TRIPODS—There are, however, certain bronze vessels which differ very little in type from the Mycenaean. These are the three-legged cauldrons or tripods of which numerous fragments have been found at Olympia,[2] and of which the shapes are easily reconstructed. The resemblance that exists between Mycenaean and Geometric tripods can only be satisfactorily explained when we have more material belonging to the intervening period : one reason, no doubt, is that the tripod, being essentially and originally a cooking pot, must have remained in use throughout the dark ages even as pottery remained in use. In the heroic age, as described by Homer, it was among man's most cherished possessions, and this suggests that it played an important part either in the Late Mycenaean or the subsequent period. Tripods were, apparently, used both for domestic purposes and as articles of value. As gifts, they are mentioned in the same breath as a pair of horses or mules, or a gold cup, or a woman.[3] They are also one of the standard prizes for games.[4] It is beyond doubt that the Homeric tripod is of the same shape as the tripods described in this section.

Though of very early date, the examples from the lowest stratum at Olympia [5] belong to an age when iron was already common. In this stratum were found miniature votive tripods of bronze and fragments of full-sized tripods, belonging to the earliest and heaviest type, the handles and legs frequently of iron. The miniature tripods are either cast or made out of a sheet of bronze. The shape of both large and small tripods is fundamentally the same as that of the tripod from Knossos, with three legs and only two handles : but, whereas the legs of the

---

[1] *J.H.S.*, 1922, p. 207.   [2] *Olympia*, IV, p. 72.
[3] *Odyssey*, XV, 84, and *Iliad*, VIII, 290.
[4] Refs., *Jahrb.*, 1921, pp. 152 ff.
[5] *Olympia*, IV, p. 72.

Minoan and Mycenaean tripods are joined to the body of the vessel, the legs of the Geometric tripods join the rim.[1]

Of the full-size tripod,[2] three main types can be distinguished. The types may be described as follows :—

1. As Fig. 5 a. The tripod is cast. The legs of the earlier examples bend inwards towards the bowl and are generally hexagonal or octagonal in section, becoming more elegant and

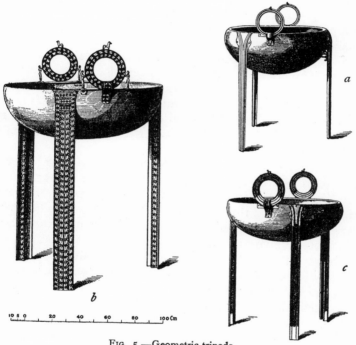

FIG. 5.—Geometric tripods.

more deeply channelled as time went on. Those legs which run straight without a bend towards the rim of the bowl belong, apparently, to the later examples.

The earliest tripods are often made either wholly or in part of iron : gradually, as the form became lighter, the use of bronze increased.

[1] There is, however, evidence that some of the very early Olympia tripods had legs joining the body ; *Olympia*, IV, p. 73.

[2] *Jahrb.*, 1921, p. 122 ; *Olympia*, IV, pp. 75 ff.

The ring-handles are first decorated with plain channellings or zigzags : later with spirals or Geometric animals.　It should be noted that some shew spiral and herring-bone ornaments like those of the sub-Mycenaean tripods.

2. Fig. 5 *b*.　This is slightly later in date than type 1, and makes its appearance in Olympia when fully developed.[1]　The tripod is of hammered plates of bronze riveted together : only small and unimportant details are cast.　The legs are made of three strips of bronze, one in front (A) and two at right angles to support it (B) and (C).　B and C were fastened to A by means of small projecting knobs which were inserted through corresponding slots in A.　All three sides of the legs are elaborately decorated by stamped patterns : concentric circles, circles with tangents, the characteristic S pattern for borders, and zigzags.

The handles, similarly decorated, and fastened by nails on to the bowl, are often supported by two figures, either of men or animals, while a small horse or bird was placed on the top of the handle itself.

The tripods of this and the following class were often extremely large, well over the average height of a man.[2]

3. Fig. 5 *c*.　This is the most mature type.[3]　It has the form of type 2 and the technique of type 1, i.e. it is like type 2 in appearance, but cast.　It is, therefore, artificial in character, for it imitates shapes that are not appropriate to casting.　It is decorated with the same patterns as those stamped on the legs and handles of tripods of the second class, but they are now either in relief or *à jour*, i.e. cut out after they have been cast.　Some shew elements usually associated with the Orientalising style that follows the Geometric, e.g. the lion on a handle from Olympia.[4]

All three types have their handles in three parts :. these are (i) the vertical handles by which the bowl was carried, (ii) an intermediate handle joining (i) to (iii), and (iii) a horizontal strip attached to (ii) and fastened to the rim of the bowl.

So far we have only spoken of the tripods from Olympia, but it must not be imagined that this was the only site where they have been found.　There were tripods among the dedi-

---

[1] *Jahrb.*, *loc. cit.*, p. 125 ; *Olympia*, IV, p. 81.
[2] *Jahrb.*, 1921, p. 133, n. 1.
[3] *Olympia*, IV, p. 90.　　　　[4] *Ibid.*, 641.

cations at most sites where Geometric remains occur : e.g. on the Athenian Acropolis, at Delphi, at the Argive Heraeum and at Dodona.

Some of the examples from Delphi and the Heraeum are remarkable because they possess later elements : [1] at the top of the leg a panel is cut off for decoration, and the decoration often has a distinct Orientalising (i.e. post-Geometric) flavour.

The three groups evidently cover a long period.   The oldest go back to the very beginning of the Geometric age, the later survive into the seventh century.   A not dissimilar type of tripod must have been made in the succeeding centuries, since it is frequently illustrated on coins and vases,[2] but of actual bronze examples there are none.[3]

GEOMETRIC DECORATION (fibulae, etc.).—The designs with which the Geometric bronze worker decorated the surface of his wares are very like those with which the potter ornamented his vases.   The repertory of patterns was a small one.   Some of them have already been illustrated by the tripods, especially by the tripods of classes 2 and 3.   They include zigzags, circles, and circles joined by tangents into a running pattern. Others, such as the swastika, are familiar to us from Dipylon pottery.

But, to get a more complete idea of what Geometric artists could do in the way of decoration and drawing, we must turn to the personal ornaments of the period, such as bracelets, diadems, and, above all, brooches.

The typical Geometric brooches have been found in large numbers or singly at various sites :—Olympia, Argos, Sparta, Delphi, Aegina, Rhodes, Amorgos, Thera, Crete and Athens.[4] They are characterised by their large ornamented " catch-plate." [5]   They evidently derive from certain proto-Geometric

[1] *Jahrbuch*, 1921, p. 124 ; *Argive Heraeum*, No. 2221, Pl. CXXIV ; *Fouilles de Delphes*, Nos. 241, 242, 243.

[2] *Jahrbuch*, 1921, p. 126.

[3] To conclude our account of Geometric tripods, mention should be made of the bronzes at Candia, *Museo Italiano Atlas*, XI.   These consist of soldiers, people in a boat, animals, that decorated a tripod now lost.

[4] References given by Reisinger, *Jahrbuch*, 1916, p. 298.   See also *Fouilles de Delphes*, V, Fig. 406.

[5] The catch-plate is that part of the safety-pin which holds and sheathes the point.

fibulae, where the bow is divided from the pin and catch-plate by two knobs.[1] In these early examples the catch-plate is small, but it gradually grew larger till it became a square field suitable for decoration, while the corresponding part of the brooch above the spiral became longer. The brooches of this shape must have been decidedly brittle, but the makers, undeterred by the danger, continued to increase the size. A catch-plate in Philadelphia [2] measures as much as 14 × 12·4 cm.

This raises the question of the purpose for which the brooches were made. The smaller ones were, of course, meant for actual use. Of the larger, many must have been intended for dedication or for burial in a tomb : there is, however, evidence that

FIG. 6.—Fibula, in Munich.

the large brooches of the half-moon type, discussed below, were worn.

There is a strong likeness between the designs on most of the fibulae, though one or two have points of special interest. Among these are the Boston catch-plate mentioned above, with Herakles and the "Hind" on one side, Herakles, Iolaos, Hydra and Crab on the other, and a fibula at Munich [3] (Fig. 6) with a race-horse standing beside the tripod he has won as a prize, obviously a tripod of type 2.

Notice the way in which the corner of the plate is filled : the usual pattern here is a diagonal line edged with dog-tooth. The outlines are frequently doubled, and the bodies of the figures hatched with lines of zigzags. Birds and fishes are used

[1] E.g. those at Mouliana ; 'Εφ. 'Αρχ., 1904, Pls. 29-30, Fig. 7.

[2] A.J.A., 1911, p. 1.

[3] Munich, Jahrbuch, 1916, p. 297, Fig. 3. Notice, on the reverse, the lion chewing up the leg of an animal.

to fill the background.   The artist draws like a child : on a fibula from Olympia, a horse is engraved in profile but with two eyes. This is a common fault with primitive draughtsmen : they know a horse has got two eyes and believe that both should appear in the drawing.   It is often possible to detect the tools used for making the different lines ; for the Philadelphia example, four different tools are used : a pointed instrument for the finer lines, a blunter instrument for the border, and two different gouges to punch out the zigzags.[1]

Another variety of brooch which lent itself to ornamentation had the bow expanded into a flat half-moon.[2]   About sixteen examples are known : the provenance of most of them is uncertain, but five were found in Boeotia, and there is every reason to believe that somewhere in Boeotia was the centre where brooches of the type were made.[3]   They include at least two pairs, possibly three ; this fact points to their having been intended for actual use, for fastening a garment, one on each shoulder.   Moreover, a fine example in a private collection at Munich has been repaired in ancient times : [4] this would hardly have occurred unless it had been worn.   The whole group is remarkable for its fine execution : the lines are neater than those commonly found on fibulae, circles are drawn with compasses, and, where the outlines are double, one line is usually thinner than the other.   The subjects and the details are those usually found on other Geometric jewellry, with one important innovation : in the centre of the field is a complex of circles or a rosette, the former recalling the patterns on certain of the gold discs from the Shaft Graves at Mycenae,[5] the latter foreshadowing the Orientalising motives that were to become popular at the close of the Geometric Period.

Four of the brooches deserve special mention.   Nos. 1 and 2, a pair, are in the Arndt collection.[6]   They were said to have come from the same grave as two bracelets decorated in the Geometric manner,[7] and both bracelets and brooches were purchased in Athens.   The preservation is good, though some

[1] *A.J.A.*, loc. cit.
[2] Reisinger, *Jahrb.*, 1916, p. 295, n. 1 ; Blinkenberg, *op. cit.*, p. 185.
[3] *Ibid.*, *op. cit.*, *loc. cit.*   [4] Reisinger, *op. cit.*, p. 288, n. 1.
[5] Schliemann, *Mycenae*, p. 167, Fig. 241.
[6] At Munich ; *Jahrbuch*, 1916, p. 288 ; Blinkenberg, *op. cit.*, p. 191.
[7] *Jahrbuch*, 1916, Figs. 1 and 2, pp. 289, 294.

4

of the patterns have been lost.   The total measurement of each fibula is 21 × 15 cm.   Above the spiral springs are knobs with spokes.

The decoration is as follows :—

On No. 1, side A (Fig. 7), is a ship, complete with mast and steering gear, and manned with a number of warriors.   One keeps a lookout from the mast,[1] supported in some erection at the masthead ; three are on deck ; the presence of the rest is indicated by their shields.   A mare and foal, in the manner of the bronze statuettes, and the usual fishes and birds, complete the picture.

On side B the details are similar, but the ship and mare are replaced by two chariots : one of their occupants carries a Boeotian shield.

On No. 2, side A (Fig. 7), is a boat in which a horse is tethered, and four warriors.   On side B is a boat and a swastika.

Nos. 3 and 4 are a pair in the British Museum.[2]   They too have knobs with spokes above the spiral spring, and the same border as the pair at Munich, though with a different type of medallion in the centre.

On No. 3, side A, are two women, each holding by the neck a brace of birds, and Herakles (?) and the Nemean lion.   On side B is a swastika and two men in a boat, which one of them rows, Mediterranean fashion, with his foot.

On No. 4, side A, are Herakles, Iolaos, the Hydra and the Crab : also a horse, which has small wheels attached to his feet.   Perhaps it is the Trojan horse ?   On side B are warriors and what may be a hunting scene.   Birds and fishes fill the background of all four pictures.

With regard to period : the half-moon brooches appear to be later than the majority of brooches with ornamented catch-plate.   The latter must have been common in the eighth century, and preferably in its second half.   The former will, therefore, belong to the close of the eighth century and to the early seventh.

Compared with the contemporary bronze statuettes, which anticipate the restraint and directness of later Greek art, the drawing on all the brooches seems surprisingly primitive.   Hence

[1] For detailed discussion, see *Jahrbuch*, 1916, p. 291.
[2] B.M., 3204, 3205.

a

b

FIG. 7.—Fibulae, in Munich.

its charm.   Just as a child, when it picks up a pencil, has very little consciousness of its limitations, and illustrates any subject it wishes, so our artists hopefully attempted a variety of scenes, and probably viewed their achievements with satisfaction.   But their satisfaction cannot have equalled ours, when we contemplate the neat details of the ship, Herakles' monstrous crab, Iolaos trying to saw the Hydra in half,[1] or the horse precariously tethered in a small and transparent boat.

An engraved bronze band [2] from a tomb at Thebes should be compared with the fibulae.   Here are beasts, birds, fishes, a warrior, a boat and a swastika ; among the beasts is a lion, a forerunner of the lions which became so common in the next period.   A double outline occurs, as on many of the fibulae.

All the designs hitherto described are drawn with a point or punched with a gouge on the bronze.   Occasionally, however, the outline was made by a series of dots.[3]   Ornaments and figures hammered from behind, so that they stand out in relief, begin to appear at the end of the period.   This technique was foreign to Geometric art, and was introduced from the East.

It will have become apparent that the big religious centres, such as Olympia, Delphi and the Acropolis at Athens, played as important a part in the development of Greek bronze-work as they did in that of Greek sculpture.   At places such as these, folk met together and bronze objects were dedicated : there also artists could form their taste, criticise their rivals, and enlarge their outlook by examining the offerings of foreigners from overseas.   There, from time to time, objects that had become out of date or otherwise spoilt were thrown away and buried.   Thus it happens that many of them have been preserved, for the pleasure and profit of our own times.

[1] On B.M., 3205.   One of the pair described above.
[2] At Athens ; *Annali*, 1880, Pl. G.
[3] *Olympia*, IV, No. 293.

CHAPTER III

THE EARLY ARCHAIC (ORIENTALISING) PERIOD, *c.* 700-575 B.C.

A. EARLY DECORATIVE WORK, VASES, ETC.

THE Geometric age in Greece was followed by what is sometimes called the Early Archaic, sometimes the Orientalising Period. It is marked by the introduction of fresh motives, either adapted from Oriental art, such as the lotus pattern, and the friezes of animals ; or produced spontaneously, the result of stimulus from without.

To define the limits of this period is not easy. We may place its upper limit somewhere about 700 B.C., always remembering that most classes of art overlap their successors, and that Geometric art, particularly, continued to exist for a long time after the Orientalising style had come to the fore.

The lower limit is marked by no very striking change. In vase painting, it would coincide with the decline of certain groups of Orientalising pottery, and the appearance of others where the Oriental motives have been more thoroughly assimilated. In bronze-work, it is comparatively obscure, since there is less material to help us. Two stages can, however, be distinguished : during the first, the artists are obviously experimenting with new and often unfamiliar material : during the second, certain themes were elaborated and perfected. Various indications shew that the first phase, the subject of this chapter, ends early in the sixth century B.C.

Accustomed to the neat, restricted Geometric ornaments, and the stiff Geometric figures, the Greeks were naturally impressed by the maturity and richness of foreign art. Instead of borrowing motives here and there, as they had done at the end of the eighth century, they now imported them wholesale : palmette and lotus patterns, cable patterns, fabulous monsters

53

such as sphinxes and griffins, wild beasts, like the lion and panther, which few Greeks could have set eyes on.

The art of Mesopotamia and Egypt penetrated into Greece through many channels. In the first place, there was the export to Greece of objects of value, such as metal-work and embroidery, many of which were carried by Phoenician traders. In the second place, these Phoenicians did an even more profitable trade in copies of Assyrian and Egyptian objects made in their own factories : more copies reached Greece than originals, so the influence of Eastern art tended to be indirect. The part played by Cyprus, whose population contained a strong Phoenician element, is not easy to estimate ; the metal-work of Cyprus stands so near that of Phoenicia, that there is often controversy as to which examples should be attributed to which of the two peoples.[1]

In the third place, Oriental influence reached Greece through the Greek colonies on the coasts of Asia Minor or Africa : these colonies must have had some direct contact with the art of their foreign neighbours, and were themselves flourishing centres whose influence affected the Greek mainland. Crete, in touch with both Egypt and the East, had a brief but interesting artistic career.

The importance of metal-work, particularly bronze, in transmitting Oriental motives, has already been mentioned. That bronze was used extensively in the seventh century is attested not only by actual remains, but by the influence of bronze on pottery. The potters began to copy features which, like the scale pattern, are appropriate to bronze, to use incision freely, and to imitate the shapes of metal vases. That so many originals have been reduced to fragments or disappeared entirely is due to the perishable nature of the material and to the possibility of melting and remoulding it.

Before giving an account of some of the surviving Greek bronzes of this period, a word must be said about certain bronzes of foreign manufacture or foreign style of which examples have been found on Greek sites.

EARLY BRONZES OF FOREIGN TYPE.

(i) PHOENICIAN BOWLS—The bronze bowls, commonly called Phoenician, are characterised by their decoration, which

---

[1] Poulsen, *Der Orient und die Frühgriechische Kunst*, pp. 34-35.

is purely Oriental in character. Sometimes the motives are Egyptian, sometimes Assyrian : some of the bowls bear inscriptions containing Phoenician words. These inscriptions, and the fact that the bowls are not homogeneous in style, suggest the attribution to Phoenicia : some authorities have favoured a Cypriote origin. Large numbers of these bowls were found at Nimrud : these must go back into the ninth century. The bowls that are important in the history of Greek art, however, are those which were made at a later period, during the eighth and even the seventh centuries. They have been found in Cyprus, Italy and Greece. Of the examples from Greek sites, two come from the Idaean cave in Crete, one from the Acropolis, one from Delphi and two from Olympia [1] (Fig. 7 a).

Exhibited at the more important shrines in Greece, these and other Oriental products could be admired and studied not only by artists, but by the large crowds that would flock to Olympia or the Acropolis or Delphi at the time of festivals. The alien scenes and surprising new designs would stimulate the imagination of sightseers, especially when contrasted with the exhibits of Geometric art, to which they were accustomed. Greek craftsmen would turn their skill to copying Oriental themes, at first too faithfully, later with discrimination ; whereupon the members of the elder generation would shake their heads and recommend the more wholesome severity of the Geometric Period.

(ii) THE CRETAN SHIELDS—One day in 1884 a peasant, watching his flock on Mount Ida in Crete, chanced to scrape away with his stick some of the soil which covered the floor of a cave. To his gratification he found the soil contained fragments of antiquities, and thus began a series of excavations, at first illicit, on the part of the peasants, later authorised, on the part of the archæologist Halbherr.[2] The finds were various, and included the Phoenician bowls already alluded to. The most famous, however, and those which concern

---

[1] Poulsen, *Der Orient und die Frühgriechische Kunst*, pp. 20 ff. ; Von Bissing, *Jahrbuch*, 1923, pp. 211-218. To the already known examples, add one from the Italian excavations at Phrati (Arkades), Crete. Fig. 7 a was found near Olympia, see *Olympia*, IV, p. 141 ; diam., ·20 m. At Athens.

[2] *Museo Italiano*, II, 1888, p. 689, and *Atlas*, Pls. I-V, IX, X ; *Jahrb.*, 1923, pp. 211 ff. ; *A.J.A.*, IV, 1888, p. 434 ; Poulsen, *op. cit.*, pp. 74 ff. The shields are in the Candia and Athens Museums.

us here, are the so-called Cretan or Idaean shields, of which
some are votive shields, others gongs or cymbals.[1] All were
used in the worship of Zeus and the Kouretes, for in this cave,
according to legend, Zeus was born and his cries drowned by
the clashing of the shields the Kouretes carried. The shields
(using the word for both shields and cymbals) are twenty-one
in number ; ten are distinguished by their larger size and striking
designs. All are of thin bronze, and some have small holes
round the border, meant for suspension or attachment to a
backing of some other material. Much of the ornament is
hammered : incision is used sparingly. The most characteristic
shape is convex, with the central boss and concentric zones of
decoration appropriate to a shield ; but there is another form,
comparatively flat, and without any boss in the centre. It is
represented by the most famous of the shields, evidently really
a gong or tympanon, on which is a single picture covering all
the surface save the border. The scene represents a god swinging a lion above his head, and accompanied by winged attendants
who are themselves striking gongs. The figures suggest, on the
one hand, the Greek Zeus and his Kouretes, and, on the other,
certain Assyrian types. This shield, though the least typical,
is the most frequently illustrated owing to its mythological
importance.

From the artistic point of view, the so-called " Shield of
Horus " [2] is the most arresting (Pl. 18 a). It is larger than the
rest, measuring 0·68 m. in diameter ; like them, it is made of a
thin sheet of metal hammered till it is extremely convex. The
central boss would be formed by the head of a bird, which is
now lost. The bird stretches its wings right across the shield,
crossing the bodies of two horned snakes ; below is a sphinx ;
in the field are two lions and a goat.

Another of the shields, the " shield of the goats," has a
central lion's head in high relief, and round it two circular
friezes, the inner frieze of goats, the outer frieze of bulls. Between are borders of single cable pattern. The edges of the
shield are missing.

The Idaean cave is not the only Cretan site where shields of

[1] *Anz.*, 1913, pp. 47-53 ; A. B. Cook, *Zeus*, I, p. 644, Pl. XXXV.
[2] At Candia. The bird's head which appears on the photograph in the
centre of the shield is modern.

this type were found. Four were unearthed during the excavations of the British School at Palaikastro in Eastern Crete,[1] one in comparatively good preservation, with the forefront of a lion in the centre, and round it two pairs of sphinxes and lions, the other three fragmentary. Two handsome shields come from the recent Italian excavations at Phrati (Arkades).

The Cretan shields are hard to place because they are hybrids. They are not pure Assyrian or Egyptian, and they are certainly not pure Greek. They would naturally be regarded as Phoenician, for Phoenician art is composed of alien elements. But certain details have been pointed out [2] which are said to be inconsistent with a Phoenician origin. The most important of these are : (1) the animals do not walk directly on the plait border, as they would if made by Phoenicians, but are separated from it by a line. (2) The goats are drawn galloping in a manner reminiscent of Minoan art, but not of Assyria or Phoenicia.

It has, therefore, been suggested that the shields are copies of Phoenician originals made by Greek artists. This could hardly have happened at any other period of Greek art, and even now is startling. The style of the shields is so un-Greek that it must surely weigh against the few details that are un-oriental.

Fortunately, the importance of the shields lies less in their origin and their artistic significance than in their presence in Crete almost before the beginning of the Orientalising period.[3] They indicate one of the channels by which Eastern motives reached Greece.

GREEK RELIEF WORK—It was the decorative arts, such as engraved metal-work, metal-work in low relief and vase painting, that were most modified by contact with the East. Sculpture in the round was less obviously affected. This is natural, for there would be no demand in the Greek market for foreign statuettes ; what the purchaser required would be orthodox representations of his own gods and their worshippers, for dedication at favourite shrines. Consequently, we should be able to arrange a series of bronze statuettes of which the first

[1] B.S.A., XI, p. 306, Pl. XVI. For other parallels, see Anz., 1913, p. 52.
[2] By Poulsen, op. cit., p. 78. The view that the shields are made by Greeks is supported by Beazley, C.A.H., IV, p. 583.
[3] They cannot be exactly dated, but may be attributed to the late eighth century B.C.

would be Geometric and the last of the ripe Archaic Period, and see clearly how each figure develops out of the one before.   With decorative art, on the other hand, the change from rectilinear or circular Geometric patterns and angular Geometric figures, to the rich and varied motives that take their place, is often so abrupt that many stages are missing.

FIG. 1.—Early engraving from the Acropolis.

A number of bronze bands from Olympia, probably diadems or strips for nailing on wooden coffers, illustrate the running patterns used at this period. There are some that differ so slightly from a certain type of pattern common on Mycenaean vases [1] that their sudden appearance in Greek art without direct antecedents is startling.   Others shew, in various forms, the palmette and lotus which play so large a part in bronze-work and vase painting, and the plait or cable pattern that was to appear so often in later archaic bronzes.

Any reconstruction of the progress of decorative bronze-work in the seventh century must be unsatisfactory until our material is considerably increased. Of the extant bronzes, some come from one school or district, some from another : local differences distract the attention from chronological development : we cannot, as in vase painting, follow the course of several homogeneous groups. Nevertheless, an attempt has here been made to collect and describe the more important pieces and to estimate their significance in the history of the art they represent.

(1) *Fragment from the Acropolis*—Among the bronzes found in the debris of the Acropolis is a fragment [2] that belongs to

[1] *Olympia*, IV, 738, Pl. XLII.
[2] Athens, 6957 ; ht., ·24 m. ; *J.H.S.*, XIII, p. 244, Fig. 17.

the very beginning of the Orientalising Period (Fig. 1). We cannot tell what purpose this fragment served, but may infer from the presence of nail-holes that it was for attachment to some object, possibly the leg of a tripod. The lines are engraved : the circles, both those on the leopard's body and those on the border, are punched with a stamp. The fragment might be considered Geometric, were it not for the fact that the leopard does not belong to the stock of subjects used by artists of that period. A close parallel in style is given by the spotted centaur from Dodona,[1] which, however, has no features that are not Geometric.

(2) *Fragment from Olympia*—An interesting fragment from Olympia [2] (Fig. 2), apparently destined to be applied to an object of another material, illustrates a different technique.

FIG. 2.—Early relief from Olympia.

The figures are in low relief, with outlines incised. Now, low relief is foreign to Greek Geometric art,[3] though it occurs occasionally before its close.[4] Combined with incision, it could be used effectively even by a not very skilful artist. The Olympia fragment represents a man sacrificing oxen, possibly Herakles, celebrating the first sacrifice under the sacred olive.

(3) *The Cretan Group*—A very close, distinctive group of objects [5] comes from Crete. The examples which compose it have not all been published, but those already known arrest attention by their remarkable style.

The first four are figures cut out of a sheet of bronze for application to a background of some other material.

---

[1] Carapanos, *Dodona*, Pl. XIX, 5. The likeness between these two bronzes has been pointed out by Bather, *J.H.S., loc. cit.*

[2] Athens, No. 6392 ; length, ·233 m. ; *Olympia*, IV, No. 694, Pl. XXXVII.

[3] *J.H.S.*, XIII, p. 244.

[4] E.g. *Olympia*, IV, Nos. 295, 296.

[5] See *C.A.H.*, IV, p. 586.

(*a*) A pair of huntsmen (Pl. 19).[1]   One carries his game, a wild goat, across his shoulders ; the feet are tied together to keep it in place.   His hair curls above his forehead, in a manner reminiscent of Minoan frescos ; he wears a sleeved tunic, fringed and embroidered.   His companion, an older man with a banded fillet round his head, wears a similar tunic.   He carries a bow, and with his free hand grasps his companion's arm, perhaps attempting to get possession of the goat.   These details are rendered by engraving on a scarcely perceptible low relief. Certain points are noteworthy : e.g. the low foreheads, the small waists and elaborate indication of muscles on the knee. Notice the nail-holes beneath the feet for attachment.

(*b*) Part of the same bronze.[2]   Head, shoulders and arm of youth with long curly hair.

(*c*) Huntsman kneeling.[3]   On his shoulder is a goat, with its legs tied to its neck : the huntsman steadies his burden by holding one horn.   He wears a sleeveless tunic and leans on a staff.   His head is hidden by the goat.

(*d*) Young huntsman with bow and quiver, carrying an ibex (identified by its large horn and its beard).[4]   A looped cord hangs over the left shoulder and must not be confused with the costume.

The other examples are bits of armour.

(*e*) *Mitra* from Rethymno [5] (Fig. 3).   The identification of this object as a *mitra* explains its semicircular shape.   The *mitra* was that part of the armour which was attached below the breastplate, and hung down to protect the lower half of the body.

The technique is a combination of low relief and incision : the figures are in repoussé work, the details engraved.

Round the edge are two main borders, the outer composed

---

[1] Louvre, 93 ; ht., ·183 m. ; *Catalogue*, Pl. 11, and p. 20, where complete references are given. See also Collignon, *Hst. de la Sculpture Grecque*, I, p. 99, Fig. 49.   " From Crete."

[2] Louvre, 94 ; ht., ·05 m. ; *Catalogue*, p. 20, Pl. 11 ; Collignon, *op. cit.*, p. 100, Fig. 50.

[3] Oxford ; *J.H.S.*, XXX, pp. 226 ff., Pl. XII, 1 ; ht., ·108 m. ; diam., ·074 m.

[4] National Museum, Copenhagen ; *J.H.S.*, XXX, p. 227, Fig. 1, and p. 228 ; ht., ·142 × ·050 m.   Another fragment in the same style as *a-d* was discovered in 1927 at Phrati (Crete), and will shortly be published by Dr. Doro Levi.

[5] At Candia ; Poulsen, *Ath. Mit.*, 1906, pp. 373 ff., Pl. XXIII.

of hatched dog-tooth patterns, the inner, a complex of pseudo-spirals (their centres are circles and dots) arranged like the true spirals in the Orchomenos ceiling, and other Minoan and Mycenaean frescos.[1]   On the *mitra*, within the main borders, is a subsidiary border of small lines shaped like a reversed S, a motive common in prehistoric Crete but occurring elsewhere. In the centre of the picture is what looks like a floral ornament : closer examination shews it to be a trophy,[2] composed

FIG. 3.—Mitra from Rethymno.

of a conventionalised breastplate above (with two holes in it for the attachment of a *mitra*), and a very Mycenaean looking palm tree below.[3] Above the tree two youths hold a wreath : behind each youth is another. Notice the device by which they are accommodated to the space they have to fill. All four have big eyes with eyelashes and eyebrows marked above, low foreheads, and hair with curled fringes, another Minoan feature.

[1] Bossert, *Alt Kreta*, Pl. 206 and Pl. 50.   See *B.S.A.*, XXV, p. 169.
[2] So Poulsen, *op. cit.*, pp. 374 ff.   Dr. A. B. Cook makes the more probable suggestion that it is a phallus.
[3] Comparisons, *op. cit.*, p. 379.

They wear belts, sleeved tunics edged with a common Mycenaean pattern, and below, what look like the elaborately folded loincloths of prehistoric Crete (see p. 23), which pass over the lower hems of the tunics. The markings on the thigh are hard to explain.[1] The muscles of the knee are drawn in a different way to those on (a).

Six other *mitrai*, from Axos,[2] are to be found in the museum at Chanea ; unfortunately, illustrations have not yet been published. One is particularly remarkable, for among the scenes engraved upon it is a tripod with an armed figure seated in the bowl.

(f) and (g) The Olympia Breastplates—Two objects of considerable importance belong to the class under discussion. These are the backs of two breastplates from Olympia ; one,[3] from the excavations, is not illustrated here, the other,[4] on Fig. 4, was found in the River Alpheios, and like all the antiquities found in that river, comes from the adjoining site. Both are by the same hand, for on both are certain lines composed of inverted scallops (e.g. on the lion's body and the outline of some of the dresses : they are an unusual feature), and both shew a curious style of drawing the human head, similar decorative motives, and almost the same heraldic sphinxes and leopards. The Alpheios breastplate, unlike its fellow, is ornamented with a group of figures at its base (Fig. 4). We cannot identify all, but it is probably Zeus who greets Apollo, and the goddess with the scaly corsage must be, not Artemis, but Athena.

There is, of course, no relief. Everything is shewn by means of engraved lines.

The arm-holes are bound with a bronze rim so as not to cut the arms : in the centre of the back are two holes which look uncommonly as though they had been pierced by the common four-sided arrow-heads. We must not assume that the unlucky

---

[1] Poulsen, *op. cit.*, p. 375, calls it a garment, comparing (p. 387) a drawing on a Boeotian vase : but,. if so, why is there no indication on the inner side of the thigh ? Perhaps tattooing is meant : instances occur in the Classical Period, and in the Prehistoric Period. Cf. the head from Mycenae, 'Εφ. 'Αρχ., 1902, Pls. I-II.

[2] *Op. cit.*, pp. 383 ff.

[3] Athens ; *Olympia*, IV, Pl. LVIII, No. 980.

[4] In a private collection when published by Furtwängler ; *Olympia*, IV, Pl. LIX, p. 154.

wearer was a runaway : he may have been making a last stand, attacked from both sides.

The breastplates have already been compared with the *mitrai*: that they are of Cretan manufacture seems beyond dispute. The unillustrated breastplate, *f*, has the same dog-tooth and zigzag pattern as the Rethymno mitra and the Axos

FIG. 4.—Breastplate from the river Alpheios.

helmet (*h* below) : the illustrated example affects the running S pattern which is also a feature of the *mitra*.[1]

(*h*) The Axos helmet (Pl. 42 *a*).[2] This beautiful bronze is described here because it belongs to the Cretan group and forms a link between the *mitrai* and the breastplates. It must, however, be later than they are ; its style is that of the sixth century.

[1] Pfuhl, *Malerei und Zeichnung*, I, p. 160 ; Poulsen, *Ath. Mit.*, 1906, p. 388.
[2] At Chanea ; ht., ·215 m.

The decoration consists of horses, rosettes and eyebrows (above the eye-sockets) in relief, and of engraved patterns. One of these, beneath the horses' feet, is the peculiar dog-tooth and zigzag already mentioned ; another is a plait and tendril which recalls the patterns on the breastplates. Between the eyebrows and the rosettes is engraved a lion's head.

All the bronzes, especially the *mitrai*, shew how individual Cretan art was at this period. It is marked, especially, by a peculiar, fine style of engraving, by a love of certain patterns, (e.g. the zigzag and dog-tooth, and varieties of honeysuckle pattern), and a tendency to group both figures and animals heraldically. Of its other products, the Praesos plate,[1] a beautiful piece of vase painting, comes nearest. The affinities of the plate and the *mitrai* with the contemporary art of the Cyclades,[2] and with Boeotian relief ware, have been pointed out by the publisher of the *mitra*, who also noted various points of contact with Minoan art.[3] But, at the time of publishing, prehistoric Crete was less familiar to us than now, and, since the parallels did not appear so striking, they were not sufficiently emphasised. Some, such as the costume and sleeved tunic and loin-cloth, are due to the survival of a fashion. Others, such as the drawing of the faces and the interlaced spirals on the border, support a suggestion recently made that here and there Minoan works of art must still have been on view,[4] and this would be especially true of Crete.

(4) *The Acropolis Bronzes* [5]—These form a series later in date than No. 1.

(a) [6] First come a group of fragments ornamented with both engraving and scarcely perceptible low relief. They must be from the leg of a tripod ; the tripod was probably more or less like the second of the Geometric types discussed on p. 46. Here are two strips of bronze united by cross-pieces like a ladder. Behind these was fastened a thin piece of bronze which would fill the spaces as a picture fills its frame, and which was, in its turn, backed by other strips. The fastenings were effected by

[1] *Ath. Mit.*, pp. 382, 391 ; *B.S.A.*, X, pp. 148 ff., Pl. III.
[2] *Op. cit.*, p. 390.
[3] Poulsen thinks the attitude of the two outer figures has Mycenaean parallels, *op. cit.*, p. 380.
[4] Beazley, *C.A.H.*, IV, p. 582. [5] *J.H.S.*, XIII, pp. 259 ff.
[6] *Ibid.*, pp. 264 ff., Figs. 30, 31 ; *Jahrb.*, 1921, p. 125.

nails. One scene illustrates part of a contest for a tripod : in the frame above it are two heraldic lions, below is a palmette. Some other fragments shew an interesting border of twisted palmettes and tendrils : they are obviously part of the same

FIG. 5.—Fragment from the Acropolis.

series as the fragments from the leg, but may belong to a different part of the tripod.

(b)[1] The fragment with the winged figure on Fig. 5, and the other with a hand and sword-pommel, come apparently from the

[1] *J.H.S.*, XIII, pp. 259 ff., Figs. 26, 27, 28, 29. The illustrations, in some cases, emphasise the boss in the centre of the palmettes, in some cases not. The boss is, of course, produced by the processes used in repoussé work : it is not marked by incision, as Figs. 28 and 32 would suggest. Athens, 6956; width, ·27 m.

5

same object ; likewise part of a boar, part of a hand and rosette, and some less important pieces which are not illustrated.   The heavy palmette border is early in style : early, too, are the proportions of the man with his unnaturally long legs.   He is the male counterpart, not without parallels,[1] of the winged female figures holding birds which are so common in archaic art.

Low relief : outline and details incised.

(c) [2] Near the end of the series comes the fragment on Fig. 6 with Herakles and an armed youth.   The figure of Herakles is

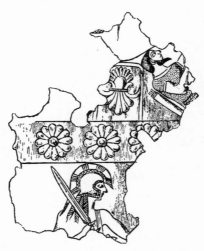

difficult to complete : the line above his head must be part of his bow, and he appears to be about to shoot, but Greek archers were accustomed to shoot with the body upright. Our archer could not have been upright if the band with the rosettes be continued in a straight line, as seems natural, making two panels at right-angles to each other.   In any case, the sheet of bronze gives the impression that it was meant to be seen from above ; if so, it may have covered the lid of a box.   There are some interesting points about

Fig. 6.—Fragment from the Acropolis.

the warrior : his helmet, with the holes round the border for the attachment of the lining (cf. the real helmet on p. 63) : his sword, with its characteristic Iron Age leaf-shaped blade (unlike the Bronze Age swords illustrated in this book), and his strands of hair, arranged in a fashion popular in the Early Archaic Period.

Though many statuettes were made at Athens, few examples of decorative bronze-work can safely be called Athenian.   The pieces just described have, however, as strong a claim as any. The somewhat Semitic profiles of Herakles and the warrior

[1] *J.H.S.*, XIII, p. 260.
[2] *Ibid.*, pp. 268 ff., Figs. 32, 33 ; Athens, 6963 ; ht., ·16 m.

resemble not only those on the Proto-Attic vase at New York,[1] but also those on certain coins and statuettes that have been classed as " Early Attic." [2] Moreover, it must be remembered that Athens probably supplied herself with metal vessels and other useful objects in ancient times as now : that so few, either plain or decorated, have survived, is probably accidental.

The chief argument against an Attic origin is provided by a bronze plaque, in a style very similar to that of our 6 c, recently discovered at the Argive Heraeum. The question must, therefore, remain open till further discoveries provide more material.

BRONZE VASES—A number of vases made at this period claim our attention by their shape, their technique, and the subjects which adorn them.

Among the *phialae* (shallow bowls for libation) found at Olympia, three, contrasting with each other in various ways, have been chosen for illustration (Fig. 7). All are made of remarkably thin sheets of bronze, thickening slightly towards the rim.

The first, a phiale with the typical boss in the centre, is ornamented with a simple pattern of lotus petals, markedly Egyptian in style.[3] The lines are drawn on the outside of the vase, where they appear concave : on the interior they stand out in relief (Fig. 7 b).

In the second phiale,[4] the central boss is surrounded by griffins' heads : there was too much room for five, too little for six, and the extra space was filled by a triangle. Both the detail of the heads, and the narrow borders above them, are very carefully drawn : as in the previous example, they were made by lines hammered on the outside of the vase, and therefore appear convex on the inside. The bowl should, however, be viewed from the outside (Fig. 7 d).

The arrangement of the griffins' heads is not uncommon at the period. Compare the plate, described below, and a vase from Naukratis, in the British Museum.[5] The heads are of the same type as those on the bowls belonging to the tripods described on p. 70.

[1] *J.H.S.*, XXXII, Pls. X, XI.   [2] *Ibid.*, XLII, pp. 216 ff.
[3] *Olympia*, IV, No. 880, Pl. LII ; diam., ·195 m.
[4] *Ibid.*, No. 883, Pl. LII ; diam., ·19 m.
[5] *J.H.S.*, 1924, p. 199, Fig. 31.

The third of the phialae [1] is fragmentary, for the central parts are missing. On the remaining portion is a procession of oxen, rendered in low relief, with engraved details. The relief is produced by repoussé work, hammered from the outside inwards : the bowl, therefore, should be viewed from inside. The oxen are fine and stately : they recall a similar procession on one of the Cretan shields and various other oxen from coins and vases (Fig. 7 d).

The *Tyszkiewicz Plate* [2] (Pl. 1 b) is one of the most important pieces of early bronze-work. Its engraved decorations, especially the animal frieze, is akin to the decoration of Rhodian pottery, and it can, therefore, safely be placed as far back as the middle of the seventh century. On the other hand, it shews strongly the influence of the Phoenician bowls, which provide approximate parallels for the central medallion, and where animals are represented, as here, contrary to Greek custom, walking on the dotted line. The griffins' heads recall those of the phiale.

It is difficult to find seventh century examples of those shapes which were to become common in the following centuries : amphorae, hydriae, jugs.

A group of *hydriae*, belonging to the late seventh century and the early sixth century, is only represented by a few surviving handles. A set of three, the one vertical handle and the two horizontal handles of a hydria, comes from Epirus and is at Berlin.[3] The horizontal handles are finished at both ends by female heads, with their hair dressed in the current fashion ; the vertical handle has a female head at its base, and at its upper junction the heads of two snakes.

The same style appears on two handles, one in the Louvre,[4] the other from Olympia.[5]

Mention should here be made of the various receptacles for holding the ashes of the dead, *urns and lidless oval vessels* shaped like a bath.[6] The latter, of which examples have been found at Olympia, Corfu, Syracuse and Megara Hyblaea, are

---

[1] *Olympia*, IV, No. 884, Pl. LII ; diam., ·16 m.
[2] Fröhner, Coll. *Tyszkiewicz*, Pl. XV ; Poulsen, *op. cit.*, p. 86 ; Pfuhl, *Malerei und Zeichnung*, Fig. 134.
[3] Berlin, 10,389.   [4] Louvre, 2645.
[5] *Olympia*, IV, No. 894, Pl. LIV.   [6] *Ibid.*, No. 646, Pl. XXXV.

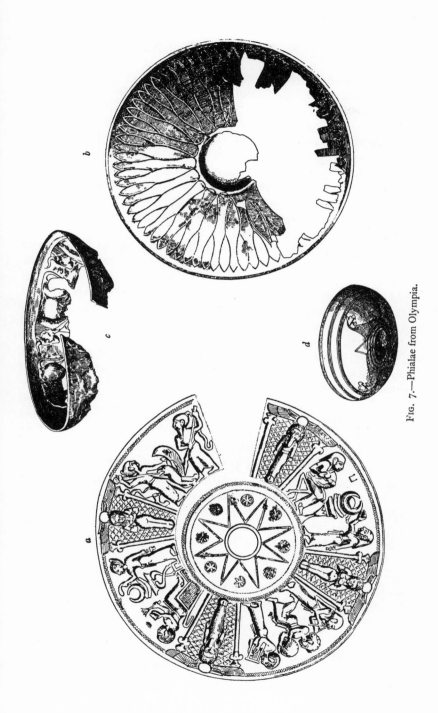

FIG. 7.—Phialae from Olympia.

particularly characteristic of the period. They have also been found in Northern Italy, whither they may have been imported from Corinth.[1]

TRIPODS AND CAULDRONS OF ALLIED TYPE—The tripods which were made after the close of the Geometric Period [2] are derived from the sub-Mycenaean or proto-Geometric type described on p. 33. There is a gap between the two groups : though we have no bronze examples to fill it, we do know of some imitations in pottery, shewing the type was not forgotten during the Geometric Period.

Whereas the Late Minoan and the bronze Geometric tripods had their legs united to the bowl, the sub-Mycenaean and Early Archaic tripods had bowl and legs separate. Above the legs was a ring on which the bowl rested. The seventh century bowls could, in some cases, be hung up, independent of this stand. The same type of bowl was also occasionally associated with a stand that was not a tripod.

These bowls are unmistakable, for round the rim are the heads of animals, usually griffins, on long curving necks.[3] Of these griffins' heads there are two classes. The first class, represented by some of the Olympia finds, and by finds in Italy, consists of heads made of bronze hammered round a core (the material of which has been identified as earth mixed with resin), and then ornamented with engraving. The earth and resin core has sometimes been found with the marks of the engraved details still upon it after the bronze shell has perished. In the earlier examples, the ears and the boss on the head are very short and clumsy in appearance. The base of the neck, where it should join the bronze bowl, is nearly always missing. The bowls with heads of this class are now regarded as imported from the East.[4]

The heads of the second class are cast, and the neck spreads at its base into a wide ring which could easily be nailed on to the vessel. They have been found at Olympia, in Etruria, on the Acropolis at Athens, in Rhodes, at La Garenne in France

---

[1] *Olympia*, IV, p. 94.
[2] *Ibid.*, p. 114 ; *Jahrbuch*, 1921, p. 105.
[3] Calves' or lions' heads also occur ; *Olympia*, IV, p. 121.
[4] Beazley, *C.A.H.*, IV, p. 584.

(Fig. 8),[1] Delphi,[2] and, more recently, at Ephesus,[3] Chios [4] and Pherae.[5] They are mostly of Greek manufacture.

Though some examples of Classes I and II are contemporary, Class I is on the whole the earlier. Class II is important as illustrating early attempts at hollow casting : griffins of this type have been found which are certainly seventh century, though many belong to the sixth.

The most interesting features of the griffins are the long spirals at either side of the neck : their likeness to the spirals on the neck of the fresco in the Throne Room at Knossos cannot be accidental, though the griffin itself is an Oriental motive, found in both Mesopotamian and Egyptian art.

Besides the griffins, winged figures often decorate the edge of the bowl. These winged figures are characteristic of the Olympia finds and have also been discovered at Delphi,[6] at the Ptoön in Boeotia, on the Athenian Acropolis, in Etruria and near Lake Van.[7]

The Oriental origin of these figures is self-evident. Sometimes their place on the rim of the bowl was taken by other creatures, such as birds or oxen. It is not certain whether, in Greece, these figures were associated with griffins of Class II as well as those of Class I.

The griffins' heads from the Greek sites have not been found attached to the bowl ; but a complete tripod from a tumulus near La Garenne [8] shews how they were used (Fig. 7). The heads are cast. A bowl from Vetulonia [9] is not unlike the last, but had originally griffins' heads of the hammered class and two small winged figures in addition.

The typical stand for such bowls is, as has been said, a ring mounted on three slender legs, with extra supports as illustrated on Fig. 8. The legs, which are often of iron, terminate in the feet or claws of animals. The La Garenne tripod is an excellent example. The ring and legs are of iron, but the lion's claws, in

[1] *Olympia*, IV, pp. 123, 115. [2] *Fouilles de Delphes*, V, Pls. X, XI.
[3] B.M., *Ephesus*, Pl. XVI, 4. [4] Δελτίον, 1915, p. 77, Fig. 13.
[5] Unpublished ; Athens National Museum.
[6] *Fouilles de Delphes*, V, Pls. XII, XIII.
[7] For all refs. see *Olympia*, IV, p. 117.
[8] *Ibid.*, p. 115 ; *Jahrbuch*, 1921, p. 105.
[9] *Notizie degli Scavi*, 1913, p. 431 ; and see p. 79, n. 1 below.

which the legs end, are of bronze, so too are the bands which
bind the ring to the legs.

Another kind of stand, has, however, been found in Etruria,
consisting of a solid core, at the summit of which is a capital
to support the bowl.   The best of these stands comes from

FIG. 8.—The La Garenne tripod.

Praeneste.   A capital of the same type from Olympia [1] proves
the existence of at least one such stand in Greece : probably it
was an offering of some Etruscan.   In Etruria the popularity of
the shape is attested by imitations in pottery, with the bowl
and griffins' heads in the same material to complete it.

[1] *Olympia*, IV, No. 810, Pl. XLVIII.

B. STATUETTES

Life-sized sculpture is, in Greece, one of the younger arts, for it began no earlier than the latter part of the seventh century. The art of making statuettes in bronze or ivory, or, more humbly, in terra-cotta, is senior by some hundred and fifty years. It follows that, of the series of bronzes discussed below, some are earlier than, some contemporary with, such statues as the Eleutherna figure, the metopes of Mycenae, or the pediment of Corfu. The earliest sculptors owed a considerable debt to the makers of the statuettes, who, for years, had been experimenting in the modelling of limbs and features. The debt was, however, quickly repaid, for a remarkable development can be observed in these bronzes, which, like Nos. 5-7, have felt the influence of sculpture. Without this influence, they might have delayed long before they passed beyond the stage represented by Nos. 1-3, descendants of the Geometric figures described in the last chapter.

(1) Near the beginning of the seventh century, and very close to the Geometric Period, comes *a* on Pl. 20, from the Athenian Acropolis.[1] It might be conceivably classed as Geometric, but it stands, not at the end, but at the beginning of a series, of which another bronze from the Acropolis and one from Delphi [2] are more advanced examples. Moreover, it presents not the indefinite features of the Geometric figures, but the heavy, rather bulbous features associated with the earliest phase of Athenian art. The man is a warrior: his right arm, now somewhat bent, once held a spear, his left a shield. His helmet is of an eastern type and occurs on other bronzes of this class.[3]

(2) The same features, and the same straight, stiff body, appear on other early bronzes from the Acropolis, of which one has been chosen for illustration [4] (Pl. 20 *b*). It represents, presumably, a warrior, but a warrior without a helmet and with some resemblance to the kouroi who were soon to become so

[1] Athens, 6612 ; ht., ·212 ; Staïs, p. 263 ; de Ridder, No. 701, p. 247.
[2] Athens, 6613 ; Staïs, p. 263 ; de Ridder, No. 702, p. 247 ; *Fouilles de Delphes*, V, Pls. 1, 4.
[3] Poulsen, *Der Orient*, p. 112.
[4] Athens, 6617 ; ht., ·215 ; Staïs, pp. 264, 265 ; de Ridder, No. 698, p. 245. I do not agree that this and similar figures represent " combatants."

important a type.   No muscles are marked on the body, but the collar-bone is in such high relief that it might almost be taken for a ring.   The left arm has been bent out of its original position.   Like No. 1, this figure is one of a series.[1]

(3) A second type of Geometric figure is recalled by the bronze in Pl. 20 c from the Tyszkiewicz Collection.   It is said to have been found in Boeotia, which is not improbable.   The most striking feature is the long neck ; this occurs, as we have seen, on Geometric warriors from Aetolia, and reappears, slightly modified, on the warrior from Delphi (Pl. 15 d).   Evidently, it is characteristic of Northern Greek art in the eighth and seventh centuries, and the Tyszkiewicz bronze belongs to this northern group.   He is nearly related to the Delphic warrior, but is a little more uncouth : this is surprising, since he is a generation younger.   The hair is arranged in strands, but smooth on the top.   A fillet confines it, and some object must have at one time capped it, nailed into holes on the forehead and the crown.   The eyes were formerly filled with another material. Notice the straight line down the front of the neck and body, the necklace and the belt : this last is a legacy from Geometric ancestors.   On the legs is an inscription, which reads :

" Mantiklos dedicated me to the far shooting (god) of the silver bow, out of the tithe.
Do thou Phoebus, give something nice in exchange,"[2]

a delightfully frank and engaging form of piety.   The bronze may be attributed to the first half of the century.

(4) A different tradition manifests itself in Pl. 23 a, from the Acropolis.[3]   It is a *protome*, a head with the upper part of the body conventionally indicated, and the arms replaced by mere projections.   Care has been expended on the head with its horizontal bands of hair : this style of hair-dressing became common in seventh century works of art, though we cannot be sure what actual arrangement is represented.   On the body is engraved the upper hem of the tunic and two rosettes, meant for embroidery.

[1] Cf. de Ridder, No. 699, p. 246, and probably No. 700.
[2] At Boston ; *Monuments Piot*, II, p. 137, Pl. XV ; ht., ·20 m.
[3] Athens, 6627 ; ht., ·093 m. ; de Ridder, No. 697, p. 244 ; Poulsen, *Der Orient*, pp. 146, 147.

(5) The bronze from Crete at Berlin (Pl. 21 *a*),[1] for all his awkward attitude and lifeless face, is a very distinct advance on the figures previously described. He is one of the first of the kouroi, the naked youths which are so characteristic of Greek art in the following century. Therefore this appearance marks a fresh stage, a stage where the conventional types of Greek art were being established, and the connections with life-sized sculpture created.

It is not surprising that the statuette should come from Crete. Crete was, at this time, an important centre of Greek art. Its other contributions to early bronze relief work have been discussed on pp. 59 ff. Life-sized sculpture was already being made in the island towards the close of the century, reminding us that here was the traditional home of the earliest sculptors. The influence of Cretan art on the early art of the Peloponnese is indicated by literary evidence and proved by the close bond between Cretan and Peloponnesian figures.

Our bronze must be dated near the end of the seventh century. With regard to detail, it should be noticed that the hands, as so often in early bronzes, are bored through, in order to hold some attribute. The muscles of the breast and the nipples are engraved.

(6) The Peloponnesian style is well illustrated by the kouros from Delphi [2] (Plate 21 *b*), a figure which has the additional merit of shewing more clearly than the kouros from Crete how much progress had been achieved during the century.

Though the legs are still too long, the arms are not glued to the sides, as they were in the Cretan figure. The modelling of the face is comparatively advanced, the hair neater. The belt recalls that worn by some of the Geometric warriors. The statuette may be dated in the last years of the seventh century, or early in the sixth century : it was possibly made at Corinth, but it is closely connected with the sculpture of the Cretan school.

(7) The youth at Stockholm (Pl. 21 *c*) [3] affords a remarkable contrast with the Cretan and Peloponnesian bronzes just described. It belongs to the Ionic group and the Samo-Milesian

[1] Berlin, 10,556 ; ht., ·173 m. ; *Anz.*, 1922, p. 63.
[2] *Fouilles de Delphes*, V, Pl. 3 ; Beazley, *C.A.H.*, IV, p. 593 ; ht., ·197 m.
[3] *C.A.H.*, Pl. I, p. 353 ; IV, p. 584 ; *Anz.*, 1921, pp. 231 ff.

school. In many ways it recalls the well-known Ephesian ivories, but these are better work, and, being fully draped, do not reveal the artist's weakness in rendering the human body. Like them, the bronze youth has a fat, good-natured face, a thick neck, and thin arms which cling to his sides. The legs, unfortunately, have got bent and broken. Date : end of seventh or early sixth century.

Female figures are, on the whole, less numerous.

(8) During the excavations of the Menelaion at Sparta, a bronze figure (Pl. 22 a)[1] was found in a stratum containing Geometric, Proto-Corinthian and Lakonian I pottery : the figure may, therefore, belong to the late eighth or to the first half of the seventh century : the square shape of the skirt and the strongly marked waist foreshadow a group of Spartan bronzes which belong to the next century. Evidently, our lady from the Menelaion was made at Sparta.

(9) The female figure on Pl. 22 b, formerly in the Tyszkie-wicz Collection, is said to have been found at Thebes together with the male figure described above [2] (No. 3). She must be a goddess, for her right hand is extended palm upwards to hold a phiale. Her hair is arranged in the same manner as No. 4 : here, also, the artist has expended all his energy on the head and features, particularly on the eyes and eyebrows, and neglected the body. Probable date, the first half of the seventh century.

(10) Female figure from Ephesus (Pl. 22 c).[3] Though some-what earlier than the Stockholm youth, she is in many ways his counterpart, and embodies the same traditions. The bronze was originally gilt. On the head was a veil held in place by a fillet : the ears appear to have been bored for ear-rings. It is remarkable how much more the artist knows about the drapery than about modelling the human form : he was unable to detach the arms from the body, though he made a success of the folds of the dress. Contrast the lady from the Menelaion, where the reverse is the case. It is, however, characteristic of the figures made in this part of the world that little or no space should be

[1] At Sparta ; ht., ·13 m. ; B.S.A., XV, Pl. X, p. 146.
[2] Ht., ·18 m. ; Poulsen, op. cit., pp. 147, 148, Fig. 171.
[3] B.M., Ephesus, Pl. XIV, p. 145. The original is at Constantinople. A cast is in the British Museum ; ht., ·243 m.

shewn between the arms and body : the ivories from Ephesus illustrate this clearly,[1] as well as our No. 7.

A few bronze statuettes of men and animals, which were not free figures but part of the decoration of some object, will conclude our account of seventh century Greece.

One of the most important is a kneeling Gorgon in the Louvre,[2] found in the sea off Rhodes. Above her head is a lion's paw ; the eyes were inlaid. She was originally one of the supports of a bowl, such a bowl, perhaps, as the bowl resting on " kneeling colossi " which the Samians dedicated to Hera on their return from Tartessos.[3] The motive is known to us from a couple of stone bowls supported by female figures, which have been associated with Naxian art. The date of the Louvre bronze must be in the last quarter of the seventh century.

From Sparta comes a pair of little men who may have decorated the handles of a bowl [4] or skyphos (Pl. 23). They were found with the Lakonian II pottery and should, therefore, belong to the very end of the seventh century ; their heavily cut features recall the Cretan style as represented by the sixth century warriors on Pl. 25, but they have more points in common with the woman from the Menelaion than appears in the photograph.

The bull's head pendants, and the lion with the serpent for its tail, on Pl. 23, come from the same deposit.[5] The lion was part of a brooch or fibula, the hinge of the pin being under his forepaws : the snake had, probably, a magic significance. Similar fibulae have been found at other Peloponnesian shrines, e.g. at Olympia,[6] the Argive Heraeum,[7] and the sanctuary of Apollo Tyritos in Kynouria.[8] One of the examples from Kynouria is inscribed Ἀπολονος ἐμ, " I belong to Apollo." Such brooches, too heavy for mortal use, were favourite offerings to god or goddess : they may have been made at Corinth.

That so many objects should come from Sparta is not mere

[1] B.M., *Ephesus*, Pls. XXI, 6 ; XXII, XXIV.
[2] Louvre, 2570 ; ht., ·55 m. ; *Catalogue*, Pl. 92.
[3] Herodotus, IV, 152 ; C.A.H., IV, 584 ; Pl. I, p. 352, 3.
[4] At Sparta ; B.S.A., XV, p. 147, Pl. IX, 1, 5 ; ht. of figures, ·053 m.
[5] At Sparta ; *op. cit.*, p. 147. There are other examples in the Sparta Museum. The illustrations on Pl. 23 are four-fifths natural size.
[6] *Olympia*, IV, p. 152, No. 966 ; and Neugebauer, *op. cit.*, Pl. 20.
[7] Athens, 14,034 ; Waldstein, *op. cit.*, Pl. 88, No. 946.
[8] Πρακτικά, 1911, pp. 264 ff.

coincidence.   Sparta is a site not only rich in seventh century products, but also well stratified and carefully excavated. Therefore, whatever was found there during the excavations can be now dated with unusual accuracy, and throws valuable light on a period when all arts save pottery are comparatively obscure.

ETRURIA IN THE SEVENTH CENTURY—The bronze-work of Italy does not come within the scope of this book till after it has felt the influence of Greek art, in the seventh century B.C.

This excludes the bronzes of the Villanova Period, and absolves us from discussing the relation of Villanovans and Etruscans.

It also excludes the earliest phase of Etruscan art, that phase which corresponds to the Geometric style of Greece.[1]

We miss thereby certain bronzes which it might have been pleasant to compare with the Greek Geometric bronzes, for instance, the procession of birds of the typical Geometric shape from the " food table " found in the " Circle of the Cauldrons " at Vetulonia.[2]   Another aspect of this early style is shewn by the bronze chair from the Barberini tomb [3] with its zones of ornament : this, too, must be passed over.   One bronze, however, belonging to the period is illustrated on Pl. 24 c, d, in order to give an idea of what Italy produced before it was affected by the art of the Orient and the art of Greece.   It comes from Vetulonia [4] and is a candelabrum ; the spikes which branch from the central stem would carry the lights : it should be contrasted with some of the later candelabra from the same part of the world.   On the top of the shaft is a sturdy little girl with a pig-tail, who has remarkably little in common with bronzes of the early iron age of Greece.

Finally, our limits exclude many of the bronzes made in Etruscan districts during the Orientalising Period, which, in Italy, as in Greece, corresponds roughly to the seventh and early sixth centuries.   The Etruscans were now going through

[1] Ducati, *Etruria Antica*, II, p. 57.
[2] Randall-MacIver, *Villanovans and Etruscans*, p. 133, Fig. 46.
[3] *Ibid.*, Pl. 42, No. 5, and p. 268.
[4] At Florence.   An example with male figures is published in *Notizie degli Scavi*, 1913, pp. 434, 435, Figs. 17 and 18, our female figure in Ducati, *Storia*, Pls. 35, 36, Figs. 120, 121.

the same experience as the Greeks : they were being introduced to the art of Mesopotamia, Egypt and Phoenicia, imported first by Phoenician traders. Therefore, we find, in Etruscan tombs, large cauldrons with animals' heads fastened round the rim (see above, p. 71), and sometimes, too, with Oriental winged semi-human figures, very similar to those described on p. 71.[1] Some were imported, some made locally. We also find details, such as the hair-dressing of the figures on a bronze bowl from Praeneste,[2] which remind us of Greek bronzes. This is, however, due not to contact between Greece and Etruria, but to the influence of the same foreign models on both.

To this stage in Etruscan art belong many of the objects from the Regolini-Galassi tomb at Caere, and from the Bernardini and Barberini tombs at Praeneste,[3] which can be dated round about 670 B.C.[4]

Gradually, however, Greek influence makes itself felt. It had been heralded by the importation of Proto-Corinthian pottery, and is characterised by the copying of this and other Greek wares. It must have been already perceptible when the Regolini-Galassi tomb was made, for it seems to have affected the palmettes which finish the handles of two jugs.[5] It is still more apparent in some of the fragments from the decoration of a chariot from Castellina di Chianti.[6] The warrior, cut out of a sheet of bronze with incised details, is quite Greek : the strip with scenes from the myth of Amphiaraos between double plaits must have been made by some one acquainted with the way in which a Greek would draw a soldier and a woman spectator.

The so-called Tomb of Isis or Polledrara Tomb at Vulci is shewn, by the pottery it contained, to be the product of an age quite familiar with Greek art. The pottery is imitated from Greek models, and can be dated about 600 B.C.[7]

---

[1] E.g. at Vetulonia (McIver, *op. cit.*, pp. 132, 133) from the Circolo dei Lebeti ; at Caere, in the Regolini-Galassi tomb (*op. cit.*, p. 202, Pl. 37, No. 87, and Bernardini and Barberini tombs at Praeneste, *op. cit.*, pp. 264, 268).

[2] Poulsen, *Der Orient und die Frühgriechische Kunst*, p. 127, Fig. 140.

[3] For general discussion see Poulsen, *op. cit.*, p. 116 ff.

[4] McIver, *op. cit.*, p. 230.

[5] Montelius, *Civilisation Primitive*, Série B, Pl. 336, 12 b and 8 b.

[6] Randall-McIver, *op. cit.*, Pl. 46, Nos. 5, 6 ; Ducati, *Storia*, Pl. 68, Fig. 207, p. 192.　　　　　　　　　[7] *Op. cit.*, p. 229.

The most remarkable of its bronzes [1] is the upper part of a female figure. She wears a necklace ; her hair falls in long ringlets : her right hand is pierced and once held some object. At the base of the figure, below a belt of meander, is a stand with two friezes. The lower, with its procession of sphinxes and chariots, must have been inspired by Greek models.

The two little bronze carts on wheels which were also among the objects found in the tomb, are decorated at the corners with protomae of horses, not unlike those on the plate on Pl. 47.

One other object deserves mention : a small tripod with side supports which cross each other and foreshadow the type which came into use in the Roman Period (p. 237).

An important group of figures, from Brolio [2] (Pl. 24 *a*, *b*), may serve to introduce Etruscan figures in the round. They belong to the very early sixth century, and must originally have supported some object : hence their symmetry and the attachments at the top of the heads.

Three represent warriors. They have a certain affinity with the Greek warrior and the Greek kouros, though they are essentially Italian. All three held spears in their right hands, javelins (apparently) in their left hands, and carried shields on the left arm.

The fourth is a woman. She is the counterpart of the Greek kore, but she also stands very close to other antiquities of Etruscan manufacture, to the stone women from the Polledrara tomb,[3] for instance, and another woman in stone from Chiusi.[4] She wears a long dress ornamented at waist, sides and hem, also a necklace. Her hair is done in the prevailing fashion. What she held in her hand is uncertain.

With these four bronzes we pass beyond the bounds of the seventh century and the Orientalising Period : Etruscan art is about to enter on yet another phase.

[1] British Museum, 434 ; Ducati, *Storia*, Pl. 65. For the other contents of the tomb, see Montelius, *op. cit.*, Pls. 265-268.

[2] At Florence ; Ducati, *Storia*, Pl. 64, Fig. 198, pp. 185-186 ; Milani, *Monumenti Scelti*, XII.

[3] Montelius, *op. cit.*, Pl. 266, No. 2.

[4] Randall-McIver, *op. cit.*, Pl. 44, No. 4.

CHAPTER IV

THE SIXTH CENTURY STATUETTES

THE great period for bronze statuettes lasts from about 575 to 450 B.C. During the sixth century they rapidly improved in quality and increased in quantity : some time before 500 they attained their high-water mark : their development during the first half of the fifth century made them less archaic but no more beautiful.

Such praise of sixth century work may be mistrusted as the mere outcome of a not uncommon preference for the primitive. Closer consideration will, however, shew that a different stage of maturity is appropriate to each material and to each branch of art : to life-sized sculpture, the perfect development of the middle years of the fifth century ; to terra-cottas, the sophistication of the fourth ; to ivories, the childish awkwardness of the seventh. To bronze statuettes certain qualities of the sixth century were especially becoming ; chief of those are an archaic severity of form, and a remarkable love of detail. The artist was still obedient to tradition, but rapidly learning to master the difficulties of his material : what he produced has the vitality and charm of adolescence.

His success, then, was assured because his medium suited his period. It was also facilitated by the independent relation in which his work stood to life-sized sculpture, an art that was now making very rapid progress. With sculpture in this, the narrow sense of the word, he was sufficiently in touch to profit by what was useful to him, and sufficiently detached to keep his individuality unspoiled.

There exist, indeed, some small bronzes which are certainly derived from famous statues, but the majority follow their own lines. Similarly, there are certain subjects, such as the nude youths or Kouroi, and the draped women or Korai, which are

6   81

common to both branches of art, but the statuettes have a much wider range. Nor is this surprising, for they have a longer tradition behind them, and an easier formula in which to express themselves. On the whole, the relationship of statues and statuettes during the sixth century was an ideal one, contrasting at once with that of the seventh century, when sculpture was disproportionately backward, and with the later fifth, in which it was unduly prominent.

A third reason for the excellence of the statuettes made in this period was the growing prosperity of Greece and the emulous patriotism of the separate states. In consequence, many shrines were rebuilt or repaired, and constantly furnished with gifts. The most suitable form of gift was a small figure of god or worshipper, preferably in bronze. These figures had, as we have seen, long been a feature of well-frequented sanctuaries such as Olympia, Delphi and the Acropolis. Now, however, they appear at shrines, which, through remoteness or poverty, had hitherto been content with humbler offerings.

The case of Arcadia is significant. Some of the most interesting bronzes we possess come from Arcadian sites : Mt. Lykaion, Tegea, Lousoi and Lykosoura, and belong to this period. There had, indeed, been dedications at all these places in earlier days, but nothing noticeable. Now, the fashion of dedicating bronzes was so strong that even the shepherds managed to contribute small figures, sometimes in their own likeness, and dressed in the same cloak with which they themselves kept off rain and snow, sometimes in the image of the god who watched over their flocks.

Given these circumstances, it is not surprising that the bronze industries, both large and small, flourished throughout Greece. Some of these, such as the Spartan and Athenian, are descended from an earlier industry, dating back to the Geometric Period, while others appear to be new. Many have left more or less distinct traces, enabling us to recognise their existence and even to reconstruct their history.

This reconstruction is only gradually becoming possible, and, save for a few isolated cases, has only lately been attempted. It depends, in the first place, on the possibility of grouping together works of art in the same style. What constitutes the " same style " will, unfortunately, always remain controversial.

The next stage is to find in what district the group was made. If a sufficient number of bronzes in the same style come from the same site, there is a strong presumption that they were made in the locality.   Again, if the group includes objects in other materials, such as terra-cotta or stone, which come from a reliable excavation, or were all found in one area, we may use these as a guide.   Thus, the terra-cottas from the Argive Heraeum and Tiryns, and the limestone reliefs from Laconia, were used in a recent reconstruction of the bronze industries of Argos and Sparta.[1]

The situation, obviously, would be simpler if we could assume a bronze to have been made where it was found, but offerings so small, solid and portable would naturally travel far.   Certain important sites, such as Olympia and Delphi, seem to have been completely stocked with bronzes from other parts of Greece.   To complicate the question yet further, there are hundreds of bronzes on the shelves of museums of which the provenance is not recorded.   It is obvious that our knowledge of the centres of bronze-working in ancient Greece will never be as accurate as our knowledge of the centres which made pottery.

CRETE—Cretan art, which had played so important a part in the seventh century, declined during the sixth ; just so a plant weakens when it has done flowering and scatters its seed on fresh soil.   Between the Cretan Kouros at Berlin, which we have assigned to the seventh century (p. 75), and early Peloponnesian Kouroi there is a close bond.   Among the sixth century Cretan bronzes there are three well-known figures : all three have an unmistakable kinship with Peloponnesian art, but display certain characteristics which are peculiar.   Two of the figures are warriors in the Louvre, heavy-featured men, one in a breastplate (Pl. 25 a),[2] one in a loin-cloth or, possibly, a *mitra* (Pl. 25 c).[3]   The former should be compared and contrasted with the warrior on Pl. 28 : the latter is interesting, because he may have been holding a pair of cymbals (see p. 56) attached to his hands by the nails which still survive.

[1] Langlotz, pp. 57, 90.
[2] Louvre, 106 ; ht., ·11 m., from Knossos, *Catalogue*, Pl. 12.
[3] Louvre, Nos. 105 ; ht., ·093 m., *Catalogue*, Pl. 12.

The third figure is the well-known Kriophoros [1] at Berlin (Pl. 25 b).

To have room for the ram, which is held stiffly above the shoulders, the boy's head droops forward. The face is distinctive, with the large eyes set somewhat aslant, the angular chin, the thick nose and smiling lips. The clothes consist of a belt and loin-cloth, and the wrapping of the loin-cloth recalls the Minoan statuettes, though its folds are less clearly understood. It should be regarded less as a survival of Minoan art than as the survival of a typically Cretan fashion. The unusual type of stand needs explanation. Just below the feet is the stand proper : it is joined by a narrow stem to a rounded mass below, the stem representing the channel through which the bronze was poured into the mould, which, with the accretion below, should have been cut off after casting. We are reminded of the prehistoric figure on Pl. 8 from Candia, and wonder if the lack of finish is a relic of Minoan technique. A glance at the Arcadian bronze on Pl. 31 will, however, prove that the phenomenon is not confined to Crete. There is, of course, a temptation to look for traces of Minoan influence in all Cretan antiquities of later date : the Rethymno *mitra* (p. 61) shews that this temptation is sometimes justified.

It is interesting to compare our boy and his ram with other representations of similar subjects : the Arcadian shepherd on Pl. 31 and the Athenian Moschophoros.[2] All these are perfectly independent, which would not have been the case a century later.

Between the three Cretan bronzes there is a common measure, amounting to style, that can be more easily detected than analysed. They are, therefore, illustrated together on Pl. 25.

THE PELOPONNESE—Passing from Crete to the Peloponnese, on the track of certain semi-legendary sculptors of ancient times, we come to what is the real home of the bronze statuette. With the Peloponnese is associated a particular style, " Peloponnesian " as distinct from Ionic, but it manifests itself in

[1] Berlin, 7477 ; ht., ·185 m. ; Neugebauer, Pl. 17, p. 35. Neugebauer considers the bronze to be seventh century, but see Beazley, *Cambridge Ancient History*, IV, p. 592 : it probably belongs to the first half of the sixth.
[2] Dickins, *Catalogue of the Acropolis Museum*, No. 624, p. 156.

several different forms, some of which can be labelled as Spartan or Arcadian, while others can, more hypothetically, be attributed to Corinth, Sikyon and elsewhere.

Of all the Peloponnesian sites, the one which produced most bronzes was *Olympia*, but, as has already been pointed out, the Olympian bronzes are a heterogeneous collection from all parts of the ancient world. Many would be the gifts of travellers and athletes who had journeyed for days to take part in the festival. It is possible that, while some people brought their gifts with them, others, less provident, bought what they wanted on the spot. The latter class would encourage bronze-vendors to attend the games in the hopes of disposing of some of their stock. Of a local Elean school there is no trace. Nor is this surprising : the demand would be too irregular.

Before describing the work of the various schools, I will give a short account of some important bronzes which are typically Peloponnesian, but which cannot safely be assigned to any school.

Two of these come from the *Sanctuary of Apollo Korynthos*, now Longa, in Messenia. One is the Kouros on Pl. 34 *a*, the other, the armed warrior on Pl. 28 *b*. The former [1] belongs to the second quarter of the sixth century and recalls, on the one hand, the somewhat earlier statue bearing the signature of the Argive [Poly]medes,[2] on the other, figures from Lakonian cups.[3]

The warrior must have been made some time between 540 and 520 B.C.[4] He is a magnificent figure, remarkable for the delicate work on moustache and beard, tunic and breastplate. The breastplate shews not only a conventional rendering of the muscles, but also a semi-floral design. The chiton is adorned with an embroidered key-pattern and a fringe. Thigh armour is worn as well as greaves. The pupils are marked by incised circles : the eyes, peering through the eye-sockets of the helmet, have a remarkably mild expression. The right hand probably held a spear, the left a shield.

It is a question whether these bronzes could have been made

[1] Athens, 14,808 ; ht., ·125 m. ; Δελτίον, 1916, p. 103, Fig. 52.
[2] *Fouilles de Delphes*, IV, Pl. 1.
[3] E.g. Pfuhl, *Malerei und Zeichnung*, Fig. 199.
[4] Athens, 14,789 ; ht., *c.* ·15 m. ; Δελτίον, 1916, pp. 106 ff. and Pl. A.

locally or not.   We should naturally expect them to have been imported from some more prosperous and productive district.[1] Nevertheless, the rather second-rate fifth century figures from the same site [2] look so provincial that they may well have been manufactured on the spot, while our two sixth century bronzes have just that misleading likeness to Spartan art which would be natural if they had been made in Messenia at this time.

The bronzes from Longa illustrate two of the favourite subjects of the period.   Other examples of the Kouros will appear among the bronzes found at Dodona, Naxos, Athens and elsewhere.   Figures of soldiers are an essentially Peloponnesian form of dedication.   The Messenian has a rival in the Spartan Karmos (p. 91 (Pl. 28 a) : attributed to Lakonia) who makes up for his small size by the truculence of his appearance. Two other warriors, from Olympia [3] and Lykosoura [4] respectively, are distinguished by the comparative plainness of their breastplates.   We can surmise that on some cold morning before the battle a Spartan, Messenian or Arcadian soldier vowed that he would dedicate a bronze in the shrine at home, if he should ever get back.   This being so, it is pleasant to think that each of our statuettes is the record of a safe return.

From these fully armed figures, it is a short step to figures of men armed with breastplate and greaves, but wearing no he'met.   Two such were found at Olympia,[5] belonging, like the helmeted warrior from Olympia mentioned above, to about the third quarter of the century.   Both, probably, come from the same workshop : this workshop may have also produced the interesting Herakles at Cassel (Pl. 26 a, b).[6]   Here is a small group of which the home is yet to be found.[7]

One of the finest early female figures is illustrated on Pl

[1] Langlotz, pp. 89, 96, attributes the warrior to Sparta.

[2] Δελτίον, 1916, p. 109, Figs. 53-57.

[3] Athens, 6233 ; Olympia, IV, Pl. VII, 41.

[4] Athens, 7644 ; de Ridder, 858.   There is also an unpublished example from Pherae at Athens.

[5] Olympia (?) ; Olympia, IV, Pl. VIII, 42, and Berlin, 4076 ; Olympia, IV, 42 b on p. 18.

[6] Bieber, Antiken Sculpturen . . . in Cassel, No. 114, p. 51, Pl. XXXVIII ; ht., ·097 m.   See also Roscher, Lexicon, s.v. Herakles, p. 2149, and Langlotz, p. 88.

[7] Langlotz, p. 88, attributes the Cassel bronze to Sparta.

35 *a* and *b*.[1]   It represents a goddess, either Hera or Aphrodite, wearing on her head a *polos* [2] ornamented with palmettes, and carrying in one hand a flower, while the other, slightly lowered, must have held a phiale for libations.   The top of the polos has been trimmed with some sharp tool in modern times : it must originally have been higher and we cannot tell exactly how it was finished at the upper edge.   The over-fold of the dress wraps the shoulders like a cape : the artist has forgotten to shew us how it is fastened, and we look in vain for any trace of a seam on the sleeves.[3]   The arrangement of the folds of the chiton recalls, among other works, the woman from the Ptoön in the Louvre,[4] and a marble fragment at Athens.[5]

It is the beauty of head and face that brings this goddess into the first rank of early bronzes.   The wide eyes with the straight lower lids, the large, smiling mouth, the hair with its carefully arranged horizontal bands, have all the charm of archaic art and little of its crudeness.   There is a definite affinity to the new standing goddess at Berlin,[6] also to the goddess at Athens from the Ptoön (Pl. 35 *c*), which is, however, a distinctly less fine piece of work.   The date must be between 550 and 530 B.C.   The figure appears to be, not a support, but votive.

CORINTH, ARGOS AND SIKYON are far the most important towns from the artistic point of view.   All three are associated with famous names : all three played a leading part in the development of sculpture.   Moreover, they formed the heart of the metal-working district of the Peloponnese, a district which produced decorative reliefs and utensils of all kinds which will be described in the next chapter.   It seems, therefore, a natural

---

[1] At the Fitzwilliam Museum, Cambridge ; ht., ·136 m.   Said to come from Athens, which need not mean that it was originally found there.

[2] The *polos* ornamented with palmettes recalls that worn by Hera on the later coins of Elis and Argos, and suggests that our bronze, too, may be Hera. I am indebted to Mr. Forsdyke for the comparison.

[3] If the artist thought about the question at all, which is improbable, he would have meant to copy an apoptugma sewn up at the sides. See Dickins, *Acropolis Cat.*, p. 224.

[4] P. 104, n. 4.

[5] *Ath. Mit.*, 1921, Pl. III, 1.   There is also a resemblance between our bronze and certain members of Langlotz' Spartan group, e.g. his Pl. 47, *a* and *b*.

[6] Rodenwaldt, *Die Kunst der Antike*, Pls. 200, 201.

inference that they were centres for the production of bronze statuettes, and that in one or another of them were made some of the finer bronzes of which the origin is unknown, but which are Peloponnesian in style. One disconcerting fact must, however, be mentioned. The Argive shrines, though they are full of objects in bronze and figures in terra-cotta, are curiously lacking in sixth century bronze statuettes. Does this mean that the statuettes were not made in any quantity at Argos till the end of the century ? [1]

Corinth is represented by a number of bronzes. One, from Dodona (Pl. 34 d),[2] bears an inscription in Corinthian characters on the base, TOIΔIBTVMΟ | ΚΝΕΔΑΜ | ΑΝΕΟΕΚΕ (Etymokledas dedicated [this] to Zeus). It is a rough little figure representing a youth, possibly Apollo, with a bow,[3] and, in view of its likeness, perhaps superficial, with the group pictured on Pl. 34 b, c, the possibility of the inscription having been added by alien hands after the bronze was finished should be taken into account. The evidence is, however, on the whole in favour of a Corinthian origin.

There is every reason to accept the attribution to Corinth of certain bronzes which have in common a peculiar type of face with compact, well-marked features.[4] These include the Zeus Lykaios from Arcadia described below, the well-known bronze rider found between Sparta and Megalopolis,[5] and a Zeus and Artemis from Olympia.

The Zeus (Pl. 28 c), standing draped in his himation, affords an excellent contrast with the naked youths and armed warriors hitherto discussed.[6] Though the pose is simple, being practically the same as that used for the Kouroi, the general character of the figure is very advanced. This is shewn by the features, the careful finish of hair and beard, and the way the form shews through the drapery. The proportions are fairly

---

[1] A large proportion of the sixth century bronzes which Langlotz (pp. 54 ff.) attributes to Argos, are assigned by me to Arcadia on account of their provincial character.

[2] Louvre, 108, Pl. 12 ; ht., ·106 m. ; Langlotz, p. 82, Pl. 42 a. Exact date uncertain.

[3] For the dedication of one deity to another, see Rouse, *Greek Votive Offerings*, pp. 129, 391.

[4] Langlotz, p. 80 ff.   [5] Athens, 7549 ; de Ridder, Pl. 2.

[6] Athens, 6163 ; ht., 0·29 m. ; *Olympia*, IV, Pl. VII, No. 40 ; Langlotz, p. 83, Pl. 40 a.

correct. These points suggest a date towards the close of the sixth century. The hair was bound by a fillet. The attribute from the right hand is missing : that from the left is broken but is usually identified as the twisted staff carried by the Zeus Lykaios on Pl. 26 c. That the Olympian bronze also represents Zeus seems highly probable. In spite of its size, it was cast solid, and fastened by a tang, which still exists, to its base.

Very close to the Zeus is the Artemis (Pl. 28 d),[1] one of the most pleasing of all archaic bronzes, which may have belonged to one of the two Artemis altars mentioned by Pausanias (Book V, Chap. XIV). The goddess probably held a bow in her right hand. She is clothed in a curious unyielding garment, embroidered but with no folds, unless the angular markings on the hanging flaps be meant for folds. What cut of garment the artist had in mind is uncertain : perhaps he misunderstood his model. By contrast, the head is remarkably delicate. The tendons of the neck are rendered with particular care, the eyebrows are very high, and there are two dainty curls upon the forehead which do not shew in the photo. One critic [2] calls attention to the likeness between our Artemis and the head of the same goddess on certain Arcadian coins.[3]

The school of Sikyon has been recognised [4] in certain bronzes whose features, like those of the group just described, are strongly marked though less compact. Bony cheeks, arched eyebrows often in relief, a love of drapery that reveals the construction of the body, a predilection on the part of the ladies for round shoulder brooches and shoes, are among its distinguishing marks.

Naturally, they are not all present in its most important representative, the Apollo Piombino, whose proportions set it beyond the scope of this book.[5]

SPARTA had a flourishing bronze industry, which can be traced back through the seventh century to the Geometric

[1] Athens, 6086 ; ht., ·188 ; *Olympia*, IV, Pl. VII, No. 55 ; Langlotz, p. 83, Pl. 40 c. Furtwängler suggests that the garment is of leather, but this is too fanciful.

[2] Furtwängler, *op. cit.*, p. 20.

[3] B.M., *Cat. Peloponnese*, Pl. 31, 13.   [4] Langlotz, pp. 30 ff.

[5] Louvre, *Catalogue*, Pl. 2, 2 ; Langlotz, p. 32, Pl. 1.

Period. Most of the bronzes found in the excavations of the various Spartan sanctuaries and many of the bronzes casually acquired in the neighbourhood are sufficiently like each other in style to be considered local work. They also resemble the local terra-cotta statuettes and votive limestone reliefs. Thus it happens that we have more ample and exact knowledge about archaic Spartan art than about that of any other Greek city save Athens.

The difficulty is to select, among the mass of material, what is most important and characteristic.

In the next chapter a description will be given of certain mirror supports in the form of naked women that are connected with Lakonia. Similar female figures have been found as free votive statuettes.[1]

Allied to these is a draped supporting figure in Berlin,[2] made about the middle of the sixth century. The clinging cloak and chiton, slanting eyes and smiling mouth, suggest certain aspects of Ionic art, as is the case with many Spartan bronzes.

Another group [3] includes women and goddesses dressed in the Doric peplos girt at the waist, usually with a remarkably short over-fold. To this group belongs the votary from the excavations of the Chalkioikos site in 1907 [4] (Pl. 27 c), with her typically Spartan features. She carries in her hand fruits and on her head a curious head-dress. Her peplos has parallel folds behind but is elsewhere plain : the square outlines of the seventh century lady from the Menelaion (Pl. 22 a) are not entirely forgotten.

The other members of the group are also more or less square in the lower half of the body. The best known of these is the Artemis Daidaleia (Pl. 35 d),[5] from the ruins of a temple at Mazi in Elis. She too has stiff folds at the back of the skirt, but the head is in a more advanced, less definitely local style.

A third group [6] comprises male figures, short in stature, reminiscent of the Central Peloponnesian or Arcadian style.

---

[1] E.g. in the Trau Collection ; Langlotz, Pl. 45 b.

[2] Berlin, 7933 ; Langlotz, p. 88, Pl. 45 a.

[3] Ibid., p. 87, Nos. 26-30.

[4] At Sparta ; B.S.A., XIII, p. 149 ; Langlotz, p. 87, No. 26 ; ht., ·135 m. Left hand split.

[5] At Boston ; ht., ·19 m. ; Neugebauer, Pl. 18 ; Langlotz, p. 87, No. 27 ; date, 540-510.   [6] See Langlotz, Pl. 89.

Here belongs the Apollo from Amyklae, who challenges attention by his curiously rayed head-dress and by the fact that he originally carried a lyre in his left hand.[1] Here, too, belongs that aggressive little soldier, Karmos (Pl. 28 a),[2] found at Selinos in eastern Lakonia. An inscription on the base reads : " Karmos (or Karilos) dedicated [this] to [Apollo] Maleatas."

Karmos wears a helmet with a beautiful plume, greaves and breastplate on which is a floral pattern, and a conventional indication of the muscles. The right hand probably held a spear, the left a shield, but, as is so often the case, the shield has left no mark. The square base is a distinctly Peloponnesian feature. A fellow soldier of Karmos has recently been identified at Oxford.[3]

Any account of Spartan bronzes would be incomplete without mention of a male head from Sparta, now at Boston.[4] It is, with the exception of the griffins described in Chapter III, the earliest surviving example of hollow casting from Greece, and must have been produced by the *cire perdue* process over a core. If the whole figure was 52-·55 m. high, as the proportion of the head suggests, this technique would be appropriate : for the ordinary small, votive statuette, however, hollow casting remained the exception, not the rule.

ARCADIA—In spite of its comparative poverty and partial isolation, Arcadia has produced a large number of bronze statuettes which are among the most delightful and distinctive of any found in the Peloponnese. They form a compact group, which begins in the seventh century, flourishes in the sixth, and survives the competition of the big artistic centres in the fifth (p. 151). The group has been recognised by specialists,[5] but

[1] 'Εφ. 'Αρχ., 1892, p. 18 ; Langlotz, Pl. 49 e ; date, 525-500.

[2] Athens, 7598 ; ht., ·084 ; Neugebauer, Pl. 21 ; date, 540-510 ; Langlotz, Pl. 49 d and p. 89.

[3] Ibid., No. 53 ; J.H.S., 1910, Pl. 12, 2 : from Dodona. For an account of the Spartan style, see Langlotz, p. 91. He notes among other points the length of leg, the rather pointed crown of the head, and stresses the way the body is carried with the abdomen drawn back.

[4] Furtwängler, *Kleine Schriften*, II, p. 429, which see for list of other examples of the technique. For the place of the head in Spartan art, see Langlotz, p. 88 and Pl. 53 d.

[5] *Ath. Mit.*, 1905, p. 65 ; B.C.H., 1903 (XXVII), p. 300 ; Neugebauer, p. 40 ; B.S.A., XXVII, pp. 133 ff. ; Furtwängler, *Kleine Schriften*, p. 458 ; *Anz.*, 1922, pp. 65 ff. Langlotz, however, does not accept the Arcadian style, and assigns some of the bronzes in question to Argos and some to Sikyon.

overlooked by most other students of Greek art, perhaps because it had very little influence on the world outside Arcadia.
Conversely, it was influenced less than most places by the move-
ments of contemporary Greek art, though it was in touch with
Argos, Sikyon and Lakonia.   This is what we should expect,
for the high road to Lakonia from Argos has to climb the mountains into south-east Arcadia, and pass through the upland
plain of Tegea, before it descends into the Eurotas valley.

The bronzes are conservative in choice of subject.   The
majority represent peasants dressed, as Arcadian shepherds
were dressed, in a conical leather cap ($\kappa\upsilon\nu\hat{\eta}$) or a felt hat ($\pi\hat{\iota}\lambda o\varsigma$)
to keep off sun and rain ; a chiton, or a short cloak for mild
weather ; a heavy, long cloak for winter ; and a pair of strong
boots for protection against stones and prickles.   Sometimes
all clothes are discarded except the cap : it can be very hot on
the Arcadian hills.   If Hermes takes the place of the shepherd,
as he does in some examples, he is distinguished by having wings
on his boots and perhaps on his cap also, but is in other respects
like his worshippers, for he, too, is a shepherd (Pl. 29 a).[1]   Like
them, he carries his ram tucked under his arm : only one Arcadian bronze (Pl. 31 a from Berekla, by Mt. Lykaion) [2] shews
a shepherd with a young animal, in this case a calf borne on his
shoulders, like our Cretan boy and the Moschophoros.

Very pious are the Arcadian shepherds : they bring the best
of their flock as an offering to the gods of the flocks, Hermes and
Pan Nomios.   Usually it is a ram or a sheep.[3]   One of their
company, small and debonair, holds by the tail a dead fox.[4]
(Pl. 29 c and d).   He is probably not a shepherd but a hunter
or trapper, and makes his livelihood by the sale of skins.   Evidently the foxes were customary gifts, for, besides that carried
by our little friend, we have a bronze representing a dead fox [5]

[1] Athens, 7539 ; ht., ·097 m. ; Hermes from Ithome (in Messenia) ; date,
540-520 B.C. ; de Ridder, 832 : or Athens, 12,347, Hermes from Andritsaena ;
B.C.H., 1903, Pl. VII ; Revue des Études Grecques, XVII, 126.

[2] Athens, 13,053 ; Staïs, pp. 311, 312 ; B.S.A., XXVII, No. 8 ; ht.,
·115 m. ; 540-520 B.C.

[3] Sheep or rams : Athens, 12,347, from Andritsaena ; Berlin, 10,781-10,783,
from Hagios Sostes (nr. Mt. Lykaion) ; 30552, " from Arcadia." Calf ; Athens,
13,053, from Berekla (Mt. Lykaion). See B.S.A., XXVII, pp. 135-137.

[4] Berlin, 10,784, from Hagios Sostes ; ht., ·067 m. ; B.S.A., XXVII,
No. 12 ; date, c. 500.

[5] Athens, 13,054, from Berekla ; ht., ·105 m. May be early fifth century.

from Mt. Lykaion (Pl. 31 *d*). Just as the statuette perpetuates the devotion of the worshipper, so the dead animal immortalises the gift : the gift may be either the flower of the flock or the proceeds of the chase.

Sometimes the man is shewn at prayer, with one hand raised ;[1] sometimes he stands, grave and aloof, with his hands wrapped in his cloak (Pl. 31). These cloaked figures form a small and distinct group.[2] They all wear caps pulled well down and pin their cloaks at the neck with an enormous pin which looks almost like a button. Once the dedicator lets us know his name :[3] on the base of his statuette is inscribed " Phauleas dedicated (this) to Pan."

There are a few female figures among the bronzes.

At Tegea was found a small statuette of Athena,[4] no doubt Athena Alea, armed with a massive helmet, aegis, spear (much bent), and shield : her short, strong figure is that of an Arcadian peasant, but the bronze is under the influence of Sparta.

Artemis appears in the guise of a girl with bobbed hair, a fringed shawl, and a necklace of large beads (Pl. 30 *b* and *c*),[5] all of which things look curiously modern to us, but might have appeared provincial to girls from less remote parts of Greece.[6] The shawl, which is worn above a Doric peplos, would have been called by the Greeks χλανίς or χλανίδιον : it is not unlike the chlamys which some of the shepherds wear. One point hangs down in front, and behind the elbows are tassels. We cannot tell whether the protuberance on the skirt is meant for the knee : if so, the artist did wrong in making both feet level. On

[1] Berlin, 10,780, from Hagios Sostes ; Neugebauer, *op. cit.*, Pl. 23, p. 42. This bronze must have been made shortly after 500 B.C., but it is in the sixth century tradition.

[2] *B.S.A.*, XXVII, pp. 138 ff. The two illustrated on Pl. 31 *b* and *c* are: Athens, 13,060 ; ht., ·085 m., from Berekla ; and Berlin, 10,786, from Hagios Sostes ; ht., ·117 m. This has bronze tangs beneath the feet, the remains of the channels through which the bronze was poured into the mould. The group may be dated from 525-480.

[3] New York, No. 58 ; *Catalogue*, p. 39.

[4] Athens, 14,828 ; *B.C.H.*, 1921, Pl. XIII ; Langlotz, p. 87.

[5] At Frankfurt-am-Main ; ht., 0·132 m. ; *Jahreshefte*, 1901, p. 34 ; Furtwängler, *Kleine Schriften*, II, pp. 461 ff. ; *B.S.A.*, XVII, No. 20 ; date, last quarter sixth century.

[6] Short hair was, however, worn in the Peloponnese as late as the second quarter of the fifth century, when the figures of Hippodameia and her mother Sterope were made for the Olympia pediment. See also the late fifth century head of Hera on the coins of Argos.

the base is a row of incised circles, an Arcadian feature that is met on the dresses of some of the other statuettes. The statuette comes from the site of Lousoi where there was once a sanctuary of Artemis Hemerasia.[1]

The finest bronzes Arcadia has produced are two seated figures.

One of these comes from Tegea and represents a goddess (Pl. 30 a),[2] Demeter or Kore, both of whom were worshipped by the citizens. The goddess sits on a throne holding in one hand a pomegranate, in the other a quince. Her dress consists of a Doric peplos with sleeves and overfold : she wears a wreath, but the ribbon which should confine the knot of hair which falls down her back has been forgotten. The face is flat and square, the mouth straight and grave. Though the eyes are poor and of the almost lidless type discussed below, the eyebrows are pleasing, and the whole effect is simple and stately. Both eyes and mouth have so many parallels in Arcadian art that an Arcadian origin is certain.

The other seated figure represents Zeus Lykaios, and was found in the precinct on Mt. Lykaion (Pl. 26 c).[3] It must have been imported, probably from some first-class centre such as Corinth.[4] It is, however, evidently modelled on an old cult statue. That is why the lower part of the figure appears more archaic and conventionalised than the head. One hand holds a curved object like a Roman *lituus ;* it has been conjectured [5] that it is of the nature of a sceptre, derived, perhaps, from the branch of a sacred tree. The other hand grasps a thunderbolt of which the top is broken off. The costume consists of a chiton and a himation : the latter has one of its ends thrown over the left shoulder and a small weight has been sewn on to the corner to keep it in place. Below the feet is a footstool. The hair, most delicately rendered, is brushed back in a fringe from the forehead, reminding us of the figures on Lakonian pottery,[6] on

---

[1] Pausanias, VIII, 18, 8.

[2] Athens, 14,922 ; ht., c. ·10 m. ; B.S.A., XXVII, No. 27 ; Langlotz, pp. 54, 59, Pl. 24 a (to Argos) ; date, c. 500 B.C.

[3] Athens, 13,209 ; ht., ·102 m. ; 'Εφ. 'Αρχ., 1904, pp. 185 ff., Figs. 12-14 ; Cook, Zeus, I, p. 86, Fig. 55 ; B.S.A., XXVII, No. 29.

[4] Langlotz, pp. 80, 83, Pl. 41 b.   [5] Cook, Zeus, I, p. 87.

[6] Cf. two of the Lakonian *kylikes* illustrated in this connection ; Cook, Zeus, pp. 93-94, Figs. 65, 66.

the François vase, and of the Kouros from Longa, all earlier in date. Our Zeus must belong to the third, not the second, quarter of the century.

From near Epidauros comes a bronze [1] which in style so closely resembles the Arcadian figures that most scholars have agreed to assign it to Arcadia (Pl. 32 *a*). The prominent, almost lidless eyes and the straight, clumsy mouth are particularly characteristic. It was made by an artist called Hybrisstas. We know the name, because he signed it at the base of the figure. In doing so he went contrary to the custom of the other bronze makers of his period. His signature is unique and gives value to what is really an unattractive piece of work. Concerning the date of the statuette there has been much controversy. The fact that the lower part of the limbs are heavier than the upper indicates an early date. One critic [2] considers the rendering of the chest muscles as well as the heavy type of face characteristic of the first half of the sixth century. Another [3] thinks that certain details, such as the way the edge of the ribs is marked, shew a more advanced style. The middle years of the century are the most probable period.

Whether the bronze represents, like the Geometric figures, a warrior striking downwards with his spear, or, like the group mentioned on p. 149, Zeus with eagle and thunderbolt, we cannot say.[4] In any case, it forms a link between the Geometric type and the Zeus figures that played so important a part at the end of the century.

The Arcadian bronzes are, during the sixth century, particularly easy to recognise, owing to their proportions, their features, and the patterns on their drapery. The proportions are distinctive : nearly all the figures are short and stocky, often with heads too large for their bodies. The few exceptions form a class apart that has been discussed elsewhere.[5] The treatment of the features varies : one group, to which belongs the Hermes from Andritsaena, has eyes with very cleanly cut

[1] Dutuit Collection, Petit Palais ; ht., 17 m. ; Neugebauer, Pl. 27, p. 48 ; Furtwängler, *Kleine Schriften*, II, p. 467.

[2] *Ibid., loc. cit.*   [3] Neugebauer, *op. cit.*, pp. 49 ff.

[4] Neugebauer, *loc. cit.*, points out that the left hand is inappropriate for the warrior's shield or the eagle of Zeus.

[5] A small group of figures with the normal slender proportions : these are all Kouroi and shepherds. See *B.S.A.*, XXVII, Nos. 22-26.

upper and lower lids, but the most characteristic, illustrated on Pls. 30 *a*, 31 *b*, *c*, 32 *a*, has almost lidless eyes, usually combined with a straight slit of a mouth and ill-modelled lips.

The patterns and trimmings of the clothes may represent embroidery : circles and half circles are much used, likewise zig-zags, and circles joined by tangents into a running pattern. The Lousoi Artemis actually has a row of circles on the base which supports her. A very similar circle, perhaps stamped, marks the heads of the pins with which the cloaks are fastened at the throat.

It is not possible, with the space at our disposal, fully to discuss the claims of the various Arcadian districts to have made the bronzes. The most we can do here is to indicate the sites from which they come.[1]

They have been found in large quantities in the south-west of Arcadia, in the district round Mt. Lykaion. This includes a site near Berekla, which is presumed to be the shrine of Pan,[2] the precinct of Zeus Lykaios, the villages of Andritsaena and Hagios Sostes, whither they must have strayed from the neighbouring sites, and two other sites not far away, Bassae and Lykosoura. Some figures come from Tegea, and a few from Kleitor and Lousoi in northern Arcadia.

It seems probable that Tegea produced some, at least, of the statuettes. The town is admirably situated for their manufacture ; its relation to Argolis and Lakonia has already been described ; we know it to have possessed works of art in the seventh century as well as in the time of Skopas, and we are practically certain it made bronzes during the fifth century.

Reviewing the Arcadian industry, we are struck by its vitality and its independence, as well as by the determination with which the Arcadian people patronised home-made goods. Moreover, two, at least, of its bronzes found their way beyond the Arcadian border, the Hermes to Mount Ithome, the Hybrisstas bronze to Epidauros.

NORTH-WESTERN GREECE AND DODONA—The half mythical sculptors, Dipoinos, and Skyllis crossed from Sikyon to

---

[1] For a fuller discussion and references see *B.S.A.*, XXVII, p. 146.

[2] See Πρακτικά, 1902, p. 72, where the Berekla site is identified with the shrine of Pan mentioned by Pausanias, VIII, 38.

Aetolia.   Other artists, nameless, but equally important, brought to Thermon the Corinthian style which we see in the metopes.   Corcyra (Corfu) was a colony of Corinth, and its art was derived from that of the mother country.[1]   It is, therefore, not surprising to find among the bronzes from Dodona, which, though far north of Aetolia, is in the same latitude as Corcyra, a strong Peloponnesian influence.   The Kouros from Dodona in Berlin [2] shews Peloponnesian art in its stiffest aspect.   The Kouros from Dodona in the Louvre is, as we have seen (p. 88), Corinthian.   At the same time, many of the Dodona bronzes have in common an individuality of style which suggests a local origin.   This is natural in a remote but important centre, and a district which had had a style of its own in the previous period (p. 43).   One of the most obvious elements of this North-Western style is the tendency to mark with small transverse cuts the hair of men and horses, and even harness and the borders of drapery.   It is the exaggeration of an ordinary technical device of the period.   Another element is the heaviness of form and feature.   A small horse in the Louvre (Pl. 38 *b*) [3] exhibits both points so clearly that, on first seeing an illustration, I assigned him to this district before ever I learned that Dodona was his provenance, or saw his typical blue-grey patina.   Another characteristic of bronzes from Dodona is a certain originality of conception and vivacity of treatment.   A prancing satyr, two riders, and a flute player [4] deserve special mention.   The flute player [5] is a figure whom we meet on vase paintings but rarely elsewhere.   Look at his long chiton, at the straps which hold the instrument in place, and at the flute-case hanging from his arm.

Still more uncommon are two girl athletes (Pl. 33), one of whom was actually found at Dodona [6] and the other in

[1] See the remarks on this subject in *C.A.H.*, IV, p. 593.

[2] Berlin, 7976 ; *Führer*, p. 37.   Most of the bronzes from Dodona are in Athens (see Carapanos, *Dodone et ses Ruines*, 1878), and Berlin (see Kekule v. Stradonitz and Winnefeld, *Bronzen aus Dodona*, 1909).

[3] Louvre, 148 ; ht., ·097 m. ; *Catalogue*, Pl. 16.   A copper rein, now broken, passed through a hole in the mouth.   There are flaws on the surface from defective casting.   [4] Athens, Nos. 22, 27, 36, 25.

[5] Athens, No. 25 ; ht., ·113 m.   The transverse cuts on the hair do not shew in the photograph.

[6] Athens, 24 ; ht., ·117 m.   Fine green patina.   Second quarter sixth century.

7

Albania [1] whither she must have penetrated across the Greek frontier.

The girl from Dodona wears a chiton with sleeves and a belt. The girl from Albania wears a chiton which is pinned on the left shoulder only. The material, which would naturally be pinned on the right shoulder, hangs down in a long flap. The chiton is bordered.

Both girls have the same type of fringe ; both hold the hem of the dress with the left hand. The Dodona statuette is the older of the two ; it belongs to the middle of the sixth century. The statuette from Albania is slightly later.

The subject is an interesting one. We are reminded of the girls' race in honour of Hera at Olympia and the copy of a fifth century statue of one of the victors now in the Vatican. Concerning the race, Pausanias says : " This is how they run : their hair hangs down, they wear a skirt that reaches to a little above the knee, the right shoulder is bare to the breast. The course assigned to them for the contest is the Olympic stadium. . . . The winners are allowed to dedicate statues of themselves." [2]

One of our two bronzes has her chiton unpinned on the right shoulder in the prescribed manner : the other has not. Nevertheless, it is tempting to imagine both were statuettes of winners at these games : winners they certainly must be, witness the satisfied expression on the face of the girl from Dodona. There is no reason to suppose that girls did not come from some distance to take part in the races : if so, the Epirotes seem to have been particularly successful.

This explanation is, perhaps, far-fetched. The girls are more probably winners in some local sports. The legend of Atalanta's race is at home not so very far from Dodona : it may testify to an athletic tradition long established in North-Western Greece.

Among the sites of Northern Greece there is one, *Delphi*, where, as far as I can see, no bronzes are of local manufacture.

[1] *B.M.*, 208 ; ht., ·11 m. Notice the cuts on the edge of the chiton. Third quarter sixth century.

Both remains are assigned to Sparta by Langlotz, p. 94. It should be noted that Spartan bronzes did penetrate into N.W. Greece, e.g. the mirror in Berlin from Vonitza (p. 128).

[2] Pausanias, V, 16. See Frazer, *Pausanias*, I, p. 260, for the translation.

It plays the same part as that played by Olympia in the Peloponnese.

ATHENS—There is every reason to believe that bronzes were made at Athens from the Geometric Period onwards. Of the offerings found on the Acropolis, a large number must have been home products. This is suggested by the constant repetitions of the same subject, and can be accepted unreservedly in the case of a subject as essentially Attic as the figures of Athena Promachos. At the same time, the wares of other states are represented, including at least one bronze from Miletus [1] and another from Vulci in Etruria.[2] One curious fact requires explanation : there are many bronzes belonging to the first two decades of the century, quantities that can be dated from 530 to 480 B.C., but remarkably few belonging to the middle years.

We should expect to find the same tendencies in Athenian statuettes as in Athenian sculpture, and to a limited extent we do : yet, on the whole, the statuettes develop on remarkably independent lines.

Affinities with certain Attic heads [3] are presented by the Athena Promachos, 6452 : [4] the Promachos on Pl. 37 *a* [5] is one of the few which recall the almost exotic beauty of those heads which some scholars connect with Chios and Chiot influence.[6] Here, as there, we find oblique, heavy-lidded eyes, a mouth drawn up at the corners and wonderfully dressed hair. The left arm once carried a shield, which has been broken from its attachment ; the right hand held a spear. Artistically, the Athena Promachos is the female counterpart of the Zeus with the thunderbolt.

One supporting figure repeats the motive of the well-known maiden votaries : [7] she differs from them only in her helmet (of which the crest is missing), and the inelegant way she fingers her drapery.

A fourth figure of Athena [8] from the Acropolis is an example

[1] Athens, 6493 ; Langlotz, p. 103.
[2] Athens, 6511 (see p. 139) ; de Ridder, Pl. V.
[3] Langlotz, Pl. 95.   [4] De Ridder, 780, Pl. VIII.
[5] Athens, 6457 ; de Ridder, 782 ; ht., ·192 m.   Last quarter sixth century.
[6] See Dickins, *Acropolis Catalogue*, pp. 20 ff.
[7] Athens, 6491 ; ht., ·17 m. ; de Ridder, 793.   Late sixth century.
[8] Athens, 6448 ; de Ridder, 794, Figs. 299, 300 ; ht., ·358 m.   Some of the rivets for attaching the two plates of bronze survive.   The left arm is broken.   The surface was originally gilt.   The figure may have decorated a rim.

of a rare technique (Pl. 44 b). It is made of two thin sheets of bronze cut out and placed back to back, so as to be seen from either side. Part of a companion figure has been put together from two fragments.[1] Both Athenas may originally have been affixed to the rim of a bowl.

Running figures of Winged Victory were also made in large numbers. The subject is associated with Chios by literary and archæological evidence : it is interesting to look at the Winged Victory from Delos in the National Museum, and then at the numerous small editions of the same subject among the Acropolis bronzes. Just as the Victory from Delos was probably destined to adorn the eaves of a temple, so the bronzes were made, not to stand alone, but to decorate bronze vessels. Most of them fall late in the sixth century or early in the fifth, but there is one fine early example.[2]

Turning to the male figures, there are three,[3] very like each other, which present a profile view, recalling the statue by the Argive [Poly]medes. But they are not Argive. Their shoulders are too narrow and sloping, and the face, seen from in front, is distinctive. They must be by an Athenian artist under foreign influence, or by a foreign artist resident at Athens. The three youths are mounted on bases of two tiers : all wear elaborate boots, have carelessly modelled ears set on obliquely, and held some object in the left hand. A fourth member of the family, now in the British Museum,[4] holds a syrinx.

Somewhat later in date comes another youth, the best known, perhaps, of the Acropolis bronzes (Pl. 37 c).[5] He has the same sloping shoulders and much the same stocky figure as the quartette just described ; his eyes, doubly outlined by their lids, are like theirs, though much less crude, but the modelling of the body and rendering of the face are more advanced. For the rest, the muscles have been studied but not emphasised,

[1] Athens, 8603 a ; de Ridder, Bronzes de l'Acropole, 795, and Bronzes de la Soc. Arch. d'Athens, 933.
[2] Athens, 6483 ; de Ridder, 800.
[3] Athens, Nos. 6597, 6607, 6598 ; de Ridder, Pl. II, 1-3.
[4] B.M., 1922, 7, 12 ; Perdrizet, Bronzes Grecs . . . Fouquet, No. 37, Pl. XV.
[5] Athens, 6445 ; ht., 0·27 m. ; Langlotz, pp. 69 and 73, attributes it to Kleonai, c. 500 B.C. See also B.C.H., 1894, p. 44, Pls. V, VI ; Furtwängler, 50th Winckelmanns Programm, p. 128 ; and Olympia, IV, p. 20. For other references, see Staïs, Catalogue, p. 283.

the shoulders, though sloping, are broad, the hips narrow, and the legs short in comparison with the body. This bronze appears to have come from the same workshop as the other four, but it is by a master hand.

The centaur had long been a familiar figure in Greek art,[1] and was a favourite one among the Athenian bronze workers. In the seventh century he had been squat and clumsy, but the sixth century artists improved his proportions. They discovered with pride that they could make his human forelegs move like those of a running man, but cheerfully overlooked the fact that his equine hind legs, planted close together, would prevent all movement.

Genial and energetic, an Athenian centaur in the Bibliothèque Nationale [2] strides forward ; in his case we are not disillusioned by the position of the hind legs, since they are missing below the hock (Pl. 39 a). The centaur's left hand holds a club which rests on his shoulder, while his right hand is drawn back like that of the runners [3] whom his human half tries to emulate. Notice the careful treatment of hair and beard, the swelling biceps of the left arm, and the casual way the human body joins the body of the horse. Another centaur from the Acropolis at Athens [4] has arms and legs in the same positions as the centaur in Paris, save for the fact that the hind legs are actually joined together.

The Athenians appear to have excelled in the rendering of birds and animals of all kinds. The fine thoroughbred head of the Pegasus on Pl. 38 a [5] is, in spite of its mutilated condition, one of the loveliest bronzes they have left us.

IONIA AND THE ISLANDS—It is disconcerting to find so few bronzes that can be attributed to the Islands or to the coast of Asia Minor. When we consider how important a part Ionia

---

[1] On centaurs, see P. V. C. Baur, *Centaurs in Greek Art.*

[2] *Bibliothèque Nationale*, 514, p. 219 ; ht., ·102 m. From the Acropolis. The human left foot, though missing in the original, is restored in the photograph ; 540-520 B.C.

[3] *J.H.S.*, XXIII, 1903, p. 269.

[4] Athens, 6680 ; de Ridder, 430, Fig. 98 ; *J.H.S.*, 1922, p. 210, Fig. 3 c. Part of forelegs missing.

[5] Athens, 6693 ; ht., ·078 m. ; de Ridder, 504.

played in the development of Greek sculpture and Greek vase painting ; when we remember the Ephesian ivory statuettes from the seventh century and study the entertaining terra-cotta statuettes of the sixth ; above all, when we read of the achievements of the Samians in bronze casting and of the Chiots in metal-work,[1] we are led to expect quantities of bronzes of Ionic provenance and with Ionic features.

In this we are disappointed. Of the six examples which are mentioned in this section, only two have the double claim of provenance and style to be of Ionic workmanship. The others can, however, be safely associated with this part of the world by their likeness to works of undoubted Ionic origin.

The type of Kouros produced by the Samo-Milesian school has already been illustrated by an early example at Stockholm. A somewhat later bronze at Delphi (Pl. 36 a) [2] shews many of the same characteristics : short, thick neck, heavy face, arms glued to the sides. There are also marked differences : [3] the Delphic bronze has the broad chest and shoulders which we know from statues found at Samos [4] as well as from Rhodian terra-cottas. Moreover, an attempt has been made to indicate the anatomy, but without much success. Still later in date, but belonging to the same tradition, comes an inferior bronze Kouros from Scala Nova near Miletus.[5]

The bronze Kouros from Naxos in Berlin (Pl. 34 c) [6] is a later work. It has a heavy chest and heavy shoulders : the face is less fleshy than the Samian type and shorter than the Naxian. Which of the island schools produced this bronze we cannot say : it is the Ionic version of a motive common at the period : the Doric version is shewn beside it on Pl. 34 a, d. The ears, fingers, finger-nails and toes are finished with remarkable care. In one hand is what may be a pomegranate. On the base is an Ionic inscription saying that the figure was dedicated by Deinagores to Apollo.

[1] Stuart Jones, *Ancient Writers*, p. 22.
[2] *Fouilles de Delphes*, Vol. V, Pl. I, 6 ; ht., ·15 m.
[3] So much so that Langlotz attributes the Stockholm Kouros to Samos, the Kouros from Delphi to Miletos, pp. 103, 118, Pl. 59.
[4] *Ath. Mit.*, 1906, Pls. 11, 12. For references and a discussion of this school, see *C.A.H.*, IV, 594.
[5] Langlotz, Pl. 59 a.
[6] No. 7383 ; ht., ·18 ; *Führer*, p. 24. Half the statue has been cleaned with a view to removing the incrustation which mars the surface.

The female type of the same or of a kindred school, fore-shadowed in the Ephesian bronze described in the last chapter, is found in a bronze from Olympia,[1] originally the support of a vessel (Pl. 36 c). She has the short neck, the flat, puffy face of the Samian figures. Other points, such as the drapery, the pillar-like chiton, and the position of the left arm, recall a group of statues of Naxian origin, but still more vividly the Ephesian ivories. Both Naxians and Samians loved to use human figures to support bowls of bronze or metal : witness the bronze kneeling woman in the Louvre (p. 77), and the women of Naxian marble below a bowl from the Acropolis.[2] That the bronze from Olympia was a support, not a free figure, is proved by the cushion-like member above the head, and by an iron bar running through the body.

Certain details deserve attention. The costume, for instance, an Ionic chiton bound with a girdle ; the bracelets, which are incised upon the wrists; the hair with its curls in front of each ear ; the eyes, which were once filled with a white composition, and some brighter material to indicate the pupil. A date in the first quarter of the century seems probable.

A younger relation of this bronze is in Berlin, and, in spite of its somewhat meagre appearance, may be assigned to the same school.[3] A dumpy little lady at Athens,[4] made at a different art centre from the two last described, completes our list of Ionic figures (Pl. 36 b).

BOEOTIA—The sanctuary of Ptoön Apollo lies among the mountains to the east of Lake Kopais. Here were found a number of antiquities of which the marble Kouroi are well known. There were also some important bronzes, both statuettes and reliefs of the Argivo-Corinthian class discussed in the next chapter.

The bronze statuettes include an armed warrior, three figures

[1] Athens, 6149 ; ht., 0·225 m. ; Olympia, IV, Pl. VII, No. 74 ; Langlotz, p. 118. Its relation to the group of works now associated with Samos was pointed out by Studniczka and Furtwängler, Olympia, IV, p. 24.

[2] No. 592 ; Dickins, Acropolis Catalogue, p. 125.

[3] Berlin, 8622 ; Langlotz, p. 119, Pl. 69 c.

[4] Athens, 6493 ; de Ridder, 772 ; Langlotz, pp. 103, 111 (Miletos). First half of sixth century; ht., ·11 m. The statuette is smooth behind, and pierced from side to side by a square hole : this should be a clue to the way in which it was mounted, but I know of no exact parallel.

of the Kouros type, two interesting female figures,[1] and an attractive series of animals, particularly bulls. Two of the male figures are inscribed with dedications to Apollo,[2] and one of these two (Pl. 34 *b*) is so like the youth from Naxos in Berlin that it might be attributed to the same school.

The female figure [3] on Pl. 35 *c* probably represents Aphrodite, since she holds in her hands a dove and a flower. The lower part of the body is square like a primitive image : the garment is embroidered in cross stitch just below the belt. The arched eyebrows, and small, curved mouth, help us to recognise the goddess' sister in a bronze from the same site in the Louvre.[4] The Louvre goddess also has a squarish appearance about the skirt : both ladies wear shoes.

They form what may be a useful clue to the Boeotian local style, which appears to have been eclectic, taking some features from Ionia, others from the Peloponnese. One of the bronze Kouroi [5] is typically Peloponnesian, and was, in all probability, imported like the Corinthian pottery and some, at least, of the Argivo-Corinthian reliefs, which are found in quantities on Boeotian sites. The country would naturally be in touch with Corinth, Athens and the Islands.

Before passing on to the bronzes of Italy, it is worth while briefly to review the development of certain types. Concerning the Kouros and the Kore enough has been said : we have discussed their origins in a previous chapter and watched their different manifestations in this. Other types of male or female figures have also appeared : seated figures like the Demeter of Tegea, running figures like the girls from Dodona, riders like the ones from Dodona and Megalopolis.

There are also many mythical creatures, which the fancy of the people created and to which the skill of the artist gave form. Sphinxes, sirens and Gorgons were usually, though not

[1] *Ath. Nat. Mus.*, 7388, 7380-7382, (male), 7389 (female) ; and Louvre, 143, Pl. 16.

[2] Nos. 7380-7381. See *B.C.H.*, 1886 (= Vol. X), 1887, 1888. A bronze in Berlin, 7100, from Thebes, should be classed with the series from the Ptoön. It was probably made in Boeotia.

[3] Athens, 7389 ; *B.C.H.*, 1888, Pl. XI. Third quarter sixth century.

[4] Louvre, 143.

[5] Athens, No. 7382 ; Langlotz, p. 55, No. 19, attributes it to Argos.

always, made for the decoration of objects in bronze.   Centaurs are interesting because of their long history : satyrs because of the variety of their attitudes.

Animals were made sometimes for decorative, sometimes for votive purposes.   Their excellence will surprise nobody who is familiar with the delightful birds and beasts of the Geometric Period.   Greek artists were as successful in this field as they were in depicting the human form.   Their statuettes of animals reproduce essential charac-teristics with the simplest possible means and are often more or less stylised.

FIG. 1.—Calf from Olympia.

The most completely stylised animals are those which the Greeks had not themselves seen ; the lions and panthers, for instance, which they took second hand from the Orient.   The familiar animals of Greece often combine a formality of shape with realism in certain particulars.

There is a calf from Olympia (Fig. 1)[1] whose skin is covered with wrinkles like those on the loose skin of a new-born creature. Votive bulls from various sites [2] have wrinkled necks.   From Dodona comes a goat [3] evidently once part of a bronze vessel, which looks as if it were getting on to its legs in the manner of its kind by straightening first the hind legs while the front legs remain bent.   With his ribbed horns and his beard and the thick hairs along his spine, he is all that a goat should be.   Two beautiful goats in the British Museum [4] are interesting for comparison.

This very cursory review of some of the more usual subjects will shew how the Greeks perfected the fine art of repeating the

[1] At Olympia ; ht., ·04 m. ; *Olympia*, IV, 961, Pl. LVI.   There is a nail to fasten the calf to some object, probably the edge of a bowl.

[2] E.g. Delphi (*Fouilles*, V, Pl. XVI) ; Athens (6705 ; de Ridder, 517) ; Ptoön (at Berlin, *Führer*, p. 34, and in quantities at Athens).   Some of these examples, e.g. the Athenian, are fifth century.

[3] Berlin, 10,584 ; Kekule von Stradonitz, *op. cit.*, pp. 1 and 43.

[4] B.M., 233, 234.   For this type see Filow and Schkorpil, *Die Archaische Nekropole von Trebenischte*, pp. 53, 54.

same theme with variations so subtle and delightful that the spectator does not tire of it.   This was one of the achievements of the Greek genius, not only in sculpture and painting, but also in literature.   The same story is told from different points of view by different writers : the same simile is consciously repeated and improved.   No one could accuse them of lack of originality, since it is often a harder task to renovate an old theme than to create a new one.

SOUTH ITALY—The Greek colonies of South Italy and Sicily played an important part, both as producers and as transmitters.   Their sculpture, their terra-cottas, their coinage are well known.   Their metal-work, long overlooked, is now fully recognised.   They distinguish themselves as makers of bronze utensils of various kinds, often adorned with figures : these will be discussed in the next chapter.   Of votive bronzes there are fewer.   Herein the Western Greeks resembled the Greeks of Ionia, who, like themselves, excelled in the making of statuettes in terra-cotta, a possible substitute for bronze.

These South Italian Greeks maintained a flourishing trade with the mother country, and with the less civilised, more northerly parts of Italy.   They imported works of art from Greece and passed them on to Campania and Etruria, together with other works of art, which they had themselves made.   Thus they were, in a large measure, responsible for the diffusion of Greek culture.

Among the bronzes from South Italy, some are purely Greek in style, the products of Greek workshops with a fully trained staff.   Others shew alien elements in a greater or less degree. These may have been made by Greek workshops with an Italian staff, or at provincial workshops started by Italian craftsmen who had been taught by Greek masters.   We have, therefore, on the one hand, the Hellenic art centres of the coast, such as Tarentum, Locri, Paestum, Cumae ; on the other hand, more obscure centres inland, especially in Campania, of which Capua must have been one.   In Campania, at this period, the Greeks were in direct contact with the Etruscans ; but Etruscan art is a subject which requires a section to itself.

Most of the figures of purely Greek style that are important enough for a detailed description belong to the next period.

Among the bronzes where an Italian element can be detected, the most conspicuous are the figures from the lids of bronze urns, of which many have been found near Capua (see p. 137).

In this style we can distinguish both Greek and Etruscan elements, and something different from Greek and Etruscan, which can be no other than South Italian. One of the most Greek of the figures is the Scythian bowman in Berlin; [1] one of the least, the figures on the urn No. 558 in the British Museum (Pl. 48 a). The long bodies of the horses on B.M. 560 are distinctive and help to connect this group with the bronze cattle from Andria in Berlin,[2] and the well-known horseman from Grumentum in Lucania (Pl. 39 b).[3] Between the cattle and the horseman a close bond exists. The latter must have been a handsome piece in its original state, with the horse's reins and the crest of the rider's helmet in some other material. The muscles on the hind quarters, very conventional, are engraved with a sharp point, while the structure of the head is rendered by the deep angular cuts that are characteristic of Italian work.

ETRURIA—By the middle of the sixth century, Etruscan art was completely under the influence of Greece. Greek wares poured into the country, where they ornamented the houses of the living and furnished the tombs of the dead. Greek artists, too, came to Etruria, particularly from Ionia. They may be responsible for some of the work which, like the Caeretan hydriae and the bronzes described on p. 121, have elements that are both Etruscan and Ionic. They certainly employed Etruscan apprentices. Thus the Etruscans had every opportunity for assimilating and copying Greek art, an occupation well suited to their taste and capacity.

Of the objects imported into the country, the vases were far the more numerous, the figures by comparison fewer. Some bronzes came direct from Greece, others by way of the Greek colonies of South Italy.

[1] Berlin, 7094; *Führer*, p. 30; Neugebauer, Pl. 33.
[2] Berlin, 8385, 8386; *Führer*, p. 30.
[3] B.M., 1904, 7-3, 1; ht., ·252 m.; *Burlington Fine Arts Catalogue*, 1904, p. 33, No. 53, Pls. 37, 38. Feet restored.

The Etruscans had a real talent for bronze work. Their own industries soon began to flourish and their output was extremely large. The presence of an Etruscan tripod on the Athenian Acropolis may be regarded as a proof of their commercial enterprise.[1] We will proceed to examine some of their achievements, the statuettes in this chapter, other bronzes in the next.

Many of the Etruscan statuettes fall into groups, each group repeating, with variations, the same subject. Thus we have a series of female figures, the equivalent of the Greek Korai ; a smaller series of male figures (Kouroi) ; a long series of warriors that does not, however, become important till the end of the sixth century ; and a series of figures of Menvra (Minerva), very like the warriors. A number of figures of Herakles can also be found which bear a strong resemblance to each other.

We will start with the female figures. Pl. 41 *a*[2] represents a type of which there are several examples in our museums. She is sufficiently primitive to have her arms attached to her sides : her costume is meant to be the chiton and himation, but the artist has got confused and made an end of drapery in front which is really out of place. On the head is the conical Etruscan *tutulus* and a diadem : on the diadem and the pointed shoes are engraved patterns. The short neck and fleshy body remind us that Etruria was much under Ionic influence. The figure, like others of its class, was meant to be attached to some object : this is shewn by the hollowing of the back and by a nail near the feet.

Contrast with her the lady from Perugia in the British Museum (Pl. 41 *c*).[3] She belongs to the second half of the century, and is a common type. She has a sister, very like her, but handsomer, in Berlin.[4] The Berlin figure also comes from Perugia. Numerous other figures repeat, more or less, the same motive.

---

[1] Athens, 6511 ; de Ridder, Pl. V. All of the tripod that remains is the group at the top of one of the supports.

[2] Bibl. Nat., 1040 ; ht., ·258 m. Cf. Louvre, 227, and a pair in the Museo Gregoriano ; Ducati, *Storia*, Pl. 102, Fig. 272. These figures may be dated about 540. The primitive arrangement of the arms may be occasioned by the needs of the object to which the bronzes were attached.

[3] B.M., 497 ; Walters, *Catalogue*, p. 68 ; ht., ·16 m.

[4] No. 2155 ; *Führer*, p. 28, Pl. 13.

The lady in the British Museum holds up her dress in her left hand, for she is trying to be as refined as the Greek girls of the period. She keeps, however, to the local fashion of wearing a *tutulus* on her head and shoes on her feet.

The youths are, on the whole, undistinguished ; they illustrate the not always painstaking and usually vain efforts of the provincial artist to get his anatomy correct. Two of the best are from Falterona, in the Louvre.[1] A real masterpiece was achieved by the maker of the dandy in the British Museum,[2] who stands so proudly conscious of his embroidered mantle and stitched leather boots (Pl. 40 b). Though the modelling is not always first class, the beauty of detail and the exquisite quality of the patina give full compensation.

The warriors will be described in Chapter VI, for they chiefly flourished in the fifth century. Most of the figures of Menvra, advancing like Athena Promachos with uplifted spear, resemble them closely.[3] Both warrior and goddess are often excessively tall and emaciated. There is a strong tendency in Etruscan art during the latter part of the Archaic Period and in the fifth century to make the cheaper figures very thin : it affected particularly the two types just mentioned and the young women.

We will pass rapidly over a number of those statuettes which have become detached from incense burners, vases, candelabra, etc. (see next chapter). Their subjects are often varied and amusing. A good example is the gesticulating satyr from a candelabrum or lid found at Chiusi.[4] Reclining figures from the rims of bowls or the framework of tripods should also be mentioned.

With the latter, compare the much larger reclining banqueter in the British Museum,[5] one of the important Etruscan bronzes of the period. It has been suggested [6] that he is by the same hand as a woman in the Bibliothèque Nationale, and

[1] Louvre, 218, 220, Pl. 21.

[2] No. 509 ; ht., ·17 m. From Pizzirimonte, near Prato.

[3] Another type, however, is represented by the Athena from near Florence, at Berlin (No. 7095 ; *Ath. Mit.*, XLVI, 1921, Pl. IV, 2), who derives from a Peloponnesian type represented by the Artemis in the British Museum from Arcadia, 1922, 11-15-1.

[4] Berlin, 715 b ; Neugebauer, Pl. 53.

[5] B.M., 556 ; Neugebauer, Pl. 54, p. 100 ; length, ·33 m.

[6] Neugebauer, *loc. cit.*

this is very probable, as both have the folds of the drapery marked in a distinctive way, by engraved lines parallel with lines of spots.

Two other important pieces will conclude our account of the sixth century.

The first is the so-called Vertumnus [1] from Isola di Fano (Pl. 40 a). It is a well made, typically Etruscan figure : notice the careful double line round the eyes, the finish of the hair in front, the slight suggestion of double chin. The under garment has sleeves ; on the right sleeve are two objects like buttons with some unexplainable object attached to one of them. The upper garment is wrapped round the body like a mantle, with a slight fold back at the upper edge which recalls the Ionic female costume. The object in the right hand has been explained as a *lituus*, the cap as an *apex*, and the statuette as an Etruscan priest taking part in some ritual unfamiliar to us. A bronze attachment below the feet would facilitate mounting : the figure, therefore, is votive.[2]

The second of our two statuettes is the Herakles of Este,[3] which can best be appreciated when seen in profile (Pl. 40 c). Herakles wears a cap with flaps descending at either side ; the back of the cap covers the nape of the neck. The lion's skin, bound by a belt at the waist, is arranged so that its head comes in front. A quiver hangs from a strap : the right hand must have held a bow : the left grasps a dead faun by the hind legs. The beard is arranged with a row of little curls at the top which match those above the forehead : it is an odd fashion, but not so odd as that adopted by the reclining Etruscan in the British Museum (p. 109). Our bearded Herakles should be compared to a young, beardless Herakles, similarly dressed, in the Louvre.[4]

There are, obviously, a number of distinct styles among the Etruscan bronzes. There are also several cities which may have had bronze industries of their own. But, up to now, very little has been done to connect any of the styles with any par-

[1] At Florence; ht., ·275, c. 500 B.C.; *Notizie degli Scavi*, 1884, Pl. III ; Ducati, *Etruria Antica*, II, 76 ; and *Storia*, p. 256, Pl. 102.
[2] Körte, *Göttinger Bronzen*, pp. 14, 15.
[3] *Bolletino d'Arte*, 1924 ; *Anno* III, Serie II (April), pp. 453 ff., Figs. 1-4.
[4] Louvre, 223, Pl. 22 ; *Bolletino d'Arte, loc. cit.*, pp. 458, 459, Figs. 5-8.

ticular city.   A guide to the style of Perugia is furnished by some of the bronzes described above, and by a whole set now at Munich.   For decorative bronzes, a beginning has been made by distinguishing the products of the district round Perugia, and those of Vulci (see next chapter).   The publication, now in progress, of the contents of Italian museums may yield important information : here is yet another field for research.

CHAPTER V

THE SIXTH CENTURY : DECORATIVE WORK AND UTENSILS IN BRONZE

IN the sixth century, as in every other period, certain groups of bronzes come to the fore, which were previously unimportant or non-existent. At its close, they either persist, as in the case of mirrors, or gradually decline, as in the case of the " Argivo-Corinthian " reliefs. With vases, which are common at all times, one shape is more interesting in one age, another in the next : or, again, one shape will be found to have been studied in connection with a particular epoch, and thus to have attained an artificial prominence.

It is the duty of anyone who chronicles the bronze industry in Greece to try and note each group as soon as it becomes conspicuous, though it is not essential for him to find space for the history of its decline. This has the drawback of making a very disconnected narrative, and also involves the risk of not seeing the wood for the trees, of neglecting the general development of art while studying particular objects. It is, however, a better alternative than discussing the general development and omitting the objects, as was often done in the last century, for if sufficient material is presented, the reader can make his own observations.

Two of these observations may, however, be anticipated. The first is that the Oriental motives described in Chapter III are now completely assimilated. The second is that the artist's interest is becoming concentrated on the human form. Animal friezes lose their place, and floral patterns become the frame for scenes where men and women play various parts.

Three main objects will be described in this chapter : reliefs, mirrors and vases : within these classes, certain groups, such as the Argivo-Corinthian reliefs and the mirrors attributed to Sparta, will be stressed as important features of the period.

A. RELIEFS

I. ARGIVO-CORINTHIAN AND SIMILAR RELIEFS—A group of bronzes in low relief and on a small scale can be detached from the rest.   The bronzes display pictures of men and animals, arranged vertically or horizontally, in panels.   The vertical strips are often finished above and below with a palmette. Mythological scenes, particularly from the Trojan cycle, are popular ; the figures are vigorous but stereotyped ; the animals are, for the most part, arranged heraldically ; the same borders —cable, egg-moulding, bosses, plaits, and, in the later examples, a plain moulding, appear again and again.   This group has been named Argivo-Corinthian,[1] for reasons that will appear below.

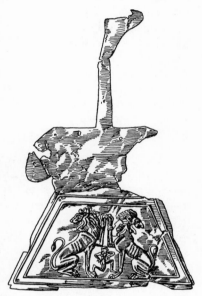

The reliefs which compose it are closely associated with others, also small, low and arranged on strips of bronze. In this allied group, heraldic animals occur but no human figures : some have heraldic animals on the same strips as bands of lotus and palmette, bands of rosettes, or manifold plaits.   These formal patterns appear, in their turn, without the animals.

FIG. 1.—Bronze of Argivo-Corinthian type from the Acropolis, Athens.

The term Argivo-Corinthian has, for the most part, been loosely applied to some of the purely animal as well as the mythological scenes ; but, since it seems inadvisable to extend it to all the bronzes with the associated types of animals and formal patterns, we confine it here to bronzes with human figures.

The same style appears on quadrangular reliefs of the shapes shewn on Fig. 1 ; the conventional decoration for these is a pair

---

[1] See de Ridder, *De Ectypis quibusdam Aeneis.* Furtwängler, *Kleine Schriften,* I, p. 428 ; and Beazley, *C.A.H.*, IV, 593.

of heraldic animals. Such bronzes appear to have been applied to the same objects as the Argivo-Corinthian bronzes, for they are frequently found together.

These objects may have been wooden chests or other bits of furniture.[1] The strips could have ornamented the sides or the lid, the quadrangular bronzes possibly covered the hinges.

The reliefs known as Argivo-Corinthian were first made familiar by the excavations at Olympia. Here were found a number of examples of which the most striking and best known represents Herakles and the " Old Man of the Sea," inscribed in unmistakably Argive characters. Fresh material was added by other sites : Corinth, Athens, Delphi, the Ptoön, Aegina and Noicattaro in Italy. With each new site, the question of where the reliefs were made became more controversial, and archæologists were divided into hostile camps, of which one claimed a Peloponnesian, the other an Ionic origin.

Before entering into so complicated a question, we will briefly describe representative reliefs from each site.

Olympia—The most important of the Olympia reliefs (Fig. 2) [2] is divided into four panels that must, on the analogy of more complete examples of this type, have been arranged vertically. One panel, much broken, shews Prometheus bound : most of the eagle was on the missing part. The scene below is ornamented with a picture of Herakles, club in hand, striking at an odd figure which some have identified as Geras (old age) : the irregular profile and unkempt hair are cleverly drawn. Another panel has a running Gorgon. Below is Herakles and the Old Man of the Sea, each character with his name inscribed beside him, ꟼᴧ.ᴧʙʙ 'Η]ρακ[λ]ῆς and ꟼᴧ MOIIᴧI ᾽Αλι(ι)ος γέρων. The lambda is characteristic of Argos and the sigma is early.

Three of these scenes bear, directly or indirectly, on the myths of Herakles : the Gorgon, less appropriate, may have been in the top panel above the other three.

Of the remaining reliefs from Olympia, some [3] resemble the last in style ; one,[4] illustrating the ransom of Hector, is almost identical in design with a mirror at Berlin (see below).

---

[1] Thiersch, *Aegina*, pp. 394 ff., advocates and then abandons the theory that they decorated the scabbards of swords.

[2] *Olympia*, IV, No. 699, Pl. XXXIX. At Athens ; diam., c. ·07 m.

[3] *Loc. cit.*, Nos. 700-702.   [4] *Loc. cit.*, No. 701.

Others [1] are a little later in date. They have less incised detail and the borders are different. The most interesting is a Rape of Cassandra, a scene which appears, in another form, on a relief from Delphi.

From *Corinth* come two mirror handles, now in the Athens Museum,[2] and a set of panels in low relief in Berlin. There can be no question that the mirror handles should be included in this

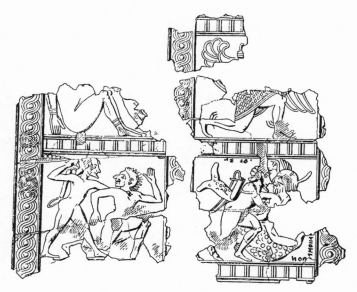

FIG. 2.—Argivo-Corinthian relief.

class, for the reliefs upon them are typically Argivo-Corinthian. Corinth, at all periods, was the chief factory for mirrors.

The panels at Berlin [3] contrast in some ways with the Olympia panels : they are arranged horizontally, they have borders of small bosses, and they have a large proportion of fantastic animals, e.g. sphinxes, griffins, heraldic lions and sirens. They include some illustrations of myths—Herakles

[1] *Loc. cit.*, Nos. 703-705. Nos. 706, 708 (*Olympia*, IV, Pl. XXXIX) differ in some details from the more conventional Argivo-Corinthian reliefs ; they are usually included in the class, but here omitted.

[2] Athens, 7687, 7691 ; de Ridder, Nos. 115, 116.

[3] *Anz.*, 1894, p. 117.

on one fragment, part of a Hydra on another, and a cheerful-looking little imp, full face, but fragmentary, who unintentionally affords comic relief.

Athens, Acropolis [1]—There are two important fragments of the conventional type (Fig. 3). The scenes are framed with cable pattern. The first (6962), from top to bottom, shews

(1) Ajax' suicide (most of this is missing).
(2) Quarrel : Ajax and Odysseus.
(3) Hector's ransom.
(4) Uncertain. Closely resembles the Olympia and Berlin reliefs.

The second (6965) is composed of the following scenes from top to bottom :—

(1) Theseus and Minotaur.
(2) Ajax' suicide.
(3) Herakles and Nemean lion.
(4) Two Sphinxes.

Besides smaller fragments with figure scenes, there are panels with heraldic lions. Below one of them is a palmette.

Delphi [2]—Two strips of bronze with vertical panels, illustrating mythological scenes. These include a Rape of Cassandra, which should be contrasted with that on the fragment from Olympia.

Below one of the strips is a palmette : these were generally used to finish off the designs at either end.

The side-border consists of bosses : between the panels occur a cable pattern, a tongue pattern and running spirals.

The Ptoön [3]—The sanctuary of Apollo Ptoön in Boeotia was remarkably rich in reliefs. Most are composed of panels arranged horizontally : two shew a second row of panels, not immediately below the first, but spaced like bricks. They are

[1] Athens, 6965, ht., ·19 m.; 6962, ht., ·175 m. ; *Ath. Mit.*, 1895, p. 473 Pl. XIV.
[2] *Fouilles de Delphes*, V, Pl. XXI, p. 123. At Delphi.
[3] *B.C.H.*, 1892, p. 357, Pls. X, XI, XIV, XV. At Athens.

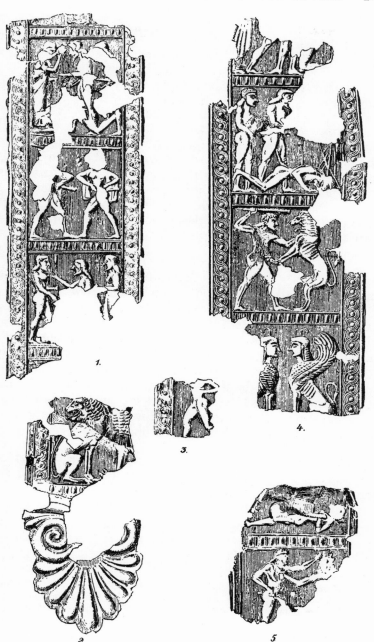

FIG. 3.—Argivo-Corinthian relief.

decorated either with heraldic animals, bordered by bosses or egg-moulding, or with figures, bordered by a cable pattern, bosses or egg-moulding On one fragment is Prometheus, on another Zeus, very determined, striking with his thunder-bolt a remarkably ugly giant ; on a third, two young men who, like those on p. 61, hold a wreath between them.

Aegina [1]—Of the fragments from the temple of Aphaia, some are very small ; the pieces large enough for one to judge the style are in the earlier manner, bordered above with an egg-moulding and at the sides with plaits.[2]   On one, there are two heroes playing dice, on another, Theseus and the Minotaur, on a third, three men, two of whom appear to be fighting.   There is also a pair of lions with the device of a tiny running man between, on a piece of bronze that is not the usual shape but a simple oblong.

Noicattaro [3]—It is interesting to find a bronze of this class in Italy. The example in question comes from Tomb IV at Noicattaro, together with vases of local Apulian ware, some Corinthian vases, fragments of a fine bronze shield, a bronze oinochoe, and a bronze belt ornamented with racing chariots in relief. The Argivo-Corinthian relief deserves attention and it is comparatively little known. It has been cut in two in ancient times. At the top is a palmette, with a plait dividing it from the top panel. All other borders are of egg-moulding. In the panels, which are arranged vertically, are the usual mythological scenes and heraldic animals.

The bronze strips with animal groups and formal patterns, to which we are not applying the term Argivo-Corinthian,[4] can be more briefly described.

The fragments from *Orchomenos*,[5] on which are griffins

---

[1] *Aegina*, pp. 392 ff., Pls. 313, 314. At Aegina.

[2] Exception : the chariot seen from the front on Pl. 113, No. 10, which has an egg-moulding at the sides.

[3] Gervasio, *Bronzi Arcaici . . . nel museo di Bari*, pp. 119, 159, Pl. XVII *Ath. Mit.*, 1927, Pl. IV.

[4] Many of these are included in de Ridder's list, *op. cit. passim*, including the Orchomenos fragments. The Argivo-Corinthian reliefs were imitated in Etruria : see Schumacher, *Beschreibung der Bronzen zu Karlsruhe*, p. 47, No 268.

[5] *B.C.H.*, 1895, pp. 219 ff. At Athens.

sirens, a bearded sphinx and a facing chariot, are interesting because they look like the work of a local and inferior artist. I think his proper trade was decorating terra-cotta pithoi with stamped designs, for in the field of one of the bronzes are two little scrolls such as are often found on the pithoi.

Several quadrangular bronzes with heraldic lions come from Athens.[1] In some cases, a minute human figure or scorpion is seen between them. Another comes from Eleutherae, on the road from Athens to Thebes.[2] Here, too, were found a number of strips [3] ornamented with lotus, plaits, rosettes and other conventional patterns, but these are occasionally combined with sphinxes, formal running figures or Gorgons' heads. The plait, rosette and lotus patterns appear in the same form on fragments of diadems from Thebes,[4] the Ptoön [5] and Corinth,[6] and on more or less complete diadems recorded as coming from Boeotia.[7]

The above account will have shewn (a) how close are the links between the true Argivo-Corinthian reliefs on the one hand and the diadems on the other, and (b) how many specimens come from Boeotia.

Many convincing arguments have been put forward in favour of assigning the Argivo-Corinthian reliefs to the North-East Peloponnese, to Corinth, or Argos.[8] In the first place, there is the Argive inscription on the Olympia fragments. In the second, there are parallels, though not, of course, an exact correspondence, between the reliefs and Corinthian pottery. Finally, Corinth was the chief factory for mirrors, and several of the reliefs decorate mirror handles. It was also the original home of the chest of Kypselos,[9] and the panel reliefs may have decorated chests.

The rival theory [10] placed the industry at Chalkis and considered the reliefs to be Ionic. The fact that so many have

---

[1] *J.H.S.*, XIII, p. 256. At Athens.
[2] At Athens ; de Ridder, *op. cit.*, No. 35.
[3] In the British Museum.   [4] *Anz.*, 1891, pp. 124, 125.
[5] Athens, unexhibited fragments.   [6] *Anz.*, 1894, pp. 116, 117.
[7] Athens, 7830-7835 ; 'Εφ. 'Αρχ., 1892, Pl. 12.
[8] See Furtwängler, *Kleine Schriften*, I, p. 428 ; and Beazley, *C.A.H.*, IV, p. 593.
[9] Which was, of course, decorated in other materials. See, however, *Ath. Mit.*, 1927, p. 1.
[10] De Ridder, *De Ectypis quibusdam Aeneis*.

been found in Boeotia would support this view. The Argive lambda is, however, not easily disposed of.

For the reliefs with mythological scenes, a North-Eastern Peloponnesian origin seems almost certain. The name Argivo-Corinthian can, therefore, be safely used. The stripes with formal patterns and some of the strips with animals have, however, been found in such large quantities in Boeotia that I am inclined to believe many were made there. Boeotia has every claim to have been a centre for bronze-work in both the Geometric and the Archaic Period. This view would imply that the same style was current in Boeotia and the North-East Pelo-ponnese, or rather, that Boeotian artists copied the work of Peloponnesian artists. A very similar problem is presented by the fibulae of the Geometric Period, of which some are ap-parently Argive, some Boeotian.

The question of date is a less difficult one : the fragments, as has long been pointed out, are not all of one date, and can be roughly assigned to the second and third quarters of the sixth century. Like much archaic work, they are remarkably finished and conventional. The hands that made the figures of youths, old men and monsters with such facility must have had years of practice.

Close enough to the Argivo-Corinthian group to have been, at one time, attributed to it is the winged figure in a chariot from the Acropolis (Pl. 42 *b*),[1] one of the finest reliefs produced at any period.

It was probably made at Athens and belongs to the later part of the century. A large percentage of gold or silver is mixed with the bronze.

Nothing could be more lovely than the delicate work on the horses' heads ; the relief is low, yet allows for variety of con-tour ; the rendering of mouth and nostril is only surpassed by the Parthenon frieze. The driver, with magnificent spreading wings, is either Eos or Nike ; either would be worthy of such a team.

II. OTHER RELIEFS—A different type of relief, but scarcely less beautiful, appears on the helmet from Axos in Crete de-

---

[1] *J.H.S.*, XIII, p. 255, Pl. VIII ; Athens, 6958 ; ht., ·068 m.

scribed in Chapter III and attributed to the first half of the sixth century (Pl. 42 a). Here, too, are winged horses, but the effect is gained by elimination rather than by elaboration of detail. Similar horses, heraldically arranged, decorate three of the *mitrai* from Axos : these *mitrai* and the helmet obviously come from the same workshop, and represent the later stages of Cretan decorative art.

Large reliefs are few, for they perish easily, and in ancient times were always in danger of the melting-pot when out of date. One of the most complete examples is the tapering relief from Olympia with the winged Artemis [1] which has been given an undeserved prominence in most text-books. It belongs to the later part of the sixth century, and may have formed part of a *thymiaterion* with three sides narrowing towards the top and three feet. The workmanship is undistinguished.

III. ETRUSCAN RELIEFS—Our study of sixth century Etruscan relief work has been handicapped by the tendency to attribute certain important bronzes to Ionia. There are, of course, many points in common between Ionic and Etruscan works of art : both have a liking for full, rounded forms, and both affect certain mannerisms of dress. This is due to the fact that Etruria was under Ionic influence : many objects were exported, and a number of artists migrated from Ionia to the west. Thus, there are three classes of work which may easily become confused : Ionic reliefs, reliefs by Ionic artists working in Italy for Etruscan patrons, and reliefs by Etruscan artists. The boundaries between these classes are like the frontiers of the Balkan states : they shift constantly in the vain endeavour to accommodate a mixed population and to satisfy the experts. We may, however, hope for a satisfactory settlement, since one has already been reached in the field of ceramics, where the same confusion once existed.

The examples of Etruscan relief described below—The Monteleone chariot, the fragments from Perugia, and the Loeb tripods—have all been at one time considered Ionic, but are now recognised by most scholars as Etruscan.

The finest surviving example of Etruscan relief work is,

[1] *Olympia*, IV, No. 696, Pl. XXXVIII.

perhaps, the Monteleone chariot (Pl. 49 a).[1] Modern criticism
has recognised its true origin, though as recently as 1905 well-
known critics attributed it to Ionian artists resident in Etruria.
It has the additional distinction of being one of the largest
monuments in bronze relief surviving from classical antiquity,
and the only complete ancient chariot from this part of the
world.

It was discovered in a tomb near Monteleone in 1902, on
the ancient Via Cassia. Subsequently it vanished out of Italy,
arrived in Paris in a fragmentary condition, and was bought by
the Metropolitan Museum, New York. Here, the bronze plates
were skilfully put together on a new wooden foundation.[2]

The bronze is thin ; the reliefs are in repoussé work, and in
places very high. Much care has been expended in chasing
and incising details such as the hair and the patterns on the
drapery. Eyes were inlaid, even the eyes of the lion and Gorgon
which decorate one of the shields, likewise the Gorgon's tongue.
Some fragments of ivory inlay which may have bordered the
inner rim of the central panel still exist. Where the green
patina has been removed, the bronze shews a particularly
bright golden colour.

With the chariot were found a number of bronze vessels,[3]
some iron objects and some pottery vases ; two of these were
Attic cups of the Kleinmeister type and served to date the
tomb in the second half of the sixth century.

The panels from the front and the two sides of the chariot [4]
are illustrated on Pl. 49 and need, therefore, no detailed description. Between the panels stand naked youths ; below the
central panel are two couchant rams and two lions : all are in
high relief.

A frieze in low relief originally ran below the panels : part
of this has been lost, but on the surviving parts can be seen a
centaur, a winged figure, a youth and a panther, a lion killing

[1] New York, No. 40 ; Catalogue, pp. 17 ff., from which the following
measurements are taken : total height of chariot, 1·309 m. ; front, ·845 m.
× ·502 m. ; sides, ·47 m. × ·375 m. An exhaustive description and complete
bibliography are given in the Met. Mus. Cat., loc. cit.
[2] Enough of the original foundation remains to shew that it was walnut.
[3] Met. Mus. Cat., pp. 177-180.
[4] For discussion of the type of chariot, see Met. Mus. Cat., loc. cit. The
small size of the chariot suggests that it was used for racing.

a bull and a lion killing a stag. Lion heads are fixed at the ends of the axles, and the fore-part of a boar at the end of the pole. At the upper end of the pole is an eagle's head, and the yoke appears to have been finished with the head of a lion.

For the interpretation of the reliefs on the panels, various theories have been put forward. One [1] would explain the scenes as illustrations of the life of the departed and heroised warrior : in the central panel, his wife hands him his armour, while the birds stand for a favourable omen ; in the left-hand panel, he vanquishes his enemy ; in the panel on the right, he mounts to Heaven in a winged chariot. Another theory [2] connects the figures with events in the life of Achilles. The most probable view,[3] however, is that all the scenes came from the stock repertory of the Etruscan artist, who had learned them and adapted them from imported Greek vases and other monuments.

The reliefs from Perugia [4] are slightly later in date, but more bizarre in style. They are believed to come, not from a chariot of the usual type, but from a four-wheeled carriage. Space does not permit a discussion of the reconstruction of all the fragments : it is enough to say that the relief on Pl. 49 c appears to come from one of the longer sides. The scale of the figures is altered to fit the space ; where a higher space has to be filled, a taller figure is made. On the left, a hunting scene is tucked into the corner among the scroll-work ; in the centre are two monsters, a sea-horse, and the Old Man of the Sea. On the right are two men (heads restored) who advance to kill a centaur.

These reliefs, too, have been attributed to Ionic artists settled in Etruria : [5] they are, however, so completely Etruscan in style that it seems unnecessary to attribute them to any other nationality.

Three tripods from the Loeb collection,[6] said to have been

[1] Furtwängler, *Kleine Schriften*, II, 322 ff.
[2] Ducati, *Jahreshefte*, XII, pp. 74 ff.
[3] G. M. Richter, *Met. Mus. Cat.*, pp. 20 ff.
[4] Perugia and Munich (Glyptothek) ; *Antike Denkmäler*, II, Pl. 15 ; *Röm. Mit.*, 1894, p. 256 ; Furtwängler, *op. cit.*, p. 331, Pls. 33, 34 ; Ducati, *Storia*, Pl. 107, Figs. 284, 285, p. 278. The illustrated fragment is 1·11 m. long.
[5] Furtwängler, text to Brunn Bruckmann, *Denkmäler*, Pls. 586, 587.
[6] Now at Munich, on loan ; *A.J.A.*, 1908, pp. 287 ff., Pls. VIII-XVIII ; *C.A.H.*, IV, pp. 595, 600.

found near Perugia, reflect Ionic models even more closely than the Perugia reliefs and the Monteleone chariot. They take the form of three-sided supports resting on three feet : the bowls which they carried have, in two cases, been restored from fragments, and lions and sphinxes replaced round the rim. All three tripods seem to be from the same workshop, but slight differences of style suggest they were by different hands.

Pl. 50 shews one side of tripod B [1] : in the top panel, Herakles strangles the Nemean lion ; in the second, Peleus, supported by Hermes, catches Thetis by the arm ; in the bottom panel, Apollo kills Tityos, who sinks to the ground supported by Ge.

This and the remaining panels give some impression of lost Ionic metal-work, but the weaknesses of Ionic art—its want of sharpness and disregard of anatomical detail—are exaggerated by the Etruscan imitator.

B. FIGURES CUT OUT FROM A SHEET OF BRONZE

Open-work figures, such as those of the Cretan style described in Chapter III, are rarer than one would expect. The best known and finest is an archer from Olympia (Pl. 43 a),[2] evidently one of a series which were fixed on to a background of another material. The bronze frame which surrounded him, and of which portions survive, has a different moulding on the right-hand side from that on the left. This shews that on the left there must have been another similar panel, probably several. What object they decorated is uncertain. Our archer's dress is somewhat barbaric : he wears a tunic without folds, and high boots. He may represent Herakles. The date will be somewhere in the second half of the sixth century.

Other open-work figures exist which may have served as devices for shields ; [3] many, however, are too small for such a purpose. Of the latter, the most interesting are a ram with Odysseus bound beneath him, and Eurystheus hiding in a jar, both from Delphi.[4] Several sites [5] have produced inferior

---

[1] Ht., c. ·438 m.
[2] *Olympia*, IV, No. 717, Pl. XL ; ht., ·53 m.   [3] *Ibid.*, p. 108.
[4] *Fouilles de Delphes*, V, p. 125, Figs. 468, 469.
[5] E.g. Orchomenos, *B.C.H.*, 1895, p. 218, and some fragments in the Nat. Mus., Athens, from Boeotia, Nos. 13,194. 13,195. 13,196.

examples of this class, roughly cut from a sheet of bronze, sometimes finished off with a few engraved details. They were, apparently, nailed up in the sanctuary, for they have either holes for nails or remains of the nail itself, and they must have been the gifts of the very poor. We are reminded of the small metal placques and figures that hang in modern Greek churches. Some, such as the rough silhouettes of horses from Olympia,[1] shew no trace of attachment—an even cheaper form of dedication.

C. GREEK AND ETRUSCAN MIRRORS [2]

A mirror as known to the people of Greece and Etruria was a polished disc of bronze,[3] usually concave. Curiously enough, this simple invention is not common to every age, and there were periods when the Greek ladies managed to exist without mirrors. This was the case with the Minoans till the sixteenth century and with the Greeks till the beginning of the sixth.

When mirrors were introduced, probably from Egypt, they became at once objects of art. Handle, back or rim were used for decoration. At first they were not made in large numbers : a few survive which belong to the first half of the sixth century, more which belong to the middle decades. Then, towards the end of the century, the demand increased, both in the foreign and home markets. Mirrors were exported to Italy, and Etruscan artists copied them or adapted them to suit the taste of their clients.

The classes into which archaic Greek mirrors can be divided are as follows :—

GREEK MIRRORS—I *a. Mirrors with handles : Peloponnesian type*—One type of mirror has a flat, rather broad handle, expanded into a small disc at the lower end. In the centre of this disc is a hole which would enable the mirror to be hung up easily. Sometimes there was an incised decoration round the hole and on the handle : sometimes the handle was inscribed.[4]

[1] Nos. 731, 732, Pl. XLI.

[2] For bibliography, see *Met. Mus. Cat.*, p. 251. A good article is in Daremberg and Saglio, s.v. *Speculum*.

[3] Mirrors were usually of bronze, occasionally of silver, sometimes of bronze silvered or gilt.

[4] Waldstein, *Argive Heraeum*, Pl. XCVI, No. 1581.

Such mirrors occurred in large numbers at the Argive Heraeum,[1] as well as other Peloponnesian sites [2] (see Chapter VI, Fig. 2) : some had evidently been used, while others were too small for any but votive purposes. Their shape is very like that of the mirrors of the Argivo-Corinthian class, which are a more elaborate development.

I b. *Mirrors with handles, Peloponnesian type, Argivo-Corinthian style*—This style is a more complex version of the " Peloponnesian mirrors " described above. The large reflecting disc and the handle were cast in one piece, and reliefs in the Argivo-Corinthian manner were affixed with lead to the surface of the handle. The shape shewn on Pl. 44 c is typical except for a small tang at the end which has been broken off : the decoration is divided into three parts : the square adjoining the rim, the oblong below it and the medallion at the end.

The best-known mirror, now at Berlin,[3] has lost all decorations save that on the square. Here is an illustration of the ransoming of Hector, very like the Olympia relief (p. 114), belonging to the middle of the sixth century.

Another example, also at Berlin,[4] consists of a handle only (Pl. 44 c). It is decorated above with a sphinx, in the middle with a bearded man, and, on the medallion, with a bird, in the typically Argivo-Corinthian manner.

A third,[5] with the disc preserved, shews two sphinxes, a youth, and, on the medallion, a Gorgon's head.

Three more ... Athens, deserve mention, since they come from known sites : two of them were found at Corinth,[6] one at Eretria.[7]

In studying museums, one should look out for undecorated examples of this class. The applied reliefs detach themselves easily, leaving an apparently plain mirror which may escape publication. There is one such mirror in the Fitzwilliam Museum, several at Athens.

[1] Waldstein, *op. cit.*, Pls. XCIII-XCV.
[2] E.g. Sparta, from the recent excavations (Woodward, *Excavations at Sparta*, pp. 271-273, Fig. 6), and Arcadia, Kotilon ; ('Εφ. 'Αρχ., 1903, p. 174).
[3] Berlin, 8099 ; Furtwängler, *Kleine Schriften*, I, p. 422.
[4] Berlin, 8629 ; *Anz.*, 1904, p. 22. " From Greece."
[5] Berlin, 8373 ; *Anz.*, 1893, p. 97.
[6] Athens, 7686, 7691 ; de Ridder, p. 31.
[7] Athens, 12,439.

I *c. Exceptional type*—A mirror from Corinth in the Louvre [1] has a handle in the shape of a figure, but a figure which, unlike those of class 3, cannot be used as a stand (Pl. 44 *a*). An archaic Athena is represented holding a wreath, and the style is like that of the lead figurines from Sparta. The date is the first half of the sixth century.

II. *Mirrors with tangs*—These mirrors consist of a disc, and a bronze tang that could be inserted into a handle of another material. Often an ornament—a palmette, flower or siren—was inserted between tang and disc. The examples illustrated in this book belong, however, to the fifth century.

III. *Mirrors with stands*—Here the handle serves as a stand, having a base which enables the mirror to be placed upright on a shelf or table.

Some of the stands are in the form of a *column :* a fifth century mirror with a columnar support is illustrated on Pl. 60.

The largest class, however, has the support in the form of a human figure. This type appears to have been introduced into Greece from Egypt in the first half of the sixth century.[2] At first only a few examples were made, but it became increasingly popular, was the favourite before the end of the century, and remained so till about 450 B.C.

One isolated mirror and one group will be described here. The former [3] belongs to the first half of the century and represents a naked woman with a small waist, long side curls and eyeballs hollowed for inlay (Pl. 27 *b*). She can be connected with certain figures from Lakonia : a supporting figure in Lakonian marble from Olympia,[4] and some terra-cottas from the Orthia site.[5] She is said to come from the Peloponnese and probably was made at Sparta.

The group begins about 560 B.C. and lasts some forty or fifty years. To it belong the following five mirror supports, all of which represent naked women. They are broad in the

---

[1] No. 1684, de Ridder, *Catalogue*, Pl. 76. On the dress of the goddess are engraved a flying eagle and a cock; ht. of figure, ·162 m.

[2] *Jahreshefte*, 1912, pp. 245 ff.

[3] Athens, 7540, ht. ·115 m.; de Ridder, No. 879, Pl. III, 2. Other refs., *Jahreshefte*, 1912, p. 226.

[4] *Olympia*, III, Pl. V, 4, 5 ; *Jahreshefte*, *loc. cit.*

[5] *B.S.A.*, XIV, p. 59, Fig. 4.

shoulder ; their waists are barely marked ; they usually have
side curls in front of each ear, wear amulets and play musical
instruments.[1]

  (i) At Athens.[2] From Amyklae. Woman playing casta-
       nettes.
  (ii) At Berlin.[3] From Vonitsa. Woman holding casta-
       nettes.
  (iii) At Vienna. From Nemea.[4] Woman holding uncertain
       attributes (Pl. 27 a).
  (iv) At New York.[5] From Cyprus.
  (v) At Munich. From Hermione.[6]

The provenance suggests the Peloponnese, the style, Sparta
(see p. 90), though it differs from the style of the earlier Spartan
mirror described above. There are, of course, differences between the members of our group. The examples from Amyklae
and Vonitsa lack finish ; a strong likeness exists between the
figures from Nemea and Cyprus ; the mirror from Hermione at
Munich attracts attention by its curiously un-Greek effect.

Allied rather by subject than by style, is a mirror from a
grave in Aegina.[7] A girl, naked save for a loin-cloth, supports
an Ionic capital on her head : above the capital is the disc of
the mirror. The most interesting feature of the mirror is the
tortoise on which she stands : the tortoise is, of course, the
device on Aeginetan coins, besides being sacred to Aphrodite.
Evidently, the mirror was made in Aegina, or expressly for the
Aeginetan market.

---

[1] *Jahreshefte*, 1912, pp. 219 ff., and *Jahreshefte*, 1915, p. 57 ; Langlotz
(Sparta), Nos. 11, 12, 13, 17, 18, pp. 86, 87, 91 ff. See *Jahreshefte*, 1912, for
other possible examples. A fresh addition to the series appears in *J.H.S.*,
1927, p. 242, Fig. 2, and will be discussed in *B.S.A.*, XXVIII.
   [2] Athens, 7548 ; Staïs, p. 308 ; Langlotz, Pl. 44 c.; *Jahreshefte*, 1912,
p. 229.
   [3] Berlin, 10,820 ; *Jahreshefte*, 1915 (XVIII), p. 57.
   [4] Vienna, 926 (2925) ; *Jahreshefte*, 1912, pp. 219 ff., Fig. 146 and Pl. V ;
ht., ·17 m.
   [5] New York, 28 ; *Catalogue*, p. 13 ; *Jahreshefte*, 1912, p. 222, Fig. 148 ;
Langlotz, Pl. 46.
   [6] *Jahreshefte*, 1912, p. 231, Fig. 152. The figure in Dresden from Caere,
Jahreshefte, 1912, p. 227, Fig. 150, is Etruscan.
   [7] Athens, 7703 ; Neugebauer, Pl. 26, p. 46, ht., ·137 m., considers there
was originally a base below the tortoise so that the figure could be stood
upright.

The motive of the naked woman may have been derived, like the mirrors themselves, from Egypt,[1] where parallels occur : more probably, it is at home in Sparta, and associated with the cult of Artemis Orthia.[2] Could we be satisfied that the inscription on a naked female figure in the Louvre reads : " I am a priestess," [3] we should be more sure of our ground.

The orthodox support—that which has been mentioned above as the type that became the favourite at the end of the century—has a draped female figure (Aphrodite or mortal ?) standing on a base which is often made to imitate a stool. Above either shoulder are two hovering figures, usually Erotes, sometimes animals, such as sphinxes. The dress and face of the figures vary considerably.

Very few examples can be dated before 500 B.C., though a number appear to have been made about that date.[4]

The chief centre for their manufacture was, no doubt, Corinth. This city was famed for its bronze-work and produced quantities of mirrors in the late fifth and fourth centuries. Neighbouring states,[5] such as Sikyon, Argos and Aegina, competed, and copies were made in more remote districts as soon as the popularity of the type was assured.

ETRUSCAN MIRRORS—The usual form is a disc with a tang which could be inserted into a handle of another material : the practice of casting disc and handle together did not, at first, appeal to the Etruscans. The mirrors are generally thicker towards the rim than those made by the Greeks, and have incised designs on the concave, i.e. the unpolished surface. Very rarely, the incised designs are replaced by designs in relief.

The archaic Etruscan mirrors are not, however, very early ; the earliest appear to have been made towards the end of the century. At the turn of the century the number increased, a fact which we can attribute to the influence of imported red-figure cups. An examination of the mirrors shews that their

---

[1] *Jahreshefte*, 1912, p. 245.   [2] Langlotz, p. 91.
[3] *Jahreshefte*, 1912, pp. 251, 252.
[4] E.g. Louvre, 1688 (Langlotz, Pl. 18 *c*), and mirrors in Petrograd and Boston (Langlotz, Pl. 54 *a* and *b*).
[5] See Langlotz, *passim*.

9

makers were indebted to the cup-painters for devices to fill the circular space : the Etruscans, however, often simplified their task by putting an exergue below the figures.   In one group of archaic mirrors, the exergue is always filled by an arrangement of dolphins.[1]   The figures are nearly always surrounded by a wreath, usually of ivy.

The mirror selected for illustration comes from Chiusi, and is now in the British Museum (Fig. 4).[2]   It may be dated about 500 B.C.   Within an ivy wreath are a woman and a naked boy, either Aphrodite and Eros, or a pair of ordinary mortals. He holds her mirror in one hand, a pomegranate in the other : she offers him a flower to smell : their little dog jumps up to greet the boy, and in the foreground, the exergue of the picture, are their cat (?) and hen.

FIG. 4.—Etruscan mirror in the British Museum.

The finest of the rare mirrors with decoration in low relief is in the British Museum.[3]   Herakles (Herecele) carries off a woman called Malache (Mlacuch).   Both in style and subject we can detect the influence of painters like Euthymides : but this influence cannot have reached Etruria immediately, and the mirrors should, perhaps, be dated beyond the limit of this chapter, in the early years of the fifth century.

[1] Ducati, *Röm. Mit.*, 1912, p. 256.

[2] B.M., 546 ; diam., ·127 m. ; Gerhard, Klügmann and Körte, *Etruskische Spiegel*, V, Pl. 14.

[3] Walters, *Catalogue*, No. 542, Pl. XVIII ; diam., ·177 ; for other mirrors in relief, see *Röm. Mit.*, 1912, pp. 258 ff.

D. PATERAE

This term is conventionally used to describe shallow pans, which, in the archaic period and occasionally in the later periods, have human figures as handles.

The " paterae " have much in common with the mirrors, for the pan is round like the mirror-disc, and the naked youths who serve as handles are the counterpart of the female mirror supports. Moreover, though in theory the youth holds the pan on his raised hands, and the girl balances the mirror-disc on her head, occasionally helping herself with her hands, in practice an extra member is inserted between figure and rim. This member may be a plain bar or a palmette more or less complicated.

One important difference between " paterae " and mirrors is that the latter are meant to stand upright, the former to be hung up or rested on the table. Therefore, there is no stand beneath the youth's feet, but often a ram's head or palmette. Another difference is that figures belonging to the " paterae " are less well made and less various than those belonging to the mirrors. The youths are often carelessly modelled, and between all of them there is a superficial likeness. A typical example is shewn on Pl. 44 _d_.[1]

E. TRIPODS

The tripods of the sixth century are a more ornate version of those seventh century tripods described on p. 71. The seventh century used its ornaments sparingly : the sixth was prodigal. They appear in numbers on the lower and upper rings, in the spaces at the upper junctions of the lateral supports, and, most important of all, at the tops of the main supports. The consequence was that the bowl could no longer rest on the upper ring, now occupied with crouching animals, horses' heads and other devices : an extra member had to be inserted.

This modified to some extent the shape. Another alteration, less obvious, is equally important. Whereas the ring used to be carried by the three main supports, those which rise

[1] Cambridge ; ht., ·24 m. From the Wyndham Cook Collection.

straight from the feet of the tripod, it is now borne by the lateral diagonal supports.[1]   In the tripod on Pl. 45 *a*, the palmettes which crown the main supports touch the rim but do not carry it.   This is structurally incorrect.

Pl. 45 *a* shews the well-known tripod from Metaponto in the Berlin Museum.[2]   The tripod is made completely of bronze, belongs to the middle sixth century, and is a fine piece of Ionian work.   Such tripods must have been not uncommon in Greece, but the complete specimens were easily destroyed.   No bowl could rest directly on the rim, and we cannot be sure how it was arranged.

For other tripods, we must turn to Etruria, where bronze antiquities live longer than in Greece.   A particular class is associated with Vulci : the industry will be discussed in connection with Etruscan vases : here we are concerned with the type.   There is general similarity between the examples, but some are more elaborate than others.   Recently, they have been arranged in chronological order,[3] according to the development of the decoration, the simpler first, the most ornate last. The tripod on Pl. 45 *b*, from Vulci, in the British Museum [4] comes near the end of the list.   In the arches formed by the accessory supports is a mesh of perforated bronze-work forming a honeysuckle pattern and finished below by a row of pendants. At the top of the vertical supports, which have no structural use, are Hermes, Thanatos carrying off a miniature Alkestis, and Herakles, figures from the same story, and all in the archaic half-running, half-kneeling attitude.   All tripods of this class are provided with the above-mentioned extra rim, rising above the rim which the legs support ; this is the typical Etruscan form.   The bowl is not a cooking-pot, but a brazier.

Another form of tripod, with human figures for supports, is represented by a female figure from Camarina belonging to the very end of the century.[5]

  [1] Schwendemann, *Jahrbuch*, 1921, p. 106.
  [2] *M.d.L.*, VII, Pl. VIII, p. 305 ; *Jahrbuch*, 1901, p. 65 ; ht., ·735 m.
  [3] Neugebauer, *Anz.*, 1924, pp. 302 ff., which see for bibliography : also Savignoni, *M.d.L.*, VII, p. 277.
  [4] B.M., Bronzes, No. 588, ht., ·66 m.
  [5] *M.d.L.*, XIV, p. 769, Pl. XLVI ; *Jahrbuch*, 1921, p. 138.

F. BRONZE VASES

The study of Greek pottery has now reached a comparatively advanced stage, a stage where we are able to distinguish fabrics, and to assign most fabrics to the district where they were made. The study of bronze vases is, on the other hand, still undeveloped. From time to time, scholars have attempted to sort the material into groups and to attribute these groups to particular towns and districts. Their classification has been much more successful than their attributions.

This is, unfortunately, inevitable, for classification depends on style, while the attribution depends on provenance. The surviving bronze vases are few, but those of which the provenance is known still fewer. Fewest of all are the vases which can, like pottery, be associated with excavation.

Given the nature of the evidence, we cannot expect to have as exact knowledge concerning bronze vases as we have concerning pots. Nevertheless, of late years, much work has been done both in collecting material and in improving the methods of investigation. One result of this work is that Chalkis is no longer considered to be the home of the most conspicuous groups. The theory of a Chalcidian origin had, for nearly half a century, gone unchallenged: there was always a tacit assumption that sufficient literary evidence supported it, and the association of the name Chalkis with χαλκός = copper, created a favourable impression. In a recent article,[1] Neugebauer has shewn that there is no reference in literature to the making of metal vases at Chalkis: nor is there any striking resemblance between the forms of Chalcidian pottery and those of our bronzes.

In place of Chalkis, he regards South Italy as the centre where most of the surviving vases were made. A large proportion of the metal vases that used to be thought Chalcidian he now considers South Italian, probably Tarentine. There is much to support this view: Tarentum is now known to have made bronze vases from the fifth century to Roman times; stylistic evidence connects a number of our metal vases with others which are certainly South Italian,[2] and many

---

[1] *Röm. Mit.*, 1923-24, pp. 341 ff.

[2] Neugebauer, *op. cit.*, p. 417, illustrates a Locrian terra-cotta plaque, shewing metal vases with egg, tongue and rope pattern, which looks like a picture of South Italian local wares.

examples come from Italy, a fact which is suggestive but not conclusive.

It seems, therefore, undeniable that the South Italian colonies produced, among their other works of art, metal vases. At present, however, there is a tendency to attribute to this district more than its proper share. In the following account I propose to examine only the most prominent groups of vases, pointing out, where possible, those that can be claimed for the mother country, and those that appear to me to have been made in the western colonies. Unfortunately, the evidence is often insufficient to justify any attribution. This account is necessarily sketchy. The material that has been studied up to date is but a small proportion of that which exists in museums. We can but hope that, in the course of a few years, the number of groups will have increased and the problems of their origin become less obscure.

It will be noticed that great importance is attached to handles, even when separated from the vase to which they once belonged. This is because so many vases have disappeared, leaving their handles, and sometimes other accessories, to indicate their shape. Most vases are perishable because made from sheet bronze : handles and accessories are durable because made of cast bronze. Students and collectors should be able to identify handles and detect, if possible, what shape of vase they came from.

The following classes are the most important that have been discussed :—

(1) *Hydriae*—An important group of hydriae, belonging to the last quarter [1] of the sixth century, is represented by a vase from Randazzo in Sicily (Pl. 46 b),[2] and another, from Sala Consilina in Lucania.[3] The bodies and necks are of sheet bronze, the rim, handles and foot cast and soldered on.

The Berlin hydria has, for the vertical handle, a youth bending backwards so that his raised hands touch the rim ; by

---

[1] Fölzer, *Die Hydria*, p. 71, dates the class in the second half of the century. The Berlin *Führer durch das Antiquarium* (Bronzen) dates the Randazzo Hydria *c.* 500 B.C. Space does not allow a description of the other types of hydriae belonging to the sixth century.

[2] Berlin, 8467 ; ht., ·46 m. ; Fölzer, *op. cit.*, No. 85 ; *Anz.*, 1925, pp. 197 ff.

[3] Paris, Petit Palais ; ht., ·42 m. ; *Notizie degli Scavi*, 1897, p. 164, Fig. 9 ; Fölzer, 86 ; *Anz.*, 1925, pp. 191 ff.

his shoulders are two lions, by his feet two rams. The finely cut palmette below his feet is distinctive of this class. Notice the decorative rendering of the rams' fleece. On the horizontal handles are swans' heads.

The hydria from Lucania has no human figure on the handle, but a head at its lower junction. A third hydria, like the one in Berlin, was seen by Furtwängler in a private collection at Messina.[1] The vertical handle was, to judge from the description, like that on the Berlin hydria, and the horizontal handles were finished at either end by swans' heads. Another pair of horizontal handles, ending in swans' heads, was found at Olympia,[2] but these are comparatively common and were used for hydriae of various kinds. Parallels to the vertical handle exist in several museums.[3] This class, formerly considered to be Chalcidian, is now attributed to South Italy.[4]

(2) *Craters with Gorgon at base of handle*[5]—The crater on Pl. 47 *a* belongs to the end of the sixth century. Formerly in an English private collection, it is now at Munich. It was said to have come from Rua in Campania, but the existence of such a place as " Rua " is doubtful.

Richness of detail and beauty of form combine to make this one of the finest vases in existence. The delicate patterns below the rim contrast effectively with the heavy beading. No photograph can do justice to the elaborate engraving of the Gorgon's eyes, or to her rows of sharp-pointed teeth, or to the pug-like wrinkles on her nose (Pl. 43 *b*). Observe, too, how her side curls repeat the twist of the beading that edges the handle.

An even more magnificent crater of the same type was discovered, during the last months of the war, in a cemetery north of Lake Ochrida ; [6] that others once existed is proved by the survival of at least three handles in London, Paris, Nîmes and Petrograd.[7] In the Paris handle, there is a

---

[1] *Olympia*, IV, p. 144.   [2] *Ibid.*, Nos. 897, 897 *a*.
[3] Fölzer, *op. cit.*, p. 70 ; Neugebauer ; *R.M.*, 1923-24, p. 344, n. 1.
[4] See Fölzer, *loc. cit.*, and Berlin, *Führer*, p. 68 ; *Anz., loc. cit.*
[5] Refs., *Röm. Mit.*, 1923-24, p. 383. See also *Burlington Fine Arts Exhibition Catalogue*, 1904, Pl. 36. The lowest part of the foot is restored. The foot and the lowest part of the body are a separate piece ; ht. of crater, ·64 m.
[6] Filow and Schorpil, *Die Archaische Nekropole von Trebenischte*, pp. 39 ff., Pls. VII, VIII.
[7] *Röm. Mit.*, 1923-24, pp. 383-390 ; Minns, *Scythians and Greeks*, p. 374, and p. 173, n. 2.

tendency to fuse together the different parts of the Gorgon : no division, for instance, is made between the body and the snakes. Evidently it is a later work.

Two other handles, with pieces of vase attached, shew a still further development. The workshop, wherever it was situated, must have flourished for several decades.

(3) *Jugs* [1]—These are far more common than hydriae, craters or amphorae. It is, therefore, particularly important to be able to assign each type to its own period. The shapes differ : some have a foot, others are footless : some have a trefoil lip, some a round one : some a beaked spout : occasionally, a human figure is used for handle, as on the Randazzo hydria.

A group of four jugs, two found in the Argolid, one at Corinth, and one at Naupaktos (which would import largely from Corinth) may be taken to represent the bronze industry [2] of the North-East Peloponnese, and as a guide for future attributions. Two are decorated, shewing a preference for tongue ornament and plaited bands : two are plain : all are of the type with a trefoil lip.[3]

The theory that bronze vases were produced in this district is supported by the new fifth century hydria at New York, which bears on the lip an Argive inscription, and has, therefore, a strong, though not irresistible claim to local manufacture (see p. 163). Moreover, various points shew that vases and mirrors were often made in the same workshops : mirrors, we know, were made in large quantities in the Argolid and the neighbourhood of Corinth.

(4) *Plates*—One important example must be described (Pl. 47 *b*).[4] It belongs to the latter half of the century and

---

[1] See, for shapes, especially Richter, *Met. Mus. Cat.*, pp. 182-195.

[2] Neugebauer, *Röm. Mit.*, 1923-24, pp. 343 ff.

[3] (i) Athens, 7586. From Corinth (Pl. 46 *a*) ; ht., ·20 m.

(ii) Louvre, 2749, has a tongue pattern on the shoulder, a lion's head and satyr's mask on the handle. From Argolis ; de Ridder, *Catalogue*, Pl. 98 ; *Röm. Mit.*, 1922-23, p. 360.

(iii and iv) Louvre, 2750, also from Argolis, and a jug from Naupaktos, in Berlin, are plain ; but their shape is that of Louvre, 2749, and parallels for their handle, with its rest for the thumb, have been found on a Proto-Corinthian and a Corinthian vase (*Röm. Mit.*, 1923-24, p. 361). Neugebauer attributes Louvre, 2749, to the Argolid, but is inclined to assign the vases with the tongue pattern to South Italy.

[4] Berlin, 10,588 ; diam., ·21 m., with handles, ·28 m. ; *Führer*, p. 38.

comes from Dodona, being covered with the wonderful blue patina which often occurs at this site. The plate was cast, then ornamented with incised patterns : the handles are riveted on. The foreparts of horses are a favourite decoration in the Archaic Period : these, however, are unusually fine. Fragmentary plates of the same pattern, though with minor differences, exist in the British Museum [1] and at Athens.[2]

(5) *Bowls and Urns*—Deep bowls or basins without feet, possessing each a pair of handles, were a favourite object for dedication.[3] As their base is slightly rounded, they need some support : two examples in the Naples Museum [4] rest on bronze rings carried by three feet. Similar rings with feet in the form of claws have been found in Olympia and elsewhere.[5]

There is another kind of footless bowl [6] that was used for holding the ashes of the dead. They are deep, with rims drawn in towards a comparatively small opening : the handles, two or four in number, pass through an attachment which was soldered on to the vessel. These bowls continued in use in the fifth century, and were probably provided with the same kind of stand as the bowls described above.

They were imitated in Italy, without their handles. To the flourishing Greek colony of Kyme, in Campania, we may assign a well-known class of urns, with figures on their lids, some of which were found near Capua. Four fine specimens belong to the British Museum,[7] two to Berlin,[8] one to Munich,[9] and one to Vienna. Round the edge of the lids are figures, usually horsemen : in the middle of three of the four lids is something higher—a standing discobolos, a goddess, a man blowing a horn or carrying a ram, a nymph and satyr. Scythian mounted archers were a favourite subject for the edge : one

---

[1] From the Payne Knight Collection.
[2] Athens, 6673 ; de Ridder (Acropolis), No. 146. Also an inferior, unpublished, example from Velestino.
[3] See *Olympia*, IV, p. 131, No. 825.
[4] Inv. 74,745 and 74,749.
[5] *Olympia*, IV, p. 136, No. 853 ; *Jahrb.*, 1921, p. 99.
[6] *Olympia*, IV, p. 134.
[7] B.M., 558-561. The example on Pl. 48 *a* is B.M., 558 ; ht., ·43 m., from Capua.
[8] Berlin, *Führer*, p. 70, Nos. 6216, 7872.
[9] For the example at Munich, see *Anz.*, 1910, p. 480. See also Sieveking, *Loeb Coll.*, Pl. 35.

archer, detached, is in the Berlin Museum.[1] Some figures are far less provincial in style than the others : compare the Berlin archer with the uncouth men who ride side-saddle on a lid in the British Museum. A tongue pattern is the conventional ornament for the shoulder of the urns, with a decorated band below it : two of these bands are engraved with animals or animals and human figures.[2] All the urns must belong to the very end of the sixth century, say about 500 B.C.

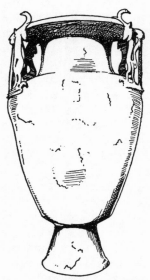

(6) *Cumaean Amphora and Grächwyl Hydria* [3]—These two vases are reproduced on Fig. 5 and Pl. 48 *b*. Both have handles consisting of a group of figures in thinnish bronze : both are now considered to be Italian and to illustrate the strong influence of mainland types on provincial Italian fabrics. The amphora has a conical foot which recalls the late Geometric and early Orientalising pottery of Euboea ; figures on the hydria suggest the early Spartan bronzes, e.g. the type of winged Artemis and the lions.

FIG. 5.—Italian amphora from Cumae.

The above account of sixth century bronze vessels does not claim to be exhaustive. Its purpose is to give some idea of the industry and to shew how Greek taste influenced the taste of the Italian colonies and provinces : unfortunately, there is not space to include those fabrics where the native elements outweigh the Greek. Wherever the bronze vases were made, whether on the Greek mainland or in the Western colonies, they are proof of the activity of Greek trade at this period.

(7) *Etruscan Vases and other Vessels*—We have had occasion

[1] Neugebauer, Pl. 33.　　　　　　　　　　　[2] Berlin, 6216 ; B.M., 560.
[3] *Röm. Mit., loc. cit.*, p. 402. For the amphora, see *Mon. dei Lincei*, XXII, 1913, p. 561, Pl. LXXVI, 3 ; ht., ·535. For the hydria, Déchelette, *op. cit.*, II, 2, 782, Figs. 305-6, Pl. VIII ; *Anz.*, 1925, pp. 183 ff. At Berne.

(p. 111) to refer to the two bronze industries that can be distinguished in sixth century Etruria. One was Perugia, the other Vulci.[1] The Perugia chariot has already been described. Its style is very distinctive. Other finds from the same district have certain characteristics in common, a fact which points to their having been made locally.

The key to the industry of Vulci is given by the bronze tripods already mentioned.[2] There are nine complete tripods, and several fragments. The former were all found at Vulci and presumably made there. Of the fragments, one was found on the Acropolis ; [3] we cannot tell if its presence is due to the respect of an Etruscan for the site, or merely to his commercial enterprise in selling a tripod at Athens.

A number of objects can be connected stylistically with the Vulci tripods.[4] There is a *thymiaterion* at Mainz, with open-work figures standing on scrolls between the legs, very like the figures and scrolls on the tripods.[5] There is a lamp in the Louvre [6] with little sirens who sit on the edge, like the sirens on the ring between the legs of some of the tripods. Collectors should look out for these creatures : they can sometimes be procured separately. There is, finally, a type of handle finished by a group of open-work figures on scrolls : it is well illustrated by handles in Trier, Berlin and elsewhere, also by a pair affixed to an alien cup in the Vatican.[7]

From this it appears that Vulci produced bronze vases, strongly resembling those from Greece. It is to be hoped that in time we shall be able to discern the products of some of the other Etruscan cities. Chiusi will, no doubt, be shewn to have played an important part.[8]

Certain bowls and dishes endear themselves to us by the figures on their rims and handles. A basin at Florence, from the district of Chiusi,[9] has three lively satyrs perched on its rim ; one in the British Museum has a man and woman reclining on each of the two handles.[10] The type is not uncommon.

[1] Neugebauer, p. 94 ; Berlin, *Führer*, p. 28 ; *Anz.*, 1923, pp. 302 ff.
[2] See p. 132.
[3] Athens, 6511 ; de Ridder, No. 760, Pl. V.
[4] Neugebauer ; *Anz.*, 1923, pp. 302 ff.
[5] *Anz., loc. cit.*   [6] *Ibid. ;* Louvre, No. 3142, Pl. 111.
[7] Refs. *Anz.*, 1923, pp. 316 ff.   [8] Neugebauer, p. 94.
[9] Florence. See Ducati, *Storia*, Pl. 107, Fig. 310, p. 289.
[10] B.M., 562.

On all these objects the Greek influence has left its stamp. Very little, on the other hand, can be traced in the one-handled vase, illustrated on Pl. 49 *b*, from a tomb at Capodimonte, and now at Florence.[1] The rim is marked with beading, the foot with tongue pattern, below the handle is a palmette. One female figure crowns the handle, a lady wearing the Etruscan head-dress (*tutulus*) and shoes, and holding a flower.

Two other women, in repoussé work, adorn the handle. The shape and the application of the figures to the handle [2] both occur in bucchero ware. The shape, moreover, recalls other bronzes of Etruscan origin. The vase is rather attractive, a little barbaric, and typical of Etruscan taste.

G. CANDELABRA

Among the most important products of Etruria are the candelabra, a name usually applied to stands both for candles and for lamps. The former have prongs which would support the candles, the latter a dish for oil on the top of a column which rests on three legs. Both were usually ornamented with figures. Sometimes one or two figures crown the shaft, sometimes animals —frogs or snakes—crawl up the shaft itself : [3] often a figure is inserted at the base of the shaft above the legs, and occasionally part way up the shaft. Closely allied to the candelabra are the incense burners and kottabos stands.[4]

Isolated figures from the tops of candelabra are often found in our museums, with the small, round bases on which they stood : they can, as has been pointed out,[5] easily be confused with figures from the tops of Capua urns, which also stand on round bases.

[1] Ht., ·28 m. ; diam., ·24 ; *Notizie degli Scavi*, 1894, p. 139, Figs. 28, 28 *a*.
[2] *Ibid.*, p. 137, Fig. 26.
[3] See Pl. 83 *a*, Etruscan candelabrum from Vulci, British Museum, 781 ; ht., ·245 m.
[4] Körte, *Das Volumniergrab bei Perugia ;* Daremberg and Saglio, *Dictionnaire*, s.v. Kottabos.
[5] Neugebauer, p. 96.

CHAPTER VI

THE EARLIER FIFTH CENTURY

A. STATUETTES

FOR the first twenty years of the fifth century, bronze statuettes maintained the high standard of the preceding period. During the next thirty years, so many masterpieces were produced and such important innovations made that we may easily ignore signs of approaching decline.

It is convenient to treat separately the statuettes made between 500 and 480 B.C. These include certain well-known figures which are all distinguished from sixth century work by reason of their more mature, more independent style, and are isolated from the great number of fifth century bronzes by their comparative archaism.[1] They are transitional bronzes which may serve as epilogue to the sixth century, or as prologue to the fifth : the second alternative has been chosen here.

I. 500-480 B.C.

The Tübingen Armed Runner (Pl. 51 c) [2] is one of the best bronzes that have survived. Its interpretation puzzled scholars for many years, until the position was recognised [3] as that of a runner in the armed race preparing to start. Originally a shield would have been carried on the left arm : this has been detached and lost. The identification was confirmed by another authority, who pointed out that the position of the feet, rather too close to suit the modern standard, corresponds to the lines marked for the start on blocks surviving in Olympia, Delphi

---

[1] Contemporary, of course, with some of the bronzes described in the last chapter, e.g. Athens, 6445 and 14,922.

[2] Ht., ·164 m.; Neugebauer, Pl. 31. See also *Jahrb.*, 1886, p. 163; 1887, p. 95; 1895, p. 182.

[3] By Hauser, *Jahrb.*, 1895, *loc. cit.*

and Epidauros.[1] Moreover, he published a vase shewing a hoplite ready to start in an attitude almost identical with that of our bronze. The Tübingen runner has much in common with the Aeginetan sculptures : there, too, we get the same combination of rather archaic faces with an advanced rendering of the muscles, and beautiful light, lean forms hidden, as our bronze was once partly hidden, by a shield.[2]

The Apollo from Delphi (Pl. 51 *a*) [3] is another example of a figure where the head is archaic, the body comparatively free. The god is represented in a three-quarter position which should be compared with that of the armed runner : there is more swing, but not the subtle antithesis between the upper part of the body and the lower. Unfortunately, comparison of details is made impossible by the bad surface of the Apollo.

He was once part of a group, where he was shewn struggling for the Delphic tripod with a Herakles, now lost. The earlier interpretation, that he was drawing his bow, does not fit in with the way the arms are held, and would necessitate the insertion of an arrow, for which there is no room in the right hand.

There is not enough evidence for assigning this bronze to any particular school. Like the Tübingen runner, it must belong to the first fifteen years of the fifth century.

A figure of Herakles, in the Bibliothèque Nationale,[4] has attracted attention both because it is a good piece of work, and because it was at one time supposed to imitate a work of Onatas of Aegina.[5] This artist made a Herakles who carried a club and a bow : the object in our Herakles' left hand was explained as a broken bow. Subsequently, the connection with Onatas was discredited,[6] the fragment in the hand considered to be the horn of his adversary Acheloos,[7] the statuette attributed to

[1] *J.H.S.*, XXIII, p. 270 (Gardiner).
[2] Neugebauer, p. 56.
[3] At Delphi; ht., ·22 ; *Fouilles*, V, Pls. V, VI ; Neugebauer, *op. cit.*, p. 58, Pl. 30.
[4] Bibliothèque Nationale, 518 ; ht., 0·135 m. ; Bulle, *Schöne Mensch.*, p. 17, Pl. 27. A curious effect is given by the oxidisation of the little knobs which represent curls : the rendering of the beard is unusual.
[5] Friedrichs, *Berlin's Antike Bildwerke*, 11, 442.
[6] Furtwängler, in Roscher's *Lexikon*, s.v. Herakles, p. 2142.
[7] *Jahreshefte*, 1899, pp. 77 ff.

Attica and associated with Kritios and Nesiotes. This, also, is mere surmise : the style of the Herakles is not decisive.

The Kanephoros from Paestum (Pl. 51 *b*) [1] is to us an intriguing and pleasant work of art : to the donor it was a souvenir of one of her greatest triumphs. Her name was Phillo : she had it inscribed on the base of the figure, where we read : " Phillo, daughter of Charmylidas, to Athena, a tenth." [2] The figure represents a young girl whose right hand originally supported an object she carried on her head, and of which traces are visible. It must have been a basket, the sacred basket carried at festivals by girls to whom the privilege was given. The base is an Ionic capital which must have been attached to a secondary base below.

The bronze shews a combination of old elements with new, and of Doric with Ionic. The stiff position, with the weight equally distributed on both feet, is archaic, and the costume is one that was soon to go out of date. The face, on the other hand, is modelled with a certain freedom and softness. The inscription is in the Doric dialect, but the dress and the rounded contours of the figure are Ionic. Two explanations have been put forward for the presence of the Doric inscription. [3] Either the bronze was made by an artist brought up in the Ionic tradition and the inscription added by some one else ; or the bronze was an attempt to copy the Ionic style on the part of an artist who spoke Doric. The general appearance of the bronze is in favour of the former suggestion. The latter is supported by a fault in the rendering of the drapery : the artist, forgetting that the outer garment was fastened on the shoulder, carried the folds right across from front to back. It is, however, improbable that any Doric copyist should have assimilated so completely the Ionic style. [4] The mixture of archaic and later elements is accounted for by the date : 500-480 B.C.

Another statuette which belongs to the beginning of the

---

[1] Berlin, 7429 ; ht., ·132 m. ; Neugebauer, Pl. 34, p. 64 ; Langlotz, pp. 104, 107.

[2] Τἀθάναι Φιλλὼ Χαρμυλίδα δεκάτα[ν] Inscr. Gr. XIV, p. 179, No. 664.

[3] Neugebauer, p. 65.

[4] Langlotz, p. 107, attributes the bronze to Miletos, and, p. 104, declares the inscription to have been added by another hand.

century—to the first ten or fifteen years—is an Athena Promachos from the Acropolis.[1] She is the best known and also
the finest of the whole series of Promachos figures from this
site, and, like the Kore of Euthydikos, shews how a new generation brought fresh life into the old forms for a short while before
discarding them.

Etruscan art gave as yet no signs of the decadence that
was about to set in. To this period belongs one of the best
Etruscan bronzes in existence, the Ajax stabbing himself, a
dramatic figure, remarkably Greek in style (Pl. 41 b).[2]

II. 480-450 B.C.

The close of the archaic period brought various changes.
In the first place, there was a rapid decrease in the number of
votive bronze statuettes. This decrease is particularly striking
at the larger shrines. The finds from Delphi and Olympia
include comparatively few bronzes that can be dated after 480
B.C., though there is a somewhat larger proportion from the
Acropolis and from Dodona. On the other hand, at minor
shrines, like Mt. Lykaion or Lousoi in Arcadia, the statuettes are
almost as numerous as before. Evidently, there was a change
of fashion in votive offerings that affected the larger sites but
had not yet reached those which were small or remote.[3]

The causes of this change are hard to find, for the fashion
had held its own from the Geometric Period onwards. One
reason, perhaps, is that religion was becoming more of a public,
less of a private concern. Therefore, the rich man and the
successful athlete dedicated expensive and beautiful statues in
the precinct of the god, but the common man, unable to vie
with him, ceased to express his piety in the form of a statuette.
An increase in the number of marble and limestone plaques,
however, corresponds to the decrease in votive bronzes.

---

[1] Athens, 6447 ; ht., ·288 m. ; de Ridder, *Cat. Acrop.*, No. 796 (which
see for references) ; also Collignon, *Histoire de la Sculpture Grecque*, I, p. 352,
Fig. 177 ; and Buschor and Hamann, p. 30. So many illustrations exist that
an extra one seems unnecessary. To the same period belongs Athens, 6504 ;
de Ridder, *Cat. Acrop.*, 784 ; Buschor and Hamann, *loc. cit.*

[2] At Florence ; Ducati, *Storia*, p. 260, Pl. 104, Fig. 278 ; ht., ·085 m.
From some object now lost.

[3] The remoteness of Dodona is, no doubt, the reason why later bronzes
are found there. They are a type of offering easily transported.

Of supporting figures, particularly mirror-supports, there is no lack. These will be used, in this chapter as elsewhere, to supplement our knowledge of the bronzes of the period.

Another change shewed itself in the concentration of the bronze industry in a few large centres, while many towns or districts that had played an important part in the previous century now ceased to be productive.

The most prosperous of the centres were, of course, those in the North-East Peloponnese, particularly Argos and Corinth. Athens also flourished, and promising work was done in the Western Colonies. On the other hand, Sparta gradually closed its workshops, of Crete we hear next to nothing, and, if any bronzes were made in Ionia,[1] they are not distinctive. Arcadia alone, with obstinate detachment and unremitting energy, continued as before.[2]

Argos and Athens were, however, primarily centres for the making of life-sized sculpture, not for the making of small bronzes. The latter was a secondary activity, the consequence of the former. Throughout the century, the influence of the large statues increased, gradually absorbing the individuality of the statuettes. Here, perhaps, we have the chief cause for the statuettes' ultimate decline. In the seventh century they took the lead ; in the sixth, the balance was more or less even ; in the fifth, they became completely subordinate. We feel the same disappointment as when a person, who used to be spontaneous and charming, starts to model himself on some one else he admires.

It is interesting to watch the way in which the little bronzes reflect the style and innovations of the great artists of the period, whose work was rapidly progressing towards the complete emancipation of the human form from archaic rigidity. One artist after another made his contribution. Hagelaidas of Argos had already improved the stance of his figures by placing the weight on one leg, and slightly bending the other,[3] though

[1] Buschor and Hamann, *Olympia*, p. 37, attribute some bronzes to Ionia. See also Langlotz, Pl. 68.

[2] The possibility of local work, allied to the Arcadian, being done in Messenia, has been alluded to on p. 86.

[3] Furtwängler, *Masterpieces*, pp. 49 ff.

10

the soles of both feet still rested heavily on the ground. This was a great advance from those sixth century figures where there was as much weight on the advanced as on the back leg. The effect of shifting the weight should be to raise one shoulder slightly above the other : this, though not always realised by artists at first, ultimately did much to give grace and balance. The head, instead of looking straight forward, was now often bent or turned to one side.

A fresh system was introduced by what is commonly, but incorrectly, called the " walking motive," another discovery of the Argive school, of which the chief exponent was Polykleitos : a pre-Polykleitan example is illustrated on Pl. 52. In these figures, one leg is bent, but behind the other, and the head is usually inclined to the side of the leg on which the weight rests, the arm on the other side being raised. This theme could be varied by changing the position of the arms or the bend of the head. Great artists delighted in making these experiments and the smaller artists were quick to follow their lead. It is not surprising that, towards the end of the fifth century, we get a number of bronzes which are copies of famous originals. They must not be confused with copies of fifth century originals made at a later date.

THE PELOPONNESE : CORINTH, ARGOS AND SIKYON

The Ligourio Bronze. Curiously enough, much of what we know concerning the earlier Argive school, i.e. the school as it was in the first half of the century before Polykleitos, is gained inductively with the help of a certain bronze statuette. The importance of this knowledge, and of our debt to the bronze, cannot be over-estimated.

It was found at Ligourio [1] near Epidauros and represents a young athlete (Pl. 52 a). He stands with his weight on the left foot and his right knee slightly bent : his right arm hangs by his side, his left hand holds an apple or ball. The right shoulder is slightly raised, and the head bent. The position should be noted, as it is repeated in other works.[2] The youth's back hair is rolled over a fillet (omitted) and combed over his

---

[1] Berlin, 8089 ; ht., ·135 m. (without base) ; 50tes *Winckelmannsprogramm*, pp. 125 ff. ; Langlotz, pp. 56, 62.
[2] See Langlotz, p. 62.

forehead in front. Beneath the feet are two projections passing through holes in the base, where they were held in place by small nails. The base itself has four tangs, so that it could be let into another larger base, presumably of a different material. The date is somewhere between 470 and 460 B.C.

The evidence [1] which connects this bronze with the early Argive school is generally accepted. It is as follows :—

The figure was found within a short distance of Argos : it is made of a bronze which resembles in appearance and composition the bronze used for shields which are undoubtedly Argive : it has the bodily characteristics we have learned to associate with Peloponnesian art, affinities with the later Argive statues, and a kinship with certain female figures in bronze and terra-cotta which have every claim to be Argive.[2]

A number of full-sized statues are sufficiently like it, in attitude and proportions, to be considered as belonging to the same school.[3] The best known of these are later copies : the Mantuan Apollo and the athletes of Stephanos and Pasiteles. These reflect original works of the first half of the fifth century. The inference is that the originals were by Argive artists of the school of Hagelaidas, who may be said to have created the type. They should give us enough data to distinguish other Argive works from works by artists from Athens, Aegina and elsewhere.

Some confusion is, however, almost inevitable, since there is a strong family likeness between all statues of the period. Moreover, the pose with the weight on one foot soon becomes common property, and many bronzes shew the influence of more than one school.

Such an one is the New York Discobolos,[4] which, though Peloponnesian, has Attic affinities (Pl. 52 d). The broad shoulders and heavy muscles are typical of the Peloponnese, but the small head and long legs are Attic. There is, indeed, a remarkable likeness between this bronze, which should be dated about 480-75 B.C., and contemporary Attic red-figure vases. Our athlete is represented preparing to throw his

[1] See *20tes Winckelmannsprogramm*, pp. 127, 134 ff.
[2] Langlotz, p. 57.
[3] See Buschor and Hamann, *Olympia*, p. 34.
[4] New York, 78 ; Richter, *Catalogue*, p. 48 ; ht., ·235 m. ; Buschor and Hamann, *op. cit.*, p. 33.

discus : he is in one of the preliminary positions.[1]   The next
stage is shewn by a bronze at Athens from Boeotia,[2] where
both hands raise the disc above his head.

A different type of male figure is represented by a group
recently attributed to Corinth.[3]   It is marked by a supple-
ness of pose, due to the weight being entirely off the free leg,
by neat, close features, and by the way in which the hair is
wound round a fillet.

To illustrate the development of the athletic type in the
second quarter of the century, two bronzes have been selected,
one from the Louvre, one from the British Museum.   Both
have one foot drawn back, a motive which we know from a base
at Olympia by Dionysios [4] of Argos to have been used before
Polykleitos' time.   The Louvre figure (Pl. 52 c) [5] has been
thought to represent Dionysos, to whom the high boots and
fanciful, though at the time not uncommon, style of hair-
dressing would be appropriate.   The study of the muscles is
careful and accurate, especially on the back.   A kantharos
(a goblet with two handles) may be restored in the right hand.[6]

The figure in the British Museum (Pl. 52 b), from Corfu,[7]
illustrates the old motive of the Ligourio figure brought to
perfection and improved by bending the head to the opposite
side.

So far we have examined the development of only one class
of figure, the athletes who are the direct descendants of the
sixth century Kouros.   The repertory of fifth century artists
was large : some subjects were inherited from the previous
generation, some were new.   Among the former was Zeus
striding forward with eagle and thunderbolt.   The statuette
of Hybrisstas (p. 95) shews that the motive was a traditional
one, and serves as a link between the group of Zeus figures
belonging to the fifth century and their remote ancestor, the

---

[1] E. N. Gardiner, *J.H.S.*, XXVII, pp. 21, 36.

[2] Athens, No. 7412 ; Staïs, *Catalogue*, p. 321.

[3] Langlotz, p. 82.   [4] Furtwängler, *Masterpieces*, p. 215.

[5] Louvre, 154 ; ht., 0·225 m.   Said to come from Olympia.   Studniczka,
Kalamis, p. 78, which see for references ; Buschor and Hamann, *op. cit.*,
loc. cit., and Langlotz, pp. 62 ff.

[6] According to Studniczka, *op. cit.* ; Langlotz, p. 64, suggests that the
head comes from a mould of earlier date.

[7] B.M., 213 ; Buschor and Hamann, *op. cit.*, p. 33.

warrior of the Geometric Period. The sudden vogue of the former early in the century (about 500 B.C.) is hard to account for : the Zeus Ithomatas of Hagelaidas, which involves so many problems of dating,[1] must have been its effect rather than its cause. We know what Hagelaidas' statue looked like, not only from the notes of Pausanias but also from fourth century coins of Messene, issued when the Messenians had been re-established by Epaminondas : it belonged to a type familiar from numerous bronze statuettes. One of these, from Olympia,[2] resembles the Zeus on the coins in having the left leg only slightly advanced. The most remarkable statuette is undoubtedly the one from Dodona in Berlin ; [3] here, however, the left leg is advanced much farther (Pl. 54 a). It is impossible, either by illustration or description, to convey an adequate idea of the beauty of this figure. The delicately engraved lines of the hair, the ripple of the muscles on the calves (not true to nature but effective), the modelling of back and chest, the careful rendering of such details as fingers and toes, finally the wonderful blue-green patina, combine to make it one of the finest surviving examples of Greek art.

The same motive, modified by the bending forward of the right upper arm, appears in a number of figures of Herakles swinging his club. The best known is the Herakles, discovered not long ago on Mt. Oeta, and considered contemporary with the Olympia metopes.[4]

One of the stock female types of Peloponnesian art was the figure of a standing woman wearing a heavy woollen dress. We can study it in endless stages and variations, such as the sixth century Artemis, from Lousoi (Pl. 30 b, c), a fifth century Artemis from Tegea (Pl. 57 b), an Athena, once in Naples, belonging to the fourth decade of the fifth century,[5] a woman with a bird from Corfu,[6] and, most of all, in the Corinthian mirrors (p. 161).

[1] Stuart Jones, p. 33. A. B. Cook dates the Zeus Ithomatas c. 455 B.C. (Zeus, II, p. 741).

[2] Olympia, IV, No. 43.

[3] Berlin, 10,561 ; ht., ·138 m. ; Neugebauer, Pl. 28.

[4] Thebes, Buschor and Hamann, op. cit., p. 33 ; Δελτίον, 1919 (supplement), p. 31 (right) ; Langlotz, p. 64.

[5] Furtwängler, Kleine Schriften, 471.

[6] B.C.H., 1891, Pls. IX, X ; Buschor and Hamann, op. cit., p. 34.

In fifth century sculpture, we know it well from the metopes and pediments of the Temple of Zeus at Olympia, and the so-called Hestia Giustiniani and her kin.[1] It was brought to perfection in the small bronze figure of a girl spinning, at Berlin (Pl. 55 b).[2] The spinner, obviously very young, stands with her head half raised as though she had just looked up from her work. Her hair is short, like that of the Lousoi Artemis, of Hippodameia at Olympia, and of many other Peloponnesian girls. Her dress has a girdle at the waist, but this is concealed by the upper part of the garment, which hangs down before and behind in almost symmetrical folds. The right knee is bent, the left hand held the distaff, and the right twisted the thread from which hung the spindle. We can speculate as to how the thread was rendered : probably by a real wire thread which must have passed in front of the breast and shoulder. The eyes were originally filled with silver : the conical base is antique.

This figure shews fifth century art at its best : a certain archaic restraint accentuates its loveliness. Technically, it is imperfect, for the holes on the surface are due, not to the wear of centuries but to original flaws in the casting.[3] Compare those on the Arcadian Pan (p. 153). The base was acquired separately but belongs without doubt. The bronze tangs below the feet fit through holes in the base and into other holes in its lead core. The shape is not common : it may be explained, fancifully, as a representation of an inverted basket, or, more scientifically, as the development of certain mirror supports.[4]

SPARTA was one of the smaller centres which were still active. Most of its fifth century work was of inferior quality, but a few bronzes deserve special mention. One was discovered during the excavations of 1907, and belongs to the first quarter of the fifth century (Pl. 56 c).[5] It probably represents a trumpeter, for the raised right hand and compressed lips

[1] Buschor and Hamann, op. cit., p. 35.
[2] Berlin, 30,082 ; ht., ·167 m., together with base, ·217 m. ; Neugebauer, Pl. 36 ; Wiegand, in 73tes Berl. Winckelmannsprogramm, 1913, pp. 3 ff. ; Anz., 1922, p. 78, No. 29.
[3] Wiegand, however, affirms that these cannot have been visible when the bronze was first made ; op. cit., p. 4.
[4] Wiegand, op. cit., p. 5.
[5] At Sparta ; ht., ·131 ; B.S.A., XIII, p. 146 ; Langlotz, Pl. 50 c, p. 89.

suggest a wind instrument. The chest, too, appears inflated as though for blowing. A plait of hair is wrapped round the head. The forehead recedes more than is usual on figures from the well-known schools of Greek art, and the face is of a type that occurs on sixth century bronzes from Sparta, e.g. some of the mirror supports described on p. 128 with which it is linked by the female figure from Sparta in the Trau Collection.[1] These facts support the view that the bronze was by a local artist.

An inferior fifth century mirror support,[2] also found at Sparta, is interesting on account of its subject. It represents a naked woman, and is, therefore, in one sense, a survival of the group made during the sixth century (see p. 128).

A local origin is less probable for the Diadumenos [3] in Berlin. The youth was engaged in tying a fillet round his hair : the fillet, now lost, must have been of silver. Eyeballs and nipples, too, must have been originally inlaid in another material, and have disappeared. The statuette has also suffered by the bending of the right arm and the left foot. It belongs to the second half of the century.

In ARCADIA, bronzes were still a favourite offering. They appear, as before, at Tegea, at Lousoi, and at the shrines of Pan Nomios and Zeus Lykaios, especially the latter. Tegea has a better claim than any other town to have been their place of origin.

They shew a combination of the old local styles with the new motives evolved by the great Peloponnesian schools : the former preponderate. So short is the journey between the eastern districts of Arcadia and the Argolid, that artistic contact is inevitable. This contact was sufficient to make the Arcadian bronze-workers acquainted with, but not master of, the more advanced technique and freer figures of Hagelaidas or Polykleitos.

The traditions of Arcadian art remain, on the whole, unbroken from the sixth century throughout the fifth. The typical Arcadian bronzes of the sixth century represented peasants, short of body, heavy of head, broad of shoulder. The same style and the same proportions reappear among the

[1] *Jahreshefte*, 1912, p. 235, Fig. 153 ; Langlotz, Pl. 45 *b*.
[2] At Sparta ; *Jahreshefte*, 1912, pp. 238, 239, Fig. 155.
[3] Berlin, 8576 ; *Anz.*, 1904, pp. 33 ff. ; Langlotz, Pl. 36.

fifth century bronzes, though the subject varies. At the same
time, another type of figure was developed, taller, slimmer, and
having more in common with bronzes from the rest of Greece.
It was, however, almost impossible for an Arcadian artist
to make a bronze which could pass as the work of any other
Greek school, for the inhibitions and mannerisms of his own
school were too deeply ingrained. Even if he improved on the
prominent eyes with their clumsily engraved lids, which were
still a common failing ; [1] even if he succeeded in making the
mouth something more than a mere slit, he was liable to
mark the hair with those too deep, too regular cuts which
are noticeable on so many Arcadian bronzes of the period.
Even if he managed to free the figure from that rigidity which
results from the weight resting evenly on both feet, he tended
to forget that, if the weight is on one leg, the corresponding
shoulder must be higher. How unsuccessful his experiments
in new positions could be is shewn by a Hermes from Mt.
Lykaion (p. 153, Pl. 57 b), who cannot bend one knee without
bending both.

A series of female figures deserves mention.[2] They are
women or goddesses, standing stiffly, each draped in a heavy
Doric peplos. It is a type that goes back to the sixth century,
where it is represented by the Lousoi Artemis. In the first half
of the fifth century it was, as we have seen, common not only
in Arcadia but throughout the Peloponnese. Two examples,
said to have been found at Kalavryta, probably come from
Lousoi ; two, at Athens, are from Tegea.

Of the four, an Artemis from Kalavryta, now in Berlin, is
the earliest (Pl. 57 a).[3] She stands on a small base and carries
a torch and a poppy head. Her short hair is bound by a fillet :
her eyes are prominent and almond shaped : her mouth is a
series of ill-drawn grooves. She is the descendant of our sixth
century Artemis : though the folds of her drapery are more
natural, they are still stiff, and both feet are planted firmly
together. Very close in style, though slightly more advanced,
comes the larger of the two figures from Tegea.[4] She also is

---

[1] See *B.S.A.*, XXVII, p. 143.   [2] *Ibid.*, pp. 144, 145.
[3] Berlin, 7644 ; ht., ·131 m. ; Furtwängler, *Kleine Schriften*, II, p. 465,
Figs. 6, 7 ; *B.S.A.*, *loc. cit.*, No. 35 ; Langlotz, p. 54.
[4] Athens, 7605 ; ht., ·106 m. ; *B.S.A.*, *loc. cit.*, No. 36 ; Langlotz, p. 54.

rigid in pose and completely frontal : her proportions, short and thick, are distinctly Arcadian. In one hand is a phiale ; a poppy head should be restored in the other. Like the goddess in Berlin, she has heavy features, almond-shaped eyes and a mouth like a narrow slit, the mouth that had marred the Hybrisstas figure (p. 95). The other statuette from Kalavryta [1] is taller and slenderer, but has the same features, the same costume and short hair.

All three belong to the second quarter of the fifth century. The smaller of the women from Tegea belongs to the second half of the century (Pl. 57 b).[2] For all her daintiness, she is one of the stock types of the period, turned into an Arcadian Artemis by the addition of a poppy head. The folds of the drapery, especially at the neck, are good, for the artist has studied his models well. The hair, on the other hand, is rendered in the manner he learned in the old workshop at home, by means of deep cuts almost parallel with each other. The awkward twist of the feet, making the right foot turn inwards, is, of course, an error ; the effect is that of a pretty peasant girl, shyly and conscientiously taking the part of a great lady.

From the sanctuary of Zeus on Mt. Lykaion comes a familiar Arcadian character, Hermes (Pl. 57 b),[3] which has something in common with the first three female figures mentioned above. One leg is advanced, but both knees are slightly bent : the position is the result of an attempt to copy Argive figures with the weight on one leg only. The Hermes has two other claims to interest : one is his base, about which are the remains of the lead which originally attached it to its mount. The other is his chlamys, which is meant to be of a very thick material : the folds on the back are rather well modelled, and the part that hangs down behind, a thin plate of bronze, implies considerable skill in casting.

Our account of Arcadian bronzes may be concluded by a description of the goat-headed Pan from Lousoi at Berlin (Pl. 54).[4] A creature of the wilds, he stands shading his eyes

[1] B.S.A., loc. cit., No. 37 ; ht., ·165 m. Present whereabouts unknown ; Langlotz, p. 54.

[2] Athens, 7565 ; ht., ·096 m. ; B.S.A., loc. cit., No. 38 ; Langlotz, p. 54.

[3] Athens, 13,219 ; ht., ·125 m. ; B.S.A., loc. cit., No. 31 ; ᾿Εφ. ᾿Αρχ., 1904, Pl. 9 ; Langlotz, pp. 56, 61. "Hermes," rather than a shepherd boy, because of the traces of wings on the boots.

[4] Berlin, 8624 ; ht., ·094 m. ; Neugebauer, Pl. 39, p. 74.

with one hand : the other may have held a pedum or short crook : his right leg is advanced as though he is ready to leap forward.   He has a beautiful fringe of hair down his back : the hair on his body and the eyelashes are most carefully engraved. Much care has also been expended on the modelling of the head, muzzle and hands : between the horns is a hole, in which some ornament could have been inserted.   The surface shews flaws from defective casting : one hole, in the right shoulder, has been filled in, but not the others.   The work is that of a skilled and practised hand, evidently not that of an Arcadian, but nowhere else, save perhaps in the Homeric Hymn to Pan, has the spirit of Arcadia been so fitly embodied.

ATHENS—The Acropolis produced a number of fifth century bronzes, most of which can safely be considered local work. One would expect nearly all of them to belong to that deposit which resulted from the destruction of the site by the Persians, and which contained, therefore, objects prior to 479 B.C.   But, since the stratification in which the bronzes are found was not recorded, and since some of them are distinctly later in style than 479, no fixed limit can be given.[1]   Undoubtedly, many belong to the two first decades of the century, but the decades which followed are also represented.

The Athenian bronze casters had, as we have already pointed out, a tendency to repeat their subjects.   This repetition is not peculiar to Athens, but is naturally conspicuous among finds that have come straight to the site from a workshop in the same town, so that the series from the shops had no chance of getting scattered.   A certain originality of subject is, however, also characteristic : it appears in the bronze figure of a boy on a dolphin,[2] in the dancing girl illustrated on Pl. 53 a, and the fine figure of a giant hurling a stone.[3]

The athlete on Pl. 53 c,[4] a good study of a body in motion, recalls, on the one hand, red-figure vase paintings, on the other, the more archaic youth on Pl. 37.   The position, long mistaken for that of a dancer, is now explained as that of an athlete

---

[1] This is also the view of de Ridder, *Cat. des Bronzes Trouvés sur l'Acropole d'Athènes*, p. 1.

[2] Athens, 6626 ; de Ridder, *Cat. Acrop.*, No. 755.

[3] Athens, 6592 ; de Ridder, *op. cit.*, No. 749.

[4] Athens, 6615 ; ht., ·201 m. ; de Ridder, *op. cit.*, No. 757 ; *J.H.S.*, 1916, p. 16 (which see for references) and Pl. I.   Date c. 480-70.

preparing to throw the discus, which would have been held in the right hand. Compare the New York Discobolos who holds it in his left : both athletes are preparing to take the discus in both hands and, probably, to raise it above the head.[1]

The athlete in the Cabinet des Médailles (Pl. 53 b) [2] is slightly later in date than the Discobolos, and contemporary with the bronze from Ligourio. The Argive and Attic figures form an effective contrast : the latter is more graceful and pleasing but less anatomically correct. His neat, regular features shew him to be own brother to the pretty dancing girl,[3] also from the Acropolis, on Pl. 53 a.

UNKNOWN SCHOOL—The Greek women and the artists who portrayed them were never tired of experimenting with the different effects to be got from the contrast of material. The lighter garment (chiton) of linen shews its more delicate folds to advantage beneath the straight folds of the woollen outer garment or cloak (himation), and the latter could be worn in various ways. We know it best fastened on both shoulders with a flap falling behind and in front, as on the Berlin spinning girl, but the Thessalian lady with a dove (Pl. 55 a) [4] prefers it unfastened and draped round her left arm like a cloak, while her left hand draws the folds together behind her. This shews to advantage its trimming, a band down one side picked out in copper which would contrast with the darker bronze. The fillet was also of copper, and the eyes inlaid with silver, a variety of metals that must have been very effective. Unfortunately, the surface has now been spoiled by the ignorant cleaning of a former possessor. A piece of cloth confines the back hair, giving from behind the impression of concentric circles. Shoes are also worn. The person represented may be Aphrodite or a mortal : the date is the second half of the century : but what district originally produced the statuette is very uncertain. A comparison can be made with a woman supporting a mirror in

[1] *J.H.S.*, XXVII, pp. 17, 18, 36.
[2] Bibliothèque Nationale, 928 ; ht., ·175 m.; Langlotz, Pl. 99, pp. 156, 164, 165.
[3] Athens, 6514 ; de Ridder, *Cat. Acrop.*, 787 ; ht., ·112 m. ; Langlotz, pp. 30, 35, attributes it to Sikyon. Buschor and Hamann, *op. cit.*, p. 30, also attribute to Athens a couple of supporting figures from the Acropolis.
[4] Berlin, 8599 ; ht., ·088 m.; Neugebauer, Pl. 38 ; Buschor and Hamann, *op. cit.*, p. 34. I do not feel convinced the bronze is Peloponnesian, and include it here for convenience.

the British Museum [1] wearing a cloak and chiton rendered in the same style as the costume of the lady from Thessaly.

SOUTH ITALY—The manner in which the Greeks of the west—Sicily and South Italy—treated the nude athletic type is illustrated by a bronze from Aderno in Sicily (Pl. 56 a).[2] It is not such fine work as the Sicilian coins of the period, though it fails in conception rather than in execution. The right hand is raised, and probably held a phiale for pouring libation. The left is also raised, for no apparent purpose. The head bends towards the right shoulder, and the weight is on the right leg. We are at once struck with the resemblance of the statuette to the well-known coin of Selinous, on which the river Hypsas pours libation in token of his delivery from pestilence.[3] The position of the body is the same, that of the arms only slightly different. Both coin and bronze belong to a date between 470 and 455 B.C. The restless movement of the arms seems to be a feature of South Italian art : we find it again in another male figure who served as the support of a mirror.[4] For the rest, attention should be called to the smooth head where no strands of hair are marked, and to the formation of the muscles of the chest.[5] It has been suggested that the figure owes its inspiration to Pythagoras of Rhegium [6] and is the replica of a statue which some victorious athlete from Italy had dedicated in one of the precincts of his mother country.

A worshipper in New York (Pl. 56 b) resembles the athlete from Aderno so closely that it can safely be considered the work of the same school [7] at a slightly earlier date. The New York figure shews the same treatment of muscles and head, and forms a link between the athlete and an isolated bronze head at New York.[8] Not far removed is a mirror support from Locri now in Berlin.[9] Two other supporting figures, in Boston and the

---

[1] B.M., 243, Pl. IV, from Corinth ; Buschor and Hamann, op. cit., p. 34.
[2] At Syracuse ; ht., ·20 m. ; Neugebauer, op. cit., Pl. 37, p. 70 ; Langlotz, Pls. 89, 90, pp. 147 ff.
[3] Hill, Select Greek Coins, Pl. XXXIX, 3.
[4] See p. 157, n. 1.   [5] Described by Langlotz, p. 148.
[6] Langlotz, p. 150.   [7] No. 79 ; Langlotz, Pl. 88, p. 149.
[8] Langlotz, Pl. 93, p. 150.
[9] Anz., 1921, p. 146, Fig. 24 ; Buschor and Hamann, p. 39 (which see for other references).

British Museum respectively [1] supplement but also complicate our knowledge of South Italian art. The figure in the British Museum, which comes from South Italy, reflects the pose of the Sicilian figure, but differs in the rendering of face, hair and muscles.

ETRURIA—We have already pointed out that in Greece, during the fifth century, the bronze industry was less flourishing than during the sixth. In Etruria, the period was one of decadence, as far as statuettes were concerned. A recent writer [2] has called attention to the fact, and suggested that the battle of Cumae and the war between Rome and Veii may be partly responsible. The battle of Cumae would damage trade relations with Greece, the war with Rome would weaken the Etruscan community.

There are very few bronzes belonging to this part of the fifth century that need be described at length.

A type of armed warrior striking downwards with a weapon in his right hand has been already mentioned in connection with the sixth century (p. 108). Many examples were produced during the fifth, of which the best known is in Florence (Pl. 65 b). [3] It is marked by an archaic stiffness of pose and formality of detail : the symmetry of the folds at the edge of the tunic is remarkable. At the same time, the features are in the manner of the fifth century.

The motive is familiar to us from the Geometric warrior (p. 41) and his descendants. Why was it popular in Etruria when it was no longer so in Greece ? Are the figures, like certain Peloponnesian bronzes of the sixth century, dedicated by soldiers on their safe return, and, if so, do they represent the mortal who dedicated them, or the god to whom they were offered ? They used to be called Mars, just as the Kouroi were called Apollo, but the former identification is more reasonable than the latter ; the Etruscan warriors are remarkably like the well-known large statue of Mars from Todi, [4] which is one of the masterpieces of fourth century Etruscan art.

[1] Furtwängler, *Kleine Schriften*, pp. 436 ff., Pls. 45 and 46 (right). The latter = B.M., 514 ; *Catalogue*, Pl. XVI.

[2] Ducati, *Etruria Antica*, II, p. 81.

[3] Ducati, *Storia*, Pl. 103, Fig. 276, pp. 259-60 ; ht., ·33 m. A modern replica is exhibited in the British Museum (No. 455).

[4] Ducati, *Etruria Antica*, Fig. 39.

The Greek Zeus, swinging his thunderbolt, and the Greek Herakles swinging his club, have their counterpart in a series of Etruscan figures of Hercules. The hero usually wears a lion skin over his left arm.[1]

It will be observed that series of figures illustrating the same subject with varying degrees of skill are a feature of all periods in Etruria. When art is vital, as it was in the sixth and fourth centuries, they are less conspicuous : when it is feeble, as now, they flourish.

B. DECORATIVE WORK, VASES, ETC:

FIFTH CENTURY GREEK AND ETRUSCAN MIRRORS—It is convenient to describe all kinds of mirrors in one section, even though some are only made important by the statuettes which support them, and have already been discussed with reference to the districts where they were produced.

The popularity of mirrors with statuettes for stands was at its height in the first half of the fifth century : towards the end of the century they began to be superseded by mirrors with a cover and no support. Mirrors with handles, like those of the present day, never played as large a part in Greece, as they did in Etruria, but occur throughout the century.

Of the *mirrors with handles*, some have a bronze handle cast together with the disc, some merely a bronze tang for insertion into a handle of another material. In mirrors of the latter kind, a graceful ornament sometimes separates tang and disc ; a palmette, a scroll, a siren. The workmanship is often very fine.

Some of the best of these ornaments have been found at Locri Epizephyrii in South Italy.[2] Occasionally part of the tang and rim, and even of the disc, has survived, but the ornament is more solid and less liable to corrosion. It usually consists of scrolls and palmettes exquisitely arranged in various ways : one has below the scrolls a calyx of three spreading leaves ;[3] on the loveliest is a siren, with feathered breast, spreading wings bent downwards, and hair in strands that rise

---

[1] A good example, B.M., 605.

[2] *Notizie degli Scavi* (Supplement), 1913, p. 12, Fig. 12 ; p. 26, Fig. 29 ; p. 31, Fig. 35. A disc with an engraved border is illustrated, p. 40, Fig. 52.

[3] *Loc. cit.*, p. 12, Fig. 12.

from the forehead like flames (Fig. 1).[1] We are reminded thereby of certain coins of Syracuse,[2] later in date but belonging, no doubt, to the same tradition. This mirror had, however, not a tang, but a bronze handle, of which about half survives : a flower is engraved upon it. The disc was originally fastened to the heart-shaped ornament above the siren. All the examples from Locri were probably made in South Italy and shew what a high standard the bronze-workers in that district had attained.

FIG. 1.—Mirror from Locri Epizephyrii.

The siren beneath the mirror on Pl. 60 b [3] is more severe, less dramatic, than the Locrian siren. It should be compared with the sirens which serve as a finish to the handles of the hydriae. The insertion of an extra set of scrolls and palmettes between the wings and the mirror disc is an unusual feature.

Many of the mirrors with bronze handles cast with the disc were cheap wares destined for less wealthy purchasers. Such mirrors are in all respects like the " Peloponnesian "

[1] *Loc. cit.*, p. 18, Fig. 18 ; *Anz.*, 1921, p. 145, Fig. 22 ; ht., ·197 m.
[2] E.g. Kimon's Arethousa.
[3] Athens, 15,127 ; ht., ·315 ; diam. of disc., ·18 m. Found at Athens near the National Museum. Hitherto unpublished.

mirrors of the sixth century : even their ornaments have changed but slightly. Punched bosses are common on the miniature votive mirrors : [1] this form of decoration was particularly at home in Argolis.

The mirror in Fig. 2, recently found at Sparta, is a fifth century version of the superior sixth century Peloponnesian type. Near the edge of the disc is an incised inscription, recording the dedication of the mirror to Athena by Euonyma, in letters which suggest the first half of the century.[2]

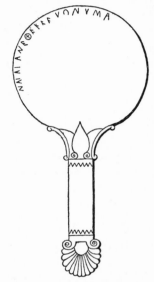

Mirrors with Stands — Columnar supports are well represented by two mirrors in the Louvre from Anthedon [3] and Hermione (Pl. 60 *a*) [4] respectively : each has a palmette and siren between column and disc ; both were probably made in the same centre as the hydriae described on p. 164. A fragment with a siren and palmette, of comparatively provincial style, from Locri Epizephyrii, shews that it was copied in South Italy.[5]

The chief centre for the production and export of mirrors with figure supports was the North-east Peloponnese, where Argos, Corinth, Sikyon and Kleonai were at work.[6] Other districts, no doubt, competed, South Italy in particular.

FIG. 2.—Mirror of Peloponnesian type, from Sparta.

These mirrors were now at the height of their popularity. It is amusing to note how the woman who carries the disc

---

[1] Waldstein, *Argive Heraeum*, Pls. XCIII, XCV ; 'Εφ. 'Αρχ., 1903, p. 17. Cf. an example from S. Russia. That the punched bosses are particularly characteristic of the Argolid is proved by the dishes, Waldstein, *op. cit.*, Pl. CIX.

[2] *B.S.A.*, XXVI, pp. 271, 272, Fig. 6 ; ht., ·29 m.

[3] Louvre, 1685, Pl. 76.

[4] Louvre, 1693, Pl. 76 ; ht., ·40 m.

[5] *Notizie degli Scavi*, 1913 ; *Suppl.*, p. 20, Fig. 20. A fourth handle with a siren, at Chicago, is mentioned by Neugebauer ; *Röm. Mit.*, 1923-24, p. 423. Neugebauer attributes all four mirrors to South Italy.

[6] See Langlotz, pp. 26 ff.

reflects, not only the advances of fifth century sculpture, but also the changing fashions of women's dress : we can see how the heavy Doric peplos became more and more popular, and how the curls and plaits gradually gave way to a neat chignon. It would, indeed, be distressing if the Aphrodite below one's mirror wore out-of-date clothes. Aphrodite she certainly is in most cases, for two Erotes usually hover at either side of her head ; more rarely, two small Victories. The scrolls and the figures by the goddess' head vary in style. The member between the head and the disc gets steadily higher as the century advances :[1] the stand below the feet is now of one pattern, now of another. A mirror in the British Museum[2] has, not the usual stool on three feet shaped like claws, but a stand flanked by fine winged horses. Other details could be added to tempt the capricious taste of the purchaser : the edge of the disc could be enlivened by animals, such as running hares, or by flowers, and a ring added above the disc for convenience. A lady at Hermione was the lucky possessor of a beautiful mirror, now in the Louvre (Pl. 60 c),[3] to which a scent bottle was attached by a chain. Among the finds from Locri Epizephyrii is a mirror[4] supported by a girl who wears, not the usual Doric peplos, but a heavy mantle swathed round her figure. It recalls the costume of the Thessalian lady with a dove. The girl herself has something in common with Phillo the Basket Bearer (p. 143). Here, however, the Ionic capital is not beneath her feet, but on her head, separated from the disc by an arc decorated with egg-moulding, like that on some of the other Locrian mirrors.

Male supporting figures are comparatively rare from Greece itself,[5] though several exist which were found in South Italy and give the impression of having been made in the South Italian colonies (see above p. 156). All are youthful figures, belonging to the second quarter of the fifth century: they shew the influence of both Peloponnesian and Ionic styles, and have already been described as representatives of South Italian bronze-work. A venerable, bearded man, draped in a mantle, is not appropriate to a mirror, and it is surprising to

---

[1] Useful for dating. See Langlotz, p. 36.
[2] B.M., 3209.   [3] Louvre, No. 1687.
[4] *Anz.*, 1921, Fig. 23, p. 145.
[5] See, however, B.M., 224, said to come from Thebes.

find even a single example, such as the one in New York.[1]   This has an attachment which could only have been meant for a mirror disc : the date is 480-470 B.C.

Etruscan Mirrors are not so numerous at this period as in the next.   Like those described in the last chapter, they were usually provided with a handle of some other material, such as wood or bone, fastened to the mirror by a metal tang which projected from the disc.   On the non-reflecting side of the disc, the edge is bent so that it forms what is almost a rim.   Inside this rim is a border of ivy leaves or tendrils, or some similar device : the engraved picture which the border frames is usually a scene from Greek mythology.

At first, the archaic style described in the last chapter prevails : then it yields to the free style.   The scenes would often be hard to identify, were it not for the names inscribed beside the characters : the names are in Etruscan, e.g. Turan for Aphrodite, Turms for Hermes, Menvra for Athena.   The standard of execution varies : sometimes the work is careless and unattractive, sometimes careful and pleasing, shewing the influence of Greek models, especially vases.   The example chosen for illustration belongs to the later part of the fifth century and will be described in the next chapter.

BRONZE VASES—The junction of the cast handle and hammered body of a vase was one of those problems which gave the craftsman an opportunity of proving his skill.   To mask a transition which might be awkward, he sometimes employed decorative devices, and with such success that they became the most pleasing features of the vase.   At other times, he left the handles plain, relying on harmony of form to make a perfect whole : this is an even greater achievement.

The fifth century Greek bronze vases are less numerous than those of the sixth, and are, therefore, less easy to group.[2]   Sometimes the most we can do is to indicate a single fine specimen in the hope that parallels, either complete vases or isolated handles, may be discovered ; occasionally two vases of a class survive, very rarely more.   On the other hand, inferior Etruscan vases, especially jugs, are not at all rare.

---

[1] New York, 77.

[2] For discussions of groups, see also Neugebauer, *Röm. Mit.*, 1923-24, p. 341, and Fölzer, *Die Hydria*, pp. 88 ff.

Starting points for any investigation of fifth century vases are given by those vases described below.

There is a hydria in New York,[1] plain save for a leaf-shaped relief on the top of the vertical handle where the thumb would rest. The wide base marks it off from most of the examples which follow, but recalls the vase with the Argive inscription (see below). With this hydria, compare another, at Athens,[2] with a similar handle but a foot of the ordinary type.

A well-known hydria in Berlin [3] comes from Eretria. Foot and horizontal handles are undecorated, but a tongue pattern and beading adorn the lip, and a silen's mask the base of the vertical handle. When the vase was published by Furtwängler, before it was acquired by Berlin, it had a lid which probably did not belong. The date is somewhere within the first half of the century.

A jug in Boston [4] from South Italy, and a beautiful hydria in New York,[5] have the upper part of a female figure rising above the rim at the junction of the handle. Both have a tongue pattern on the shoulder, but this feature is not unusual. On the jug, at the base of the handle, is a siren. Both belong to a date between 465 and 450 B.C.

The New York hydria (Pl. 59 a) has an Argive inscription on the rim stating that it came from the games in honour of Hera. The style of the female figure is Peloponnesian. It seems evident that the hydria was made in the North-east Peloponnese, in which case it carries on the tradition of the sixth century Argive vases mentioned in the last chapter. We have, therefore, a not inadequate idea of the type of vase produced in this part of Greece for well over a century.

A favourite finish for vertical handles, already popular in the sixth century, and already illustrated by the fifth century jug at Boston, was a siren flanked by palmettes.[6] This admitted

---

[1] New York, 525 ; *Catalogue*, pp. 197, 198 ; ht., ·38 m. From Galaxidhi.
[2] Unnumbered.
[3] Berlin, 7907 (Fölzer says 7807) ; ht., ·43 m. ; *Führer*, p. 99 ; Fölzer, No. 183 ; Furtwängler, *Sammlung Sabouroff*, II, 149.
[4] Boston, *Ann. Report*, 1899, p. 139, 7 ; *Röm. Mit.*, 1923-24, p. 347.
[5] Ht., ·514 m. ; *Bulletin, Met. Mus.*, 1926, April, II, p. 8 ; Richter, *Festschrift für Amelung*, pp. 182 ff. ; Langlotz, pp. 68 and 76.
[6] See Weicker, *Die Seelenvogel*.

of variations. There are many different kinds of siren : some
have arms, some are armless ; some spread their wings one way,
some another ; they affect different styles of hairdressing.[1]
There are still more different kinds of palmette.

From the many vases thus adorned, one class of hydria
stands out. Its distinguishing mark is that the palmette
below the siren's feet is carried upwards, at either side, by
a fourfold scroll pattern, with a small boss in the centre of
each scroll. This is both dainty and effective. The vases
have a tongue pattern on the lip and ridged handles : the
attachments of the horizontal handles and the upper attachment of the vertical handle are, at first, in the form of a rosette
or tongue pattern, though towards the end of the century they
become more elaborate. The complete examples belong mostly
to the second half of the century,[2] but a vertical handle at New
York [3] and a hydria in the British Museum represent the type
in the first half. The British Museum hydria lacks only the
foot, but the vertical handle has, at one time, been removed
and then soldered on in a slightly different place. Whether
this was done in ancient or modern times is uncertain : one of
the horizontal handles has, however, been reattached comparatively recently. In the centre of the scrolls that flank the
sides are silver studs.[4]

These hydriae are associated with a particular part of
Greece : Boeotia and Euboea. Abroad, they are more widely
spread, for they have been found on the coast of Asia Minor and
the shores of the Black Sea.[5] In spite of modern prejudice,
one is tempted to think that they were made in that part of
Greece where they have been found, and to locate the factory
in Euboea, whence they could have been exported by Chalcidian traders.

The superior *Italian products* are represented by a few vases,
or groups of vases and isolated handles. The examination

[1] See Weicker, *die Seelenvogel.*
[2] See list on p. 183. To the first half of the century belongs a hydria in
Munich with a siren and palmette below the vertical handle, which must be
distinguished from the rest of the class (the body is restored too high).
[3] No. 80, *Catalogue*, pp. 53, 54 ; ht., ·212 m.
[4] B.M., 1927, 7, 13-1 ; ht. *c.* ·38 m. On the body is a patch shewing
the marks of a cloth with which the bronze had been covered.
[5] See below, p. 183.

and classification of the material has only just begun : at a later stage it may be possible to discover the centres where the groups were produced.

There is a hydria in Ancona from Castelbellino of which the handles closely resemble a set of handles in Berlin.[1] It is of a different type to most of the hydriae hitherto described, for its vertical handle joins, not the neck, but the lip, like the handle of a jug. Two large discs with Gorgon's heads mark the junction. On the shoulder of the vase is a tongue pattern, and the handles are heavily decorated with beading.

A slender amphora in the British Museum [2] might be Greek, but is more probably made in a South Italian colony. Two youths bending backwards form the handles ; below their feet are sirens and palmettes. On the lip is a silver bar with a scroll pattern above and below it. Whether the foot belongs to the vase is uncertain.

A pair of amphorae in Berlin and Rome respectively deserve mention. The former comes from Schwarzenbach,[3] to which place it must have been exported from Italy. It is fitted with a lid. Below each handle is a siren with horse's hooves. The other amphora, from Etruria, now in the Vatican,[4] has no lid, but is in most details similar (Pl. 59 b). The shape is unconventional, with narrow neck, wide shoulder, and body narrowing to a small base. Their date is somewhere in the first half of the century.

The chief products of the *Etruscan bronze industry*, besides the mirrors described on p. 162, were objects such as lamp stands, kottabos stands and incense burners. In all these, figures could be used to crown or support the shaft. One of the finest of the figures comes from Vetulonia, and represents a satyr, who, with one arm raised, supports the cup into which the dregs were thrown.[5] Of the candlesticks, the best known is, perhaps, in the Vatican,[6] with a horse held by an armed man.

---

[1] *R.M.*, 1923-24, p. 371, Figs. 10-13.
[2] No. 557 ; Walters, *Catalogue*, p. 79.
[3] *Röm. Mit.*, 1923-24, pp. 365-366, No. 18, Fig. 8.
[4] Vatican ; ht., ·058 m., including probably alien stand ; *loc. cit.*, 365, No. 17.
[5] At Florence ; Ducati, *E.A.*, II, p. 83, and *Storia*, Pl. 139, Fig. 361 ; Pl. 141, Fig. 364. [6] Neugebauer, *op. cit.*, p. 96, Fig. 5.

A handsome bucket from Offida, in the British Museum,[1] deserves attention.   It is large and rather ornate : below the two handles are attachments in the form of a winged harpy with two little victims : above the three feet are groups of Hercules and the Nemean lion : the honeysuckle patterns in low relief contrast with the hatched triangles which border them. The vase impresses more by its size than by its beauty, and a photograph does not do it justice.

[1] No. 650 ; Walters, *Catalogue*, p. 107.

CHAPTER VII

THE LATER FIFTH AND THE FOURTH CENTURY

A. STATUETTES

SOON after 450 B.C. the last traces of the strong style give place to the perfect free style associated with the later part of the century. This style is, in its turn, replaced in the fourth century by something more elegant, more facile, and more sophisticated.

Bronze statuettes remain in a transitional stage. They are no longer much used as votive offerings, and not yet in great demand as objects of art. Hence the comparatively small number made at this period.

They have now lost their independence and originality. Nearly all reflect, more or less, the motives of well-known statues. Among the rare exceptions is the Resting Maenad from Dodona described below.

As far as we can judge, all the smaller industries declined during the second half of the fifth century and disappeared early in the fourth. The last survivor was Arcadia. Nor is there much individuality about the products of the larger centres, Corinth, Sikyon, Argos, Athens and South Italy :[1] contact between schools of art had become so easy, an eclectic style so inevitable, the makers of small bronzes so subordinate. Scholars may theorise about the origin of certain bronzes, but their attributions rest upon little that is not extremely controversial.

Dating, also, becomes a problem after the close of the fifth century. Hitherto, we have been able to mark the improvements of each generation as it moved a step further from archaism towards complete freedom. Freedom is now attained.

The dominant influence of great sculptors such as Praxiteles,

---

[1] As far as the small bronzes are concerned.

Skopas and Lysippos, is, to a certain extent, a guide. But the presence of features characteristic of these artists merely gives a *terminus post quem*. Imitations and adaptations made at a much later date can often be mistaken for contemporary works. In the case of the fourth century bronzes, we are safe in adopting the somewhat negative methods of eliminating, on the one hand, figures of which the poses, subjects and proportions are known to be Hellenistic ; on the other, bronzes in the comparatively severe style of the fifth century.

All these difficulties of dating and attribution are, in themselves, inconvenient. They also tend to make any account of the period into a disjointed catalogue, where bronzes appear as isolated objects of beauty, not as representatives of a group.

BRONZES AFTER POLYKLEITOS—The small figures of athletes belonging to the late fifth and early fourth centuries are usually under the direct inspiration of some famous work of art : many, indeed, appear to be copies of well-known statues by the artist's pupils. Since Polykleitos has the double distinction of " having brought the bronze casters' art to perfection " and having discovered one of the most rhythmical and satisfying poses a statue can embody, the number of Polykleitan bronzes is not surprising.

The finest of all is an athlete from Sikyon, in the Athens Museum (Pl. 62 *a*) [1] which must have been made by some one in very close touch with the master himself. Scarcely less beautiful is an athlete in the Louvre (Pl. 61 *b*) [2] which has been attributed to a pupil of Polykleitos,[3] partly because of its style, partly because it is attached to its base by nails through the feet, a method of fastening which suggests a comparatively early date. The eyes were inlaid with silver, the nipples with copper : the right hand is like that of the Idolino and may have held a kylix. The treatment of the surface is surpassingly fine ; the chasing of the hair, and of the veins of the abdomen, is in the manner of Polykleitos at his best. The position of the feet is the same as those of a statue of Xenokles by Polykleitos at Olympia, of which the base survives.[4]

---

[1] Athens, 7474 ; ht., ·21 m. ; Furtwängler, *Meisterwerke*, p. 475. The eyes were originally inlaid : the copper inlay on the nipples is preserved.
[2] Louvre, 183, Pl. XIX ; ht., 0·21 m.
[3] Furtwängler, *Masterpieces*, p. 279, Pl. XIII.   [4] *Ibid.*, p. 279.

Another athlete in the Louvre,[1] reflecting a Polykleitan original, is illustrated on Pl. 61 *a*.   One scholar has suggested that it is a fourth century adaptation by Kleon of Sikyon,[2] but the way the hair is finished with little round holes, looking like the work of a drill, points to a still later period.   The muscles on the sides, and the finish of the ribs are beautifully rendered : but the modelling of the abdomen is neglected.   The hands may have held a fillet, or, more probably, the right held a flask for pouring oil.

Though many statuettes reproduce Polykleitos' two most famous statues, the Doryphoros and the Diadumenos, scarcely any of these reproductions can be claimed with certainty for the later fifth and the fourth centuries.   The Diadumenos from the Janzé Collection (Pl. 61 *c*)[3] may, perhaps, be early fourth century : were his legs less long in proportion to his body, we could have attributed him to the fifth.   He is bending his head to bind round it the victor's fillet, which was of silver, to contrast with the bronze.   Of the other Polykleitan figures, some are certainly late Hellenistic or Roman,[4] others of indefinite date.   To the undatable class belongs the pretty Amazon in Florence,[5] who, in style and attitude, so closely resembles what we believe to be the Amazon of Polykleitos.

ISOLATED FIGURES—One of the most beautiful late fifth century bronzes is the Resting Maenad from Dodona (Pl. 64 *a*).[6] The bronze is something new in this department of art : it might have been translated from a painted vase, for the theme is one that had been used by vase painters, and the rock, with its suggestion of leaves and flowers, would look more realistic in outline.   There is, too, a flavour of romance about the slightly weary figure bending to fasten her sandal, which is still foreign to sculpture, though in painting not unfamiliar.   The artist knew how to contrast the surface of the fawn skin the girl has

---

[1] Louvre, 184, Pl. 19 ; ht., 0·218 m. ; Furtwängler, *op. cit.*, p. 278.

[2] *Ibid.*, *op. cit.*, *loc. cit.*

[3] Bibliothèque Nationale, 927 ; ht., ·143 m.   Surface much rubbed. Furtwängler, *op. cit.*, p. 239, n. 7.

[4] They will be discussed in Chapter IX.

[5] Photo Alinari, 17,051.

[6] Berlin, 10,582 ; ht., ·103 m. ; Neugebauer, p. 75 ; Pl. 40 ; *Münchner Jahrbuch,* 1922, p. 123 ; *Anz.*, 1922, p. 79, No. 30.

knotted round her with that of the dress, and how to render the tightly drawn folds across the legs : moreover, he has managed to achieve a statuette that can be looked at with satisfaction from various angles.   He was, perhaps, a native of South Italy. There is a distinct likeness between his work and certain objects of South Italian origin.[1]   South Italy and Sicily have already been represented in this book by the Kanephore from Paestum, the athlete from Aderno, and others : the maenad, if added to our list, would show how high a standard western art could attain.

The Bathing Girl from Beroea [2] belongs to a somewhat later date, probably to the first years of the fourth century (Pl. 62 *b* and *c*).   This bronze is evidently not Praxitelean, and more than one archæologist [3] considers that it is under Argive influence.   But, though there is a pleasing severity about the youthful figure, standing with her head bent as though looking at some drapery she has laid aside, it is a subject alien to the Argive tradition.

The girl has none of the self-consciousness of the Medici Venus : on the other hand, she is shyer than the mature Knidian Aphrodite.   Probably she is shrinking rather from the cold water than from a possible onlooker.   There exist a number of glass paste intaglios of Roman date with the figure of a woman in the same attitude, removing her mantle preparatory to bathing : a bowl of water stands before her.   These evidently go back to the same original.

The figure is cast hollow, a technique comparatively rare in statuettes (see p. 91).   This may be an indication that the artist was more used to making life-sized statues than small ones.[4]   The arms were cast separately and attached.   The hair over the forehead, and the fringed edges of the snood are finely engraved : the eyeballs are engraved and pierced, but less attention has been paid to the modelling of the feet than we should expect.

---

[1] *Münchner Jahrbuch, loc. cit.*   The bronze has also been considered Attic, Kekule von Stradonitz, *Bronzen aus Dodona*, pp. 20 ff.

[2] Munich ; ht., ·25 m. ; *Anz.*, 1910, p. 480 ; Neugebauer, p. 79, Pl. 42.

[3] *Ibid., op. cit.*, p. 81 ; Sieveking, *Anz., loc. cit.*

[4] The suggestion is Neugebauer's, *op. cit.*, pp. 79, 80.

PRAXITELEAN BRONZES—Whether our bronze represents Aphrodite herself is uncertain, but she is the forerunner of many Aphrodite figures made during the fourth and following centuries. The immediate cause of these figures was the work of Praxiteles, particularly his Aphrodite of Knidos. The subject was popular at this period and became gradually more so : in a small edition it was particularly appealing. Hence the number of statuettes of the goddess, bathing or adorning herself, or tying her sandal. Some of these are Roman, some Hellenistic, but a few must be genuine fourth century.

A date in the second half of the fourth century may be claimed for the Pourtales Aphrodite,[1] who is engaged either in binding a fillet round her hair, or clasping a necklace round her neck (Pl. 62 d). Fillet or necklace must have been in gold or copper wire.

This fine bronze is evidently derived from a fine original. At least two replicas exist,[2] and, at a much later date, a variant of the type came into fashion. This new Aphrodite is distinguished by wearing a diadem, and has all the faults and vulgarities associated with Roman Provincial bronzes, but her attitude is the same. The two types have, somewhat inappropriately, been associated with Praxiteles' Pselioumene.[3]

It will be apparent that the Praxitelean Aphrodite statuettes are the female counterpart of the Polykleitan athletes. Both subjects become part of the bronze-workers' stock in trade from now onwards.

BRONZES AFTER LYSIPPOS AND OTHER ARTISTS—Of the bronzes found at Paramythia in Epirus,[4] which form an important exhibit in the British Museum, nearly all are later than the fourth century : two, however, the so-called Poseidon and Zeus, belong to the fourth century tradition. The " Poseidon " (Pl. 63 a) [5] may equally be a Zeus, with his right hand holding a sceptre, his left an eagle. The nipples are inlaid with copper, the eyes were inlaid with some other material. One of the

---

[1] B.M., No. 1084 ; ht., ·257 m. From the Peloponnese. Feet and left hand restored ; *Berl. Phil. Wochenschrift*, 1900, p. 628 ; Paciaudi, *Monumenta Peloponnesia*, p. 286 ; Klein, *Praxiteles*, pp. 286 ff.

[2] At Cambridge and in London (B.M., 1079).

[3] Klein, *op. cit., loc. cit.*

[4] Walters, *B.M. Cat.*, p. 36.   [5] B.M., 274 ; ht., ·22 m.

most successful points is the modelling of the veins on the feet. The conception is Lysippaean, so, too, are the proportions, the shortness of the body, for instance, compared to the length of leg. The base, though antique, does not belong. The second statuette (Zeus) [1] has similar proportions and may have held the same attributes : here, too, the eyes were inlaid with silver. Both are examples of a new athletic type, taller and more slender than that popularised by Polykleitos ; both are among the finest specimens of Greek bronze casting.

The Paramythia bronzes may have come originally from Dodona. They should be compared with a Poseidon from Dodona, now in Berlin (Pl. 63 c).[2] The Berlin bronze is, like them, beautifully cast and finished ; like the bronze on Pl. 63 a, it has carefully engraved veins on the feet ; but it excels in the careful marking of the joints and nails of toes and fingers. Balance, now lacking, would be given by the trident which the god held in his left hand. The body is a shade lighter, the legs comparatively longer than those of the Paramythia bronzes. All shew a marked contrast with the Hellenistic Poseidon in the Loeb Collection (p. 196).

Another bronze in the fourth century tradition is the Herakles in Berlin (Pl. 63 b).[3] It is modelled on a well-known statue by Lysippos, the same statue that, later on, appears distorted into the Farnese Hercules. The eyes were once inlaid and the left shoulder supported by a club with the lion skin hung upon it.

ETRUSCAN AND LATIN STATUETTES—During the last years of the fifth century, Etruscan art revived ; during the fourth century it flourished. The new motives and devices of the Greek masters had at last reached the Etruscan craftsman, who assimilated enough to reform and rejuvenate his art, but not enough to make it entirely Hellenic.

The Greek bronze-worker of the fourth century adapted his figures from some statue, perhaps by Skopas or Lysippos or

[1] B.M., 275 ; ht., ·193 m.
[2] No. 10,581 ; ht., ·26 m. ; Sieveking, *Loeb Coll.*, pp. 46 ff. ; *Führer*, p. 36.
[3] Berlin, 8395 ; ht., ·217 m. ; *Zeitschr. d. Münch. Altertumsvereins*, 1902, pp. 1 ff. ; *Führer*, p. 25.

Praxiteles : the Etruscan bronze-worker modelled his figures on those of the Greek : Etruscan bronzes are, therefore, a stage or two further removed from the same originals as Greek bronzes. At the same time, they have about them something unmistakably Italian.

The word Italian is here used instead of Etruscan, firstly because the style to which it refers is found at Latin Praeneste as well as in Etruria, secondly because this style has little in common with sixth century Etruscan art but persists throughout the Hellenistic age and is conspicuous in Roman bronzes.

It is not possible to identify and tabulate all its elements : one, however, is so characteristic that it can be described here and will be emphasised again in connection with the Roman Period. This is the sharpness of folds of drapery, of hair, of eyelids, and of other details, produced by overmuch chiselling after the bronze has been cast.

Look at the three figures from the lid of the Praenestine Cista on Pl. 66.[1] The cloak of the central figure falls in heavy folds below the waist, and these folds are almost angular in section. There are sharp incised lines marking wrinkles on the necks of all three figures, and sharp outlines to the strands of hair. The trio represent Dionysos—more or less—accompanied by two satyrs. Turn from them to the Roman bronzes on Pl. 85, where all these tendencies are enhanced.

The same style appears on the woman worshipper in the British Museum (Pl. 66),[2] one of the finest of all Etruscan bronzes, and belonging to the late fifth century. Everything is clean-cut, from the folds of the drapery to the neatly waved hair above the forehead. On clothes and diadem are patterns, incised or made with a stamp : dots, lines and circles. They form a link between this bronze and the Mars figures.

There is a " Mars " from Lake Falterona (Pl. 65 a),[3] also in the British Museum, which can be dated in the early years of the fourth century. It is interesting both for the fineness of its technique and the fact that it forms a link between the

[1] The Ficoroni Cista : for description and date see p. 190.

[2] B.M., 613 ; ht., ·14 m. ; cf. Louvre, 323, *Catalogue*, Pl. 28.

[3] B.M., 459 ; ht., ·32 m. ; Walters, *Catalogue*, p. 64. The eyes were originally inlaid ; Ducati, *op. cit.*, p. 83, places it in the fifth century. There is no explanation of the different patina of the left arm and shield, which appear to be original.

earlier warriors (p. 109) and the large bronze "Mars" from Todi in the Vatican. Here, too, the sharpness of detail is remarkable: not, however, on the small hem of drapery which shews beneath the tunic, but in the eyes and the plates of the cuirass.

A Minerva from Apiro, at Berlin (Pl. 65 c),[1] is an interesting example of the survival of archaic tradition into the fourth century, to the earliest years of which she may belong. She is one of the latest of a group of East Italian bronzes, representing the same subject : she wears an undergarment, and a sleeved chiton with two girdles. The lower girdle is concealed by the pouch, the upper marked by incised lines. She also wears an aegis and a helmet of which the plume has been lost : the shield is attached to the left arm by a nail. Notice the archaic style of the drapery, especially the lines on the skirt. The stamped patterns she has in common with the " Mars," the British Museum worshipper, and various other figures of the period.

B. DECORATIVE WORK, VASES, ETC.

RELIEF-WORK AND ENGRAVING—The statuettes give a fair idea of one aspect of the bronze-worker's activities in the later fifth and fourth centuries. They show his excellent technique, his facility, his dependence on life-sized sculpture for his models.

His real masterpieces, however, are in relief. This branch of art now attained a standard of perfection that has never since been equalled. The greatest achievements were in high relief, a technique which requires considerable skill in a material that can so easily become brittle. The sheet of bronze was hammered from behind, with the result that it remains thick when the relief is low and is reduced to a surprising thinness when it is high. Details could be added with graving tools when the hammering was finished, and very salient pieces made separately and attached.

Of the many examples of relief, the finest and most famous are, perhaps, the Siris bronzes in the British Museum (see Pl. 67 b).[2] They were said to come from near Siris in South Italy,

---

[1] No. 10,819 ; ht., ·243 m. ; *Führer*, Pl. 21, p. 42 ; *Anz.*, 1922, pp. 95, 96.

[2] *B.M. Cat.*, No. 285, pp. 39, 40, which give references up to 1899 ; *Jahreshefte*, XIX-XX, p. 201, Fig. 128. For discussion of provenance, see Michaeli, *Ancient Marbles*, p. 152.

and were made during the early part of the fourth century. They are from the shoulder-pieces of a cuirass, where they decorated the clasps which joined front and back. There is a certain symmetry between the pair : both show variations of the theme of a Greek and a fallen Amazon. The relief is often so high that it seems to be undercut : the very prominent parts, such as the heads of the Greeks, were, apparently, made in separate pieces. The way in which the shield on the right-hand shoulder-piece projects towards the spectator is clever, but not unusual at the period : it is rendered more effective by the projection of the background in that place. The folds of the drapery are fine and delicate. The shields on the ground are marked with an engraved pattern that forms a contrast to the relief.

From the same workshop as the Siris bronzes comes a fragmentary relief from Palestrina (Pl. 67 a),[1] representing a Greek seizing an Amazon by the hair. The Greek and Amazon come particularly near to the British Museum bronzes in composition, in the detail of the drapery, and in the successful illusion of an arm and a shield coming towards the spectator. Much care has been spent on the folds of the neck, the nails of the fingers, and the decoration on the inside of the shield.

The three reliefs are now considered to be part of a group of South Italian products, which include the Boston Situla (p. 187 below), the Tarentine silver rhyton (p. 186), some of the finer mirror cases, and perhaps a splendid cheek-piece from a helmet found at Dodona.[2]

The beautiful figure of a youth from near Lake Bracciano (Pl. 64 b) deserves mention here.[3] Two holes are pierced in the drapery, and must have served to attach it to some object : it is possible, however, that they were pierced at a later date. The surface shews a good deal of chiselling, made after the bronze had been cast, and producing a certain angularity in the drapery. This, as I have already pointed out, is a feature of bronzes made

---

[1] Now in the Villa Giulia ; *Anz.*, 1910, pp. 185, 186, Fig. 4 ; Della Seta, *Cat. Villa Giulia*, p. 452, No. 13, 220. Cheek-pieces of helmet ?

[2] *Röm. Mit.*, 1923-24, pp. 469 ff. The relief in the Louvre, No. 1839 (*Cat.* II, pl. 88), has also been included in the group. There is a second Palestrina relief with a seated Herakles which is usually not attributed to the group. Della Seta, *op. cit.*, p. 451.

[3] *B.M.*, 286 ; ht., ·17 m.

by Italians ; yet the head looks like the work of a Greek.   In any case, the bronze must have been made in Italy.

It is remarkable how much of the fine work of the period was put into the decoration of armour, no doubt meant for state occasions only.   A fair proportion of the fourth century reliefs are from cheek-pieces ; [1] some, as we have seen, from the clasps of breastplates.   A large percentage, however, come from mirrors, and these will be examined below.

A favourite device of the late fifth and fourth century artist should be noticed : it consisted in marking rocks on the ground with little depressions made with the punch, an attempt at realism as naïve as the " tree-touches " of our grandfathers : it persisted, however, for several centuries.

MIRRORS : (i) *With covers*—A new type of mirror was put on the market some time in the second half of the fifth century.   It was handleless and protected by a cover : both cover and mirror had rims which fitted each other as a box fits its lid.   The result was two discs and four surfaces, of which one, slightly convex, was polished for reflection : its reverse was often adorned with concentric circles.   To a third surface was attached the main design, either of figures hammered in relief and filled with some substance to preserve the contours, or of plainer patterns or circles : the fourth could be ornamented with an incised picture, or concentric circles, or polished like the mirror.   Rarely, a polished disc was enclosed in two covers, or a mirror had both back and cover decorated with reliefs.[2]   Some mirrors had rings for suspension, or a ring on the cover to help raise it, or a hinge attaching mirror and cover.

A beautiful series of mirrors with covers was found at Vonitsa in Akarnania.   One belongs to the British Museum,[3] the other six to New York.[4]   Four of the New York examples are noteworthy : one has an incised design inside the cover,[5] one a particularly fine ornament applied to the back, composed

---

[1] For instance, the Odysseus, Berlin, 7863, or the plaque with a battle scene from Dodona ; Carapanos, *Dodona*, Pl. XV.

[2] E.g. Athens, 7669 (Eretria) ; de Ridder, Nos. 161-162.

[3] *Inv.*, 1904, 7-8, 1.

[4] Richter, *Catalogue*, Nos. 758, 759, 760, 761, 766, 767.

[5] No. 760.

of a flower, an acanthus and palmette.[1]   On the other two [2] are female heads, one full face, one three-quarter face (Pl. 68), which recall certain coin types of the period.   They are, in fact, the outcome of the same impulse which, toward the end of the century, produced the Apollos of Choirion and Herakleidas, and Kimon's Arethousa.   These coin engravers were making the experiment of decorating their coins with a facing or three-quarter head :   Choirion made the head absolutely frontal, Herakleidas almost frontal ;   Kimon, more subtle, turned it slightly to one side.   Just so, one of the artists of the New York mirrors preferred a head facing the spectator, and the other a head in three-quarter view.

A completely frontal head is, for a coin, unsuitable : for, " since the nose of a facing head is the first detail to suffer in circulation, such a design rapidly becomes a caricature." [3]   On a mirror, it is not quite so dangerous.   The designer of New York No. 759 took the risk, tempted by the decorative effect of the head, with its framework of hair, in the circular field.

No. 758 (Pl. 68 b), the mirror with the head in three-quarter view, is in very high relief.   This beautiful woman must be Aphrodite :   her lips are slightly parted and she seems to be fingering a lock of her hair.   Eyebrows, lashes and the short hairs on the forehead are carefully engraved.   The introduction of the hand alone mars the picture.   The facing head on No. 759 has, however, no such blemish, and makes us regret the decision of artists not to use this position more often.

The profile heads, like those in full face and three-quarter view, have much in common with contemporary coin types. The influence of coinage was, naturally, strong on any kindred branch of art, owing to its easy circulation, and the fame which the die-engravers enjoyed.   On the mirrors, the heads in profile usually represent mature ladies of fashion, with elaborately dressed hair, expensive ear-rings, and a tendency to double chin. Occasionally, the same lady, by the same artist, appears on more than one mirror.[4]   To the second half of the fourth century

[1] No. 761.
[2] No. 758 ;   diam., ·20 m. ;   No. 759 ;   diam., ·155 m.   Notice the earrings, shaped like flowers.
[3] Hill, *Select Greek Coins*, p. 12.
[4] For instance, the lady in a fillet on an unnumbered Athens mirror is the same as the lady on B.M., 301 (from Corinth).

12

belongs a series of mirrors bordered with cable pattern and featuring a handsome woman whose hair is dressed in what is irreverently called the "melon style." The heads shew her at various ages, quite young on a mirror at New York (Pl. 68 c),[1] older on two mirrors at Athens,[2] and middle-aged on an example in the British Museum.[3] We must not allow ourselves to be tempted to believe that the mirrors are portraits, and to date them accordingly, though the New York mirror is distinctly earlier than the mirrors in the British Museum.

Other designs shew other ways of decorating the circular space. Sometimes the subject fills the circle [e.g. a mirror in New York (Pl. 69 a),[4] with two Pans quarrelling and Eros trying to force them apart]. Sometimes it contrasts with the circle [e.g. a mirror in the British Museum from Anaktorion with Herakles and the Nemean Lion].[5] The treatment of relief is often masterly : this is well shown by the figures of a Greek and an Amazon on a mirror in the British Museum from a tomb in Elis.[6] The way the Greek warrior's shield projects towards the spectator repays study, likewise the minute incised palmettes marking the attachments of the strap through which the arm passes. Another mirror [7] in the British Museum with Nike sacrificing a bull, is interesting because the knife in the goddess' hand is cast separately and fastened with solder behind the hand. These reliefs, like all the best, are in repoussé work. They are first hammered and chased, and then fastened in place with solder.

(ii) *Mirrors with covers and engraved designs* [8]—A distinct class of mirror came into existence at the end of the fifth century and flourished during the fourth. Its speciality was the engraved decoration on the inside of the cover or the back of the mirror, a decoration which, for delicacy and sureness of

---

[1] No. 767, one of the Vonitsa Mirrors ; diam., ·158 m.
[2] Nos. 16,863 and 14,326 (the latter from Hermione).
[3] No. 3211.   [4] New York, 765 ; diam., ·133 m.
[5] B.M., 1904, 7-8, 1.
[6] B.M., 1906, 4-5, 1 ; *J.H.S.*, XXIX, p. 161. Originally silvered.
[7] B.M., 290 ; *J.H.S.*, VII, pp. 275 ff., Pls. D, E. The sword of the Greek on the mirror from Elis is one of several parallels, but is less well preserved.
[8] See Pfuhl, *Malerei und Zeichnung der Griechen*, pp. 719 ff. ; bibliography, p. 722.

touch, is practically unsurpassed.   The best-known examples
are a mirror-cover in the British Museum with Aphrodite and
Pan playing a game called πέντε λίθοι (Pl. 69 b),[1] and on a
mirror in the Louvre (Fig. 1) [2] with personifications of Corinth
and its colony, Leukas.   Korinthos is a venerable man, reminiscent of Zeus, and Leukas is a stately woman crowning him.
A lovely but less-known mirror in the Louvre [3] has its circle

FIG. 1.—Engraved mirror in the Louvre.

well filled by the drapery of two dancing women of familiar
type.   Another mirror, at Berlin,[4] has a nymph in a cave,
kneeling to wash her hair.   The rocky entrance of the cave,
which the artist had some difficulty in depicting, occupies a
large part of the space and acts both as exergue and frame.   The
New York mirror, with an engraving of Atlas and Herakles,
from Vonitsa,[5] has already been mentioned.

[1] B.M., 289; diam., ·185 m.   On the cover, relief of Phaedra and
Hippolytus; Pfuhl, op. cit., p. 720.
[2] Louvre, 1699, Pl. 81; diam. ·165 m.; Pfuhl, op. cit., Fig. 624, pp. 719,
720.
[3] Louvre, 1703, Pl. 75, and Pfuhl, op. cit., Fig. 623, p. 720.
[4] Berlin, 8148.   On the exterior is a relief of Pan and a nymph; Pfuhl,
op. cit., 625, p. 721.
[5] New York, 760.

On many of the mirrors we can see remains of the silver with which the figures were often covered. It is well preserved in the example described above with the nymph and rock-work. The drawing is frequently composed, not only of engraved lines, but of lines of punctured dots. We must not forget that the engraving was merely the decoration of the inside of the cover : on the outside was the usual relief, which, however, has occasionally disappeared, leaving only a discoloration on the surface to shew where it had been.

The majority of the mirrors with engraved designs are reported to have come from Corinth. Though it behoves us to be wary when any class of objects becomes associated in the minds of dealers with a particular place, we can here safely assume the industry to have been at Corinth. The mirror with Korinthos and Leukas is an eloquent witness in favour of this theory : moreover, Corinth was still a well-known centre for bronze work, and the neighbouring Sikyon was, in the fourth century, renowned for its school of painting.

Apart from their beauty, the engravings are important because of certain points in common with a group of fourth century vases. These are the vases of the so-called Kertsch style, made in Attica. Sometimes particular figures on the bronzes recall figures on the vases, e.g. Korinthos recalls the Zeus on two pelikae in the Hermitage,[1] and our nymph in the cave suggests the kneeling girl on a pelike in Petrograd.[2] Sometimes methods or mannerisms occur on both classes of objects, e.g. the employment of short, broken lines to indicate drapery, and the rendering of the nipples through the drapery by a small circle.[3] If we possessed any paintings of the great Sikyonian artists, who at this time played so important a part, we should probably find that they showed all these characteristics, and that it was their influence which affected the two minor branches of art. The engravings, at least, must be directly inspired by the drawings of really first-class artists.

(iii) *Mirrors with open-work plaques between disc and handle*[4] —The bronze industries of South Italy no doubt produced

[1] Furtwängler-Reichhold, Pls. 69 and 70.
[2] *Ibid.*, Pl. 87.   [3] *Ibid.*, II, pp. 42 ff.
[4] Pollak, *Jahreshefte*, 1904, p. 203 ; Petersen, *Röm. Mit.*, XII, 1897, p. 117.

mirrors of the ordinary type with reliefs on the cover. Their speciality, however, was a mirror with a plaque inserted between handle and disc, the plaque being decorated with an open-work design, usually of figures framed by the trunks of trees or the pillars of a little shrine. There is a fine specimen in the British Museum from Locri (Pl. 70 *a*) : [1] on the plaque are Aphrodite and Adonis in a frame ornamented with tendrils, and on the top of the disc is another open-work decoration with two Erotes between foliage. The border is inlaid with silver. On the back of the mirror is a four-spoked wheel, which is rare.

Mirrors of this class have been found in Sicily and South Italy. The chief find-spots are Locri and Catania. It is highly probable that they were made somewhere in this region : the city which was at this period famed for its metal-work was, as we have seen, Tarentum. The fondness for scenes framed by pillars or taking place within a shrine is a feature of South Italian art familiar from vases. The mirrors can, therefore, be taken as representing one branch of the South Italian or Tarentine industry in the second half of the century.

HORSE-TRAPPINGS—The ideal setting for a full-face head in relief is not a coin or a mirror, where it is liable to get damaged, but a disc sufficiently concave to afford it some protection. Three such discs from a tomb in Elis are illustrated on Pl. 70 *b*. They are of bronze, but the backgrounds were originally silver-plated. They belong to a set of five : [2] there are two young satyrs, two old satyrs, and one bearded man in a Phrygian cap. The pupils of the eyes are pierced : they may once have held silver nails but could scarcely be as effective as they are now. The curls, too, are improved by having become partly detached from the background.

In a tomb at Alexandropol in S. Russia were found skeletons of horses and fragments of bridles.[3] One bridle was decorated

---

[1] B.M., 303 ; ht., ·483 m.

[2] In New York and the British Museum ; *J.H.S.*, XXIX, pp. 157 ff., and *Met. Mus. Cat.*, Nos. 111 and 112, pp. 68 and 69. The silver in the background is discernible in the British Museum examples : those at New York I have not seen. The examples on Pl. 70 are in the British Museum ; diam. of man in Phrygian cap, ·10 m. ; of young satyr, ·081 m., of old satyr, ·09 m.

[3] *Recueil d'Antiquités de la Scythie*, 1866, pp. 18 ff., Pl. XIV. For discussion of *phalerae* or horse-trappings, see A. B. Cook, *Zeus*, I, p. 336.

with five discs of the type just described, four being placed where the straps crossed, and one on the forehead.   Another tomb in South Russia, at Kertsch, contained similar ornaments[1] together with the skeletons of four horses, who were evidently intended to appear beautifully caparisoned in the next world.   Both the Russian tombs and the tombs in Elis produced other bronze trappings for which place could be found on the various straps of the bridle.[2]

The Greek examples have been attributed to Tarentum.[3] One feels much diffidence in disagreeing with experts, but remembering that horse-trappings were one of the commonest products of South Russia,[4] and with an eye on the coin types of Panticapaeum, especially the stater with the three-quarter view satyr's head,[5] one is tempted by the idea that our *phalerae* too may have been made in that district.[6]   So close a bond exists between South Russia and South Italy [7] that in either case they belong to the same artistic tradition.

THE LATE FIFTH AND FOURTH CENTURY VASES—There are three important groups of hydriae.   The first is the group with scrolls and sirens, which started in the first half of the fifth century and ended early in the fourth.

The second consists of three plain hydriae belonging to the late fifth or early fourth centuries.

The third has distinctive reliefs below the handle, is assigned to Rhodes, and belongs to the fourth century.

The hydriae with scrolls and sirens below the vertical handle have already been discussed, since they had been made since 480 B.C.   In the second half of the fifth century they became more numerous, and certain details were modified.   For instance, the siren's hair followed the fashions, and, on the attachments of the horizontal handles, the upper attachment of the vertical handle, and the foot, a new, more ornate pattern

---

[1] *Compte Rendu,* 1865, pp. 164 ff., Pl. V, 2-6.

[2] See also Pernice, *Griech. Pferdegeschirr.*

[3] Pernice, *Hellenistische Kunst in Pompeji,* p. 7.

[4] Rostovtzeff, *Iranians and Greeks,* p. 89.

[5] Hill, *Select Greek Coins,* Pl. VIII, 4.

[6] The style of the other bits of harness decoration found with the *phalerae* is not inconsistent with this view.

[7] Pernice, *op. cit.,* p. 6.

tended to displace the tongue and rosette. This pattern is a form of egg and tongue with tiny palmettes in the spaces : it remained, from now onwards, the favourite, and was used, with slight variations, on the hydriae of the other fourth century class, attributed to Rhodes.

Four complete hydriae and several handles represent the scroll and siren group at this period. The complete hydriae are as follows :—

(1) Early example (before 450 B.C., described in the last chapter, p. 164).

(2) In the Louvre : from the Kopaïs district.[1]   Rosette at attachments of handles. The siren and scroll differ considerably from those of Nos. 1, 4 and 5.

(3) At Petrograd :[2] from Kertsch. Traces of gilding. Rosettes at attachments of handles.

(4) At Athens : from Thebes.[3] De Ridder notes traces of gilding. Egg and tongue with palmettes in the spaces on handle-attachments and foot.

(5) At Athens (Pl. 71 a).[4] Slight differences in Sphinx and palmette from No. 4. Body somewhat repaired. Foot broken off, but belongs.

Four elegant, *plain hydriae* represent a class which must have been produced in the late fifth and early fourth centuries. One is in the British Museum,[5] one at Vienna, one at Athens,[6] one in Berlin.[7] None have any decoration save a tongue pattern on the lip. The Berlin hydria is the most important of the four : it comes from Notion, near Lampsakos, and bears an inscription saying it was the prize, won at Lampsakos, of Leophantos.

[1] Louvre, 2673 ; Fölzer, *Die Hydria*, No. 188.
[2] Petrograd ; Fölzer, No. 190 *a* ; and Reinach, *Antiquités du Bosphore Cimmérien*, Pl. 44, 7. The reproduction leaves a doubt as to whether this vase does not belong to the first half of the century, and I have not seen the original. I do not include Fölzer's No. 190 *c*, as I have not identified it or seen an illustration.
[3] Athens, 7914 ; ht., ·40 m. ; Staïs, *Catalogue*, p. 300 ; de Ridder, No. 30.
[4] Athens, unnumbered ; ht., ·37 m.
[5] 67, 5-8, 719 ; ht., ·38 m. ; Fölzer, No. 180, p. 88. I cannot identify Fölzer's No. 181 in the British Museum.
[6] Unnumbered.
[7] Berlin, 30,636 ; *Führer*, p. 99. This hydria has been dated in the fourth century by Neugebauer. The fragments of which it is composed have been riveted on to a modern core ; Fölzer, No. 182.

Rhodian Group—A group of hydriae, destined, like so many bronze hydriae, to hold the ashes of the dead, belongs to the fourth century and is associated with the eastern Mediterranean. Reliefs from vases of this class have been found in Chalke, Telos and Kalymnos near Rhodes, and at Mesembria ; further afield, in Locris and at Eretria. The inference is that the fabric should be sought in Rhodes or the neighbourhood. It is pleasing to find evidence of a flourishing bronze industry in this part of the world, which has been for some time in the background.

The hydriae in question have a sloping shoulder and a gradual transition from shoulder to neck. It is the typical fourth century form. The foot, which is, as usual, cast separately, is decorated with the beautiful and elaborate pattern which can be distinguished on Pl. 71 *b* : a pattern very similar, but often modified to suit a smaller space and giving more the impression of a rosette, adorns the attachments of the horizontal handles. Below the vertical handle is a relief : the handle's upper end spreads into a shield-like plaque richly ornamented with leaves. All handles are channelled. A tongue pattern adorns the lip.

The relief below the handle consists of figures standing on a raised bar which serves as ground line and helps us to identify detached reliefs as having belonged to hydriae of this class. Between the figures and the handle is usually an extra plate of metal ornamented with two rosettes or daisies. In cases where the handle alone survives, this plate tends to disappear with the vase instead of being preserved with the relief.

The chief examples of this class are as follows :—

(1) Hydria in Berlin, from Locris.[1] Under vertical handle, Eros playing ball.

(2) Hydria in the British Museum, from Chalke.[2] Under vertical handle, Dionysos and Ariadne.

(3) Hydria in the British Museum, from Telos.[3] Horizontal handles and foot missing. The relief under the vertical handle with Eros and Psyche looks suspicious ; but cleaning may have brought out the differences of style between it and the other reliefs. From the lip hang chains.

---

[1] Berlin, 8068 ; *Führer*, p. 67 ; Fölzer, *op. cit.*, p. 91, No. 192.

[2] B.M., 312 ; Fölzer, *op. cit.*, p. 91, No. 193.

[3] B.M., 313 ; Fölzer, *op. cit.*, p. 92, No. 194.

(4) Hydria at Athens, from Eretria (Pl. 71 b).[1] Beneath vertical handle, Dionysos and Ariadne. Lip and body partly made up. Lower attachment of vertical handle slightly unconventional.

(5) Three handles and relief, in the British Museum, from Kalymnos.[2] On relief, Boreas and Oreithyia.

(6) Three handles, relief and foot. In the British Museum, from Chalke.[3] On relief, Dionysos and Ariadne. Foot inlaid with silver.

(7) Hydria at Sofia, from Mesembria. Beneath vertical handle, Boreas and Oreithyia. Lid preserved. The hydria originally contained bones and ashes.[4]

With these, contrast the hydria from Kyzikos in the Loeb Collection.[5] It, too, has a relief below the handle : on the relief is Boreas carrying off Oreithyia, which only varies in detail from No. 310 in the British Museum. Nevertheless, the hydria is of quite a different shape : it is broader and its shoulder flatter : the foot is plainer and the horizontal handles quite plain. The vertical handle is, unfortunately, missing.

One is tempted to suggest that the relief was from the workshop which produced the group described above, and that it has been used to decorate a hydria made elsewhere. It is certainly large in proportion to the vase.

Cups and Goblets of the type illustrated on Fig. 2 were made, during the fourth and third centuries, in large numbers : [6] to judge from the style, more belong to the third century than to the fourth. The handles are long and slender, with a characteristic twist at the top, and often with a leaf-shaped attachment where they join the body. The shapes vary : some of the cups have high feet, some low ones : some have a moulding, concave or convex at the lip, some none : all have the curves of the body more rounded, less gradual than is common.

[1] Athens, 7913 ; ht., ·48 m. ; Staïs, *Catalogue*, p. 301 ; de Ritter, No. 29.
[2] B.M., 310.   [3] B.M., 311.
[4] *Ath. Mit.*, 1911, pp. 308 ff., Figs. 4, 5. Several handles of this class, without vase or relief, exist in our museums. These have not been included in the above list. A good example is B.M., 1918, 11, 27 : a fine set, gilt and silvered, and with backgrounds covered by punctures, is at Munich.
[5] Sieveking, Loeb Collection, *Bronzes*, Pls. 36, 37.
[6] Examples, British Museum, *Inv.*, 78, 10-12, Nos. 1 to 11, 14, 15, 18, 20, 21 (from Galaxidhi), and 82, 10-9, 1 to 3, 9, 11, 12 : (Galaxidhi), 73, 8-20 ; New York, Nos. 595, 596 ; Loeb Collection, No. 44. For other references see Richter, *Catalogue*, p. 216.

The chief factory for these vases was probably Corinth.[1]
The majority come from Galaxidhi,[2] not far from Corinth, on
the Gulf of Itea.   Galaxidhi has been identified with the ancient
Oenanthea,[3] a small town which was much addicted to piracy.
Why it should have acquired all these cups we cannot say.

Silver cups of the class in question were imported into South
Russia, and have been found in tombs in the Crimea.[4]   Among
the black glaze vases of the period, there are many which copy
the forms of the bronze.   Evidently, the rich bought a set in

FIG. 2.—Kylix of " Galaxidhi type."

silver, the less wealthy, a set in bronze, and the poor bought
pottery.

South Italian Situlae—The metal-work of Tarentum and
South Italy has already been mentioned in connection with
mirrors, the Siris bronzes and the *phalerae*.   It included objects
in silver, and, probably, in gold.   A silver rhyton, from Tarentum, now in the Museum of Trieste,[5] shows us the high standard
attained, and serves as a guide for assigning other objects.

Of these, the most important are the vases : they must
have served as models for South Italian pottery, and as proto-

[1] See Richter, *op. cit., loc. cit.*   A cup of this class was found in the same
grave as a fourth century Corinthian coin ; Von Stackleberg, *Gräber der
Hellenen*, Pl. VII, 13.
[2] See n. 6, p. 185.
[3] Frazer, *Commentary on Pausanias*, X, 38, in Vol. V, p. 466.
[4] Reinach, S. *Antiquités du Bosphore Cimmérien*, Pl. XXXVIII.
[5] Pernice, *Jahrbuch*, 1920, pp. 90, 91, Figs. 3-5 ; *Röm. Mit.*, 1923-24,
p. 451 ; and *Jahreshefte*, V, 1902, p. 112.

types for the handsome Hellenistic bronze vases found in Herculaneum and Pompei.[1]

In the last years of the fifth century, one of the South Italian towns, possibly Tarentum, began to produce pails (situlae) sometimes ornamented with reliefs, sometimes plain.

The attribution of the pails to South Italy [2] rests on the fact that all, save two, of which the provenance is known, come either from Italy or the borders of the Black Sea. The same can be said of their imitations in pottery. Moreover, the style of some of the reliefs which decorate them resembles that of the relief on the Tarentine silver rhyton.

Only the pails with reliefs will be described here.

The earliest example, made, apparently, in the last years of the fifth century, is an incomplete pail in Berlin [3] (Pl. 72). It is ornamented in repoussé work with reliefs of Perseus pursuing a Gorgon ; Perseus on one side, the gorgon on the other. Perseus is depicted mounting a rocky slope, with his *harpe* and Medusa's head in his hand. A winged and not unlovely Gorgon, perhaps one of the remaining sisters, flies before him. Another pail (Pl. 73 *a*), different in shape [4] and of cast bronze, has reliefs of Nike driving a team of panthers in a style recalling that of Sicilian coins of the late fifth century. This has been attributed to the same hand as the Perseus pail. It is, however, as one critic [5] points out, later in date, for the chariot wheels are in perspective : it was probably made early in the fourth century.

A third pail is in Boston,[6] and, like the last, is said to have come from South Italy. The shape is that of the Perseus pail, but the details are more ornate. Instead of having a figure at either side, it has a frieze of figures in repoussé work, round the upper part of the body. On one side, Dionysos is seated stroking a panther ; to right and left of him are a satyr and

---

[1] See Pernice, *Hellenistische Kunst in Pompeji*.

[2] Schröder, 74tes *Winckelmannsprogramm* ; Pernice, *Jahrbuch*, 1920, pp. 83 ff. For the derivation of situla (" little thirsty one ") see A. Walde, *Lateinisches Etymologisches Wörterbuch*, under *situla*.

[3] Berlin, 30,399 ; upper diam., ·21 m. ; Schröder, *loc. cit.*, Pl. II ; Pernice, *Jahrb.*, p. 84, Figs. 1 and 2.

[4] Berlin, 677 ; from S. Italy ; Schröder, *loc. cit.*, Pls. I, III.

[5] Pernice, *Jahrbuch*, 1920, p. 93, Fig. 7.

[6] Boston, Fine Arts Mus., *Ann. Report*, 1903, p. 61, No. 13 ; diam., ·253 m. ; *Jahrbuch*, 1920, p. 91 ; Pernice, *Hellenistische Kunst in Pompeji*, Pl. V.

maenad, behind him is a tree in very low relief. On the other side, where the preservation is poor, is a seated woman, Ariadne (?) with panther, satyr and maenad. Above the relief is a band of laurel.

This class is important, since it shews the effect of a Greek design applied to a shape that was essentially Italian. Economically, also, it is important, since it illustrates the close trade relations between South Italy and the Black Sea, and foreshadows the important part South Italy was to play in the Hellenistic period.

From the Greek workshops we turn to those where Italian elements predominate.

The showy *hydria* in Naples (Pl. 73 *b*),[1] said to come from Locri, presents some unusual features. Such are the gorgoneion and horses at the base of the vertical handle, the youths in relief on the horizontal handles, the combination of lotus and plait in the band below the tongue pattern. A lion's head adorns the front of the vertical handle : its rough mane can be seen at the top of the handle in the photograph. The eyelids of the Gorgon overlap at the outer corners, which indicates a date in the second half of the century.

PRAENESTE AND   ETRURIA : THE RISE OF PRAENESTE : *Cistae*—A description of the objects usually called cistae is the best introduction to the important Latin fabric of Praeneste. The popularity of these cistae dates from the close of the fifth century : they were made in large numbers during the fourth, and, to a certain extent, in the third. They are deep boxes, fitted with a lid, carried on feet, and designed to hold toilet articles. Usually they are round (Fig. 3), occasionally oval, rarely square. They have been found in graves, mostly at Praeneste (Palestrina) : evidently they were buried with the dead as treasured possessions. During the life of the owner, they had probably stood on the dressing table, holding odds and ends. Some, when found, still contained hairpins, brooches combs, mirrors, strigils and pincers ; one held a rouge pot, another a bit of cloth.

There is a great similarity about most cistae in all points save the designs with which they are decorated. They possess

---

[1] *Röm. Mit.*, 1923-24, p. 378, No. 23 ; ht., ·545 m.

a lid, and on the top of the lid are figures arranged to form handles : sometimes two men carry a dead comrade, whose body, being horizontal, can easily be grasped by the hand : sometimes two figures place their arms on each other's shoulders or clasp each other's necks like wrestlers, allowing the hand to pass between.   Round the middle of each cista are rings, through which a chain or strap would be threaded to facilitate carrying.   Three feet support the round cistae, four the oval and the square : they end in animals' claws, and their junction with the body is masked by a figure, human or otherwise.

On the lid and body of the cistae are designs engraved with a sharp-pointed instrument.   The lines are angular in section.[1] They follow a preliminary sketch which the artist made with an instrument of another kind.   Apparently, this instrument was sometimes blunt, making a compara-tively shallow line ; sometimes it was a cleft metal pen, making a line that tends to become double ; sometimes it was very finely pointed.

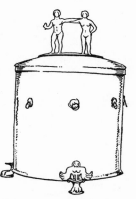

FIG. 3.—Typical Etruscan cista.

There is one group of cistae,[2] dated about 400 B.C., of which the body is partly of bronze and partly of wood covered with leather.   The wooden part is exposed in the centre of the body, and into it are fixed the rings.   Where the bronze meets the wood, it is cut into an elaborate open-work pattern.   The lids are surmounted with figures and decorated with animated engraved scenes.   These cistae have been found at Praeneste and many appear to have actually come from the same workshop.

The most typical cistae, however, have bodies altogether of bronze.   These, too, have been found mainly at Praeneste ; such examples as have been found elsewhere, e.g. at Vulci and Corneto, are so like the others as to leave little doubt that they come from the same centre.   We can safely identify this centre as Praeneste : additional evidence is afforded by the Praenestine mirrors which are similar in style (see below).

[1] Matthies, *Pränestinische Spiegel*, p. 17, Fig. 3.   [2] *Ibid.*, p. 35.

Nevertheless, one cista,[1] and that one the most famous of all that survive, was made at Rome.   This we learn from the inscription :—[2]

Dindia Macolnia fileai dedit.
Novios Plautios med Romai fecid.

" Dindia Macolnia gave (me) to her daughter.
Novios Plautios made me at Rome."

FIG. 4.—Engraving from the Ficoroni cista.

The handle (Pl. 66) has been described on p. 173.   Of the three feet, one is original, one an antique copy, one a more recent copy : [3] they consist of claws resting on frogs : at the top of each foot is a group of Eros, Herakles, and a third, more indefinite figure.

On the lid are engraved an inner circle of heraldic beasts, and an outer circle of hunting scenes.   On the body, between ornamental patterns, is a scene from the adventures of the Argonauts (Fig. 4).[4]   Amycus, the aggressive boxer, is being bound to a tree by Pollux ; a slave boy sits at the foot of the tree

---

[1] Behn, *Die Ficoronische Ciste*, which see for bibliography.
[2] *C.I.L.*, I, 54 ; XIV, 4112.   [3] Behn, *op. cit.*, p. 9.
[4] Pfuhl, *Malerei und Zeichnung*, Fig. 628.

holding Pollux' shoes, while the boots of Amycus lie on the ground beside him. Victory flies up with a crown ; Minerva watches ; the Argonauts, not always easy to identify,[1] gather round. Close at hand is the Argo, from which one of the crew descends by means of a ladder ; he carries a basket and an odd vessel, perhaps a water-can.[2] Further on there is an amusing group round a fountain which gushes from a lion's head spout and splashes into the mouth of an amphora. Beside the fountain sits a Papposilenos ; near it, from a nail, hangs a kylix, obviously decorated with figures in the late Attic style ; another kylix is in the hands of a youth who drinks from it thirstily. There are trees, olive, pine, and perhaps laurel, conveniently lopped to be within the limits of the design ; there are also rocks and flowers.

Various technical points deserve notice : the three-quarter views of faces and figures ; the perspective of an overturned amphora ; the way some muscles are shewn by hatched lines ;[3] the hair on a Silen's chest. The heads recall those on a particular group of South Italian vases.[4]

This cista, usually called the Ficoroni cista, has been much discussed, partly for its own sake, partly because of its supposed connection with important Greek paintings. The influence of the Greek originals no doubt reached the Latin draughtsman via South Italy, but their effect on him must not be exaggerated.[5] Both style and epigraphy suggest a date about 400 B.C.

Next in importance comes a cista in Berlin,[6] representing the triumph of a Latin commander, the only cista decorated with a historical Latin subject. It belongs to the second half of the fourth century.

A third masterpiece, formerly in Napoleon's collection,[7] has a handle which may be by the same hand as that of the Ficoroni cista.

The workshops of Praeneste form an interesting study.

[1] For possible identifications, see Behn, *op. cit.*, pp. 24 ff.
[2] *Ibid.*, p. 39, points out a parallel in Patroni, *Ceramica Antica*, Fig. 68.
[3] Behn, *op. cit.*, p. 54, compares the Talos vase, Furtwängler-Reichhold, Pls. 38, 39.   [4] Behn, *op. cit.*, p. 55.
[5] Pfuhl, *op. cit.*, II, p. 793. See also p. 722, where he proposes a date in the second half of the fourth century.
[6] *b* 238, *Führer*, p. 93, Pl. 57.
[7] Behn, *op. cit.*, p. 13 ; *Mon. del Inst.*, VI, 64.

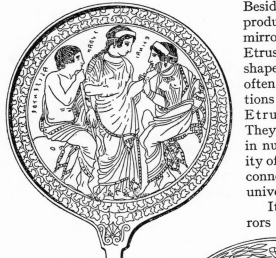

FIG. 5 *a*.—Etruscan mirror in New York.

Besides the cistae, they produced *mirrors*. These mirrors differ from the Etruscan by being pear shaped instead of round: often they bear inscriptions which are not in Etruscan but Latin. They have been found in numbers in the vicinity of the town, and their connection with it is universally accepted.

It appears that mirrors had been made at Praeneste before the fourth century,[1] but these were of the usual Etruscan type. This was natural, for Praeneste was subject to Etruscan influence until the end of the fifth century: its emancipation began a period of artistic activity which lasted

FIG. 5 *b*.—Praenestine mirror in London.

[1] Matthies, *Pränestinische Spiegel*, pp. 20 ff.

throughout the fourth century and into the early years of the third.

The pear-shaped mirrors were easier to decorate than the round. Often the narrow space near the handle was filled with a floral motive or some subsidiary design : above this the figures were grouped. . The subjects vary : a group of mirrors illustrates the binding of Amycus,[1] the myth which had been chosen for the Ficoroni cista. Round the design usually ran a border of leaves : laurel leaves were the favourite, whereas the Etruscans preferred ivy.

A Praenestine mirror is given on Fig. 5 b ; a somewhat earlier Etruscan mirror is placed by its side (Fig. 5 a) for contrast. The former [2] shews Menelaus preparing to kill Helen, and can be dated well within the fourth century. The latter,[3] illustrating an earlier chapter of the same story, is also earlier in date. Aphrodite (Turan) is persuading Helen (Elinai) to elope with Paris (Alcsentre). The goddess places her hand under Helen's chin, wishing to make her look up, while Helen tries to push her away and Paris looks on

FIG. 6.—Typical Etruscan pointed situla.

philosophically. This mirror belongs to the late fifth century. In spite of the differences of shape, subject and date, there is an affinity of style between the two. The art of Praeneste can scarcely be separated from that of Etruria, and probably Etruscan workmen found employment in the Latin city.

Though the cistae and mirrors are the most characteristic and best-known products of Latin or Etruscan art at this period, the manufacture of candelabra, kottabos stands, vases and

[1] Matthies, *op. cit.*, p. 73. Matthies divides the mirrors into a number of classes, of which the first belongs to the early fourth century, the latest to the early third.

[2] Louvre, 1744 ; diam., ·313 m. ; Gerhard, *Etruskische Spiegel*, CCCXCIX ; Matthies, *op. cit.*, p. 75, Fig. 13, and p. 61, where it is assigned to group B 1.

[3] New York, 797 ; diam. ·154 m. ; Gerhard, Klügmann and Körte, *Etruskische Spiegel*, V, Pl. 107.

other utensils continued.   The *candelabra* form an unbroken
chain from the seventh century B.C. to the fourth century A.D.,
but only its later phases, the Hellenistic and Roman periods,
have been adequately studied (see below, p. 239).

Among the *vases*, a particular type of situla with a pointed
base attracts our attention.   An example is illustrated on Fig. 6.[1]
The type had been made during the fifth and perhaps the later
sixth century : the execution is usually very fine : the patterns
which decorate the body of the vase are graceful and well chosen.
A tongue pattern is common ; still more characteristic is what
might be called a " feather pattern," as on Fig. 6.   The most
interesting of these situlae, at Florence,[2] is adorned with a
bacchanalian procession in very low relief and probably belongs
to the late fourth or early third century.

[1] See Schröder, 74*tes Winckelmannsprogramm*, p. 20 ; examples, *loc. cit.*,
n. 9, to which add B.M., 51, 9-6 : 5.
[2] *Drittes Hallisches Winckelmannsprogramm* (1878), Pl. IV, 3.

CHAPTER VIII

THE HELLENISTIC PERIOD, OR THE HELLENISTIC TRADITION [1]

A. STATUETTES

A NEW age begins with the conquests of Alexander, which spread Greek culture over a comparatively large area. The division of his empire among his successors resulted in the establishment of flourishing states, some mainly Greek, but most with a strong foreign element, in the Middle East and in Egypt. Mainland Greece, in the meantime, decayed. Consequently, new art centres came into being in Pergamon, Alexandria, and, later, in the island of Delos, while the old schools of the mother country worked half-heartedly and lost their reputation. The more commercial forms of art, such as the making of bronze utensils, were even more quickly affected by the new conditions : with the strengthening of the industries of Asia Minor, Egypt and Italy, the main currents of trade and manufacture withdrew to the east and west, leaving Greece in a backwater.

At the same time, the standard of living among individuals became higher. Hellenistic houses were far more comfortable than houses of the fifth century, and it was the fashion to furnish them with objects that were not only useful but also ornamental For instance, more care was bestowed on decorating tables, chairs and couches than in the earlier periods, and, as parts of these articles were often of bronze, the bronze industry profited. Statuettes in various materials, including bronze, were now in demand as cabinet pieces for rich connoisseurs, and even for ordinary householders. This implies that the transitional period mentioned in the last chapter is at an end. Statuettes have entered on a new and very definite phase.

[1] This chapter will include not only Hellenistic bronzes, but bronzes in the Hellenistic tradition made after the Roman Period had begun.

Political and economic changes involved a change of temperament in the population. The Hellenistic Greek was more complex and more self-conscious than his predecessors, and his ideals in art were different. He liked things which were sensational or dramatic or daring, and things which had a purely sensual appeal. We must not be surprised if his taste was often lacking in subtlety and occasionally vulgar. He was, after all, a member of a cosmopolitan civilisation in which the cultured element was smaller than the semi-cultured. What strikes us most, however, in the art of the earlier Hellenistic age is its vitality. It had been transplanted to a new soil and flourished : later, because the soil was too rich, it became luscious and overblown : finally it decayed. Its earlier stages make a not unpleasant study, for they shew that artists once more felt the inspiration of discovery : they invented, or at least elaborated, a new treatment, new positions and new subjects.

The Loeb Poseidon (Pl. 80 c) [1] is a good example of the new treatment of an old subject. Contrasted with the Poseidon from Paramythia, the god appears theatrical and restless. His attitude is traditional, save for one rather unsuccessful innovation in the position of the right hand. This is extended with an imperious gesture which might be thought appropriate to his character, but which mars the harmony of the composition. His face is fretful and passionate, as befits a personification of the sea. The proportions are Lysippean.

The new poses are legion. Most striking, and most important in the history of art, are those which are multi-facial, i.e. of which a pleasing view can be obtained from several angles.

DANCING FIGURES can easily be treated this way, for the effect of a dance depends on the contrary motions of the different parts of the body. A number of statuettes represents boys dancing with castanettes,[2] the body being swung to one side with a sharp turn at the waist, and the arms to the other side. Figures such as these can be seen in Berlin, Munich and the Fouquet Collection : the bronze on Pl. 74 c is at Munich.[3]

---

[1] Sieveking, *Bronzen der Sammlung Loeb*, Pls. 17 and 18, p. 41 ; ht., ·305 m. ; Neugebauer, Pl. 44. Feet restored. Patina mostly spoiled by cleaning. A trident should be restored in the left hand.

[2] Perdrizet, *Bronzes Grecs de la Coll. Fouquet*, p. 63, Pls. XXIX-XXXI. The Berlin example, 2120, is classified as Roman (*Führer*, p. 64).

[3] Ht., ·110 m. ; Perdrizet, *op. cit.*, p. 65, Pl. XXX.

The Dancing Faun from Pompeii,[1] now generally regarded as an heirloom dating from the Hellenistic Period, shews a somewhat different theme treated with much skill.

SLEEPING AND CROUCHING FIGURES, too, became popular during the Hellenistic Period. In the Sleeping Eros [2] in New York, the artist has attempted to shew how the limbs relax, and has made the head rest very prettily on one arm. The folded wings, too, are pretty, but the whole effect is marred by a piece of carelessness : both legs and one arm are entirely unsupported. Crouching figures at once recall the well-known statue of the Persian from the dedication of Attalos on the Acropolis, and the famous " Crouching Aphrodite " : the motive appears to be associated with Pergamon.[3] It is pleasing to find it among the small bronzes representing Gauls and other barbarians, which are ultimately derived and adapted from the Pergamene dedication (see below, p. 199), even though the figure in question copies no known original and is of inferior quality. It represents an Oriental soldier hunched up with his shield across his knees (Pl. 76 b).[4]

The new subjects are of great importance. Once more, however, the word " new " needs apology and qualification, since isolated examples of all the subjects enumerated below have appeared in earlier art, mainly in vase-painting. Now, from being the exception, they become the rule : from being proof of the originality of one or two artists, they have become significant of the mentality of the age.

Among bronzes, many illustrate, in different aspects, the Hellenistic tendency towards realism. Realistic art admits and encourages subjects which other forms of art exclude : the classical Greeks, with their love of beauty and restraint, had little use for representations of hard-featured peasants, of uncouth barbarians, of worn old men and women. Their painters attempted such subjects occasionally, their sculptors rarely.

One might expect the most important manifestations of realism to be in portraiture. This, however, is not the case :

---

[1] Pernice, *Hellenistische Kunst in Pompeji*, p. 3, Fig. 2.
[2] No. 132 ; length, ·21 m. Cast hollow.
[3] G. Dickins, *Hellenistic Sculpture*, p. 6.
[4] Louvre, 696 ; ht., ·048 m. ; *Catalogue*, Pl. 48. The bronze may be of Roman date, but it is Hellenistic in conception, and bears none of the marks of Roman manufacture.

moreover, portraiture develops too steadily throughout the centuries for any aspect of it to be associated closely with one particular age.

We will, therefore, leave it aside for the moment and consider first certain typically Hellenistic subjects : foreigners, children, old people, sick and deformed people, grotesques.

First the FOREIGNERS. These are no longer only the handsome Persians that had won their place in art two hundred years before, but the races with which the Greeks in their new cities came in contact. Imagine the cosmopolitan crowd that must have filled the streets of Alexandria ; Egyptians, Jews, negroes and other races from Asia and Africa. Some of these the artists selected for models. Semitic types are rare : I know of no certain example.[1] Egyptian types are represented by figures of priests, whose shaven heads and enveloping mantles are very distinctive. A good example, from the Fouquet Collection,[2] is shewn on Pl. 80 *a* carrying a vessel of Nile water beneath his cloak. The most popular models were, however, the black races, who were represented in all possible variations.

The finest of all is in the Bibliothèque Nationale (Pl. 74 *a*).[3] He stands as though he were singing to the accompaniment of a small harp which he could have held in his right hand : one can imagine the slightly nasal voice droning an eastern tune. The tight curls are typical, so, too, are the thin legs, the heavy body, and a certain pathos in face and attitude.

Among the northern Barbarians, the Gauls furnished the favourite subjects. Their invasions of Greece and Asia Minor,[4] and their sensational withdrawal and repulse, gave them a place in the popular imagination, the sculpture commemorating those events kept them there. The monuments erected by Pergamene artists are known to us from reliable copies ; a

[1] Certain heads that serve as weights may be a caricature of the type, e.g. Perdrizet, *Bronzes Grecs de la Coll. Fouquet*, p. 60 and Pl. XXVIII. The subject is to a certain extent " made up," e.g. the hair.

[2] Perdrizet, *loc. cit.*, p. 48, No. 82, Pl. XXII ; ht., ·133 m. Now exhibited at the Louvre. The statuette was found at Erment (Hermonthis).

[3] Bibl. Nat., 1009 ; ht., ·202 m. Found at Châlon-sur-Saône. Harp missing. Particularly fine modelling on back.

[4] They were driven back from Delphi in 279 B.C. : their defeat in Asia Minor at the hands of Attalos took place *c.* 230 B.C. See Bienkowski, *Die Darstellungen der Gallier in der Hellenistischen Kunst*, and Kekulé von Stradonitz, 69*tes Winckelmannsprogramm*.

monument at Delphi has been inferred by works less directly inspired.[1]   Of the Pergamene dedications, the one that concerns us is the collection of bronze figures, about three feet high, dedicated by Attalos on the Acropolis at Athens.

Naturally, small souvenirs of these larger statues were in demand among patriotic Greeks and tourists : the makers of bronze statuettes took advantage of the situation.   Their figures, although, apparently, free adaptations not exact copies, nevertheless reproduce the spirit of the originals well enough for us to distinguish one bronze that may be derived from an earlier source, perhaps connected with the victory at Delphi, and any number of bronzes that reflect the fallen and crouching barbarians by the artists of Pergamon.

We will examine the single figure first (Pl. 75 a).   It is a good piece of work, belonging to the second half of the third century, and represents a Gaulish slinger,[2] who grasps a sling-stone in his left hand, while his right must have originally held the sling.   His right knee rests on the ground : the position is not unlike one which is used for a slinger on the interior of a kylix.[3]   He wears a helmet adorned with horns, a torque and a belt.   The eyes had, apparently, no filling in the hollowed pupils.   Very little chasing has been done after the casting was finished.   This Gaul is quite different from the Pergamene figures. In spite of his torque, his helmet and his rough hair, he is less foreign than they are, and the modelling is more restrained.   He appears to represent another tradition : hence the supposition that he derives from a monument associated with the defeat of the Gauls in Greece.

To return to the bronzes inspired by the Pergamene dedication.   Their manufacture appears to have been taken up by some well-known centre, possibly Alexandria, a town which specialised in the production of marketable wares to sell in its bazaars, and to have been continued for several generations. Then came a time when another series of Gallic victories stirred popular imagination.   These were the victories of Caesar and

---

[1] Kekulé von Stradonitz, *op. cit.*, pp. 17, 22.

[2] Berlin, 11,876 ; ht., 0·135 m.   Published by Kekulé von Stradonitz in 69th *Winckelmannsprogramm*.   See also *Anz.*, 1922, p. 98, No. 4 b.   Neugebauer and Winnefeld consider it Italian.

[3] Hartwig, *Meisterschalen*, Pl. XVIII, 1.

his successors. At once the output increased : statuettes of dying or captive Gauls found favour with Roman purchasers and with Roman settlers in Gaul, where many examples have been discovered. When Gaul had become thoroughly Romanised, the Gauls themselves would not be averse from possessing these representations of their ancestors, since they were, on the whole, both flattering and romantic.

This being so, the surviving bronzes ought to include both Hellenistic and Roman statuettes in the style of Pergamon. As a matter of fact, though there are many which are obviously inspired by the Pergamene series, they are of such poor workmanship that even approximate dating is impossible ; probably all are of Roman date. They have, nevertheless, a grace and originality that atone for their lack of finish, and recall, even if they do not repeat, the motives of the Hellenistic originals. They will, therefore, be included in this chapter.

They can be roughly divided into figures of dead or dying Gauls completely extended on the ground,[1] and figures of vanquished and wounded Gauls half supported on the ground.[2] The former are usually meant for attachment to some object, and are too thin to be called figures in the round. They are frequently found in Gaul, which suggests a Roman origin.

The division we have made corresponds to the two types of figure on the Pergamene dedication, where some figures are laid flat on a slab of marble,[3] others not.[4] In comparing the statues and the statuettes, we find that the latter are eclectic : they combine motives taken from more than one statue, and also achieve variety by elaborating the armour and costume.

A third victory over the Gauls took place in Italy : the Italians defeated the invaders at Telamon in 225 B.C. A bronze

---

[1] (i) B.M., 815 ; from France ; *Jahrb.*, I, p. 86.

(ii) B.M., 816 ; *Jahrb.*, I, p. 86, and VIII, p. 127.

(iii) Alesia : a cast in St. Germain ; *Inv.*, 50,816 ; *Mon. Piot.*, XVIII, 1910, p. 88, Fig. 20.

(iv) Musée Calvert : a cast in St. Germain ; *Inv.*, 60,874.

[2] (i) B.M., 814 ; *Jahrb.*, I, 85 ; *Mon. Piot.*, 1910, p. 92, Fig. 22.

(ii) B.M., 817 ; *Mon. Piot.*, 1910, p. 91, Fig. 21.

[3] E.g. the Gaul in Venice, Bienkowski, *op. cit.*, Fig. 50, p. 37.

[4] Cf. the Gaul at Naples, Bienkowski, *op. cit.*, Fig. 60, p. 48 ; and at Venice, Bienkowski, *op. cit.*, Fig. 53, p. 40.

from near the site of Telamon, and now in Florence,[1] represents a barbarian, who, though he looks like a Persian, has the shield and sword-belt of a Gaul (Pl. 75 b). The drapery has been heavily chased after casting : this is a mark of Italian origin. The figure may, therefore, be considered as the record of a historic event, and, like the slinger at Berlin, be dated well within the Hellenistic period.

CHILDREN—The fourth century had begun to understand what the fifth century had overlooked : that children have not the proportions of adults on a small scale. The Hellenistic Greeks grasped this completely, and delighted in portraying children or babies. Boethos of Chalcedon, who made a famous statue of a small boy struggling with a goose, was not only a sculptor of children, but also a silversmith. This suggests that he made figures of children in the precious metal in minia- ture : he probably made small bronzes as well, and his imi- tators certainly did so. There are numerous bronze statuettes of babies in our collections, and it is, therefore, difficult to select one for illustration : moreover, they were so popular in the succeeding Roman period that we are often at a loss how to distinguish the Roman from the Hellenistic. One of the nicest children in either Greek or Roman art is the fat, plain little girl at New York,[2] holding a resigned but anxious puppy (Pl. 76 a) in her arms.

OLD AGE—Most of the surviving examples of this subject are in marble, but one of the finest is in bronze (Pl. 78 a). It is the figure of an Old Woman, in Vienna,[3] which came from Krain (Jugo-Slavia), a district of which the Roman town Neviodunum was the centre. The statuette has been the sub- ject of much discussion : the provenance, and certain technical defects may indicate Roman manufacture, but the fine style looks like the work of a great artist. The inference is that our bronze is a copy, some say a Roman copy : the original is,

---

[1] See Kekulé von Stradonitz, 69tes Winckelmannsprogramm, p. 23.

[2] New York, 375 ; ht., ·06 m. Cast hollow. Has been catalogued as Roman, but may well be Hellenistic.

[3] Vienna, 3218 ; ht., ·148 m. ; Neugebauer, Pl. 49 ; Jahreshefte, 1919 (XIX-XX), p. 296 ; (Bankó), 299 ; (Reisch).

according to one scholar,[1] a good Hellenistic bronze statuette :
according to another,[2] it is a statue of the fourth century B.C.,
by the artist Nikomachos representing the temple attendant
Syeris.   Such a statue is known by an inscription, and was
dedicated on the Acropolis of Athens.   This identification is,
however, too ingenious : the bronze is evidently meant to
represent an old peasant, and is not appropriate to a temple
attendant.   Moreover, its style is markedly Hellenistic, and its
conception is entirely in the spirit of the Hellenistic age.   Indeed, there is so little specifically Roman in its execution that
a good case could be made out for its being itself an original.
In any case, it should be discussed among the works of this
period.

The old woman wears two garments, an upper and a lower :
the former is draped over the left shoulder and girt up round
the waist.   A piece of cloth confines the hair.   The right
shoulder and part of the chest are bare, and we can see how
tightly the skin is drawn across the collar-bone.   The missing
right hand, no doubt, carried some heavy object : the left
forearm passes through the handle of a basket, and is ornamented by a bracelet.

Our bronze owes its distinction to the treatment of the
face.   There is no obvious attempt at pathos ; the tired
eyes, sunken cheeks and lines round the mouth are never
exaggerated ; yet the effect is curiously moving.   Here is a
person who has worked unsparingly all her life, and is resigned
to working still in her old age.

It is a short step from representations of old age to those
of SICKNESS.   Half-way between the two stands the excellent
figure of a bald man in the Bibliothèque Nationale.[3]   From
him we pass to the well-known sick man, formerly in the Wyndham Cook Collection (Pl. 77 a).[4]   The extreme emaciation is
certainly due to sickness, and not, as one critic has suggested,
to asceticism.[5]   As an anatomical study, the bronze deserves
praise, though less attention has been paid to familiar points
like fingers and toes than to effective details like the hollows
by the collar-bone, the vertebrae and the bones of the lower

---

[1] Neugebauer, p. 91.   [2] Reisch, *loc. cit.*   [3] No. 854.   Cast hollow.
[4] *Burlington Fine Arts Cat.*, 1904, No. 50, Pl. LII. ; ht., ·115 m.
[5] *Loc. cit.*, p. 27.

arm. Across the knees there is a punctured inscription,[1] Εὐδαμίδας Περδίκ[κα] in lettering which must be of the first century B.C., or later. The legs of the chair are missing. The eyes were once inlaid with silver. The statuette was found near Soissons, and may, therefore, have been at one time in the possession of a Roman colonist or of a rich Gaul.

The humpbacked beggar in Berlin (Pl. 77 c) [2] shews a different treatment of a similar subject. There, again, the figure is emaciated, but less stress is laid on anatomical details, more on general effect, and particularly on the head. The latter is made painfully effective by the eyes, set between overhanging brows and pouches of wrinkled skin. Beneath the humility of the expression there is hidden resentment, and the spectator feels at once embarrassed and repelled, as he would if he met a real Oriental beggar to-day. The rock on which the beggar sits should be contrasted with the rock beneath the maenad on Pl. 64 a.

In the Berlin figure, the characterisation is more important than the deformity. Another step brings us to figures where the deformity is the main feature : often it is exaggerated, in which case they are classed as GROTESQUES. These bronzes exist in large numbers : many come from Egypt, many from Italy, some from elsewhere. They belong both to the Hellenistic Period and to the Roman Period which succeeded it. They include hunchbacks, dwarfs, negroes, and creatures with large heads like Punch. In style, they are often rough and unfinished. Were they made merely to titillate the morbid taste of a degenerate population, such as would be found in the Graeco-Egyptian towns, or had they some other function ? A good case has been made for the use of such bronzes as charms to keep off the evil eye : the charms worn nowadays in South Italy are often in the form of hunchbacks, continuing the old tradition that ugliness is prophylactic.[3] At the same time, there is no doubt that the grotesques appealed to the Hellenistic public, apart from their protective qualities. Just so, our

[1] C.I.G., 6855 B ; *Burlington Fine Arts Cat.*, p. 50, gives the name as Ἐυθαμίδας.

[2] Berlin, 30,894 ; *Anz.*, 1922, p. 88 ; ht., ·158 m. The beggar and rock are cast hollow. Right foot missing. Eyeballs, originally inlaid, missing.

[3] Wace, *B.S.A.*, IX, p. 226 ; and X, 103 ff.

own mascots, which are less offensive but decidedly ugly, are
bought partly for luck and partly because we like their looks.

It is a question to what extent the grotesques were made in
Alexandria. Obviously, their popularity originated there : that
is why they are so often found in Egypt, and why they tend to
represent negroid types. They correspond, moreover, to a certain coarse strain in the Alexandrian temperament, of which we
read in a letter of Synesios. Describing the crew of the boat
from which he landed at that city, he says that each member
addressed the other by a nickname derived from some physical
deformity.[1] The bronzes are, however, so easy to make that
other countries would have copied them, especially Italy.

A well-known grotesque of unusually careful workmanship
is now in New York (Pl. 77 b).[2] The figure, which may be meant
for a comic actor, has a humped back, a crooked nose like a
beak and two protruding teeth. He wears sandals and a
sleeved tunic. The forearms were made separately and inserted ;
they are now lost like the irises of the eyes. The whites of the
eyes and the protruding teeth are of silver, and perhaps the
slight depression on the crown of the head was also once filled
with silver inlay. Niello is used to cover hair, whiskers and
buttons : this is unusual, and the effect must have been most
striking.

The grotesques from the cargo of the ship wrecked off
Mahedia will be described on p. 206. They are important because they can be dated, though not exactly, because they
appear to have once been in an Athenian collection, and because of their individual though unpleasing style.

PORTRAITS—Classical Greek art idealised its portraits :
Roman art treated them, on the whole, realistically. Hellenistic art stands midway between the two. It was well on the
way to realism, but restrained by being often concerned with
princes and other influential people. Realism in portraiture
is, in fact, dependent on the courage of the artist and the good-
nature of his model. In Roman art, however, there were
peculiar causes at work to produce a stronger realism than we
should have expected.

[1] Hercher, *Epistolographi Graeci*, p. 640.
[2] No. 127 ; ht., ·10 m. ; *Catalogue*, pp. 81 ff.

It was not till the Hellenistic Period that portraits became sufficiently popular to be adapted to the form of art under discussion : the statuette. It was then found that the small size had many advantages. Enthusiastic admirers could have in their houses little portraits of their favourite poet or philosopher. A compliment could be paid to the ruler by giving his features to a statuette of Hermes or some other god.

Unfortunately, there is even more controversy about the identification of small portraits than about that of large portraits. Two bronzes are exhibited in Naples : one has been called Antiochos II or Antiochos VIII by different critics (Pl. 78 c),[1] the other, Demetrios Poliorketes or Seleukos I.[2] The former has the body of a Hermes. It is interesting because it was found in Pompeii on a base which had originally belonged to another statuette.[3] It had evidently been preserved as a work of art by several generations and at one time remounted.

The so-called Hermarchos in New York (Pl. 78 b) [4] is a fine piece of work, whether the identification, which rests on its resemblance to an inscribed bust of Hermarchos in Naples, be accepted or not. The figure is typically Hellenistic. It stands, however, on the remains of an Ionic column finished with hook-like projections suitable for the attachment of small vases ; the capital of the column looks Roman. The question whether it belonged originally to the statuette has not been decided.

The examples of Hellenistic work that have been so far examined illustrate either the new departures or the realistic tendencies of the age. Many bronzes, however, cannot be so easily labelled and are yet equally important.

The Satyr from Pergamon (Pl. 74 b) [5] might well be regarded as the counterpart of one of the jolly shepherd boys out of Theokritos. He has the features of a plain, good-natured

---

[1] Wace, *J.H.S.*, 1905, pp. 95, 98 ; and Pernice, *Hellenistische Kunst in Pompeji*, p. 2, Pl. I ; Naples, Inv., 126,170.

[2] Wace, *J.H.S.*, 1905, pp. 87, 94 ; Naples, Inv., 5026.

[3] Pernice, *Hellenistische Kunst in Pompeji*, p. 2, Fig. 1.

[4] Met. Mus., No. 120 ; ht., ·263 m. Cast hollow. Neugebauer, Pl. 50. See also Lippold, *Griechische Porträtstatuen*, p. 82. Miss Richter tells me she queries the identification with Hermarchos in the forthcoming text for the Brunn-Bruckmann plates of sculpture at New York.

[5] Furtwängler, *Kleine Schriften*, I, pp. 190 ff., Pl. IV ; Neugebauer, 47. Found in a private house. Ht., ·15 m.

peasant, and grins cheerfully as he prepares to beat off the animal who attacks him.   Whether the said animal was left to the spectators' imagination or represented and brought into relation with the satyr, we cannot say.   As the satyr was originally fastened to a background by a small tang on the panther skin behind, his adversary could easily have been attached in the same way.   His right hand may have held a short stick, his left, half-wrapped in the panther skin, grasps his pipes. These are of the older form, with all reeds of nearly the same height, not steeply graduated, as in the later form.

The technical details can be summarised as follows :—All parts were cast together except the stick, which is now lost. The right foot has at one time been bent, owing to the absence of a base.   The toes of both feet have no surface that could have been used for fastening, therefore the only support must have been by the tang on the back of panther skin.   Here there is sufficient flat surface to have made attachment easy.[1]   The pupil of the eye is marked by a hollow.   The panther skin is chiselled, the hair is not.

The pose was not a new invention : it occurs as early as the fifth century in the Satyr of Myron.   It was developed by the Pergamene school and used with variations, the constant elements being the raised right hand and the weight carried on the tips of his toes.   Hence the number of dancing fauns and satyrs made in this and the following period.

Many museums possess personifications of cities in the manner of the allegorical Antioch of Eutychides.   There is, for instance, a small Antioch in New York,[2] and a small River Orontes,[3] like the Orontes beneath the feet of Eutychides' statue, in the Louvre.   Though the motive is Hellenistic, the statuettes are usually of Roman date.

This is the place to describe the *bronzes from the cargo of a ship wrecked off Mahedia*,[4] on the coast of Africa.   That the ship was on its way from Athens is shewn by the fact that it

---

[1] Other Hellenistic works were fastened in the same way, e.g. the Theseus or Minotaur, Berlin, 7382 ; *Führer*, p. 71, Pl. 49.

[2] New York, 259.   For other references see Richter, *Catalogue*, p. 131.

[3] Louvre, 520, *Catalogue*, Pl. 39.

[4] *Mon. Piot.*, 1909, p. 29 (Vol. XVII) ; 1910 (Vol. XVIII), pp. 5 ff. ; *Anz.*, 1909, pp. 207 ff. ; 1910, pp. 258 ff. ; 1912, pp. 387 ff. ; Reinach, *Rep.*, IV, p. 557.

carried several Athenian inscriptions. It must have been bound for some Italian port and have been driven off its course on the way. The date of the catastrophe was between 150 and 50 B.C., for a terra-cotta lamp, some pottery and bars of lead inscribed in letters current at the end of the Republic, all belong to this date. It has been suggested that the cargo consisted of booty brought from Athens after its conquest by Sulla.[1]

Among the objects of bronze which the ship carried, the following ten deserve special mention :—

(1), (2) and (3) are a set of grotesque dancers [2] with disproportionately large heads.

(1) A woman playing castanettes and wearing a single shawl-like garment drawn round her, shoes with thick soles and a sort of bonnet (Pl. 79 b).[3]

(2) Woman, younger, with a childish dimpled face and a wreath round her head. She wears a single garment and sandals and holds castanettes. Eyes inlaid : the inlay of one now lost (Pl. 79 a).[4]

(3) Man with a piece of cloth wrapped round his body and a cap. The eyebrows are drawn down at the inner corners and the lips parted ; and, to make the figure more repulsive, the iris of one eye was omitted.[5]

(4) Eros with cithara. This figure has, like the last three, remarkably large eyes, a round fleshy face, and a peculiar hardness of finish. Like No. 2, it was fitted with a ring so that it could be hung up. Though apparently by the same hand, it is not a grotesque, and is somewhat larger. The Eros is remarkable for the number of charms or fillets he wears ; one set hangs down his chest, another is knotted round his leg. He also wears a bracelet, anklets and a necklace with a charm attached. His eyes were originally inlaid (Pl. 79 c).[6]

(5) A satyr ready to leap forward, found in another part of the ship. Good, typical Hellenistic work.[7]

[1] See Reinach, *Rep.*, IV, p. 557.
[2] See Perdrizet, *Bronzes Grecs de la Coll. Fouquet*, p. 66 for parallels.
[3] Ht., 0·295 m. ; *Anz.*, 1912, p. 387, Fig. 2 ; and *Mon. Piot.*, 1910, Pl. II.
[4] Ht., ·315 m. ; *Mon. Piot.*, 1910, Pl. III.
[5] Ht., 0·32 m. ; *Anz.*, 1912, p. 388, Fig. 3 ; and *Mon. Piot.*, 1910, Pl. IV.
[6] Ht., ·42 m. ; *Anz.*, 1912, Fig. 5, p. 391 ; and *Mon. Piot.*, 1910, Pl. I. Are Nos. 1-4 a set ? *Mon. Piot.*, 1910, p. 14, mentions a set of terra-cottas, similar in subject, belonging to the first century B.C.
[7] Ht., 0·35 m. ; *Anz.*, 1912, p. 389, Fig. 4 ; and *Mon. Piot.*, 1910, Pl. V.

(6) Eros advancing with torch (taking part in a torch race ?).[1]

(7) A small bronze representing an actor in a mask seated on a pillar, a not uncommon type.[2]

(8) A bronze herm, ht. 1 m., signed Βοηθὸς Καλχηδόνιος ἐποίει. Boethos was probably the copyist, not the originator of the work.[3]

(9, 10) Two bronze mouldings, one ornamented with the head of Dionysos, the other with that of Ariadne. The heads are 0·20 m. high. It has been conjectured that they covered the ἐπωτίδες (the " cat heads ") on the bows of some ship of state, possibly an Athenian state trireme.[4]

The above account will serve to illustrate the taste of the period, for the objects must have been first the property of Greek collectors, and later the selection of some well-to-do Roman. The grotesques and the Eros are particularly characteristic : they were probably made in Alexandria, though their hard finish contrasts with the softness affected by other branches of Alexandrian art. The satyr is the one really pleasant piece. The minor objects are useful for dating purposes : they serve as proofs that the types they represent were current in the period between 150 and 50 B.C.

ETRURIA—The Hellenistic Period which had been so stimulating to the art of Southern Italy produced a decadence in the art of Etruria, and the Etruscan bronzes now interest us less for their own sake than because they form a link between the Roman bronzes and those made by Etruscan artists during the fourth century. They also entertain us by shewing the effect of Hellenistic motives on the local art.

Two examples will suffice to illustrate both points.

The first is the statuette of a child,[5] from Trasimene, now in the Vatican (Pl. 76 c). On the right leg is an inscription. The child wears bracelets (two), an anklet, and a charm which hangs from his neck by a chain. His right hand holds a bird.

---

[1] Ht., 0·50 m.; *Anz.*, 1910, Fig. 2, p. 262 ; and *Mon. Piot.*, 1909, p. 54, Fig. 5.

[2] *Anz.*, 1912, p. 394, Fig. 6.   [3] *Ibid.*, 1909, p. 211, Fig. 5.

[4] *Ibid.*, 1909, p. 215 ; and 1912, p. 392.

[5] Ducati, *Etruria Antica*, II, p. 111 and Fig. 41 ; *Storia dell' Arte Etrusca*, Pl. 231 *b*. Compare other children, one in the Vatican from Tarquinii, *Storia dell' Arte Etrusca*, Pl. 231 *a* ; and one at Leyden, *Etruria Antica*, p. 111.

The bronze is obviously inspired by the figures of children by Boethos and other Hellenistic artists : the body is awkward but the head realistic. This is what we should expect, for the Etruscans, and the Romans after them, had a gift for portraiture.

The outlines are less hard in this figure than is usual in Etruscan or Roman art : this is due to the absence of drapery. But turn to the Minerva from Orte on Pl. 80 b,[1] who holds a bird, evidently meant for an owl, on her hand. The folds of her garments are sharp and angular, and the same angularity is discernible, in spite of poorer preservation, on hair and face. She may have been made at any date between the end of the fourth century and the end of the second, and has features in common with the figures on the lid of the Ficoroni cista, as well as with the Roman bronzes on Pl. 85.

With the exception of those from Etruria, the bronzes described in this chapter are a cosmopolitan company, and, like true cosmopolitans, lack individuality. They serve to illustrate the mentality of the Hellenistic Age, but throw very little light on its industries. The most we can do is to surmise that certain subjects originated at a particular centre : we cannot assume that the surviving examples were made there. We know, for instance, that the popularity of Gaulish types was due to Pergamene artists, but the bronze statuettes of Gauls may have been made in Alexandria, Italy or France. Similarly, there is good reason to think that grotesques were particularly plentiful in Alexandria, but the extant grotesques might have been made almost anywhere.

There are one or two really fine Hellenistic bronzes, the old woman at Vienna, the negro in Paris, the portrait at New York. Of the others, some are fair, many bad : the latter have little artistic value, but shew that cheap wares were made in large quantities for an undiscerning public, then as now.

The similarity of Hellenistic and Roman bronzes is most misleading. An early Hellenistic bronze can, of course, be easily distinguished from a late Roman, and certain subjects can be set aside as definitely Roman.

[1] In the Vatican ; ht., ·128 m. ; *Ausonia*, V, pp. 101-103, Figs. 21, 22.

14

Apart from these, there is room for infinite confusion. Nor is this surprising. Towards the end of the Hellenistic Period art became stereotyped. The same workshops continued to produce the same motives, unaffected by the gradual advance of the Roman dominion. The main element among their customers was the same, and the new Roman element liked to buy something approved by Greek taste. Artists often migrated to Italy, creating a fresh demand for their own wares. In consequence, there are many indefinite bronzes which might have been made any time between 200 B.C. and 100 A.D. and which a conscientious student can only label " Graeco-Roman ": some are of the inferior, commercial type described above, others are good work, but conventional. Certain bronzes are " Graeco-Roman " in a slightly different sense : their subject and style are characteristic of Greek work of the Hellenistic Age, but there is every reason to think they were made in a period which historians would call Roman. A good example is the sick man from the Wyndham Cook Collection, and several others will have been noted by the reader. For, in this chapter, style and subject have been used as grounds for classification : statuettes in the Hellenistic tradition are obviously more at home here than in the next chapter, whatever their date.

During the first half of the last century before Christ, certain new elements, which can only be Roman, make their appearance, and certain technical peculiarities associated with Roman subjects become increasingly common. The bronzes which exhibit these features form a class apart, and will be the subject of Chapter IX.

B. DECORATIVE WORK, VASES, ETC.

(i) SOUTH ITALY—For elegance of form and perfection of detail, the Hellenistic vases and utensils of metal deserve high praise. They may have been produced at several centres, but we can write with certainty of one centre only. This is South Italy, where the workshops began as long ago as the sixth century, flourished and prospered during the fifth and fourth, and, in the Hellenistic Period, became the most important in the ancient world. Its wares were exported to the rest of Italy, to Greece, Egypt, Asia Minor, Thrace and South Russia.[1] No

---

[1] Pernice, *Hellenistische Kunst in Pompeji*, pp. 6-8.

doubt there were rival centres which threatened its trade, but they have so far failed to make an impression on posterity.

It is safer to speak of South Italy in general than of Tarentum in particular, as many do. The vicissitudes through which that city passed cannot have favoured the uninterrupted output of works of art ; probably other towns contributed their share.

Our knowledge of the South Italian fabrics has not been easily supplied to us by the excavation of Hellenistic sites or by a large and convincing number of undoubted examples. It is a still unfinished structure of which each stone has been painfully collected, and at first a reliable foundation was hard to find.

The process of investigation was as follows :—

We know of several earlier types of metal-work that were undoubtedly made in South Italy: the pails described on p. 187, the mirrors described on p. 181, and the silver rhyton.[1] Recently, work has been done in identifying certain stone reliefs as Tarentine.[2] Hence, students are fairly competent to recognise the style of South Italian works from the fifth century onwards, and have been able to attribute to South Italy a number of bronzes of which the copper *emblema* inside a bronze bowl from the Kuban is a good example.[3] Of all branches of South Italian art, however, we know most about the pottery. The pottery vases often have very individual features : they display variations of shape which must be local, and their profiles, even when conventional, are easily distinguished from those of earlier Greek vases. Therefore, it is safe to assign to South Italy any metal vases which shew the same features, and to consider them, other things being equal, as not far from the pottery vases in date.

One remarkable result of this process is that if we apply the test to vases from Herculaneum and Pompeii, some of the best metal vessels appear to be Hellenistic.[4] This, on second thoughts, is not surprising. Pompeii was a flourishing city during the whole of the period, and buildings dating from the second century B.C. were still in existence when the great

[1] *Jahreshefte*, V, 1902, p. 112.
[2] *Münchner Jahrbuch*, XII (1923), p. 117.
[3] *Anz.*, 1906, p. 111.   [4] Pernice, *op. cit.*, p. 8.

eruption occurred in 79 A.D. Herculaneum, too, had a long history behind it.

Many Hellenistic bronze statuettes were preserved by the inhabitants and handed on from generation to generation,[1] and it is not to be wondered at that the bronze vessels, many of which are equally fine, should have been treasured with equal care. The fact that some have been obviously adapted and repaired shews that they must have long been in use.

The beautiful calyx *crater* on Pl. 82 *b* has a good claim to be Hellenistic.[2] It is the earliest of four types common in Herculaneum and Pompeii. The handles of this type are always finished below with Silens' masks. There is usually a stand below the foot of the crater, which, in some of the examples at Naples, is not the one originally belonging to the vase. The column crater on Pl. 82 *a*, from Herculaneum, is one that would, on stylistic evidence, have been attributed to the fourth century, and might have been made in the Hellenistic Period but scarcely later.[3] It finds its counterpart in vases like the Orestes amphora from Ruvo.[4]

The South Italian *situlae*, or pails, of the fifth and fourth centuries have already been described. In the third and the succeeding centuries several new shapes were evolved, while the elegant shape that had been used for the Perseus pail was still popular. A number of pails of this shape are simply decorated with an egg-moulding, while the outline is enlivened by the two handles and their attachments. In other pails, there is a palmette, more or less elaborate, below the handles. Both the simplest and the most ornate examples come from Pompeii, and can safely be attributed to a pre-Roman Period.[5] Pails of all kinds became a very profitable article for export : some went east, others north : in the course of time they penetrated into most northerly countries of Europe.

Two bronze *vessels* from Pompeii, which are more interesting than beautiful, deserve mention here. One, nicknamed the " samovar " (Pl. 81 *b*), is obviously meant for some hot liquid, for it has a conical outer lid and an inner lid, as well as a

[1] See p. 197.
[2] Naples, 73,098 ; Pernice, *op. cit.*, pp. 38, 42, Pl. XI.
[3] *Ibid.*, p. 9, Fig. 9.   [4] *Ibid.*, Fig. 8.
[5] See *ibid.*, pp. 21-29.

spout.[1] Conical lids are not common, but they occur in South
Italian pottery : a vase already mentioned, shewing Orestes
and the Furies,[2] had both a conical lid and handles like those of
the samovar and the column crater.   Similar legs can be found
on another vase at Naples.[3]

The other vessel is the big hot-water jar with pairs of wrestlers as handles for the lid (Pl. 81 a).[4]   By means of these handles
the whole upper part of the vessel could be lifted out.

The lower part contained hot coals which could be inserted
through the small door.   The wrestlers, the hands which serve
as finish to the lower pair of handles, the patterns on the lid,
the supporting feet, the little upright rosettes on the lower
handles are all early in type and suggest a date in the second
century B.C.[5]   Whether the small Eros on the top of the vase
and the masks belonged to the original vase must remain
uncertain.

Candelabra with feet like those on Pl. 84 a [6] can be safely
assigned to the Hellenistic Period, or to an even earlier date,
for one of the same type came from a fourth century grave at
Roccanova [7] now at Tarentum.   It was a type which probably
remained in use some time, and, though originally meant to
carry candles, was often adapted for lamps at a later period.

A certain type of *askos* now plays an important part.   Its
shape was suggested by a wine skin half filled ; a conceit that
had caught hold of the Italian imagination, though never that
of the Greek.[8]   Like so many vases of the period, these askoi
testify rather to the vitality and ingenuity than to the taste of
the workshops which produced them.

Another aspect of South Italian art is shewn by the ornamented breastplates made, probably in Campania, during the
third century B.C.   The best known of these comes from a tomb
at Ksour-es-Saf in North Africa.[9]

[1] Pernice, *op. cit.*, p. 9, Pl. II.   [2] *Ibid.*, Fig. 8.
[3] Photo Allinari, No. 11,296.
[4] Pernice, *op. cit.*, Pl. VII, and pp. 30 ff.   One pair of wrestlers has disappeared.   The other has been resoldered on to the lid in modern times.
[5] *Ibid.*, pp. 30-34.
[6] *Ibid.*, p. 43, Fig. 53.   At Naples.   [7] *Ibid.*, p. 45.
[8] *Ibid.*, p. 14.   Examples from Greece are very rare.   Pernice quotes one
from Dodona.
[9] *Mon. Piot.*, XVII (1909), p. 131, Pls. XIII, XIV.

(ii) ETRURIA—Of the Etruscan bronze utensils, some are decadent survivals of an earlier period, others vital forerunners of the art of Rome. To the first class belong the mirrors, to the latter most of the candelabra.

The fault of the mirrors lies in the carelessness of the engraving, and the fact that the figures which adorn them have become stereotyped. This is well shewn by the many mirrors on which are drawn the two Dioskouroi, Castor and Pollux, recognisable by their Phrygian caps. Another favourite subject was the winged Lasa, a spirit who, as far as we can judge, presided over women's toilet.

The Lasa was also used as a handle for the bronze bowls (paterae) which are found in Etruscan tombs,[1] and which are comparatively well made. She usually stands in an elegant attitude with her pretty wings spread beneath the rim of the bowl, unconscious of the weight above her head. There is often a ring beneath her feet which enables the bowl to be suspended.

Among the various candelabra, kottabos stands and incense-burners, one lamp stand has been selected (Pl. 83 c) [2] which shews a typical blend of Etruscan and Greek elements. Whether the upper part really belongs is uncertain, though it harmonises well enough with the lower.

The slave boy, who holds up the bowl, and balances himself so neatly, is a figure not uncommon on bronzes of this kind. Here he is accompanied by a little dog, who imitates him, standing on his hind legs and completing the group. The motive is pleasing to us, and would have appealed to Hellenistic taste. Below the shaft is another slave, this time a negro, carrying a bowl in his right hand, a wine skin in his left. He is the counterpart of the foreign figures described above, and might have been made by a Greek. Three bending women support the shaft in place of feet. This is a well-known Etruscan device, but one which no Greek would have tolerated.

The excessive number of human figures, too, is Etruscan. The artists of that country had not sufficient discernment to realise the beauty of a plain, well-proportioned object, therefore they found it necessary to embellish the objects they made,

---

[1] Richter, *Catalogue*, p. 217.
[2] Rome, Vatican ; ht., ·53 m. ; Neugebauer, p. 102, Fig. 6.

either with human figures, or with animal and floral motives. Now, the combination of human figures, plants and animals is a feature of the later Roman bronzes from Pompeii and Herculaneum. By that time, practice had made perfect : the different elements harmonise better than they had done in Etruria, and the result, though florid, is no longer bizarre. The obvious conclusion is that the makers of the Pompeian bronzes owe a great deal to the Etruscan, more, perhaps, than is generally admitted. The former were the heirs of the latter, but better educated by closer contact with Greek art.

CHAPTER IX

ROMAN BRONZES

A. STATUETTES

THE last of the periods which concerns us is marked by the appearance of certain bronzes which, in subject and technique, are definitely Roman. We cannot say exactly when it began, though we know it was in existence before the end of the first century B.C. It may have been produced by the artistic revival under Augustus, but was probably earlier. Its lower limit is even more uncertain than its upper, owing to the scarcity of bronzes which are definitely late. Nor is it easy to date bronzes within the period. Some, of course, can be placed before or after a certain date, if they come from a site of which we know the history. Those from Herculaneum and Pompeii, for instance, must be earlier than 79 A.D. Some can be dated by the fashion of their dress and hair ; busts can be dated on the same principle as marble busts. All this, however, is very inadequate. Further evidence may come with fresh excavation, or with intensive study of the bronzes themselves, which have, hitherto, been sadly neglected.

The term *Roman bronzes* must now be explained more fully. It is here applied to bronzes of which the subjects are obviously Roman, such as Lares, men sacrificing dressed in the toga, priestesses, attendants on priests (*camilli*), gladiators, etc. To these we may add certain portraits, including the numerous small busts of Roman emperors, and the figures of less-known men and women dressed in the Roman fashion.

Subject is here the most certain basis for definition. An examination of the bronzes will, however, shew that the majority are characterised by a technique sufficiently marked to constitute a distinct " Roman style." This discovery may help us to reduce that large group of indefinite bronzes that lies between the Hellenistic and the Roman (see p. 210). For, if we find the " Roman style " present in any of the " indefinite " bronzes, we can safely assign that bronze to the Roman Period.

Apart from these considerations, the Roman bronzes merit closer acquaintance. They are, on the whole, unimportant from the artistic point of view, but not without dignity ; moreover, they form a useful illustration of contemporary life and religion. Their technique errs on the side of hardness, and this is a fault in the right direction.

ROMAN SUBJECTS : (1) *Lares*—The cult of the Lares Compitales, those spirits worshipped at the *compita*, or cross roads, was revived and stimulated by Augustus to such an extent that it influenced the corresponding cult of the Lar Familiaris. The results were, firstly, that the Lar Familiaris becomes duplicated to match the Lares Compitales : secondly that, like them, he was represented dancing.

Wall paintings, such as those in Pompeii, shew a pair of dancing Lares flanking the Genius of the master of the house.[1] Bronzes found in the household shrines resemble very closely the Lares in the paintings, and can safely be regarded as the actual images which the family venerated. Countless similar bronzes line the shelves of our museums, looking so unassuming that it is pleasant to think what an important part they once played. Few of them have any claim to be considered earlier than the Empire : they are an indirect result of Augustus' reforms.

They take the form of youths with rather long hair, wearing a short-girt tunic,[2] sometimes also a scarf or mantle, and boots or sandals. One hand is raised holding a drinking horn, the other is extended and usually holds a patera. We must picture them in pairs, with the outer arms raised, as in the paintings. A nice pair was found in a Pompeian house, where it shared the Lararium with Jupiter, Juno and Minerva, a seated Mercury and a bronze oinochoe.[3]

Sometimes we get an exceptional figure, e.g. a Lar in the

[1] See Roscher, II², p. 1883, Fig. 2, which also shews a typical group of figures ; and Mau, *Pompeii in Leben und Kunst*, p. 279, Fig. 143, p. 254, Fig. 128 (in the House of the Vetii).
[2] The example on Pl. 85 *a* is Louvre, 686 ; ht., ·137 m.
[3] *Notizie degli Scavi*, 1907, pp. 564 ff. Casa degli Amorini Dorati.

Louvre,[1] who wears a dog-skin (see Plut., *Quaest. Rom.* 51) ;
sometimes we get representatives of the older type of Lar
Familiaris, who stand quietly holding a cornucopia.[2]

The style is undistinguished, as one would expect. The
drapery is marked with many folds which are often rather hard
and angular. The details of face and hair also tend to be hard
and angular : this is the result of the bronze having been worked
on after casting.

(2) *Men sacrificing*—They were made in large numbers.
One of the best is No. 1584 [3] in the British Museum. It has an
excellent patina, and was in ancient times embellished by an
inlaid stripe on the right shoulder of the tunic : the eyes were
also inlaid. The toga is drawn over the head, and, while one
end was thrown over the left arm, the other was tucked into a
transverse fold round the waist. The effect was to make a
number of close, semicircular folds in the drapery : in many
examples, the folds have become almost too symmetrical. The
shoes leave the toes uncovered ; the right hand holds a fruit,
the left, now lost, must, on the analogy of similar figures, have
held a patera.

The folds of drapery on all bronzes of this class closely
resemble the folds on the togas of countless marble portrait
statues. A question arises as to whether the bronzes represent
ordinary Roman citizens and priests or have some religious
significance. They are remarkably like the Genius of the house-
holder, as he appears in paintings between the two Lares.
Probably they could be used both to personify the Genius in
the Lararium and for purely decorative purposes.

Curiously enough, Pompeii and Herculaneum produced very
few examples.

(3) *Women sacrificing*—These are the counterpart of the
men just described. They are often of poor quality,
which shews itself, in particular, by the extreme thinness of
the statuettes. This thinness recalls many of the inferior
Etruscan bronzes from the sixth century onwards : as the subject in question appears to go back at least as far as the third

---

[1] Louvre, 683 ; ht., ·15 m. ; Pl. 47.
[2] Roscher, II², p. 1892, Fig. 4 ; and B.M., 1566.
[3] B.M., 1584 ; ht., ·135 m.

century B.C., we can regard it as one of the links between Etruscan and Roman art.

The women are represented standing, with the right hand raised to pour libation from a patera, while the left often holds a small box (*acerra*). They wear a tunic with a high girdle, a cloak (*palla*), and a diadem of the form shewn on Pl. 86 c. The cloak, like the men's toga, is drawn over the head in accordance with the custom of pious Romans performing their religious exercises.

The most distinguished of these figures is now,in the British Museum (Pl. 86 c).[1] It shews how effective the motive could become in the hands of a careful artist. There is an individuality about the features, which are those of a woman no longer young, and a distinct grace in the angular figure. She belongs to a set of seven, which were said to come from one of the sunk "galleys," more accurately described as pontoons, in Lake Nemi.[2] These galleys are associated with the name of Caligula. The bronzes from the "galleys" were salvaged in 1895, whereupon they mysteriously leaked out of Italy. Some were recovered for the Terme Museum, others remained in the market.

It is, however, improbable that any of the seven here mentioned come from Lake Nemi. In the first place, had they been immersed so long, they would have been more corroded. In the second place, their connection with the late fourth and early third century types of Praeneste and Etruria is so close that they cannot be later than the first century B.C.

Of the six companion figures to the British Museum priestess, three were women like herself, and three youths wearing a rayed head-dress of a type common in Roman bronzes.[3] All carry paterae, and all are marked by the same sharply cut lines and the same narrowness of shoulder, a fact which shews that even the better artists were affected by the meagre proportions of the common type.

(4) *Gladiators*—The figure of a gladiator was an appropriate

---

[1] B.M., 1913, 5-29 ; ht., ·263 m.   [2] *Revue Archéologique*, 1909, p. 177.

[3] These figures are exceedingly characteristic of the period, but since their subject has not yet been satisfactorily identified, they are not described in this book. They wear the radiated head-dress and are draped in a cloak.

Usually they are found with the figures of women sacrificing, which should be borne in mind by those who attempt to identify them.

finish to a knife.   Many of the bronze gladiators in our museums
shew traces of the knife blade to which they were once attached.
Examples have been found in Italy, Gaul, Egypt, Spain and
South-Eastern Europe : one of the finest is in Berlin.[1]   It
is remarkable for its decorative detail : engraved spirals on
greaves, shield and thighs ; silver bosses on belt ; silver ribs on
shield ; a silver visor.   The knife was attached to the back.
    Other typically Roman subjects will suggest themselves :
e.g. *camilli* [2] (boys who assisted certain priests in religious
ceremonies), *Roman officials* carrying fasces or other insignia
of office,[3] or personifications of the *Genius Castrorum*.[4]
    Portraits are not uncommon, especially in the form of busts.
Some of these busts were intended for attachment to an object,
and some served as weights : in such cases they have, of course,
no artistic merit.   Others appear to have been ornamental
rather than useful : if portraits of the reigning emperor, they
would indicate the loyalty of their possessor.   The bronze
busts can be classified, like the larger marble busts, according
to their proportions.[5]

THE " ROMAN STYLE "—None of the bronzes here described is of first-class workmanship, though each is among the
best of its own class and stands at the head of a quantity of
humbler examples.   No doubt, the Roman citizens whose houses
they adorned were no more fastidious than those of us who to-
day crowd our mantelpieces with cheap figures of crockery and
plaster.   First-class bronzes would, however, have had more
individuality and less, therefore, of those elements which are
the common measure of the Roman style.   The style, if analysed,
will be seen to depend on a certain hard precision : eyes and
eyelids, hair, and drapery are clean-cut, angular, regular.   In
other words, the Roman bronze-worker relied too much on the

---

[1] Berlin, 8583.   Described by Neugebauer, p. 110, Pl. 60.   He suggests
that the engraving on the thighs may represent tattooing.
    [2] A fine example in New York, No. 271 ; ht., 1·17 m. ; Richter, *Catalogue*,
p. 135 ; and Strong, *Scultura Romana*, p. 89, and p. 92, Fig. 63.
    [3] E.g. B.M., 1585, 1586.   [4] Vienna, 1282.
    [5] I.e. in the Julio-Claudian Period, the " bust " includes the collar-bone ;
in the Flavian Period, the shoulders and pectoral line ; in the Hadrianic and
Antonine Periods, the upper arm and lower chest ; in the third century A.D.,
the whole upper part of the body.

effect he could get by chasing the bronze when it had been cast :
the inference is that he did not trouble enough about the actual
casting.

This procedure is, of course, liable to occur in almost any
workshop, at almost any period, but with the Romans, as with
their Etruscan and Italian predecessors, it was so common that
it can be regarded as characteristic.   Its most shameless mani-
festation was, perhaps, the way folds in drapery were accentuated by lines cut beside them in the surface of the bronze.

The style which I have attempted to define has a twofold
importance.   In the first place, it may be useful for classifying
doubtful bronzes.   There is, for instance, in the British Museum,
an attractive statuette of a Gaulish prisoner, standing with his
hands bound behind him, wearing a tunic and trousers (Pl.
86 a).[1]   His dress, face and hair are all worked over, sharply
cut and polished.   We are pleased by the result, just as we
should be pleased by a neat, efficient piece of draughtsmanship.
Now Gauls, as we have seen, can be either Hellenistic, Greek
or Roman, and the manner in which this Gaul has been tooled
is typically Roman.   He should probably be dated in the first
century A.D.

In the second place, this style is significant because it shews
that the makers of the Roman bronzes were the descendants,
metaphorically speaking, of the Etruscan and Italian artists
of the late fifth and succeeding centuries.   The fourth century
figures on Pl. 66 shew the same clean-cut lines, the same re-
liance on the chisel rather than on the mould.   Though some
of the craftsmen who worked for the Romans may have been
immigrants from South Italy or the Greek East, many must
have been of Etruscan or Latin stock, and the apprentices of an
earlier generation of Latins and Etruscans.

OTHER BRONZES OF THE PERIOD : COPIES AND ADAP-
TATIONS—Side by side with the Roman bronzes in the strict
sense of the word are others.   Many of these, as has already
been pointed out, carry on the Hellenistic tradition, which was

---

[1] B.M., 1913, 4-16 ; ht., ·108 m.   From Umbria.   The back of the
figure is concave and the backs of the arms are flat.   Therefore, the bronze
must have been meant for attachment to a vase.   Compare the captives on
the handle described below, p. 236.

weakening in power of invention, though not in its hold on the popular taste. Some appear more Hellenic than Hellenistic, being copies of Greek originals of the fourth, fifth or even sixth centuries. By all these, the true "Roman bronzes" were outnumbered.

Concerning the original works of art which were imported into Rome, either acquired by legitimate purchase or looted during various campaigns, so much has been written that there is no need to repeat it here. Roman authors speak chiefly of life-sized sculpture, but bronze statuettes were more portable and equally popular. They may have helped to fill the 240 chariots which carried works of art in the triumph of Aemilius Paulus.

The more intelligent Roman connoisseurs really appreciated good Greek originals, the less intelligent acquired them because it was fashionable to do so. Since the supply was unequal to the demand, reproductions were made : some reproductions are close to the originals, some shew variations which were designed to please Roman taste. Drapery, for instance, was added, or the position of the arms transposed, or an athlete turned into a god by the addition of attributes. Such variations can be studied in certain bronzes which appear to be ultimately derived from the Doryphoros of Polykleitos : one of these, a Hermes in the Bibliothèque Nationale (Pl. 87 b),[1] wears a chlamys which covers his body, and held some object in his right hand : another, the Hermes from Fins d'Annecy,[2] raises his right hand and lowers his left, thus reversing the action of the Doryphoros, though perhaps recalling some other Polykleitan statue : [3] a third, also a Hermes, in the British Museum [4] wears a torque, possibly added in modern times, and a chlamys, and carries a purse and a herald's staff (Pl. 87 a).

All these examples bear, in some way or other, the Roman stamp. Our first, which Furtwängler attributes to the Augustan Period, has a characteristic smoothness of surface accompanied

[1] No. 838 ; ht., ·195 m.
[2] In the Dutuit Collection, Petit Palais, in 1909 ; Furtwängler, *Masterpieces*, p. 231.   [3] *Jahrb.*, 1909, p. 3, Fig. 2, and p. 6.
[4] B.M., 825 ; ht., ·153 m. without base ; Furtwängler, *loc. cit.*, p. 232. The statuette has also been called Lysippean (Walters, *Catalogue*, p. 149). The eyes were inlaid. The surface of the whole has, like that of most bronzes from the Payne Knight Collection, been spoiled by polishing.

by faulty proportion in the arms, which are too short. There are also late elements in the rendering of the hair.

The second has not only a very smooth surface, but drapery cut in the Roman manner. The third betrays its Roman origin in many ways : the motive of the purse is Roman and likewise the treatment of the hair : moreover, the copyist has been influenced by the Lysippean proportions and has made the legs longer than Polykleitos himself would have done. For the rest, chlamys and caduceus are restored. The possibly modern torque is of gold, as are the bosses which fastened the chlamys on the shoulders. The base is original, and has been inlaid with silver. The statuette was found by some peasants in a cave at Pierre-en-Luiset near Lyons.

It was natural that, as collectors and connoisseurs, the Romans should interest themselves in works of the sixth century as well as in those of the fifth. We possess various copies and adaptations of sixth century bronzes, and it is probable, though not certain, that they were made at this period. We can attribute them, provisionally, to a date between 50 B.C. and 50 A.D.

One of them is the Payne Knight Apollo in the British Museum (Pl. 88 c) : [1] the motive is archaic, but the rendering (though not the arrangement) of the hair is free. This bronze is considered to be a copy of the famous Apollo Philesios of Kanachos, a Sikyonian artist of the sixth century B.C.[2]

Two other bronzes resemble their originals sufficiently closely to have been mistaken for genuine archaic works. The first is the lovely Kore with diamond eyes in the British Museum [3] (Pl. 88 a), the second is a Hermes in Boston [4] (Pl. 88 b). The latter is after an Arcadian model by an artist steeped in the Neo-Attic tradition.

HERCULANEUM AND POMPEII—The bronzes from Herculaneum and Pompeii are the best possible comment on the

[1] B.M., 209 ; ht., ·18 m. ; Langlotz, pp. 31, 46.

[2] K. O. Müller has suggested that the statuette would have approached more nearly to the style of the original were it not the product of a mould that had lost its sharpness through being too much used (*Kleine Schriften*, p. 357, quoted by Langlotz, p. 46).

[3] B.M., 192 ; ht., ·153 (without base).

[4] Boston, Fine Arts Mus., 99, 489 ; ht., ·25 m. ; Langlotz, p. 31.

taste of the provincial middle-class Roman of the first century
A.D., and the shelves of the Naples Museum, where they are
arranged, are as good as an art exhibition of the period.   A
written account of them cannot fail to give a distorted impression, for it will inevitably stress the good pieces, and give inadequate space to those poorer pieces, which are really far more
numerous and characteristic.   This is particularly undesirable,
for some of the best bronzes from Pompeii and Herculaneum
were not made in the Roman Period but were Hellenistic works
cherished as heirlooms.   All the bronzes must, as already stated,
belong to a date before 79 A.D.

The *Dancing Faun*, from the House of the Faun in Pompeii,
is one of these heirlooms, and has already been mentioned in connection with Hellenistic art.[1]   Like many household treasures,
ancient as well as modern, he got broken : apparently the base
was damaged and the left ankle cracked off.   Thereupon the
owner sent him to be repaired : the ankle was neatly mended
and a base originally made for something else took the place
of the old base.   The back of this second base appears to be
soldered on, not, as usual, cast with it : this suggests that the
original proportions had been longer from back to front and
that the back part was subsequently cut off.   On the front
corners are inlaid silver designs ; the corresponding designs at
the back went with the missing piece.

The *Portrait of a Hellenistic Ruler* from Pompeii, described
on p. 205, and also remounted, is another example of the survival of earlier works (Pl. 78 c).

The *Nocera Venus* [2] has also been considered Hellenistic,
though, if so, she must be very late Hellenistic (Pl. 89 a).   Her
drapery is sharply chased in the manner we associate with the
" Roman Period," and the surface is diversified by minute
punctures, a device which, in this connection, suggests Roman
work.   Her type is not far from that of the Venus of Milo, and
she belongs to that class of Aphrodite whose garment remains
miraculously unsupported.   Pieces of plaster, inserted beneath

[1] See p. 197 ; and Pernice, *Hellenistische Kunst in Pompeji*, pp. 2-4, and
Figs. 2 and 3.

[2] Naples, 4998 ; Pernice, *op. cit.*, pp. 3, 4, Fig. 4.   The left hand may have
held a mirror, but I have not been able to examine the figure closely enough
to verify this.

both feet, disguise the fact that she too has been mounted, perhaps in modern times, on an alien base.   The base is not of a very late form, and may have belonged to a lamp stand.

Though she is not actually from Pompeii or Herculaneum, she is from the same district, and can most fitly be described here.

There is more difficulty in placing the well-known " Narcissus," who is really *Dionysos* [1] beckoning to a panther which is left to the spectators' fancy.   He may well be one of the better examples of the survival of the Hellenistic tradition in works made during the Roman Period.   The same may be true of the equally famous *Satyr with a wine-skin.* [2]

An original by Lysippos is usually inferred for the bronze statuette of a Macedonian horseman, often called Alexander : [3] the statuette itself is clearly Roman.   It shews the Roman copyist at his worst, and we ought not to libel the Greek artist by stressing the connection.

How the Italian spirit could affect an Alexandrian motive is shewn by the figure of a rather florid young *fisherman* [4] armed with rod and fish-basket, and seated on a rock.   He retains little of the realism which marks most Hellenistic genre figures : instead, he looks like certain Neapolitan townsfolk of to-day, fleshy, common and rather handsome.   This bronze is one of the many which once ornamented a fountain.

Among the more recent finds from Pompeii [5] is a set of four grotesques, probably representing itinerant vendors of cakes, for they carry plates.   The plates are inlaid, and the perfection of the technique is in striking contrast to the repulsive ugliness of the subject.

A still less-pleasing aspect of South Italian taste is shewn by those fat, complacent cupids with top-knots, and those bloated, hairy silens, which catch the unwilling eye as one passes through the galleries of the Naples Museum. [6]   The silens recline on rocks and clasp or bestride their wine-skins ;

---

[1] Naples, 817 ; *Guida*, pp. 202, 203, Fig. 47.   From Pompeii.
[2] Naples, 815 (III, 495); *Guida*, p. 202; Overbeck, *Pompeii*, p. 548, Fig. 285.
[3] Naples, 1487 ; *Guida*, p. 353, Fig. 80.   From Herculaneum.
[4] Naples, 825 (4994) ; *Guida*, p. 204.   From Pompeii.
[5] *Bolletino d'Arte*, 1925 (December), p. 268, from the new excavations in the Via del Abbondanza.
[6] Comparetti and de Petra, *La Villa Hercolanese dei Pisoni*, Pl. XVI.

15

the cupids rest their arms on pillars and often hold dolphins or wine-skins or torches ; usually the figures are in pairs with the attributes reversed.   Such figures were part of the proper equipment for a gentleman's garden : a typical example is shewn on Pl. 89 c.[1]

It is interesting to speculate how many of the bronzes described above were made locally.   No doubt, works of art still came in from abroad, but there must have been, at this time, many workshops in Campania itself, staffed by workmen of mixed origin and varied capacity.   Their wares would be easily accessible to the Pompeian tradesman when he became rich enough to build himself a villa and lay out his grounds : he would avail himself of the opportunity to order a set of cupids or any other suitable figures.   With these, he would crown his pedestals and fountains, and sit, on hot afternoons, listening to the trickle of the water with satisfaction tinged with vague regret because his bronzes were so like the set next door.

Within the house, he would furnish his Lararium with its pair of bronze Lares, and perhaps two or three gods and goddesses : in other spots, he would arrange a selection of Minervas, Mercuries, Fortunas, actors, barbarians and grotesques.   If he wished to appear as a scholar, he would display somewhere the small bust of a well-known philosopher.[2]   There would also be many figures serving as supports to lamps, tables and other articles of furniture.   All these would, he hoped, shew him a man of taste, a man of property, and a man who conformed to the conventions of the society in which he lived.

THE ROMAN PROVINCES—In the Roman provinces to the East—Egypt, Greece, Asia Minor and Syria—many bronzes were made that were Hellenistic in motive and tradition.   Of those from Greece and Asia Minor we know comparatively little, of those from Egypt and Syria somewhat more.

Egypt—The bazaars of Alexandria still provided tourists and residents with figures that differed very little from those

[1] Naples, 5030 ; ht., ·49 m.   From Comparetti and de Petra, *op. cit.*, Pl. XVI, Fig. 4.

[2] Cf. the busts of philosophers from Herculaneum, inscribed with their names and therefore useful for identifying other portraits ; Comparetti and de Petra, *op. cit.*, Pl. XII.

made in the Hellenistic Period. From Alexandria, probably, come many of the statuettes of Isis, Serapis and Harpokrates, gods of Egyptian origin, more or less Hellenised, who had a marvellous hold on the popular imagination. Isis, with her lotus head-dress, we know well : in Roman times, she often borrowed the attributes of other deities, Venus, Fortuna, Hygieia. Harpokrates is the child asking for silence with finger on lip :[1] like Isis, and like many gods at this period, he becomes confused in the mind of artist and public with other gods, and so is seen with the wings of Eros, the ivy wreath of Bacchus, and other things that did not originally belong to him.

We owe our knowledge of *Syrian bronzes* in a large measure to the de Clercq Collection.[2] The statuettes in this collection were acquired, with a few exceptions, from Syria and the Phoenician coast, and the majority belong to the Roman Period. Their technique is undistinguished, as is that of most bronzes from the Eastern provinces, but they shew what subjects were in vogue in this part of the world. The favourite is, on the whole, an Aphrodite of a type with which most people are familiar. She is crowned with a head-dress of spreading palmettes : to these, the figure on Pl. 89 b [3] adds a complicated device of uraeus and horns borrowed from Isis.

From north Syria and Commagene came the cult of Jupiter Dolichenus, a cult that was carried north and west by the army.[4] The god is generally represented like a soldier fully armed, but carrying an axe. Such figures have been found as far north as Germany and the Island of Fünen : [5] their inspiration comes from Syria, but there is no reason to think they were made in that province. On the other hand, a small bronze figure of the Genius of Jupiter Dolichenus, in the likeness of an armed child running, comes actually from Marash, which is not very far from Doliche itself.[6] It was not till the second century A.D. that the cult became really popular, which suggests that all the figures are comparatively late. This conclusion is supported

---

[1] Originally the infant Osiris sucking his thumb, which was later misinterpreted (Dr. A. B. Cook).

[2] De Ridder, *Cat. de la Collection de Clercq*, III.

[3] Ht., ·36 m. ; de Ridder, *op. cit.*, No. 106, p. 77, Pl. XXI. The right hand originally held a mirror. The necklace and bracelet are of gold.

[4] A. B. Cook, *Zeus*, I, p. 607.

[5] Neugebauer, p. 121. [6] *Op. cit.*, p. 118, Pl. 65.

by the fact that some of the bronzes have, on independent grounds, been attributed to the time of Caracalla.[1]

Many bronzes have been found in the *Northern Balkans*, in *Austria* and in *Hungary*. Among those which appear to have been imported, I would mention a group of small figures found near Starigrad in Dalmatia.[2] The group consists of a Roman emperor charging, his standard bearer, a follower, and two barbarian enemies, probably Dacians, one fleeing, one fallen. The bronzes made locally are poor and clumsy. There are several Venuses,[3] often very stiff and elongated, including an adaptation of the inevitable Medici type : [4] there is also an interesting Diana from Scheibbs.[5] Diana picks an arrow from her quiver with an affected gesture obviously copied from Graeco-Roman sculpture, but her dress is that of a peasant, thick, full and unyielding, and her head-dress, though meant for a stephane, looks like a frilled cap (Pl. 91 *a*).

Turning to the *northern provinces*, we pass from a part of the world where classical culture had long been established to one where it was new and alien. Nevertheless, many bronze statuettes found their way even to remote *Germany*, though they were not so many as the bronze pails and cooking pots of which more will be said in a later section. Some of the statuettes were procured for decorating the house and the household shrine : some, if we believe a recent authority, were bought second-hand as toys for children.[6] Near Marren in Oldenburg two statuettes have been discovered, together with a coin of Decentius (350-353 A.D.), carefully buried inside a little ring of stones : [7] it is amusing to speculate what purpose they had served, and why they were so concealed.

The statuette of Jupiter Dolichenus on Pl. 90 *b* comes from a German grave at Lichtenberg, and is considered to be the

---

[1] *Op. cit.*, p. 121.

[2] Vienna, 1328. The present grouping of the figures commends itself, though we cannot be certain if it is the original one.

[3] Vienna, 1293. (From Thorda, Siebenburgen.) Vienna, 1296. (From Unterach, Altensee.) Vienna, 1291.

[4] Vienna, 1295. (From Unterach, Altensee.)

[5] Vienna, 1292 ; ht., ·163 m. ; Kenner, *Fündchronik, IX* (*Archiv für Künde Oesterreichischer Geschichtsquellen XXXVIII*), p. 155, No. 2, Fig. 15.

[6] Willers, *Neue Untersuchungen*, p. 98.

[7] *Op. cit.*, p. 95.

work of a provincial artist whose home was north of the Alps.[1]
Originally, the right hand held a double axe, the left a thunderbolt, and inlay of copper and silver brightened the armour. The
date is probably somewhere in the third century A.D.

A decidedly more provincial Dolichenus was found in the
Island of Fünen.[2] In many points, including the curious form
of the base, he resembles the bronze from Lichtenberg.

The Roman civilisation in *Britain* brought with it Roman
objects of art. Of these, one of the finest is a naked bowman [3]
discovered in London (Pl. 90 *a*). He waits with his left arm
extended, so that the muscles on the forearm stand out. His
left hand must have grasped the bow while his right hand drew
back the string. The modelling of the lower part of the body
is excellent, so too is the finish of the toes, but the right hand is
rather clumsy. This is the only fault we can find. For the
rest, nothing could be finer than the hawk-like face, and the
way the head is sunk so that the eye can sight along the arrow
to its mark. The bronzes made locally are, on the other hand,
crude and unattractive.

Of all the provinces, *Gaul* is, perhaps, the most interesting
to those who make a study of bronzes. Here, the south had
long been civilised : the city of Massilia (Marseilles) dates back
to about 600 B.C., and had attracted trade from all parts of the
ancient world. Through Marseilles and Nismes, where a colony
of Alexandrian veterans had been established by Augustus,
Alexandrian influences reached south Gaul.[4] Through Marseilles and over the Alps, a number of really fine bronzes, of
Hellenistic and Roman date, were imported, for in Gaul as in
Italy ambitious collectors, native as well as Roman, were to be
found. We have already had occasion to illustrate one or two
good bronzes from Gaul (Pl. 77 *a* and Pl. 86 *b*). A number can
be seen in the British Museum : the Hercules from Bavay,[5]

---

[1] Berlin, 2129 *a*; ht., ·145 m.; Neugebauer, Pl. 63, p. 120, which see
for more complete description.

[2] At Copenhagen ; Neugebauer, p. 121.

[3] With the Romano-British bronzes in the British Museum. Ht., ·275
m.; Neugebauer, Pl. 67; *Archaeologia*, XXX, Pl. 22. From Queen Street,
Cheapside.

[4] Reinach, *Antiquités Nationales*, pp. 11 ff.

[5] B.M., 787.

the Jupiter from Lyons,[1] the Apollo from Orange,[2] to mention only a few.   Among the bronzes in French museums, perhaps the most famous, apart from the Hermes mentioned above from Fins d'Annecy, are the Épinal Hermaphrodite,[3] considered by many to be pure Hellenistic, the warrior defending himself from Vienne,[4] also probably Hellenistic, and the Jupiter from Vieil Évreux,[5] a Roman work in the Lysippean tradition.

The local bronzes form a group that is more interesting to the mythologist and the ethnologist than to the student of art.[6] Here we find statuettes in the elegant attitude of a Greek god, but wearing, perhaps, checked trousers and a tight-fitting jerkin with long sleeves.   Sometimes Dispater is represented, a Gaulish version of Jupiter, carrying a hammer in one hand, a jar (*olla*) in the other, and wearing native costume.[7]   Such an one is reproduced on Pl. 91 *b*,[8] though the *olla* from the right hand and the hammer from the left have disappeared.   Many bronzes shew a still more barbarian Jupiter, uncouth and ill-finished, carrying a wheel, the significant symbol of the solar disc (Fig. 1).[9]   Purely local gods also occur, but it would take too long to discuss the Gaulish pantheon.

The most attractive divinity comes, not from Gaul itself, but from Muri in Switzerland, and is now at Berne.[10]   She is the goddess Artio, originally, perhaps, a bear-goddess, and a giver of the fruits of the earth : to her, one Licinia Sabinilla de ʾicated the small group illustrated on Pl. 92.   The goddess is romanised, and the bear, though a little pressing in his attentions, is tame.

All kinds of workmen seem to have tried their hand at bronze

[1] B.M., 786.   [2] B.M., 799.
[3] Neugebauer, Pl. 45, p. 82.   At Épinal.
[4] Bibliothèque Nationale, 815.
[5] At Évreux.   A cast at St. Germain-en-Laye ; Reinach, *op. cit.*, p. 29, and frontispiece.
[6] See Reinach, *Antiquités Nationales ;* and *B.M. Cat.*, pp. liii and 142-148. Bronzes found in Gaul can be admirably studied in the Museum of St. Germain-en-Laye, where the originals are supplemented by casts, making a very exhaustive collection.
[7] Reinach, *op. cit.*, pp. 137 ff.
[8] B.M., 790 ; ht., ·172 m.   From Tournus.   Notice the hunting knife in the belt.
[9] At St. Germain ; ht., ·227 m. ; Cook, *Zeus*, I, pp. 288 ff., Fig. 208.
[10] J. J. Bachofen, *Der Bär in der Religionen der Alterthums*, pp. 3, 34-38, Pl. I.   The throne is missing ; ht. of goddess, ·154 m. ; of bear, ·116·m.

casting. Some copied classical models successfully ; others
conscientiously imitated the shape, but had no idea how to produce the effect they wanted and did disastrous things with their
graving tools after casting. Others,
again, went their own way, and any
classical features they reproduce are
more accidental than intentional.

A number of busts [1] and heads
illustrate the vagaries of partially
trained artists. The heads are often
very flat from front to back, which
may be the exaggeration of a national
characteristic (Fig. 2).[2] The faces
amuse us by their double chins and
staring eyes, by their spiral curls,
and carefully hatched eyelashes and
eyebrows. In some, the crown of the
head has been made into a small lid.
They look like modern inkpots and
were probably receptacles of some
kind. One was meant to be nailed to
a temple wall, for there are holes
through which the nails would pass,
and an inscription in front which says
that Cnusticus dedicated it in pay-
ment of a vow.[3]

The end of the making of bronze
statuettes, in Gaul as elsewhere, came
with the advance of Christianity. The
small figures of Roman or Gaulish
divinities were heathen idols, like the
larger statues ; they carried with them
disturbing associations, and were dangerous in a country which had not yet
forgotten its paganism. So the priests bade their flock destroy
all such figures, and the order was usually obeyed. But

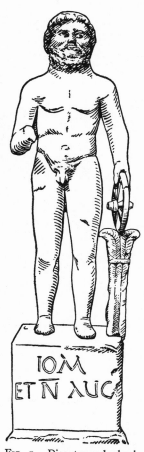

FIG. 1.—Diapater and wheel.

[1] Reinach, *op. cit.*, pp. 224 ff.
[2] *Ibid.*, p. 225. The two examples in Fig. 2 are from near Compiègne,
op. cit., Nos. 217, 219. Now at St. Germain.
[3] *Ibid.*, *op. cit.*, pp. 230-231, No. 223. From near Évreux.

there were still a few folk who clung to the old beliefs, or who felt uncomfortable at the thought of desecrating that which they had been used to venerate. To some of them occurred a plan by which the figures might be saved and the priests none the wiser. They hastily constructed a small chamber underground, and placed within it a number of bronzes that had been sacred to the god Rudiobus.

In 1861 the chamber was discovered :[1] of the bronzes which

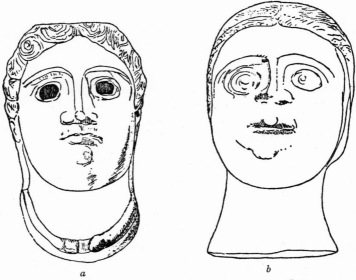

a   b

FIG. 2.—Heads by Gaulish artists at St. Germain-en-Laye.

it contained, some had been cast, and these sustained little if any injury, others had been hammered, and these were in bad preservation.[2] They included a large horse inscribed with the dedication to Rudiobus, a fairly large stag, some pigs and a boar. There were also twelve small figures, three imported, the rest local work.[3] They may have been made in the third century A.D.

---

[1] Reinach, *op. cit.*, pp. 241 ff. Originals at Orléans. Casts at St. Germain-en-Laye. The place of their discovery was Neuvy-en-Sullias.

[2] Said to have been broken before being buried, *op. cit.*, p. 243.

[3] I consider the Mars (Reinach, *op. cit.*, No. 37) to be local. Reinach, p. 242, implies eleven figures.

Hidden in their secret chamber so many centuries ago, they escaped alike Christian iconoclasts and barbarian invaders, and re-emerged at last to gladden the antiquaries of our own time.

B. DECORATIVE BRONZES AND BRONZE UTENSILS OF THE ROMAN PERIOD

INLAY—The people of prehistoric Crete were, as we have seen, past masters in the art of inlaying bronze with other precious metals. The Greeks used inlay to a large extent for the details of their bronze statues and statuettes, to a more limited extent for decorative work on armour and utensils of bronze, but not with the same perfection as their Minoan predecessors. Towards the end of the Hellenistic Period, however, and during the Roman Period which succeeded it, the inlaying of objects, other than statuettes, became supremely important, and artists attained such skill that their work ranks next only to that of the Cretans.

Two comparatively early examples usually assigned to the Hellenistic Period, though probably later, are the pan and hydria found in 1831 at Egyed in Hungary.[1] Both are inlaid with gold and silver : for the pan, a background of niello is used. In both cases, an Egyptian origin seems almost certain, for on the pan is inlaid a Nilotic landscape, in the centre of which a hippopotamus chews up a crocodile, while on the hydria are Egyptian divinities and motives obviously adapted from Egyptian art.

Many vases from Pompeii and elsewhere owe their beauty to their inlaid patterns or silver-studded handles : the formality of an inlaid jug from Pompeii,[2] belonging to the first half of the first century A.D., contrasts with the naturalism of the hunting scene on a second century jug at Berlin.[3] The finest inlay is, however, found on certain chariots, couches and litters : to the narrow surfaces which these objects offer for decoration, such treatment is peculiarly appropriate.

A number of fragments of a chariot from Thrace were some time ago acquired by a private collector in Paris.[4] On what

[1] *Jahrb.*, 1909, pp. 28 ff., Pls. III and IV. I would be inclined to place both pieces later than Hekler does : the hydria is the earlier of the two.
[2] Naples, 118,295.   [3] Berlin, 30,244 ; *Führer*, p. 94, Pl. 78.
[4] *B.C.H.*, 1904, pp. 210 ff. Bought at Salonika.

appears to be the rim of the platform are hunting scenes : there is an indication of landscape by incised lines, and leaves and boughs are intermingled with the figures. Huntsmen ride after their quarry with their dogs : there is also a bacchante and a fisherman with his line in his hand. The lines are engraved neatly, and certain points, such as the panther's eye and the leopard's spots, are picked out in silver. On the rim of the breastwork are lozenge-shaped panels, each containing an animal inlaid in metal of a suitable colour, copper for a hare, silver for a dog or a deer. Similar hunting scenes can be seen on a bronze plaque now in the Louvre.[1]

A good example of Augustan work is given by a litter, much reconstructed, in the Conservatori Museum,[2] from the Esquiline. The framework has an inlaid pattern of running vine sprays and rosettes. The carved end-rests,[3] with their panthers' heads in high relief, are adorned with inlaid acanthus and other leaves of a type recalling the Ara Pacis. The herms of Herakles and an Idaean Dactyl which help to carry the canopy, the heads of an Amorino and a satyr at the end of the carrying poles, illustrate the Roman love of human figures as adjuncts of furniture. The litter in its present form would only be long enough to carry a person sitting ; this may be due to the reconstruction.

Better preserved, in spite of its faulty restoration, and still more elaborately decorated, is the inlaid couch in the same museum (Pl. 93).[4] It is of a type which is known from other examples, from Boscoreale, Pompeii, Priene.[5] The Conservatori couch comes from a tomb at Amiternum. The type probably originated in Asia Minor. Between the various examples quoted there are, of course, certain differences of detail. The couch with which we are at present concerned has four legs of a shape suggesting turned wood, though they really have a bronze casing and a wooden core. At each end of the bed are two end-rests, on which would have lain the pillows and cushions. The end-rests are highly ornamental. They

[1] Louvre, 3448, Pl. 116.
[2] Stuart-Jones, *Conservatori Cat.*, p. 178, No. 12, Pls. 64-66.
[3] I.e. the equivalent of the curved piece with the mules' heads on Pl. 93.
[4] *Conservatori Cat.*, p. 175, No. 11, Pls. 62-63. I have accepted the system of dating there proposed. *J.H.S.*, 1927, p. 146, querries *maenad* and *genius fulcri*.
[5] References, *op. cit.*, *loc. cit.*

are finished with a mule's head, which suggests a well-known passage in Juvenal, *Satires*, XI, 97, " Vile coronati caput ostendebat aselli : " the claims of metre, no doubt, made him put " donkey " for " mule." Evidently an ass or mule was a traditional motive. Our mule wears silver trappings and an ivy wreath, and a collar with a bell attached (the bell has been lost from one of the two heads). He also wears a skin, which would prevent him being rubbed by the harness. His ears are laid back, his teeth bared, and he looks thoroughly vicious. There is also a maenad's bust on the lower part of the end-rest, which may stand for the *genius fulcri* mentioned by Juvenal, *Satires*, VI, 21-22 : the maenad has silver wings and an ivy wreath and carries a curved falchion.

In the panels between the mule's head and the maenad's bust are vintage scenes, beautifully framed. The one on the left is the one which appears in the plate. Two satyrs are fruit gathering : one picks fruit and the other holds a basket or bucket. There is also a goat going into an arbour, a high candlestick before which stands Priapus, a vine tree ornamented with *oscilla* and tambourine, a bowl and an amphora. This sounds rather a queer mixture, but all motives could be found in a crowded vineyard at the proper season, and the right effect is produced. There are two other figures, a girl and a satyr treading the grapes. Our plate shews part of the frame of the bed with its exquisite inlaid rosettes, but does not include the legs with their crouching sphinxes, or the foot-rest with its seated sphinx beneath the ends.

The busts of the maenads are of the shape associated with the Trajanic Period : it is probable that the same principles should be applied to decorative busts, like these, as to portrait busts. The rest of the decoration has no elements which would be inconsistent with the date proposed.

RELIEF—Since the most distinctive and epoch-making achievement of Roman art is found in its sculptured reliefs, namely the illusion of space produced by treating the background pictorially, we turn with curiosity to those bronze reliefs which are small enough to be included within this book, and sufficiently distinguished to merit description.

One of the most striking decorates the high handle of a

jug.[1] At the lower end are two barbarian captives, Gauls or
Dacians.   Above, another barbarian, a handsome man with
a bundle over his shoulder, appears to be moving rapidly away.
At either side of him are shields of a northern type with a central
boss.   A woman, perhaps personifying Dacia or Sarmatia, sits
crowning the handle : she is of an unclassical type and a melan-
choly aspect.   Below her is a wall, complete with towers and
regular masonry.   Over the wall two warriors are peering, with
their bow and their two spears beside them.   It is here that
we see most clearly the features that recall other Roman reliefs :
the figures and the tower might have come straight from the
column of Trajan, and the style of the whole piece suggests the
Antonine Period.
     A number of reliefs, important both for their style and be-
cause they can be dated to the third century A.D.,[2] ornament
what was once a *tensa*, or sacred car in which the images of the
gods were carried at the opening of the games.   The reliefs,
representing Dionysiac processions and scenes in the life of
Achilles, are eclectic : some have a completely neutral background, others a background such as we find in the Neo-Attic
reliefs, others, again, a background of elaborate architecture
that recalls Trajan's column.   Heads in medallions, in the
manner of the period of the Severi, facilitate dating.   Little,
if any, chasing was done after casting.   This is a contrast
to the usual practice that should warn us not to dogmatise
about technique.

UTENSILS AND VASES — Among the many and varied
achievements of the bronze-workers of antiquity, none are more
widely known than the objects from Pompeii, Herculaneum,
and the villas at Boscoreale near Pompeii. All these sites were
destroyed by the eruption of Vesuvius in 79 A.D., but the two
cities had a long, though somewhat obscure, earlier history.
It is not, therefore, surprising that, at the time of the destruction, a number of objects were buried that dated from the

---

[1] Louvre, 2825 ; *Mon. Piot.*, XVIII (1911), Pl. IX, pp. 89-91. The
handle may originally have been covered with silver incrustation. There is
no reason to doubt its authenticity. Ht., ·165 m.
[2] Stuart-Jones, *Conservatori Cat.*, pp. 179 ff., Pls. 68-73. The preservation is too bad to allow reproduction except on large plates.

Hellenistic Period (see p. 211). Besides these, the houses contained bronzes made during the later Republican Period, and during the reigns of several emperors. A complete account would not be possible in this book, but a selection will be made to comprise on the one hand the most beautiful and on the other the most characteristic pieces.

The *tripod* stand on Pl. 81 *c* was said, at one time, to come from the Temple of Isis at Pompeii, and has also been claimed for Herculaneum.[1] The supporting ring with the garlands and boukrania is a later addition : originally, as far as we can judge, a table was carried on the very top of the legs. Subsequently, the ring was inserted at a point a little way down, as can be seen in our plate. This necessitated (1) sawing the legs through at the place where the ring was fixed, and (2) cramping and hiding the upper part of the sphinxes' wings. The ring is inferior in style, and does not match the good Augustan work on the rest of the tripod.

This tripod should be contrasted with the well-known support composed of three Satyrs,[2] of which the date is somewhat controversial, and with another more common type of tripod,[3] represented in Pompeii and elsewhere, and often used for tables to stand before the couches during dinner. In tripods of the latter class, the legs can be drawn together so as to fit whatever object they carry, or folded up like a camp-stool, for the trellis-work between them contracts, owing to its lower attachment being movable. The legs were often adorned with human figures.

On Pls. 95 *a* and 96 *c* are illustrated two *craters* which belong to the Roman Period. Whereas the handles of the Hellenistic craters were always finished by a satyr's mask, they are now finished by heads of various types. The crater on Pl. 95 *a* is from Boscoreale :[4] notice the rings on the shaft of its support

---

[1] *Jahrbuch*, 1908, pp. 107 ff. See Fig. 4, p. 110, for restoration of original shape (Pernice).

[2] Pernice, *Hellenistische Kunst*, p. 37 (Hellenistic Period suggested), and Pl. X.

[3] *Jahrbuch*, 1921, pp. 107-113. This is the common Roman and Hellenistic type (the Klappendreifuss), foreshadowed in a somewhat similar early tripod from the Polledrara Tomb, Vulci.

[4] Berlin, 8850 ; ht., ·64 m. ; *Anz.*, XV, 1900, p. 182, Fig. 8 ; Pernice, *op. cit.*, p. 40.

which may be intended to facilitate the grip. The example on Pl. 96 *c* is from Pompeii,[1] of a type made unmistakable by its elaborate handles. These handles recall the tendrils of a plant : below each is a beautiful head and a pair of spreading wings.

The *jugs* from Pompeii and other Roman sites are remarkably varied in shape, and we have room to illustrate only two of the most common types. One of these has a round mouth and a distinctive handle : at the upper end of the handle is a leaf-shaped projection on which the thumb could rest, at the lower, a medallion, a mask, or some other device (Pl. 96 *a*).[2] The other has a good spout for pouring, and a high swung handle, with the forepart of an animal, usually of a horse or griffin, where handle and lip meet (Pl. 96 *d*).[3] The leaf-shaped projection was in use as early as the second century B.C., for we find it in the cemetery of San Bernardo, conveniently dated by coins [4] between 150 and 50 B.C.

Passing over the dishes and bowls, in which both Pompeii and Herculaneum were rich, we come to the *pails*, remote descendants of those fourth century pails from South Italy described on p. 186 and near descendants of the Hellenistic pails discussed on p. 212.

The most distinguished examples are of the " bell-shape " and have a frieze running beneath the handles, sometimes continuous, sometimes interrupted by decorative motives below the handles. These friezes shew the art of the Roman Period at its best. They have the same perfection as many of the sculptured reliefs, where flowers, birds and beasts are combined in a half-decorative, half-naturalistic style. The decorative element predominated over the naturalistic in the sculpture of the Augustan Period ; this is also true of the friezes of the pails belonging to the time of Augustus or to the end of the Republic. We know that the pails were made by the artists of South Italy : concerning the identity of the sculptors we are ill-informed. We can, however, surmise that they were not uninfluenced by the South Italian bronze-workers, who had

[1] Naples, 109,697 ; Pernice, *op. cit.*, p. 41, Pl. XIV.
[2] At Naples, from Pompeii.
[3] Bibl. Nat., 1390 ; ht., ·265. On lower attachment of handle, gorgon's head, eyes inlaid. Handle probably alien.
[4] Willers, *Neue Untersuchungen*, pp. 14-19.

long been established in the country. On Pl. 95 *b* is the well-known bronze pail bearing the stamp, Cornelias Chelidonis.[1] It must be assigned to the last decades of the Republic on grounds of epigraphy and of style. The frieze that decorates it consists of semi-floral motives, broken by griffins under the handles, and by long-necked birds half-way along each side. Details are picked out in copper and silver, and silver studs form the centres of the spirals on the handle, a characteristic Pompeian device.

Of the dozens of *candelabra* [2] or lamp stands from Pompeii and Herculaneum, some examples have already been distinguished as heirlooms preserved from an earlier period. Pl. 84 *b* shews a candelabrum of the Augustan age,[3] easily recognised by the plate above the feet. The support at the top of the shaft is covered with decoration, and is shaped like a crater ; even the curious swelling which facilitates the grip on the supports of certain craters is here reproduced and exaggerated into a separate member. The other candelabrum on Pl. 84 *c* [4] belongs to a common type which has some claims to be earlier than that last described. It has very bent legs with an ivy leaf between each pair, and, for the support of the lamp, a wide-lipped crater, often with little handles at each side. The candelabrum on Pl. 84 *d* [5] imitates a reed : one can see the joints and the overlapping leaves, and the three little branches which carry the plate for the lamp. This type appears to go back to Republican times, but it had a long period of popularity. Besides the ordinary large-sized examples, which stood on the floor, shorter examples were made which could be placed on the table. Other candelabra shew other variations of form. Some, decorated with Herms, could be taken apart, a further proof of the ingenuity of Roman craftsmen.[6]

It is the astonishingly free use made of human figures and of representations of twigs, leaves and the like that strikes the student most when he looks at the smaller lamp stands. Not that such devices appear here alone : they are liable to occur as decorations of all kinds of furniture in all parts of the Roman

---

[1] Naples, 68,854 ; Schröder, 74*tes Winckelmannsprogramm*, p. 9, No. 14 ; Pernice, *op. cit.*, p. 22, Pl. IV.
[2] *Ibid.*, pp. 45 ff.   [3] *Ibid.*, p. 46, Fig. 56.
[4] *Ibid.*, p. 48, Fig. 61.   [5] *Ibid.*, p. 55, Fig. 73.   [6] *Ibid.*, pp. 55, 56.

world. Nowhere else, however, are they more numerous or more daring. Twigs and tendrils spring from the junctions of the three feet and curl upwards : sometimes they expand into branches from which hang lamps on chains, sometimes they fork into three and support a flat stand on which the lamp is placed. Occasionally they sprout out from the back of a silen who is either seated or staggering backwards as though intoxicated. A few of the satyrs appear decorous and hard-working, and carry on their head what seems to be a round box above which is the support for the lamp. One such satyr, in the British Museum, comes from Aigion in Achaia, and must have been made at the same workshop as the examples in Pompeii.[1]

Among the objects from the excavations at Ephesus is a lamp stand which shews the same love of figures and flowers that we meet at Pompeii, though expressed in a different style.[2] The lamp stand is in the form of a column, and it is said to be one of a pair which supported large lamps. Beneath the capital and its elaborate scrolls are heads of Herakles and Omphale, back to back. The hero wears the lady's kerchief, and she his lion skin. A youthful Herakles with his club on his shoulder [3] is the finish to each of the four tendrils that depend from the volutes of the capital : a reclining Herakles with two cupids lies between the volutes. The shaft of the column is missing, but a bronze group, from somewhere at its base, survives, representing Herakles and a centaur in mortal combat. The whole must have been an imposing piece of furniture, but it does not bear comparison with the better bronzes from the workshops of the west.

The small tripod stands [4] which served to support lamps on the table, also fall into certain well-defined types. In examining the specimens at Naples, it must be remembered that the lamps placed on the stands are not those which originally belonged, just as the candelabra and other objects are often "made up" from parts of different specimens.

---

[1] *B.M. Cat.*, 284. See also *Anz.*, 1922, pp. 100, 101.

[2] *J.H.S.*, XX, p. 180 ; and XXIII, p. 347, Figs. 10, 11 (attributed to the Hellenistic Period) ; and *Anz.*, 1922, p. 86, where Neugebauer attributes them to Roman Imperial Period. At Vienna.

[3] Compare the very similar Herakles and acanthus from Egypt ; *Jahreshefte*, 1912, p. 76.

[4] Pernice, *op. cit.*, pp. 57 ff.

Countless *small vases*, both ornamental and useful, were made during the Roman Period. Some, like the lamp stands, are fantastic in shape : askoi copy wine skins and small dishes copy shells. These askoi and dishes were put on the market during the Hellenistic Period and enjoyed a long popularity.[1] Among the plainer vases are bottles, jars, pans, strainers, and ladles for mixing wine. The three last-named claim our attention, less for their own sake than because many are inscribed with the names of their manufacturers in a form which throws light on contemporary industrial conditions (see below).

This is the occasion to give a brief account of the types of *mirrors* [2] in use among the Romans. Those with covers and those with handles still remained popular, but Roman taste shews itself by the introduction of certain new features. The edge of the disc, for instance, was often pierced with small holes, which, according to the suggestion of an ingenious French scholar,[3] may have served the purpose of a pincushion. Sometimes the edge was bordered with scallops and other devices, which broke the previously plain rim of the circle. Square and oblong mirrors, also, were favourites. For the mirrors with covers, a fashion arose of setting a coin in the centre of the cover, like a medallion.

In the time of the Elder Pliny,[4] however, silver mirrors were becoming common, so common, indeed, that even servants possessed them. From this we infer that bronze mirrors were beginning to take a back place.

CENTRES FOR THE MAKING OF ROMAN BRONZE WARES— Where were all these objects made ? We hear much from Roman authors about the factories of *Capua*, which seem to have had a reputation for bronze wares. Cato (*De Agricultura* 135) [5] recommends Capua as a place where one should buy " buckets, vessels for oil, pitchers for water, vessels for wine, and other bronze vases." Horace, in two passages, mentions Campanian goods as though they were cheap and common

---

[1] Pernice, *op. cit.*, pp. 14, 17.
[2] Daremberg and Saglio, s.v. *speculum*, p. 1429.
[3] de Ridder, in Daremberg and Saglio, *loc. cit.*
[4] Pliny, *Nat. Hist.*, XXXIV, 48.
[5] " Hamae, urnae oleariae, urcei acquarii, urnae vinariae, alia vasa ahenea Capuae."

16

(*Sat.*, I, 6, 116 and II, 3, 142).   Pliny (*N.H.*, XXXIV, 20) says,
" in other classes the prize should be given to Campania, which is
excellent for useful wares." [1]   All these writers suggest that
Campanian bronze vessels were, not works of art, but useful
household goods produced in large quantities.[2]   The factories
would be the indirect descendants of those workshops of Capua
which made the urns described on p. 137.   From the Roman
Capua, then, would come the less ornamental vessels of Pompeii
and elsewhere.

For the more artistic bronzes which are the main subject
of this book, an origin must be sought in that district which
for many centuries had produced work of high quality and had
transmitted its wares and its inspiration to the rest of Italy.
A close examination of the details of these Roman vessels
shews so many points that can be linked with the Tarentine
bronzes of earlier periods, that we are forced to the conclusion
that the same traditions and more or less the same *South
Italian workshops* produced both.

Another centre for bronze-work was *Brindisi*, which had
been famed for its mirrors in the Republican Period, and probably continued to produce bronze wares at a later date.[3]

PRODUCTS OF THE WORKSHOPS OF CAPUA—Even among
the " useful wares " made at Capua, there were many which
had claims to beauty and were highly valued by their posses-
sors.   The handsome pails, of the type illustrated on Pl. 96 *b*,
belong to a comparatively early date (125-25 B.C.).[4]   To the
Romans they may have been mere temple or household furniture, but to those northern barbarians who strove to acquire
even second-hand and damaged specimens, they were works
of art.   Certainly, they are remarkably well made, for, though
cast, they have walls so fine that one would consider them ham-

---

[1] " In reliquis generibus palma Campano perhibetur, utilensibus vasis
probatissimo."

[2] See Pernice, *op. cit.*, pp. 29, 30.

[3] Pliny, *Nat. Hist.*, XXXIII, 45.

[4] Willers, *Neue Untersuchungen*, p. 22.   The handles and the attachments
are sometimes of iron, replacing original bronze handles.   A relief from the
theatre at Capua shews one of the pails, not quite similar in profile, among a
group of sacrificial objects ; *op. cit.*, Pl. V, 4.   The pail on Pl. 96 is from
Nienbüttel, Germany.

mered were it not for a small depression on the base, proving
that they had been finished on a turning wheel.[1] Below the
handles are usually heart-shaped leaves or a pair of dolphins.
It would be illuminating if we could trace the different routes
by which these pails penetrated into the more distant parts of
Germany, and even into Laaland and Seeland, off Denmark.

From Capua, too, must come many of the cullenders pierced
with holes in elaborate patterns, that were found in Pompeii,
and were copied by provincial fabrics.

FIG. 3.—Saucepans from the workshop of C. Cipius Polybius.

A type of pan made during the Empire [2] deserves mention
because it is an important record of the vicissitudes of a prominent Roman industry. The shape is illustrated on Fig. 3.
Some of the pans shew traces of three feet ; some have an
interior lined with a white metal, just as our own copper saucepans are lined with tin. The earliest have a device of two swans'
heads at the end of the handle, but the later examples have
holes, and the shape of the hole often indicates the date. On

[1] *Op. cit.*, p. 12.   [2] *Op. cit.*, pp. 73 ff., Pl. VI, 3, 4.

the handle is a stamp with the maker's name, and it is from comparing these stamps and names that we learn something of the history of the factory.

The vessels with two swans' heads on the handle flourished in the Augustan Period : a noted manufacturer, one Trebellius Romanus, used to engrave a thyrsus on the handles of his wares. We cannot exactly call it a trade-mark, because it was imitated by other firms.

The handles with holes at the end, at first half-moon shape, then round, then trefoil, filled a period that lasted from the time of Augustus to some time in the second century. P. Cipius Polybius and L. Ansius Epaphroditus, whose pans had a round hole, worked in the generation before the destruction of Pompeii, under Claudius and Nero. This was the time when the Capuan industry reached the highest point of prosperity, exporting its wares to Italy and more northern countries.

After the first century it began to decline. The old families ceased to manufacture, and a few big establishments, delegated to slaves, controlled what trade was left. This we learn from the names on the handles, single names in the nominative case, which could only belong to a slave working on his own account.

PROVINCIAL INDUSTRIES—In Gaul, however, towards the end of the first century A.D., a number of workshops had come into existence which supplied the neighbourhood with imitations of the wares of Capua. Some had imitated the pans of the Cipii and Ansii, some copied them with slight changes. A pan from Évaux is marked STEPAPROD,[1] which is evidently intended for the signature of L. Ansius Epaphroditus. The pan is, however, of a shape that would never have been adopted by Ansius himself. A Gaul called Draccius [2] appears to have had a factory near Lyons in the second century A.D., for five of his pans were found there.

The most typical Gaulish pans, however, have highly decorated handles inspired by the handles of Roman gold and silver vases. On the handles we see figures, garlands, birds or masks.

A certain Ianuaris seems to have made such pans at Lyons,

[1] *Op. cit.*, p. 80, Fig. 46.   See *Bull. Épigraphique*, 1881, p. 129, Pl. 4.
[2] *Op. cit.*, p. 79.

while Boduogenus was responsible for an excellent specimen, quite in the classical manner, which was found in England.[1]

In other parts of Western Europe besides Gaul, local trades-men flourished under the Roman rule. We have the names of several makers of cullenders from Holland—Agorix, Adraxius, Cannimasus, not, apparently, late in date (c. 100 A.D.). There were also fabrics in Belgium and South Germany.[2]

Of all the centres of provincial bronze-work, however, the most important at this time must have been the one which produced pails of the so-called " Hemmoor Type ".[3] These pails were, by the middle of the second century A.D., on their way towards supplanting the Italian wares of Capua. They have been named from the site, Hemmoor in Germany, where so many have been found : other examples come from other German sites, and from England, France, Denmark and Nor-way. They are cast, with very fine walls, and are finished by being turned on the wheel. The site where they were manu-factured in such quantities and from which they were sold with such success was long sought in vain. The most convincing suggestion is one that identifies it with Gressenich between Aix and Cologne. Here are Roman remains and traces of a bronze industry, here cadmium could be obtained for brass, and hence the bronze vessels could be exported, not via the Yssel and the Zuyderzee, which would be in hostile territory, but starting from Vechten (Fictio in Roman times) via the Roer and the Maas.[4] The industry must be dated between 100 and 250 A.D.

It will have become apparent that the history of Roman bronze wares in the provinces is a long one. The way north-ward had been prepared for them many centuries before, by certain fifth and sixth century vases, Italian and Etruscan, which penetrated beyond the Alps. The Roman rule, as it spread to east, west and north, not only gave a stimulus to trade, but caused a high value to be set on objects from Italy by friend and foe alike. However far the Roman boundary extended, the objects were always in advance of it, and in time they reached places where no Roman was ever to set foot.

[1] Willers, op. cit., p. 81.   [2] Ibid., p. 84.
[3] Ibid., pp. 30 ff. ; and Willers, Die Bronzeimer von Hemmoor.
[4] Willers, Neue Untersuchungen, p. 47.

Exactly when they arrived we cannot say, but some are so carefully patched and repaired that we cannot avoid the conclusion that they were not only bought second-hand, but also remained a long time in use.   They included vessels, statuettes and second-hand furniture.   In a grave near Sackrav, north of Breslau,[1] was discovered the four-legged support of a table, the legs decorated with panthers and satyrs and crowned with busts.   It bore an inscription NUM AVG (Numini Augusti, " to the divine Augustus ").   Having, therefore, at one time of its life graced a temple of the deified emperor, it wandered north, became the treasured possession of some rich German chieftain, and was finally given a resting place in his grave.   Evidently, the collectors in these northern districts, like many collectors of to-day, coupled a love of real works of art with a disarming partiality to anything of Greek or Roman origin.

[1] Willers, *op. cit.*, pp. 96-97.

SUBJECT INDEX

ACROPOLIS, objects from: Argivo-Corinthian reliefs, 116; Athena Promachos, 144; centaur, 101; chariot relief, 120; dancing girl, 155; early Archaic statuettes, 73; early reliefs, 58, 64; fifth-century bronzes, 154; Geometric animals, 37; griffins, 70; Phœnician bowl, 55; protome, 74; sixth-century bronzes, 99; tripods, 47, 108, 139; warrior, 41; winged figures, 71, 100.
Actor, 208.
Aderno, figure from, 156, 170.
Adraxius, 245.
Adriatic coast, bronzes found on, 38.
Aegean Islands, 2, 4.
Aegina, Argivo-Corinthian reliefs, 118; Geometric bronzes, 37; Geometric brooches, 47; mirrors, 128, 129. See also Museum index.
Aegion, satyr from, 240.
Aetolia, Geometric bronzes from, 43. See also North-Western Greece.
Agorix, 245.
Agrinion, Geometric bronze from, 37.
Aidepsos, copper found at, 4.
Ajax, 116, 144.
Albania, 98.
Alesia. See Museum index.
Alexander, 195, 225.
Alexandria, 195, 204, 208, 227.
Alexandropol, 181
Ἅλιος γέρων, 114.
Alpheios, breastplate from, 62.
Amiternum, couch from tomb at, 234.
Amorgos, 47.
Amphipolis, 38.
Amphora, Italian, fifth century, 165.
Amycus, 190, 193.
Amyklae, 91, 128.
Anatoli, 22.
Ancona. See Museum index.
Andria, 107.
Andritsaena, 95, 96.
Animals, statuettes of, 36 ff., 39, 40, 105.
Antioch, 206.
Aphaia, temple of, 118. See also Aegina.
Aphrodite: decorating mirrors, 161, 177, 192, 193; Syrian type, 227. See also Venus.
— of Knidos, 170, 171.
— Pourtales, 171.

Apiro, Minerva from, 174.
Apollo, 62, 88, 91, 142, 147, 230.
— Korynthos, 85.
— Maleatas, 91.
— Philesios, 223.
— Piombino, 89.
— Ptoös, 103, 116.
— Tyritos, 77.
Arcadia, bronzes from, 37, 82, 91 ff., 151 ff.; characteristics of style, 91 ff., 152-3.
Archaistic bronzes, 223.
Archers, 124, 137, 229.
Argive Heraeum, Geometric bronzes from, 37; daggers, 11; fibulae, 77; mirrors, 126; early relief, 67; terracottas, 83; tripods, 47.
— School, bronzes of, 87, 147. See also North-East Peloponnese.
Argivo-Corinthian reliefs, 113 seq., 126.
Argolid, the, 136, 160.
Argos: lack of sixth-century statuettes, 88; coins of, see coins; Geometric brooches, 47; mirrors, 129, 160; fifth-century statuettes, 147.
Arkades. See Phrati.
Armour, early Archaic, 60; decoration of, 176.
Arndt collection. See Munich: Arndt collection (in Museum index).
Arrow-heads, stone, 3.
Artemis, 43, 62, 89, 93, 96, 149, 152; on relief from Olympia, 121.
— Daidaleia, 90.
— Orthia, 129.
Artio, figure of, 230.
Ashmolean Museum. See Oxford: Ashmolean Museum (in Museum index).
Asia Minor, use of copper in, 3.
Asine, 16.
Askos: Hellenistic, 213; Roman, 241.
Assyria, influence of on Greek art, 54.
Athena, 62, 99 ff., 149. See also Minerva.
— Alea, 93.
— Promachos, 99, 144.
Athens, bronze industry at, 66, 67, 99 ff., 154 ff. See also Acropolis and Museum index.
— objects from, 33, 47, 119, 159 n. See also Acropolis.
Austria, bronzes found in, 228.

Axe, development of, 7.
— double, 7, 11.
Axos, helmet from, 63, 120; mitrai, 62, 121

BALKANS, Northern, 228.
Bands. *See* Diadems.
Barbarians, 236. *See* Gauls.
Barberini tomb, 79.
Base. *See* Stand.
Bassae, 96.
Bavay, 229.
Beads, of Geometric period, 38.
Bear, 230.
Beetle, 40.
Belgium, bronze industry in, 245.
Berekla, 92, 93, 96.
Berlin. *See* Museum index.
Bernardini tomb, 79.
Berne. *See* Museum index.
Berœa, bronze from, 170.
Bibliothèque Nationale. *See* Paris : Bibliothèque Nationale (in Museum index).
Birds, 34, 36, 37, 40, 48, 50, 52, 56, 78. *See also* Eagles, Cocks, etc.
Boar, 7, 232.
Boduogenus (manufacturer), 245.
Boeotia, copper found in, 4; diadems, 119; discobolos from, 148; early Archaic statuette from, 74; half-moon fibulae, 49; hydriae, 164; bronze industry in, 120; sixth-century statuettes from, 103.
Boethos of Chalcedon, 201, 208.
Boscoreale, objects from, 234, 236, 237.
Bosnia, primitive settlements in, 38.
Bosses, as decoration, 115, 116, 118, 160.
Boston. *See* Museum index.
Bowls, early Archaic, 70; sixth-century decorated, 137. *See also* Phialae.
Bracciano Lake, 175.
Bracelets, 49.
Breastplates : representation of, 61; from Olympia, 62; S. Italian, 213.
Brindisi, 242.
Britain, bronzes from, 229, 245.
British Islands, tin mines of, 5.
— Museum. *See* London : British Museum (in Museum index).
Brolio, figures from, 80.
Bronze, decorative use of, 2; discovery of, 4; proportion of tin, 5; smelting and casting of 5. *See also* Technique.
— Age, 1, 29.
Brooches. *See* Fibulae.
Bucket. *See* Pail.
Buda-Pesth. *See* Museum index.
Bull and acrobat, 27.
Bull, representations of, 7, 27, 35, 36, 59, 68, 105.
Busts, dating of, 220 *n.*, 235; of philosophers, 226; Gaulish, 231.

CAERE, objects from, 79.
Calf, statuette of, 105.
Camarina, support from, 132.
Camilli, 220.
Campania, art centres in, 106, 242.
Candelabra, Etruscan, 78, 140, 165, 194, 214; Hellenistic, 213; Roman, 239.
Candia, statuette from, 21; Geometric tripods, 47. *See also* Museum index.
Cannimasus (manufacturer), 245.
Capodimonte, 140.
Capua, bronze industry at, 106, 241; bronzes from, 241 ff.; pails, 242; urns from, 107, 137.
Carts, 80.
Cassel. *See* Museum index.
Castelbellino, 165.
Castellina di Chianti, 79.
Casting, of animal statuettes, 39; of folds of garment, 153; metal for bronzes, 5. *See also* Technique.
Catania, mirrors from, 181.
Catch-plate, of fibulae, 38, 47.
Cato, 241.
Celts, bronze, 6.
Centaur, representations of, 40, 42, 59, 101, 105.
Cesnola collection. *See* Museum index, New York.
Chalcolithic Age, 3.
Chalke, hydria from, 184; handles and relief from, 185.
Chalkioikos site, 90.
Chalkis, theory of bronze industry at, 119, 133; copper at, 4.
Chanea. *See* Museum index.
Chariot 42, 50, 79, 80, 119, 123, 233.
— Monteleone, 121 ff.
Chauchitza, 38.
Chests, decorated, 119.
Chieftain's grave, 16.
Children, statuettes of, 201, 208.
Chios : bowls and tripods, 71; influence on Attic art, 99; winged victory motive, 100.
Chiusi, 109, 130.
Χλανίδιον, Χλανίς, 93.
Choirion, 177.
Christianity, effect of on bronze-making, 231.
Chrysokamina, 5.
Circle of the Cauldrons, Vetulonia, 78.
Cire perdue process. *See* Technique.
Cistae, 188 seq.
Coins, Aeginetan, 128; Arcadian, 89; influence of on other arts, 177; ornaments to mirrors, 241; Sicilian, 156; Syracusan, 159; types of head on, 177; Zeus on, 149.
Compiègne, 231 *n.*
Cook, A. B., 37 *n.*, 61 *n.*, 149 *n.*, 227 *n.*

Cooking utensils, Roman, 243.

Copenhagen. *See* Museum index.

Copper, defects of metal, 4; discovery of working of, 3; sources of supply, 4; used in inlay, *see* Inlay.

Corcyra. *See* Corfu, 97.

Corfu, objects from, 68, 148, 149; early art of, 97.

Corinth: Argivo-Corinthian work, 115, 119; cups and goblets, 186; diadems, 119; fifth century, 146; mirrors, 126, 127, 129, 160, 180; sixth century, 88, 136.

Cornelias Chelidonis pail, 239.

Corneto, 189.

Costume: Cretan, 21, 26, 27; Doric peplos, 90, 161; Etruscan, 108, 110; female, sixth century, 87; girl athletes', 98; Greek experiments in, 155; mirror figures, 161; of Artemis, 89, 93.

Couch, inlaid, 234.

Cover, of mirrors, fifth century, 176.

Cows, statuettes of, 36, 40. *See also* Bulls.

Crater, archaic Greek, 135; Hellenistic, 212; Roman, 237.

Crete, artistic influence on Peloponnese, 75; decline of art in sixth century, 83; early metal work, 3, 5, 12; Geometric brooches, 47; Minoan art in, 7-28; orientalising period, 59 *seq.*; transitional period, 35.

— Eastern, 35.

Crimea, tombs in, 186.

"Crouching Aphrodite," 197.

Crouching figures, statuettes of, 197.

Cullenders, Capuan, 243.

Cumae, as art centre, 106.

— battle of, 157.

Cumaean amphora, 138.

Cupid, S. Italian figures of, 225. *See also* Eros.

Cups and goblets, of fourth and third centuries, 185. *See also* Kylikes.

Cyclades, bronze statuette from, 3, 18; daggers, 6.

Cycladic, use of term, 2 *n.*

Cymbals, Cretan, 56.

Cyprus, bronze objects from, 3, 34; daggers, 7; early metal working in, 3, 4, 5; Geometric bronzes, 43; in Orientalising period, 54, 55; in Sub-Mycenaean period, 30; mirror support from, 128.

DACIA, 236.

Daggers, Cretan, 6, 7; hilt, from Troy, 18; Mycenaean, 7 ff.

Dancers, representations of, 42, 155, 179, 196.

"Dancing Faun," 197, 224.

Davies, O., 4 *n.*

De Clercq Collection. *See* Museum index.

Decoration of bronzes, Geometric, 47 *seq.*; Prehistoric, 1, 8; Sub-Mycenaean, 32. *See also* Decorative motives and designs.

Decorative motives and designs: acanthus, 177, 234; animal friezes, 68, 112, 118; beading, 165; circles, 46, 47, 94, 96; claws, 71, 161; criss-cross, 16; dog-tooth, 61, 63, 64; egg *and* egg and tongue, 118, 161, 183, 212; feather, 194; flying gallop, 33; hatched triangles, 166; heraldic animals, 113, 115, 116, 118; herringbone, 33, 46; honeysuckle, 64, 132, 166; ivy, 130, 162, 193; laurel, 188, 193; leaves, 12, 184, 243; lily, 10, 12; lotus, 53, 58, 67, 119, 188; palmette, 53, 58, 65, 66, 79, 87, 113, 116, 131, 135, 158, 160, 163, 164, 177, 178, 183, 212, 227; rope, cable and plait, 32, 33, 34, 53, 56, 58, 64, 113, 116, 118, 119, 178, 188; rosette, 10, 49, 64, 66, 113, 119, 183, 184, 213, 234, 235; S pattern, 46, 63; scallops, 62, 241; scrolls, 158, 165, 182; spirals, 10, 11, 33, 34, 46, 61, 64, 71; swans' heads, 135, 243, 244; swastika, 50, 52; tendrils, 181, 240; thyrsus, 244; tongue pattern, 116, 136, 163, 165, 183, 184, 188, 194; zigzag, 46, 47, 48, 63, 96.

Deer, 10, 40.

Delos, 100, 195.

Delphi, objects from: Argivo-Corinthian fragments, 116; bowls, 71; cut-out figures, 124; early Archaic statuette, 73; Geometric brooches, 47; Geometric statuettes, 41, 43; Kouros, 75; Phoenician bowls, 55; Samo-Milesian bronze, 102; sixth-century bronzes, 98; tripods, 47, 71; winged figures, 71. *See also* Museum index.

Demeter, 94.

Dendra, 16 *n.*

Denmark, bronzes found in, 245.

Diadumenos (statue), 151, 169.

Diana, 228.

Dindia Macolnia, 190.

Dionysios of Argos, 148.

Dionysos, 148, 187, 225.

Dipoinos, 96.

Discobolos, representations of, 147, 148, 154.

Dispater, 230.

Dodona, askos from, 213 *n.*; characteristics of bronzes from, 97; cheekpiece from helmet, 175; Corinthian bronze, 88; decorated plate, 137; fourth-century bronzes, 172; goat,

105; horses, 37, 97; Kouros, 86; Peloponnesian influence, 97; spotted centaur, 59; tripods, 47; Zeus statuette, 149.
Dog, 18, 40, 130.
Dolphins, 130, 243.
Dorian Invasion, 30, 38.
Doryphoros, 169, 222.
Draccius (manufacturer), 244.
Drill, 6.
Dutuit Collection. *See* Paris: Petit Palais, Dutuit Collection (in Museum index).

EAGLES, 123, 127 *n.*, 148.
Early Archaic period, 35, 53, 79.
Egyed, 233.
Egypt, bronze technique, 8, 19; contrast to Crete, 19; copper in, 3, 4; influence on Greek art, 54; inlaid utensils, 233; Roman bronzes in, 226. *See also* Alexandria.
Elatea, 37.
Electrum, use of in inlay, 9 *n.*, 10.
Eleutherae, 119.
Elis, no local style, 85.
— tomb in, 181.
Enkomi, objects from, 31, 33, 34.
Epaphroditus, L. Ansius, 244.
Ephesus, bowls and tripods from, 71; excavations, 240; female statuette, 76; ivories, 76, 102, 103.
Epidauros, 95, 96.
Epinal, 230. *See also* Museum index.
Epiros, 68.
Eretria, objects from: hydriae, 163, 184, 185; mirror, 126.
Eros, 161, 207-8. *See also* Cupid.
Etruria, bronze work in: bowls, 70; candelabra, 78, 140, 214; influence of Greek art, 78, 107; local styles: *see* Chiusi, Vulci, Perugia; mirrors, 129 ff., 214; reliefs, 121 *seq.*; tripods and stands, 70, 72, 132; statuettes, 78, 107, 144, 157, 172, 209; vases, 138 ff., 165, 193; winged figures, 71.
Euboea, 4, 164.
Εὐδαμίδας Περδίκ[κ]αι, 203.
Evans, Sir A., 21, 22, 27.
Évreux, Jupiter from, 230. *See also* Museum index.
Ewers, prehistoric, 6, 13, 15, 16, 17.

FABRICIUS, 21.
Falterona, statuettes from, 109, 173.
Female figures: Cretan, 26 *seq.*; Early Archaic, 76; Etruscan, 80; fifth century, 149, 152; Roman, 218; sixth century, 87. *See also* Korai.
Fibulae, development of, 31; Geometric period, 36, 47 *seq.*; Greek type, 38; lion and snake type, 77.

Ficoroni cista, 173, 190.
Fins d'Annécy, 222, 230.
Fish, 48, 50, 52.
Fisherman, 225.
Fitzwilliam Museum. *See* Cambridge: Fitzwilliam Museum (in Museum index).
Florence. *See* Museum index.
" Flying gallop," 10.
Forsdyke, E. J., 87 *n.*
Foundry site, Enkomi, 34.
Fouquet Collection. *See* Museum index.
Fox, 92.
France, 245. *See also* Gaul.
Frescoes, compared with Minoan bronzes, 8-10, 20, 27, 60, 61.
Fünen, bronze found in, 229.
Furtwängler, A., 89 *n.*, 135, 163, 222.

GADES. *See* Tarshish.
Galaxidhi, 186.
Gaudos, 4.
Gaul, bronzes from, 200, 229, 244.
Gauls, 198 *seq.*
Genius Castrorum, personification of, 220.
Geometric period: bronzes of, 36 *seq.*; character of decoration, 30; decorative designs, 47; Etruscan bronzes, 78; local styles, 43; tripods, 44.
Germany, bronzes from, 228, 243, 246.
Gilliéron, Emile, 8 *n.*, 9 *n.*, 10 *n.*
Gladiators, figures of, 219.
Glasinatz, 38.
Glyptothek. *See* Munich: Glyptothek (in Museum index).
Goats, statuettes of, 40, 105; as decoration, 56 ff.
Gold, in inlay, 9, 233.
Gongs. *See* Cymbals.
Gorgons, 77, 104, 114, 119, 122, 135, 165, 188.
Gournia, metal workings at, 5; statuette, 21, 23, 28.
Grächwyl hydria, 138.
Graeco-Roman bronzes, 210.
Griffins, 54, 67, 68, 70, 71, 115, 118, 239.
Grotesques, 203 ff., 207, 225.
Grumentum, 107.

HAGELAIDAS of Argos, 145, 147, 149, 151.
Hagia Triadha, dagger from, 5; fresco, 9; statuettes, 25, 26, 27, 35.
Hagios Sostes, bronzes from, 92 *nn.*, 96.
Hairdressing, seventh century, 74.
Halbherr, 21, 55.
Half-moon fibulae, 49.
Hallstatt, 38.
Handles of vases, 68, 135, 162, 164, 182, 185; importance of, 134; of mirrors, 126, 158 ff., 181; of tripods, 46.

Hare, 40.
Harpokrates, 227.
Harpy, 166.
Hazzidakis, 12 *n.*
Heads, as vessels, 231.
Helen, 192, 193.
Helladic, use of term, 2 *n.*
Hellenistic period, choice of subjects in, 198 ; in Etruria, 208; inlaid utensils, 233; portraiture, 204; statuettes, 195; vases and utensils, 210.
Helmets : Early Archaic type, 66, 73 ; Geometric period, 42 ; Phoenician type, 28. *See also* Axos helmet.
Hemmoor, pails from, 245.
Hera, 77, 87, 93 *n.*, 98.
Herakleidas, 177.
Herakles : archaic, 66, 86 ; early fifth century, 142 ; Este figure, 110; Etruscan, 108, 158 ; Lysippaean, 172 ; Mt. Oeta statuette, 149 ; on reliefs, 66, 114. *See also* Hercules.
Herculaneum, column crater from, 212 ; heirlooms at, 197, 211, 224; Hellenistic period, 212; Roman bronzes, 223 ; utensils and vases, 236.
Hercules, Gaulish figure of, 229. *See also* Herakles.
Hermaphrodite, 230.
Hermarchos, 205.
Hermes, 92, 95, 96, 152, 153.
— Kranaios, cave of, 28, 35.
Hermione, mirrors from, 128, 161.
Herms, 234, 239.
Herodotus, 5.
Heroic Age, 1.
Hesiod, 1.
Hestia Giustiniani, statue of, 150.
Hierapetra, 35 *n. See also* Museum index.
Hippodameia, 93 *n.*, 150.
Hiram, King of Tyre, 35.
Holland, bronze manufacturers in, 245.
Hollow casting, 19, 70, 91, 170, 202 *n.*
Homer, 1.
Horace, on Campanian bronzes, 241.
Horses, statuettes, 36 ff., 40, 97, 107, 232 ; as decoration, 49, 50, 64, 80, 121, 137, 165, 188.
Horse-trappings, ornamented, 181.
Hounds, 40.
Hungary, bronzes found in, 228.
Hunting scenes, 233, 234.
Hybrisstas, 95, 148, 153.
Hydriae, Early Archaic, 68 ; fifth and fourth century, 163, 164, 182; Rhodian, 184 ; sixth century, 134.

Ianuaris (manufacturer), 244.
Iberian peninsula, tin mines in, 4.
Idaean cave, objects found in, 55.
Incense burners, 140, 165.

Inlay : daggers, 7 ff. ; particular figures, 151, 155, 204, 218, 219; Hellenistic vases, 233 ; Roman, 233 ff.
Inscriptions on bronzes, 74, 77, 88, 91, 93, 102, 114, 129, 143, 160, 183, 190, 203, 231, 232.
Iolkos. *See* Volo.
Ionia, 101.
Ionic Art, 75, 101, 119, 143.
— — and Etruria, 121.
— — and Sparta, 90.
— capitals, 33, 34, 143, 205.
Iron Age, date of, 2 ; art of, 30.
Iron, use of, 2, 31.
Isis, figure of, 227.
— temple of, Pompeii, 237.
— tomb of. *See* Polledrara tomb.
Isola di Fano, 110.
Italy, Southern, art of, 106, 156 ; male figures, 156-7 ; mirrors, 158, 180 ; vases and vessels, 133, 186 ff., 210 ff.
Ithome, Mt., 96.
Ivories, 76, 77, 81.
Ivory, as inlay on bronzes, 122.

Joins, methods of making, 6. *See also* Rivets, soldering, welding.
Jugs, archaic, 136; Roman, 238; S. Italian, 163.
Jupiter, Gaulish figures of, 230. *See also* Zeus.
— Dolichenus, 227, 228.

Kalathiana, 12.
Kalavryta, 152, 153.
Kalymnos, 184, 185.
Kanachos, 223.
Kanephoros, 143, 170.
Kardhitza, 43.
Karmos, 86, 91. *See also* Warriors.
Kassiterides, 5.
Kertsch, objects from, 182, 183.
Khorassan, tin mines of, 4.
Kimon, 177.
Kirrha, tin mine at, 4.
Knidos, Aphrodite of. *See* Aphrodite.
Knife-handle, bronze, 18.
Knives, development of, 7.
Kleitor, 96.
Kleonai, 160.
Knossos, clay tablet from, 17 ; decorated bowl, 6 ; faïence votary, 26 ; frescoes, *see* frescoes ; geometric cemetery, 33; snake goddess, 22, 23; temple repositories, 22; tombs, 16; vases, 12 ff. ; warrior from, 83.
Kopaïs, Lake, 183.
Korai, 80, 104, 108, 144.
Korinthos, on mirror, 179.
Kotilon, 126 *n.*
Kottabos stands, 140, 165, 214

Koumanoudes, 8.
Kouretes, 56.
Kouroi, Cretan, 75; Etruscan, 108; Pelo-
ponnesian, 86, 95 n., 104; Samo-
Milesian, 75, 102.
Krain, 201.
Kriophoros, 84.
Ksour es-Saf, 213.
Kuban, the, 211.
Kurion, objects from, 32, 33.
Kylikes, Attic, 122; designs influence
mirrors, 130; bronze, 185.
Kyme, 137.
Κυνῆ, 92.
Kynouria, 77.
Kypselos, chest of, 119.
Kyzikos, 185.

LA GARENNE tripod, 71.
Laaland, bronzes found in, 243.
Lakonia, objects from: 83, 90, 127. See
also Sparta.
Lakonian Pottery, 76.
Lamps. See Candelabra.
Langlotz, 88 n., 91 n., 102 n.
Lares, the, 217 ff.
Larnaka, 34.
Lasa, 214.
Lasethi district, 7.
Leukas, 37; on mirror, 179.
Leyden. See Museum index.
Libation table, from Psychro cave, 21.
Lichtenberg, 228.
Licinia Sabinilla, 230.
Ligourio, bronze from, 146, 155.
Lions, figures of, 77, 105; as decoration,
10, 46, 52, 54, 56, 57, 62, 65, 115, 119,
122, 188.
Litter, inlaid, 234.
Locri Epizephyrii, as art centre, 106;
hydriae from, 188; mirrors, 156, 158,
160, 161, 181.
Locris, hydria from, 184.
Loeb Collection. See Museum index.
Longa, 85.
Lousoi, 82, 151; Artemis from, 94, 96,
149; horses from, 37; Pan from,
153.
Louvre. See Paris: Louvre (in Museum
index).
Lykaion, Mt., objects from, 82, 93, 94, 96,
151, 152.
Lykosoura, objects from, 82, 86, 96.
Lyons, bronzes from, 230, 244.
Lysippos, 168, 171, 225.

MACEDONIA, 37.
Maenad, 169, 188, 235.
Mahedia, bronzes from ship wrecked off,
204, 206 ff.
Mainz. See Museum index.

Malache, 130.
Male figures: Arcadian, 92; Minoan, 21
seq.; Early Archaic, 73 seq.; fifth
century, 146 seq. See also Athletes,
Kouroi, Warriors.
Maleatas, 91.
Malia, 28.
Manufacturer's marks, on bronzes, 244.
Marash, 227.
Marren (Oldenburg), 228.
Mars, figures of, 157, 173.
Marseilles (Massilia), 229.
Mazi, 90.
Megalopolis, 88.
Megara Hyblaea, 68.
Melos, 19.
Menelaion, the, 76, 90.
Menvra, Etruscan figures of, 108, 109.
See also Minerva.
Mesembria, objects from, 184, 185.
Mesopotamia, influence of on Greek art,
54. See also Assyria.
Messenia. See Longa.
Metaponto, tripod from, 132.
Miletus, 99. See also Samo-Milesian
school.
Minerva, figures of, 174, 209. See also
Menvra.
Minoan Art, 7 ff.; reminiscence of in later
art, 60-62, 64, 84.
— Periods, dating, 2.
Minotaur, 42.
Mirrors: Argivo-Corinthian, 115, 126; en-
graved (Greek), 178 ff.; Etruscan,
129 ff., 162, 193; Hellenistic, 214;
Peloponnesian type, 125-6, 159;
Praenestine, 192; prehistoric, 7; with
covers, 176, 177 ff.; with open-work
plaques, 180; with stands, 127 ff.,
160 ff., 214; with tangs, or handles,
127, 158; Roman, 241. See also
Supports.
Mitrai, Cretan, 60 ff., 83, 121.
Monsters, Mycenaean, 32.
Monteleone chariot, 122.
Moschophoros, 84, 92.
Moulds, for casting, 5. See Technique.
Mouliana, 48 n.
Mule's head, 235.
Munich. See Museum index.
Muri, 230.
Mycenae, 2, 7, 13-16.
Mycenaean art, possible reminiscence of,
60-62, 64, 84. See also Minoan Art.
— civilization, influence of in Cyprus, 5,
32; definition of, 2.
— painting. See Fresco.

NAKED women, figures of, 127, 151.
Naples. See Museum index.
"Narcissus," 225.

Naukratis, vase from, 67.
Naupaktos, 136.
Nauplia, vessels from, 16. *See also* Museum index.
Naxos, 77, 86, 102, 103.
Nemea, 128.
Nemi, Lake, 219.
Neolithic period, 1; figures, reminiscent of, 28.
Neugebauer, 84 *n.*
Neuvy-en-Sullias, bronzes discovered at, 231, 232.
Neviodunum, 201.
New York. *See* New York: Metropolitan Museum (Museum index).
Niello, use of, 9, 204, 233.
Nike, 100, 120, 161.
Nikomachos, 202.
Nîmes, 135, 229. *See also* Museum index.
Nimrud, 55.
" Nocera Venus," 224.
Noicattaro, 118.
North-Western Greece, 43, 96.
Norway, bronzes found in, 245.
Notion, 183.

Ochrida, Lake, 135.
Oeta, Mt., 149.
Offida, 166.
Old age, representations of, 201.
" Old Man of the Sea," 114.
Olympia, archer, 124; Argivo-Corinthian reliefs, 114, 121; bands, 58; bowls, 55, 70, 137; breastplates, 62; calf, 105; chariots, 42; female figures from, 89, 103; fibulae, 36, 77; geometric animals, 36, 39 ff.; hydriae, 68, 135; phialae, 67; Phoenician bowls, 55; relief, 59; riders, 42; sculpture, *see* sculpture; silhouettes of horses, 125; sixth-century statuettes, 85; stand, 72; supporting figure (marble), 127; tripods, 34, 44; warriors, 41, 86; winged figures from bowls, 71; urns, 68; Zeus, 89, 149. *See als)* Museum index.
Onatas, 142.
Open work: figures, 124; on cistae, 189.
Orange (town), 230.
Orchomenos, 61, 118.
Orestes amphora, 212.
Orientalising period. *See* Early Archaic period.
Orontes, river, 206.
Orthia, 127, 129.
Othrys, Mt., 4.
Oxen. *See* Bulls.

Paestum. *See* Kanephoros.
Pails: Etruscan, 166, 194; from Offida, 166; provincial, 245; Roman, 238,

242; South Italian, 186 ff., 212 ff. *See also* Situla.
Painting. *See* Frescoes.
Palaikastro, objects found at : ewer, 15; moulds, 6; pin, 18; shields, 57; statuettes, 25, 26, 28.
Palestrina. *See* Praeneste.
Pan, figure of, 153.
— Nomios, shrine of, 151. *See* Berekla.
Panthers, 54, 58, 187, 234, 246.
Panticapaeum, 182.
Paramythia, 171.
Paris (Alexander), 193.
Paros, 4.
Pasiteles, 147.
Pateli, 38.
Paterae, decorated, 131; Hellenistic, 214. *See* Phialae.
Patina, of bronzes, 97, 109, 137, 149, 218.
Pausanius, 96 *n.*, 98.
Peacock, 37.
Pegasus, head of, 101.
Peloponnese, art of, 37, 75, 84 ff., 146; copper in, 4; mirrors, 125, 160. *See* Argos, Corinth, etc.
Pendants : bull's head design, 77; Geometric period, 38.
Pergamon, satyr from, 205; school of, 195, 197, 198.
Pernice, 5.
Perseus pail, 187.
Perspective, 191.
Perugia, Etruscan statuettes from, 108; reliefs, 123. *See also* Museum index.
Petrograd. *See* Museum index.
Petsofa, terra-cottas from, 21, 22, 24 *n.*, 26.
Phaistos, objects from, 5, 16, 23.
Phauleas, 93.
Pherae, objects from, 37, 71.
Phialae, from Olympia, 67, 68.
Phillo, 143, 161.
Phoenician art, bowls, 54; characteristic motive, 57.
— coast, statuettes from, 28.
— trade, 54.
Phrati, 55 *n.*, 57, 60 *n.*
Phylakopi, 19.
Pierpont Morgan Collection. *See* New York: Pierpont Morgan Collection (in Museum index).
Pierre-en-Luiset, 223.
Pigs, figures of, 232.
πῖλος, 92.
Pins, Minoan, 18; Geometric, 36.
Plates, sixth century, 136.
Pliny, 242.
Pnyx, the, 33.
Podlaze, 38.
Polledrara tomb, 79, 237 *n.* *See also* Vulci.

Polos, of female figures, 87.
Polybius, P. Cipius, 244.
Polykleitos, 146, 151, 168, 169, 222.
Pompeii, cullenders from, 243 ; heirlooms at, 197, 211, 224 ; hot-water jar from, 213 ; inlaid utensils, 233 ; Lares, 217 ; pails, 212 ; portrait, 205 ; Roman bronzes, 223 seq. ; "samovar," 212 ; utensils and vases, 236 seq.
Portraiture, Hellenistic, 197, 204 ; Roman, 220.
Poseidon, 171, 196.
Pottery, continued use of, 44 ; cups, fourth century, 186 ; development, 29 ; influence of bronze on, 17, 54, 186 ; Kertsch style, 180 : Polledrara tomb, 79 ; Praesos plate, 64 ; Proto-Attic vase, New York, 67 ; South Italian, 211 ; tripods, 72. See also Lakonian pottery, Proto-Corinthian pottery, and Vase painting.
"Pourtales Aphrodite," 171.
Praeneste, objects from : bowl, 79 ; cistae 188, 189 ; pear-shaped mirrors, 192 ; relief, 175 ; stand, 72 ; tombs at, 79.
Praesos, male figure from, 28 ; plate, 64.
Praxiteles, influence of, 167.
Prehistoric period, 1.
Priene, 234.
Proto-Corinthian pottery, 79.
Proto-Geometric period, 30, 35.
Protome, 74.
Psychro cave, objects from : knife-handle, 18 ; libation table, 21 ; statuettes, 21, 25, 26, 27, 35.
Ptoön, the, 103 ff. ; objects from : Argivo-Corinthian reliefs, 116 ; diadems, 119 ; statuettes, 37, 87, 103, 105 n. ; winged figures from bowls, 71.
Pythagoras of Rhegium, 156.

RAMS, 92, 122, 135.
Randazzo, 134.
Rapiers, Minoan, 7, 11.
Razors, bronze, 6.
Realism, Hellenistic tendency towards, 197.
Regolini-Galassi tomb, 79.
Reliefs : Argivo-Corinthian, 113 ; Etruscan, 121 ; late fifth and fourth century, 174 ; on pails, 187 ; Roman, 235 ; Tarentine, stone, 211 ; votive, 90.
Repoussé work, in bronzes, 68, 140, 178.
"Resting Maenad," 169.
Rethymno, mitra from, 60.
Rhodes : bowls from, 70 ; Cretan art traditions, 3 ; Geometric period, 37, 47 ; Gorgon statuette, 77 ; hydriae, 184.
Rhyton, silver, 186, 211.
Riders, statuettes of, 42, 88, 107.
Ring, from Mycenae, 26.

Rivets, of bronzes, 6, 17.
Roccanova, candelabrum from, 213.
Rocks, 10, 176, 203.
Roman bronzes, 216 seq.
— provinces, bronzes from, 226.
Rome, Ficoroni cista, made at, 190.
Rua, crater from, 135.
Rudiobus, bronzes sacred to, 232.
Russia, South, objects from, 181, 182, 186, 188.
Ruvo, amphora from, 212.

SACKRAV, 246.
Sala Consilina, Lucania, 134.
Samo-Milesian school, 75, 102.
Samos, art of, 103.
San Barnardo, 238.
Satyrs, 105, 109, 139, 165, 173, 188, 205, 207, 235 237, 240, 246.
Satyr with wine skin, 225.
Scala Nova, near Miletus, 102.
Scheibbs, bronze from, 228.
Schliemann, 8.
Schwarzenbach, 165.
Sculpture: Cretan, 19 ; development and relation to statuettes, 73, 75, 81, 145, 150. Particular statues : archaic goddess at Berlin, 87 ; Hestia Giustiniani, 150 ; marble fragment at Athens, 87 ; Moschophoros, 84, 92 ; Naxian marble figure, 103 ; Olympia metopes, 150 ; Olympia pediments, 93, 150 ; Pergamene, 198 ; Syeris, 202 ; Zeus Ithomatas, 149. See also under particular artists and Diadumenos, Discobolos, Doryphoros, Aphrodite, etc.
Seeland, bronze pails from, 243.
Selinos, 91.
Selinous, coin of, 156.
Serapis, 227.
Sesklo, 6.
Shaft-Graves, Mycenae, vases from, 13, 15 ; swords and daggers, 6, 7.
Sheep, 92.
Shepherds, figures of, 92 ff.
"Shield of Horus," 56.
"Shield of the Goats," 56.
Shields, Cretan, 55, 56 ; devices for, 124.
Ships, 50, 52.
Sickness, representation of, 202.
Sicily : athlete from, 156 ; coins of, 156, 177 ; Greek art in, 106 ; mirrors, 181.
Sikyon, figure from, 168 ; mirrors, 129, 160 ; school of painting, 180 ; sixth-century bronzes, 89.
Silens, 225, 240. See Satyrs.
Silver, coating on mirrors, 180 ; mirrors, 180, 241 ; inlay and accessories, 9 ff., 204, 220, 233 ff. ; vases, 186.

Sirens, 104, 115, 119, 139, 158, 159, 160, 163, 164, 182.
Siris reliefs, 174.
Sitanos, pendant from, 18 *n.*
Situlae, derivation of word, 187 *n.*   *See* Pails.
Skopas, influence of, 168.
Skyllis, 96.
"Sleeping Eros," 197.
Sleeping figures, statuettes of, 197.
Smelting, of metal for bronzes, 5.
Smyrna, 25.
Snake, 56.
— goddess, or attendant, 22, 23, 26.
— in fibulae, 77.
Soissons, 203.
Soldering. *See* Technique.
Solomon's temple, 35.
Sparta: excavations at, 78; fifth-century bronzes, 150; Geometric bronzes, 36, 47; mirrors, 151, 160; seventh-century bronzes, 77; sixth-century statuettes, 86, 89 ff. *See also* Museum index.
Spear-heads, development of, 6, 7.
Spectacle fibulae, 38.
Sphinx, 54, 56, 57, 62, 80, 104, 115, 119, 183, 235.
Spratt, Capt., 22.
Stags, figures of, 40, 232.
Stamped decoration, 173, 174.
Stands and supports: of animal statuettes, 39, 40; of Arcadian Hermes, 153; columnar, 127, 160, 240; of mirrors, 127, 160; mounted on wheels, 34, 35; of bowls, 72, 132; stalk-like, 22, 84, 93 *n.*
Starigrad, 228.
Stephanos, 147.
Sterope, 93 *n.*
Stockholm. *See* Museum index.
Stone implements, 3, 4.
Studs, as decoration, 239.
Sub-Mycenaean period, 30, 32.
Supports. *See* Stands and Supports.
Swastika, as decoration, 47, 50.
Swords, bronze, 7; iron, 37; iron age type, 66; decoration of, 7.
Sybrita, figure from, 28, 35.
Syracuse, vessel from, 68.
Syria, bronzes from, 227.

TANG, use of, 21, 127.
Tarentum: as art centre, 106, 211, 242; horse-trappings, 182; metal-work, 181; pails, 187; rhyton, *see* Rhyton.
Tarshish, tin mines of, 5.
Tattooing, 62 *n.*, 220 *n.*
Technique: casting, defective, 150, 154; channel left, 22, 84, 93 *n.*; chasing, on Italian and Roman bronzes, 173,
209, 220; Cretan, 8, 19; cire-perdue, 91, *and see* hollow casting; engraving tools, 49, 189; Geometric figures, 39, 41, 49, 52; figures from sheet-bronze, 39, 100, 124; hammered figures, 41, 70; high relief work, 174, 178; hollow-casting, 19, 70, 91, 170, 202 *n.*; primitive, 5; rivets, *see* Rivets; Roman, 217, 220, 236; welding and soldering, 6, 12; wheel, vases turned on, 245.
Tegea, objects from: Artemis, 149; Athena, 93; female figures, 152, 153; seated goddess, 94; votive bronzes, 82, 96, 151.
Telamon, site, 201.
Telos, 184.
Tensa, 236.
Terra-cottas: as evidence for attribution, 20, 83, 90; as mould, 20; bronzes in style of, 39, 41; of Argive shrines, 88; Rhodian, 102; South Italian and Ionian, 106; Spartan, 90.
Thebes, objects from: diadem, 52, 119; hydria, 183; statuettes, 37, 76. *See also* Museum index.
Thera, objects from, 11, 47.
Thermon, objects from, 37, 43.
Thessaly, objects from: Geometric bronzes, 37, 43; silver figure, 28; statuettes, 43, 155; stone implements, 4.
Thrace, inlaid chariot from, 233.
Throne Room, Knossos, 71.
Tin, sources of supply of, 4; used in bronze, 4.
Tiryns, objects from, 10, 28, 34, 83.
Todi, Mars statue from, 157, 174.
Toga, arrangement of, 218.
Toilet accessories, 7.
Tombs, bronze vessels in, 15, 16.
Tools, bronze, 6, 7. *See* Technique.
Tortoise, 128.
Transitional period, 30.
Trasimene, 208.
Trau Collection. *See* Vienna: Trau Collection (in Museum index).
Trebellius Romanus, 244.
Trees, 35 *n.*, 181, 188, 191.
Trier, bronze at, 139.
Trieste. *See* Museum index.
Tripod Hearth, Tomb of the, 16.
Tripods: Cretan, 15, 16; Early Archaic, 70; Etruscan, 80, 123, 132, 139; Geometric, 44 ff.; Roman, 237; sixth century, 131; sub-Mycenaean, 32.
Troy, objects from: copper utensils, 12; decorated dagger, 18; moulds, 6; primitive statuette, 3, 18.
Tübingen. *See* Museum index.
Turan, 193.

Tutulus, Etruscan, 108, 140.
Tweezers, bronze, 6.
Tylissos, objects from: basins, 12; statuettes, 22, 23, 25.
Tyszkiewicz plate, 68.

URAEUS, 227.
Urns, 68, 137, 184.

VAN, Lake, 71.
Vapheio, 11.
Vase painting, Attic, 130, 169, *See also* Pottery, Praesos plate, etc.
Vases, bronze: Early Archaic, 67; Etruscan, 138, 194; fifth and fourth centuries, 162, 182 *seq.*; prehistoric, 7, 11 ff.; Roman, 241; sixth century, 133. *See also under* Amphora, Hydria, etc.
Vatican. *See* Rome: Vatican (in Museum index).
Velestino. *See* Pherae.
Venus, Medici type of, 228; Nocera, 224. *See* Aphrodite.
Vertumnus, 110.
Vesuvius, eruption of, 236.
Vetulonia, objects from, 71, 78, 165.
Victory. *See* Nike.
Vienna. *See* Museum index.
Volo. 37.

Vonitza, mirrors from, 128, 176.
Vrokastro, objects from 33, 35.
Vulci: bronze industry of, 99, 132, 139; cistae from, 189; tripods, 132, 139. *See also* Polledrara tomb.

WALKING motive, introduction of, 146.
Warriors, bronzes of, Etruscan, 80, 108, 109, 157; Geometric period, 41, 157; Peloponnesian, 86.
Weapon, bronze, 6, 7.
Welding. *See* Technique.
Wheels, 181, 230, 231.
Windows, 34.
Winged figures, horses, 101, 120, 121; male, 65; Oriental, on tripods, 71 ff. *See also* Artemis, Nike.
Wyndham Cook Collection. *See* Museum index.

XENOKLES, statue of, 168.

ZAFER Papoura, cemetery, 11.
Zeus, and Idaean cave, 56; representations of, 62, 88, 94, 148, 149, 172. *See also* Jupiter.
— Ithomatas, 149.
— Lykaios, 94, 96, 151, 153.
— Temple of, Olympia, 150.

MUSEUM INDEX

Clarendon type numerals refer to Museum numbers ; roman type numerals to pages.

AEGINA.
Argivo-Corinthian reliefs, 118.
ALESIA.
dying Gaul, 200.
ANCONA.
hydria, 165.
ATHENS, National Museum.
  I Mycenaean bronzes :
    187 dagger from Vapheio, 11 ;
    394 dagger from shaft graves, 9 ;
    395 dagger from shaft graves, 10 ;
    604 vessel from shaft graves, 13, 14 ;
    683 vessel from shaft graves, 13-15 ;
    744 dagger from shaft graves, 10 ;
    747 dagger from shaft graves, 10 ;
    748 dagger from shaft graves, 10 ;
    764 dagger from shaft graves, 10 ;
    765 dagger from shaft graves, 9 ;
    daggers from Argive Heraeum, 11.
  II Greek bronzes :
    22 satyr from Dodona, 97 ; **24**
    girl from Dodona, 97, 98 ; **25** flute-
    player from Dodona, 97 ; **27** rider
    from Dodona, 97 ; **36** rider from
    Dodona, 97 ; **223** fibula from Dodona,
    37 ; **296** fibula from Dodona, 37 ;
    308 fibula from Dodona, 37 ; **640**
    Geometric horse from Dodona, 37 ;
    645 Geometric horse from Dodona,
    37 ; **646** Geometric horse from
    Dodona, 37 ; **6086** Artemis from
    Olympia, 89 ; **6149** supporting figure,
    103 ; **6163** Zeus from Olympia, 88 ;
    6177 warrior from Olympia, 41 ;
    6178 warrior from Olympia, 41 ;
    6190 chariot and driver, 42 ; **6193**
    deer and fawn, 40 ; **6199** mare and
    foal, 40 ; **6229** tripod from Tiryns,
    34 ; **6233** warrior from Olympia, 86 ;
    6236 dancers, 42 ; **6392** relief from
    Olympia, 59 ; **6445** youth, 100 ; **6447**
    Athena Promachos, 144 ; **6448**
    Athena, 99 ; **6457** Athena Promachos,
    99 ; **6483** Nike, 100 ; **6491** support,
    99 ; **6493** Ionic female figure, 99, 103 ;
    6508 Geometric bird, 37 ; **6511** Etrus-
    can tripod, 99, 108, 139 ; **6514** dancing
    girl, 155 ; **6534-6555** Geometric horse,

37 ; **6592** giant hurling stone, 154 ;
6597 male figure, 100 ; **6598** male
figure, 100 ; **6607** male figure, 100 ;
6612 early male figure, 73 ; **6613**
early male figure, 73 ; **6615** athlete,
154 ; **6616** geometric warrior, 41 ;
6617 early male figure, 73 ; **6626** boy
on dolphin, 154 ; **6627** protome, 74 ;
6673 fragment of plate, 137 ; **6679**
Geometric bird, 37 ; **6680** centaur, 101 ;
6693 Pegasus, 101 ; **6956** relief from
Acropolis, 65 ; **6957** engraving from
Acropolis, 58 ; **6958** Nike in chariot,
120 ; **6962** Argivo-Corinthian fragment, 116 ; **6963** relief from Acropolis,
66 ; **6965** Argivo-Corinthian fragment,
116 ; **7380** Boeotian male figure, 104 ;
7381 Boeotian male figure, 104 ; **7382**
Kouros, 104 ; **7388** Boeotian male
figure, 104 ; **7389** Boeotian female
figure, 104 ; **7412** discobolos, 148 ;
7474 Polykleitan athlete, 168 ; **7539**
Arcadian Hermes, 92 ; **7540** mirror,
127 ; **7547** Apollo from Amyklae, 91 ;
7548 mirror support, 128 ; **7549** rider
from Megalopolis, 88 ; **7565** woman
from Tegea, 153 ; **7586** jug, 136 ;
7598 Karmos, 91 ; **7605** woman from
Tegea, 152 ; **7644** warrior from Lykosoura, 86 ; **7686** Argivo-Corinthian
mirror, 126 ; **7687** Argivo-Corinthian
mirror handle, 115 ; **7691** Argivo-
Corinthian mirror handle, 115, 126 ;
7703 Aeginetan mirror, 128 ; **7830/5**
fragments of diadem, 119 ; **7913**
hydria, 185 ; **7914** hydria from Thebes,
183 ; **7940** tripod from Pnyx, 33 ;
8603a fragmentary Athena, 100 ;
11711 figure from Phylakopi, 19 ;
12347 shepherd, 92 ; **12439** Argivo-
Corinthian mirror, 126 ; **12831** warrior
from Kardhitza, 43 ; **13053** shepherd,
92 ; **13054** dead fox, 92 ; **13060**
peasant, 93 ; **13209** Zeus Lykaios, 94 ;
13219 Arcadian Hermes, 153 ; **13788**
group of dancers, 42 ; **14034** lion
fibula, 77 ; **14326** mirror with cover,
178 ; **14494** Artemis from Thermon

43; **14563** Geometric bronze from Thermon, 37; **14755** figure from Thermon, 43; **14756** figure from Thermon, 43; **14757** figure from Thermon, 37; **14789** warrior from Longa, 85; **14808** Kouros from Longa, 85; **14828** Athena from Tegea, 93; **14839** horses from Lousoi, 37; **14922** Demeter, 94; **15127** mirror with siren, 159; **16863** mirror with cover, 178; bronzes from Velestino, 37; bronzes from Argive Heraeum, 37; engraved band from Thebes, 52; Phoenician bowls, 55; shields from Idaean cave, 55; engraved fragment from Dodona, 59; breastplate from Olympia, 62; relief from Argive Heraeum, 67; griffin from Velestino, 71; reliefs from Ptoön, 116; Orchomenos fragments, 118; reliefs from Athens, 119; hydria, fifth century, 163; plain hydria, 183; fifth-century hydria, 183.

BARI.
Argivo-Corinthian relief, 118.
BERLIN, Altes Museum, Antiquarium.
677 cast bronze pail, 187; **715b** satyr, 109; **2120**, dancer, 196; **2129** Jupiter Dolichenus, 229; **2155**, Etruscan woman, 108; **6216** urn, 137, 138; **6238** cista, 191; **7094** Scythian bowman, 107; **7095** Athena from Florence, 109; **7342** bronze from Agrinion, 37; **7383** Kouros, 102; **7429** Kanephoros of Paestum, 143; **7477** Kriophoros, 84; **7644** Artemis, 152; **7863** Odysseus, 176; **7872** urn, 137; **7907** hydria, 163; **7933** draped woman, 90; **7976** Kouros from Dodona, 97; **8068** hydria from Locris, 184; **8089** Ligourio bronze, 146; **8099** Argivo-Corinthian mirror, 126; **8148** engraved mirror cover, 179; **8373** Argivo-Corinthian mirror, 126; **8385-86** cattle from Andria, 107; **8395** Herakles, 172; **8467** Randazzo hydria. 134; **8576** Diadumenos, 151; **8583** gladiator, 220; **8599** lady with dove, 155; **8622** Ionian bronze, 103; **8624** Pan, 153; **8629** mirror handle, 126; **8702** Geometric dancers, 42; **8850** Boscoreale crater, 237; **10389** hydria handles, 68; **10518** Minoan male worshipper, 24; **10556** Cretan Kouros, 75; **10561** Dodona Zeus, 149; **10581** Poseidon from Dodona, 172; **10582** Maenad, 169; **10584** goat, 105; **10588** plate from Dodona, 136; **10819** Minerva from Apiro, 174; **10820** mirror support, 128; **10825** Minoan

male figure, 28; **11876** Gaul, 199; **30023** Minoan worshipper, 24; **30082** girl spinning, 150; **30244** inlaid jug, 233; **30399** Perseus pail, 187; **30636** plain hydria, 183; **30894** beggar, 203; **Fr. 674**. Schwarzenbach amphora, 165; **Fr. 768** tripod, 132; woman worshipper, 26; stand from Larnaka, 34; Locri mirror support, 156.
BERLIN, Museum für Völkerkunde.
Figure from Troy, 18.
BERNE, Historisches Museum.
Grächwyl hydria, 138; Artio and Bear, 230.
BOSTON, Museum of Fine Arts.
Early male figure, 74; Artemis Daidaleia, 90; Spartan male head, 91; mirror support, 156; jug, 163; situla, 187; Hermes, 223.

CAMBRIDGE, Fitzwilliam Museum.
Minoan worshipper, 23; Geometric bronzes, 37; Archaic goddess, 87; Peloponnesian mirror, 126; patera, 131; replica of Pourtales Aphrodite, 171.
CANDIA.
Sword from Zafer Papoura, 11; basin from Kalathiana, 12; basins from Tylissos, 12, 14; vases from Knossos, 12, 16; ewer from Palaikastro, 15; vases from Phaistos, 16; vases from tombs, Knossos, 16; knife handle from Psychro cave, 18; pin from Palaikastro, 18; knife from Psychro cave, 18; worshipper from Candia, 21; worshippers from Gournia, 21, 23, 28; worshippers from Tylissos, 22, 23; worshipper from Knossos, 24; figure from Palaikastro, 25; figures from Psychro cave, 25, 26, 27, 35; female worshipper from Hagia Triadha, 26; female worshipper from Palaikastro, 26; primitive figure from Palaikastro, 28; figure from Malia, 28; figure from near Praesos, 28; tripod from Knossos, 33; tripod from Vrokastro, 33; figure from Vrokastro, 35: figures from Sybrita, 35; fragments of tripods, 47; bowl from Phrati, 55; objects from Idaean cave, 55; shields from Palaikastro, 57; mitra from Rethymno, 60.
CASSEL.
Herakles, 86.
CHANEA.
Mitrai, 62; Axos helmet, 63, 121.
CONSTANTINOPLE.
Bronzes from Pateli, 38; Artemis from Ephesos, 76.

COPENHAGEN, National Museum.
Dagger from Thera, 11 ; Archaic Cretan fragment, 60; Jupiter Dolichenus, 229.

DE CLERCQ COLLECTION.
Aphrodite, 227.

DELPHI.
Geometric objects, 37; Geometric woman, 43 ; Kouros (Peloponnesian), 75; Kouros (Ionic), 102; votive bulls, 105; Argivo-Corinthian fragments, 116 ; Apollo, 142.

DRESDEN.
Female figure from Caere, 128 n.

EPINAL, Museum.
Hermaphrodite, 230.

ESTE, Museum.
Herakles, 110.

ÉVREUX, Museum.
Jupiter, 230.

FLORENCE, Museo Archeologico.
Candelabrum from Vetulonia, 78 ; orientalising bronzes from Vetulonia, 79; figures from Brolio, 80; 'Vertumnus,' 110; basin from Chiusi, 139; one-handled vase, 140 ; Ajax, 144 ; Etruscan warrior, 157; satyr, 165 ; Amazon, 169; Etruscan situla, 194; Gaul, 201.

FOUQUET COLLECTION.
Dancing figure, 196; grotesque, 198; Egyptian priest, 198.

FRANKFURT-AM-MAIN.
Fragment of Minoan worshipper, 25 ; Artemis from Lousoi, 93, 96.

FROEHNER COLLECTION.
Tyszkiewicz plate, 68.

HIERAPETRA.
Early figure, 35.

LEYDEN.
Minoan male figure, 23, 26.

LOEB COLLECTION.
Etruscan tripods, 123; hydria, 185; cups, 185 ; Poseidon, 196.

LONDON, British Museum.
182 Cypriote Geometric figures, 43 ; **192** Archaistic kore, 223 ; **208** girl athlete, 98 ; **209** Payne Knight Apollo, 223 ; **213** youth from Corfu, 148 ; **224** mirror support, 161; **230** Dispater, 230; **233** goat, 105 ; **234** goat, 105 ; **243** mirror with stand, 156; **274** Poseidon, 171; **275** Zeus, 172; **284** silen, 240; **285** Siris reliefs, 174; **286**

Lake Bracciano figure, 175 ; **289** mirror-cover, 179; **290** mirror with cover, 178; **303** mirror from Locri, 181; **310** handles and relief, 185; **311** handles, relief and foot, 185; **312** hydria, 184; **313** hydria, 184; **434** female bust, 80; **459** Mars, 173 ; **497** Etruscan woman, 108; **509** Etruscan youth, 109; **514** mirror support, 156, 157; **542** Etruscan mirror, 130; **546** Etruscan mirror, 130; **556** Etruscan banqueter, 109; **557** amphora, 165; **558** urn, 107; **560** urn, 107, 138 ; **562** basin, 139; **588** Vulci tripod, 132; **605** Etruscan Hercules, 158; **613** Etruscan woman, 173 ; **650** pail, 166; **781** candelabrum, 140; **786** Jupiter, 230; **787** Hercules, 229 ; **790** Dispater, 230; **799** Apollo, 230; **814** Gaul, 200; **815** Gaul, 200; **816** Gaul, 200; **817** Gaul, 200; **825** Hermes, 222 ; **1079** Aphrodite, 171; **1084** Pourtales Aphrodite, 171; **1585** Roman official, 220; **1586** Roman official, 220 ; **3204** fibula, 50, 52 ; **3205** fibula, 50, 52 ; **3209** mirror support, 161 ; **3211** mirror with cover, 178 ; **67**, 5-8, **719** plain hydria, 183 ; **78**, 10-12, 1 to 11, 14, 15, 18, 20, 21 ; **82**, 10-9, 1, 2, 3, 9, 11, 12 ; **73**, 8-20 cups and goblets, 185 ; **97**, 4-1, **1296** stand from Enkomi, 34 ; **97**, 4-1, **1516** tripod from Enkomi, 33 ; **97**, 4-1, **1571** tripod from Enkomi, 34 ; **1904**, 7-3, 1 horseman from Grumentum, 107 ; **1904**, 7-8, 1 mirror with cover, 176, 178 ; **1906**, 4-5, 1 mirror with cover, 178 ; **1913**, 4-16 Gaulish prisoner, 221 ; **1913**, 5-29 Roman woman, 219 ; **1920** 12-20, 1 stand from Cyprus, 35 ; **1922** 7, 12 youth with syrinx, 100 ; Minoan worshipper, 22 ; bronzes from Rhodes, 37 ; cast of woman from Ephesus, 77 ; tripod from Polledrara tomb, 80, 237 ; reliefs from Eleutherae, 119 ; crater handle, 135 ; plate from Payne Knight Collection, 137 ; horse-trappings, 181 ; **1927**, **13-1**, **7**, hydria, 164 ; archer from London, 229.

MAINZ, Museum.
Thymiaterion, 139.

MUNICH, Arndt Collection.
Geometric fibulae, 49.

MUNICH, Museum Antiker Kleinkunst.
Fibula, 48; mirror support from Hermione, 128 ; urn, 137; hydria, 164, n. ; bathing girl, 170; dancing figure, 196.

MUNICH, Glyptothek.
Reliefs from Perugia, 123.

NAPLES, Museo Nazionale.
74745, 74749 bowls, 137; hydria, 188; dancing faun, 197; 126170, 5026 portrait statuettes, 205; 73098 calyx crater, 212; hot-water vessels, 212, 213; Hellenistic candelabrum, 213; 4998 Nocera Venus, 224; 815 satyr with wine skin, 225; 817 Dionysos, 225; 1487 horseman, 225; 825 (4994) fisherman, 225; grotesques, 225; 5030 cupid, 226; bust of philosophers, 226; 118295 inlaid jug, 233; 109697 crater, 238; jug, 238; 68854 pail, signed, 239; candelabra, 240.

NAUPLIA, Museum.
Bronze vessels, 16.

NEW YORK, Metropolitan Museum.
28 mirror support, 128; 40 Monteleone chariot, 122; 58 Phauleas, 93; 77 male mirror support, 162; 78 discobolos, 147; 79 worshipper, 156; 80 hydria handle, 164; 111, 112 horse-trappings, 181; 120 Hermarchos, 205; 127 grotesque, 204; 132 sleeping Eros, 197; 259 Antioch statuette, 206; 271 camillus, 220; 375 child and puppy, 201; 525 hydria, 163; 595 cup, 185; 596 cup, 185; 620 rim and handles from Cyprus, 32; 758 mirror, 176; 759 mirror, 176; 760 mirror, 176, 179; 761 mirror, 176; 765 mirror, 178; 766 mirror, 176; 767 mirror, 178; 797 Etruscan mirror, 193; 1180 tripod from Kourion, 33; inscribed hydria, 163.

NÎMES, Museum.
Handle with Gorgon, 135.

NORTHWICK PARK, Spencer-Churchill Collection.
Bull and acrobat, 27.

OLYMPIA.
Geometric animals, 39; horse, 40; bull, 40; deer and hounds, 40; phialae, 67; phiale with oxen, 68; man in breastplate, 86; calf, 105; silhouettes of horses, 125.

ORLÉANS.
Bronzes from Neuvy-en-Sullias, 232.

OXFORD, Ashmolean Museum.
Bronzes from Psychro cave, 21, 25, 26, 35; silver figure from Thessaly, 28; bronzes from Sybrita, 28, 35; bronze from East Crete, 35; Cretan openwork bronze, 60.

PARIS, Bibliothèque Nationale.
514 centaur, 101; 518 Herakles, 142; 815 Vienne warrior, 230; 927 Diadumenos, 169; 838 Hermes, 222; 854

bald man, 202; 928 athlete, 155; 1009 negro, 198; 1040 Etruscan woman, 108; 1390 Pompeian jug, 238.

PARIS, Louvre.
2 Apollo Piombino, 89; 80 Cretan woman, 27; 93, 94 Cretan openwork figures, 60; 104 minotaur, 42; 105 Cretan soldier, 83; 106 Cretan soldier, 83; 108 kouros from Dodona, 88; 143 woman from Ptoön, 87, 104; 148 horse from Dodona, 97; 154 Dionysos, 148; 183 athlete, 168; 184 athlete, 169; 218 Etruscan youth, 109; 220 Etruscan youth, 109; 223 young Hercules 110; 520 Orontes, 206; 683 Lar, 218; 686 Lar, 217; 696 barbarian, 197; 1684 mirror, 127; 1685 mirror, 160; 1687 mirror and bottle, 161; 1688 mirror, 129; 1693 mirror, 160; 1699 engraved mirror, 179; 1703 engraved mirror, 179; 1744 Praenestine mirror, 193; 1839 relief, 175; 2570 Gorgon, 77; 2636 handle with Gorgon, 135; 2645 handle of vase, 68; 2673 hydria, 183; 2749 jug, 136; 2750 jug, 136; 2825 handle with figures, 236; 3142 lamp, 139; 3448 inlaid plaque, 234.

PARIS, Petit Palais, Dutuit Collection.
hydria, 134; Hybrisstas' bronze, 95; Hermes, 222.

PERUGIA.
Etruscan reliefs from carriage, 123.

PETROGRAD, Hermitage.
Crater handles, 135; hydria from Kertsch, 183.

PHILADELPHIA.
Fibula, 49.

PIERPONT MORGAN COLLECTION.
Centaur and man, 42.

ROME, Conservatori Museum.
Inlaid litter, 234; inlaid couch, 234; tensa, 236.

ROME, Museo Kercheriano.
– Minoan worshipper, 25 n.

ROME, Vatican.
Etruscan vase, 139; candelabrum, 165; statuette of child, 208; Orte Minerva, 209.

ROME, Villa Giulia.
Reliefs from Praeneste, 175; Ficoroni cista, 190.

ST. GERMAIN-EN-LAYE.
50816, 60874 casts of bronzes of Gauls, 200; cast of Jupiter, 230; 217, 219 Gaulish heads, 231, 232; casts of bronzes from Neuvy-en-Sullias, 232.

SOFIA.
Crater from L. Ochrida, 135; hydria, 185.
SPARTA.
Female figure from Menelaion, 76, 90; male figures from Menelaion, 77; lion fibula, 77; bull's head pendant, 77; woman votary, 90; trumpeter, 150; mirror support, 151.
STOCKHOLM.
Ionic kouros, 75, 102.
SYRACUSE, Museum.
Athlete from Aderno, 156.

THEBES.
Herakles statuette, 149.
TRIER, Museum.
Handle with openwork figures, 139.
TRIESTE.
Tarentine silver rhyton, 186.

TÜBINGEN, Museum.
Armed runner, 141.
TYSZKIEWICZ COLLECTION (formerly).
Early Kore, 76.

VIENNA, Kunsthistorisches Museum.
921 Minoan worshipper, 21; 922 Minoan worshipper, 24; 926 (2925) mirror support, 128; 1282 Genius Castrorum, 220; 1292 Diana, 228; 1293 Venus, 228; 1295 Venus, 228; 3218 old woman from Krain, 201; 1292 Diana from Scheibbs, 221; 1328 Starigrad bronzes, 228; urn, 137; plain hydria, 183; stand from Ephesus, 240.
VIENNA, Naturhistorisches Museum.
Geometric bronzes from Amphipolis, 38.
VIENNA. Trau Collection.
Female figure, 151.

WYNDHAM COOK COLLECTION (formerly).
Sick man, 202.

PLATE I

INLAID DAGGER FROM MYCENAE

PLATE II

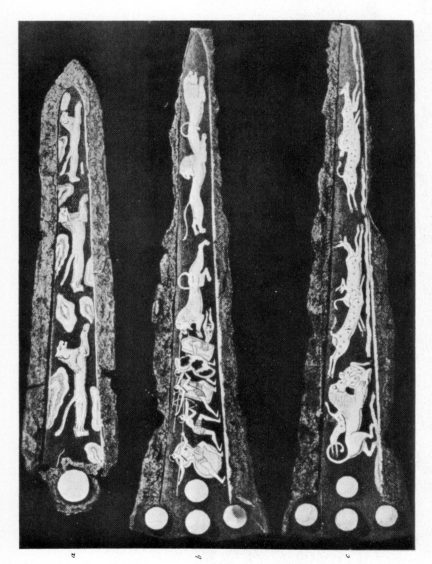

DAGGERS FROM MYCENAE

PLATE III

SWORDS FROM MYCENAE

DAGGER FROM CRETE

PLATE IV

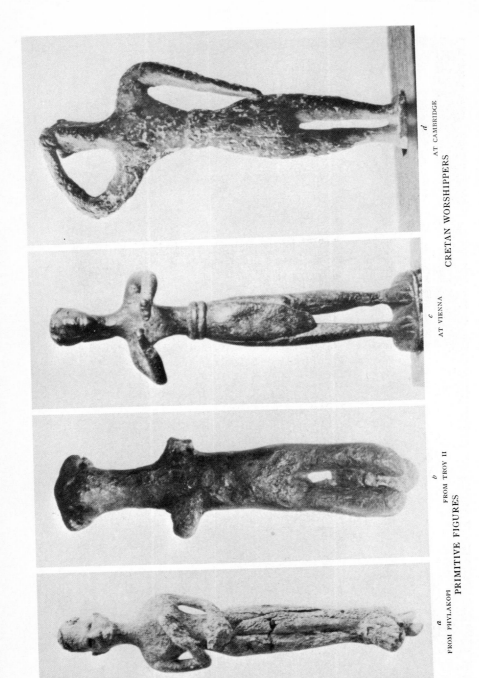

a
FROM PHYLAKOPI

b
FROM TROY II

PRIMITIVE FIGURES

c
AT VIENNA

d
AT CAMBRIDGE

CRETAN WORSHIPPERS

PLATE V

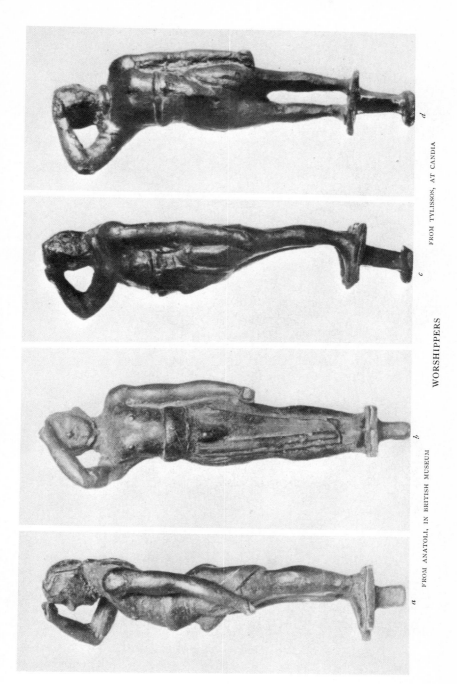

WORSHIPPERS

a FROM ANATOLI, IN BRITISH MUSEUM *b* *c* FROM TYLISSOS, AT CANDIA *d*

PLATE VI

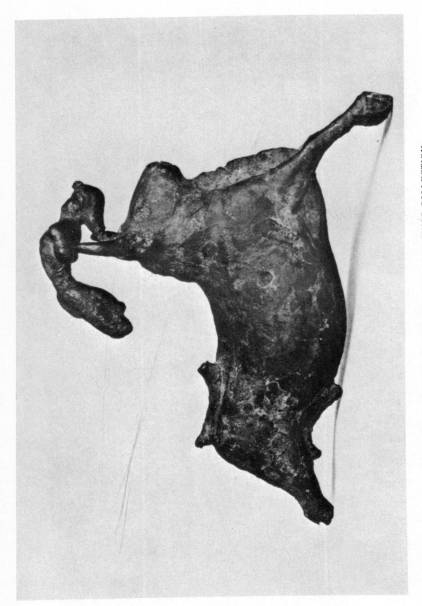

BULL AND ACROBAT IN THE SPENCER CHURCHILL COLLECTION

PLATE VII

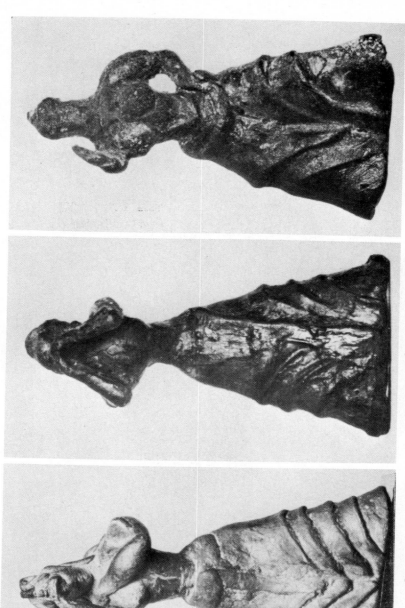

AT BERLIN   *a*   *b*   FROM HAGIA TRIADHA, AT CANDIA   *c*

WOMEN WORSHIPPERS

PLATE VIII

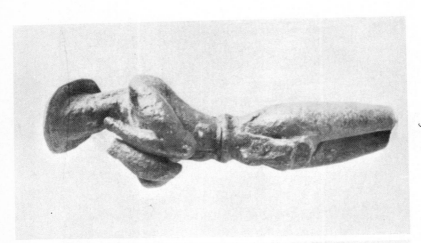

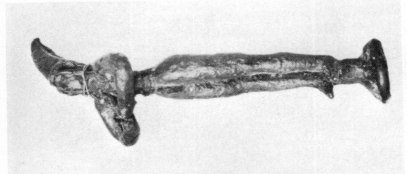

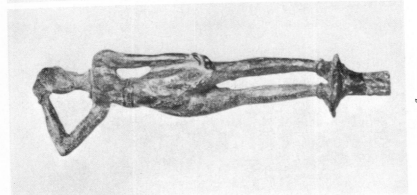

a

FROM TYLISSOS, AT CANDIA

b

FROM THE HARBOUR TOWN, AT CANDIA

WORSHIPPERS

c

AT LEYDEN

PLATE IX

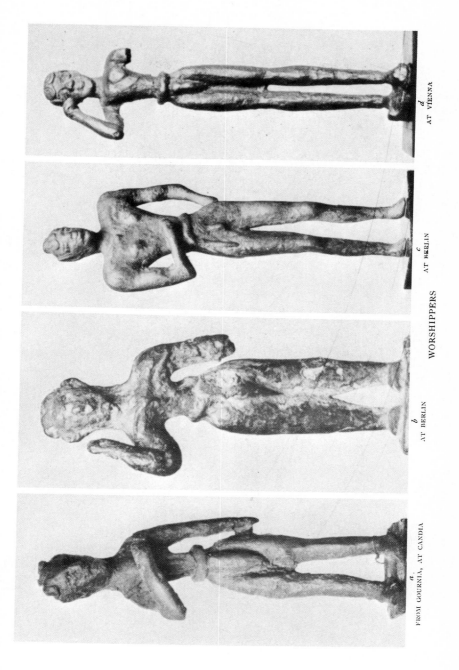

FROM GOURNIA, AT CANDIA

a

b
AT BERLIN

WORSHIPPERS

c
AT BERLIN

d
AT VIENNA

PLATE X

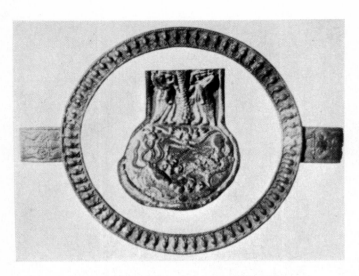

a. SUB-MYCENAEAN BOWL FROM CYPRUS
IN THE CYPRUS MUSEUM

b. TRIPOD FROM CYPRUS
AT NEW YORK

PLATE XI

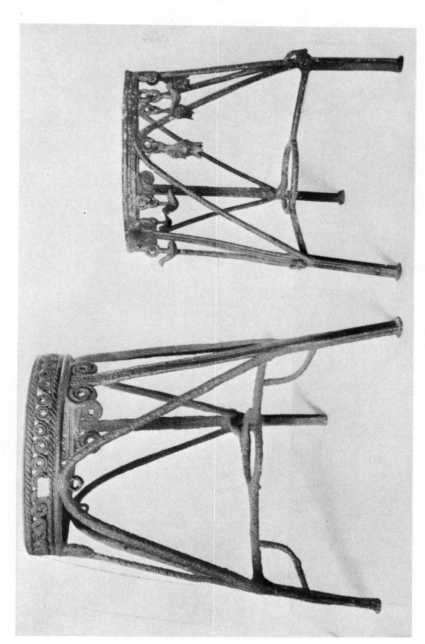

PROTO-GEOMETRIC TRIPODS AT ATHENS

PLATE XII

a. STAND FROM LARNAKA
AT BERLIN

b. STAND FROM ENKOMI
IN THE BRITISH MUSEUM

PLATE XIII

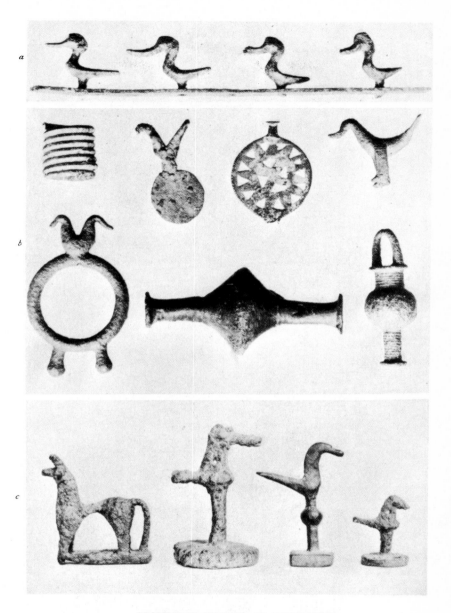

GEOMETRIC OBJECTS AT CAMBRIDGE

a. DUCKLINGS
b. RING, BIRDS, PENDANTS, AND BEAD
c. ANIMALS ON STANDS

PLATE XIV

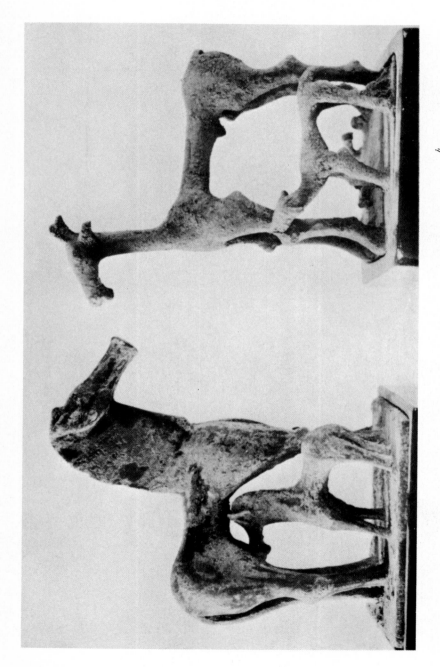

a
MARE AND FOAL.

b
DEER AND FAWN

BRONZES FROM OLYMPIA, AT ATHENS

PLATE XV

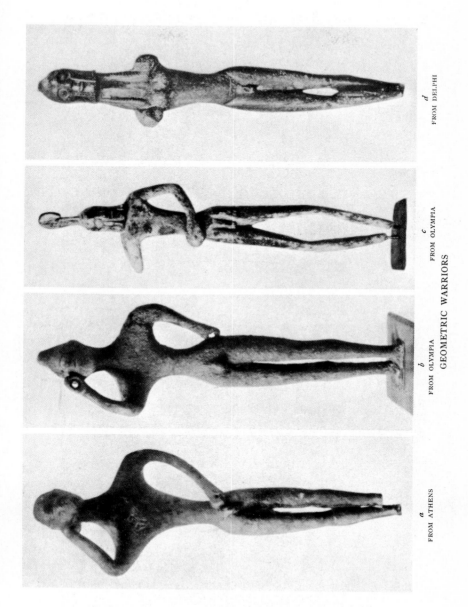

a
FROM ATHENS

b
FROM OLYMPIA

c
FROM OLYMPIA

d
FROM DELPHI

GEOMETRIC WARRIORS

PLATE XVI

a. CHARIOTEER

b. WOMEN DANCING

BRONZES FROM OLYMPIA
AT ATHENS

PLATE XVII

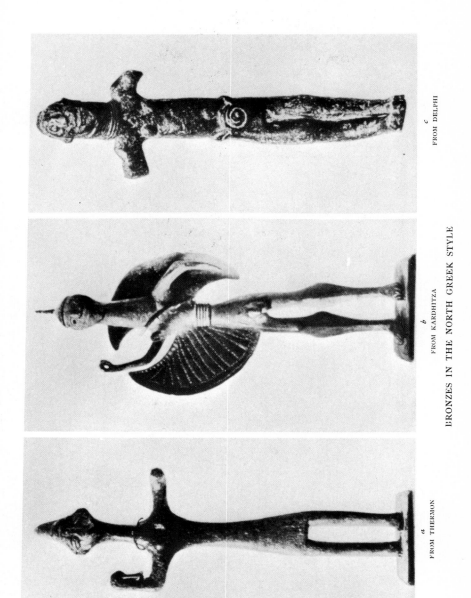

c
FROM DELPHI

b
FROM KARDHITZA

a
FROM THERMON

BRONZES IN THE NORTH GREEK STYLE

PLATE XVIII

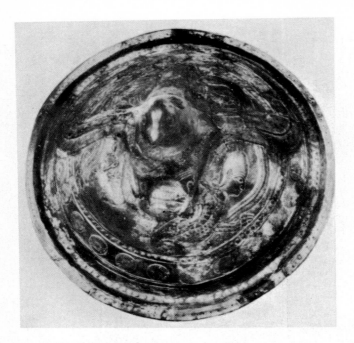

a. CRETAN SHIELD
IN CANDIA

b. TYSZKIEWICZ PLATE

PLATE XIX

FIGURES OF HUNTSMEN FROM CRETE
IN THE LOUVRE

PLATE XX

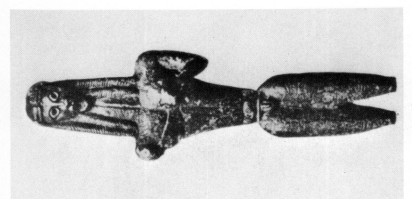

c

FROM BOEOTIA

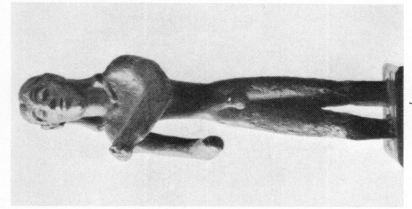

b

FROM ATHENS

EARLY MALE FIGURES

a

FROM ATHENS

PLATE XXI

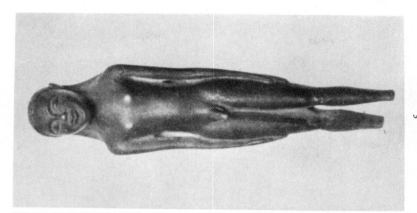

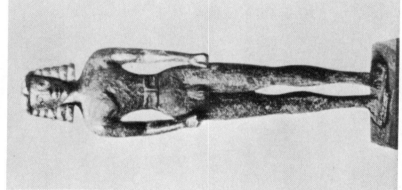

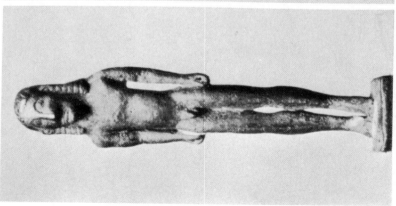

a

FROM CRETE

b

FROM DELPHI

c

AT STOCKHOLM

EARLY KOUROI

PLATE XXII

FROM EPHESUS

FROM BOEOTIA

FROM SPARTA

EARLY KORAI

c

b

a

PLATE XXIII

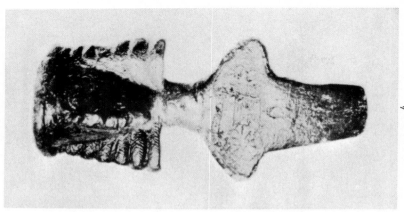

b

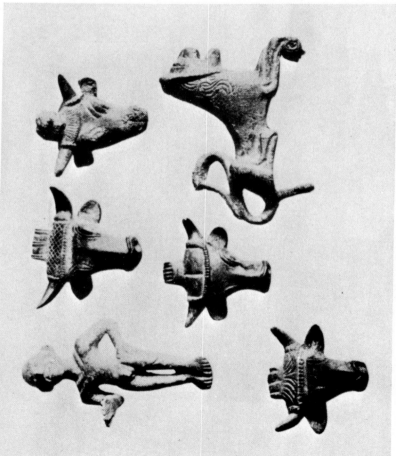

a

BRONZES FROM SPARTA

PLATE XXIV

a EARLY FIGURES FROM BROLIO

b

c CANDELABRUM FROM VETULONIA, AT FLORENCE

d

ETRUSCAN BRONZES

PLATE XXV

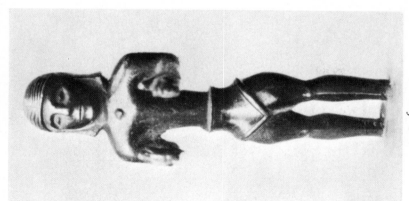

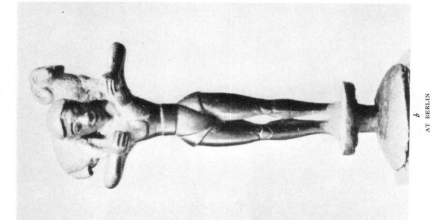

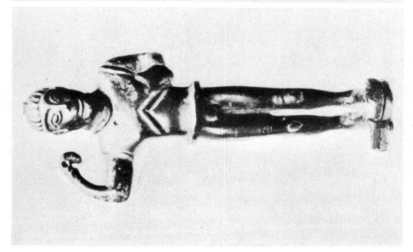

c

IN THE LOUVRE

b

AT BERLIN

CRETAN BRONZES

a

IN THE LOUVRE

PLATE XXVI

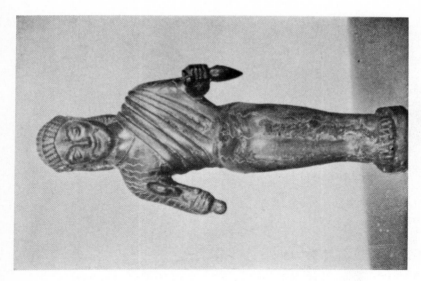

c. ZEUS LYKAIOS
AT ATHENS

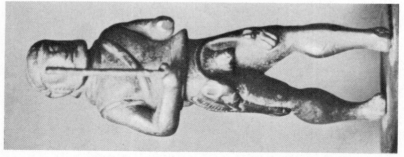

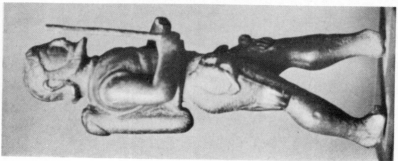

a. b. HERAKLES
AT CASSEL

PLATE XXVII

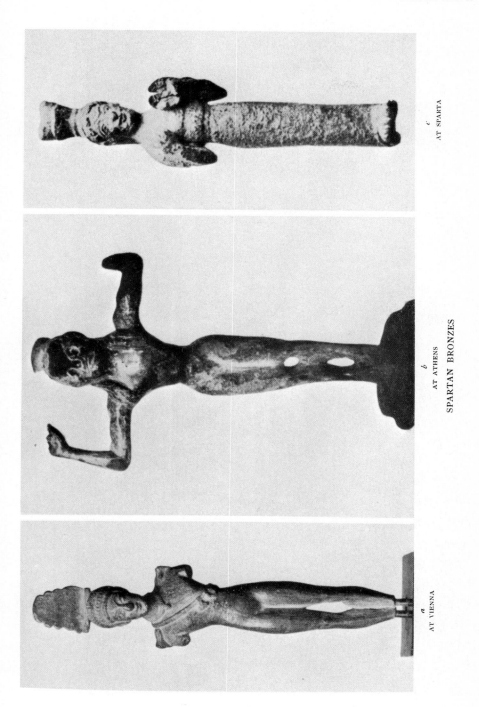

c
AT SPARTA

b
AT ATHENS
SPARTAN BRONZES

a
AT VIENNA

PLATE XXVIII

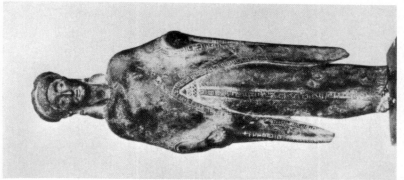

a. SOLDIER FROM LAKONIA

b. SOLDIER FROM MESSENIA

c. ZEUS FROM OLYMPIA

d. ARTEMIS FROM OLYMPIA

BRONZES AT ATHENS

PLATE XXIX

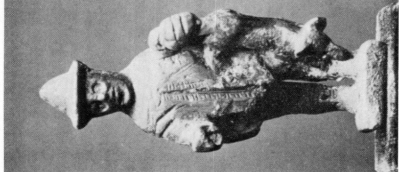

c. d. MAN WITH FOX, AT BERLIN

b. SHEPHERD AT BERLIN

a. HERMES AT ATHENS

ARCADIAN BRONZES

PLATE XXX

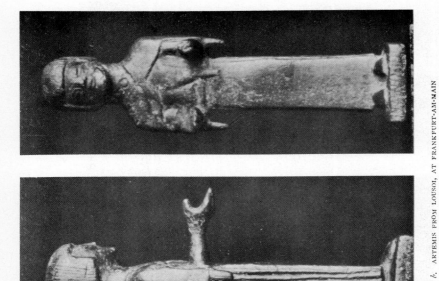

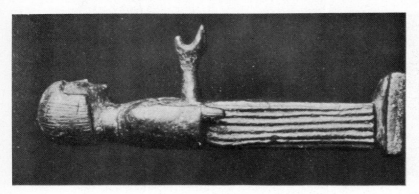

b. ARTEMIS FROM LOUSOI, AT FRANKFURT-AM-MAIN

a. GODDESS FROM TEGEA, AT ATHENS

ARCADIAN BRONZES

PLATE XXXI

a. SHEPHERD AT ATHENS   b. PEASANT AT BERLIN   c. PEASANT AT ATHENS   d. DEAD FOX AT ATHENS

ARCADIAN BRONZES

PLATE XXXII

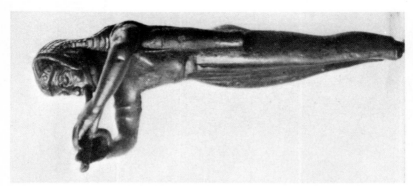

c. FLUTE PLAYER FROM DODONA
AT ATHENS

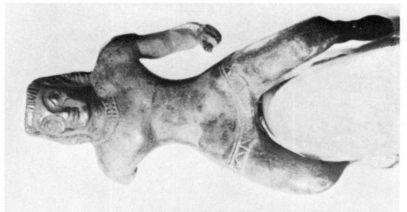

b. RIDER FROM DODONA
AT ATHENS

a. STATUETTE BY HYBRISSTAS
IN THE DUTUIT COLLECTION

PLATE XXXIII

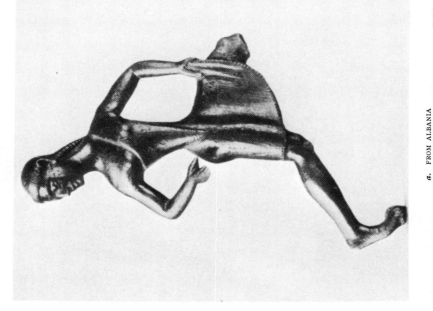

b. FROM DODONA

GIRL ATHLETES

a. FROM ALBANIA

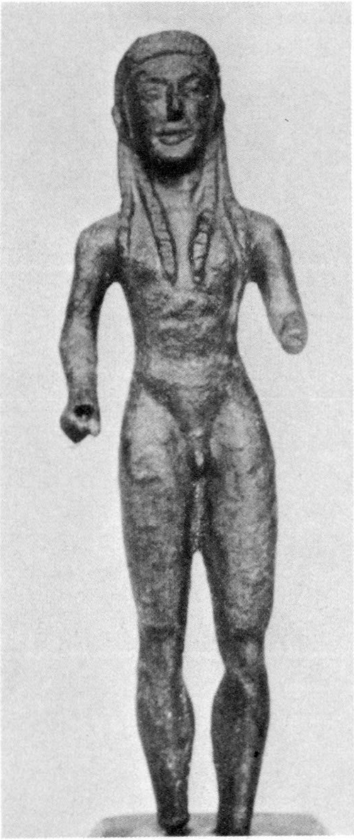

PLATE XXXIV

a. FROM LONGA, AT ATHENS    *b.* FROM THE PTOON, AT ATHENS 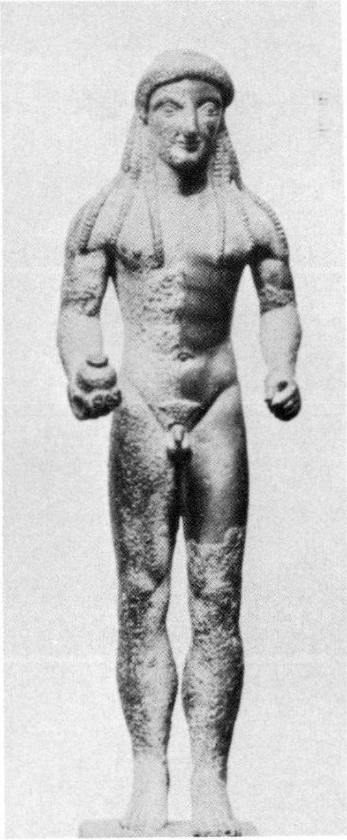   *c.* FROM NAXOS, AT BERLIN 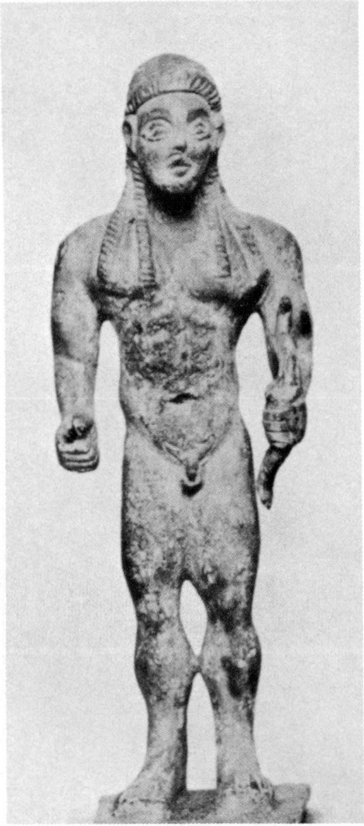   *d.* FROM DODONA, IN THE LOUVRE

KOUROI

PLATE XXXV

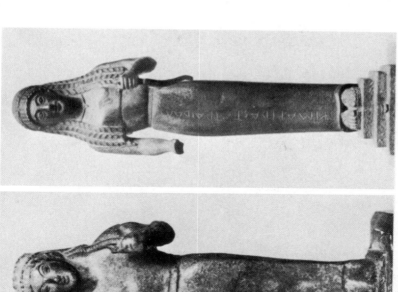

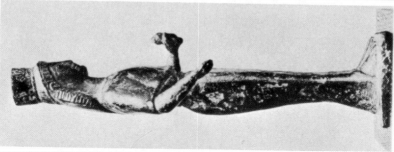

b. ARTEMIS DAIDALEIA,
AT BOSTON

c. FEMALE FIGURE FROM THE
PTOON
AT ATHENS

a, b. GODDESS
IN THE FITZWILLIAM MUSEUM

PLATE XXXVI

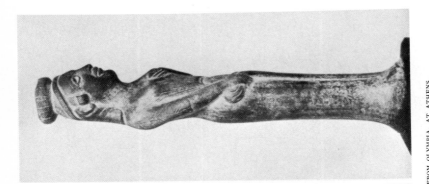

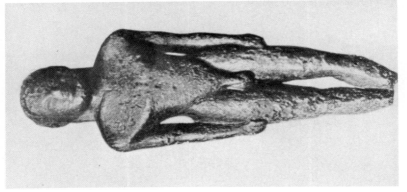

a. KOUROS AT DELPHI

b. KORE FROM THE ACROPOLIS, AT ATHENS

c. FEMALE FIGURE FROM OLYMPIA, AT ATHENS

IONIAN BRONZES

PLATE XXXVII

a. ATHENA   *b.* KORE   *c.* KOUROS

ATHENIAN BRONZES

PLATE XXXVIII

a. PEGASUS, FROM THE ACROPOLIS
AT ATHENS

b. HORSE FROM DODONA
IN THE LOUVRE

PLATE XXXIX

a. CENTAUR FROM THE ACROPOLIS
IN THE BIBLIOTHÈQUE NATIONALE

b. HORSEMAN FROM GRUMENTUM
IN THE BRITISH MUSEUM

PLATE XL

c. HERAKLES AT ESTE

b. YOUTH IN THE BRITISH MUSEUM

ETRUSCAN BRONZES

a. PRIEST (?) AT FLORENCE

PLATE XLI

c

FEMALE FIGURE FROM PERUGIA, IN THE
BRITISH MUSEUM

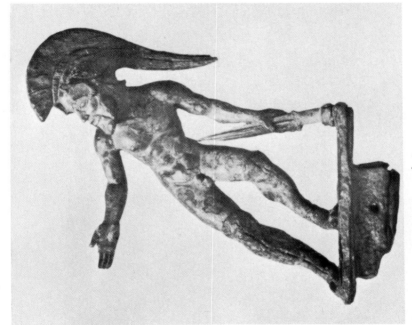

b

AJAX STABBING HIMSELF, AT FLORENCE

ETRUSCAN BRONZES

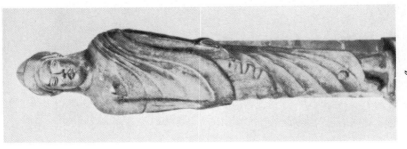

a

FEMALE FIGURE IN THE BIBLIOTHÈQUE
NATIONALE

PLATE XLII

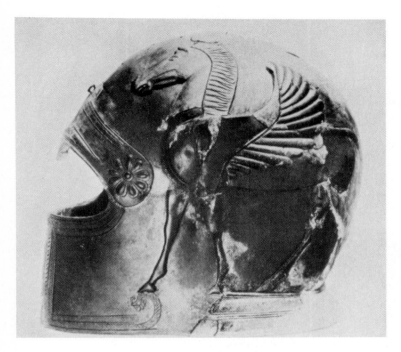

a. HELMET FROM AXOS
AT CANDIA

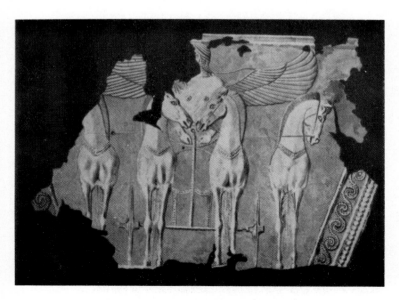

b. RELIEF FROM THE ACROPOLIS

PLATE XLIII

a. ARCHER FROM OLYMPIA
AT ATHENS

b. DETAIL OF HYDRIA
AT MUNICH

PLATE XLIV

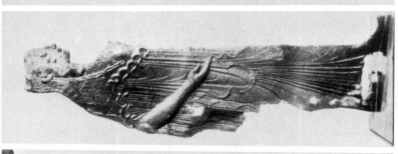

d. PATERA HANDLE
AT CAMBRIDGE

c. MIRROR HANDLE
AT BERLIN

b. ATHENA FROM THE
ACROPOLIS
AT ATHENS

a. MIRROR HANDLE
IN THE LOUVRE

PLATE XLV

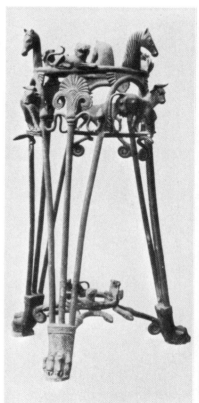 

a. TRIPOD FROM METAPONTO,
AT BERLIN

b. TRIPOD FROM VULCI
IN THE BRITISH MUSEUM

PLATE XLVI

b. HYDRIA FROM RANDAZZO

AT BERLIN

a. JUG FROM CORINTH

AT ATHENS

PLATE XLVII

b. PLATE
AT BERLIN

a. CRATER
AT MUNICH

PLATE XLVIII

b. THE GRÄCHWYL HYDRIA
AT BERNE

a. VASE FROM CAPUA
IN THE BRITISH MUSEUM

PLATE XLIX

b. VASE FROM CAPODIMONTE. AT FLORENCE
c. RELIEF AT MUNICH

a. THE MONTELONE CHARIOT
AT NEW YORK

PLATE L

RELIEF FROM TRIPOD
IN THE LOEB COLLECTION

PLATE LI

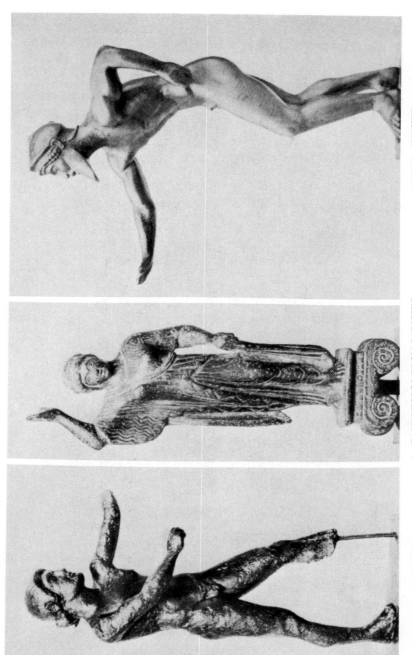

c. ARMED RUNNER
AT TÜBINGEN

b. KANEPHOROS FROM PAESTUM
AT BERLIN

a. APOLLO
AT DELPHI

PLATE LII

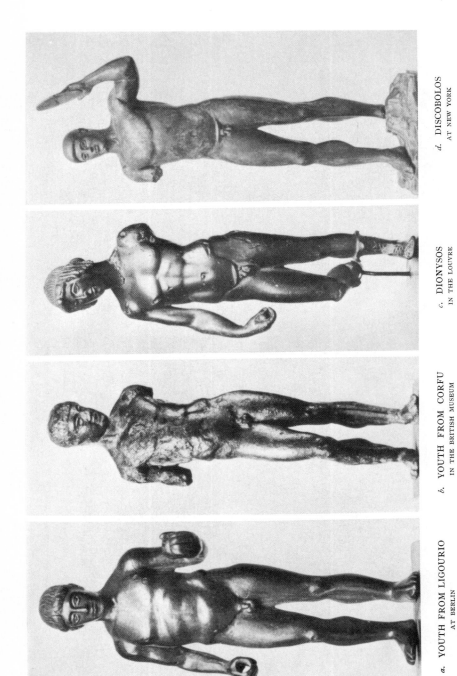

a. YOUTH FROM LIGOURIO
AT BERLIN

b. YOUTH FROM CORFU
IN THE BRITISH MUSEUM

c. DIONYSOS
IN THE LOUVRE

d. DISCOBOLOS
AT NEW YORK

PLATE LIII

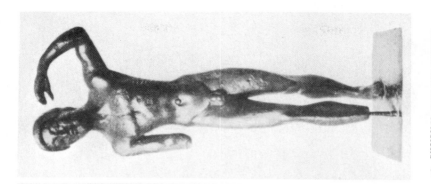

c. DISCOBOLOS, FROM THE ACROPOLIS

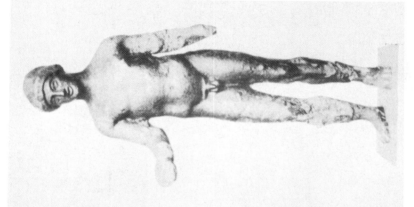

b. ATHLETE IN THE LOUVRE

ATHENIAN BRONZES

a. WOMAN DANCING, FROM THE ACROPOLIS

PLATE LIV

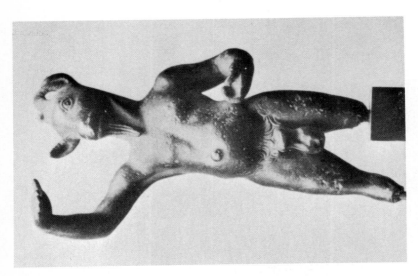

b. PAN FROM ARCADIA

a. ZEUS, FROM DODONA

BRONZES AT BERLIN

PLATE LV

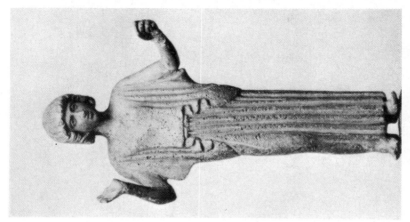

b. GIRL SPINNING

a. GIRL WITH DOVE FROM THESSALY

PLATE LVI

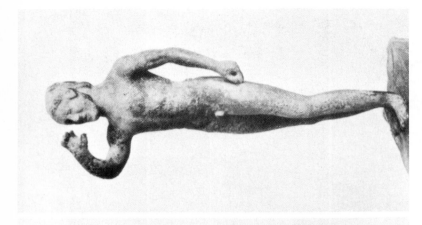

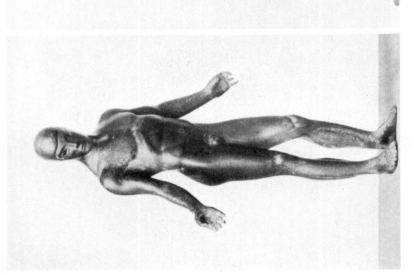

c. TRUMPETER
FROM SPARTA

b. ATHLETE
AT NEW YORK

a. ATHLETE
FROM ADERNO

SOUTH ITALIAN AND SPARTAN BRONZES

PLATE LVII

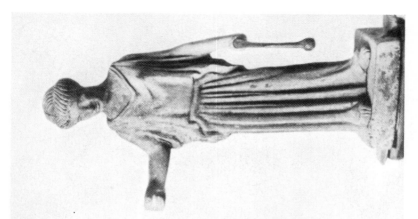

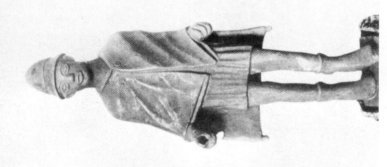

c. ARTEMIS AT ATHENS

b. HERMES AT ATHENS

ARCADIAN BRONZES

a. ARTEMIS AT BERLIN

PLATE LVIII

HYDRIA
IN THE BRITISH MUSEUM

PLATE LIX

AMPHORA
IN THE VATICAN

JUG WITH ARGIVE INSCRIPTION
AT NEW YORK

PLATE LX

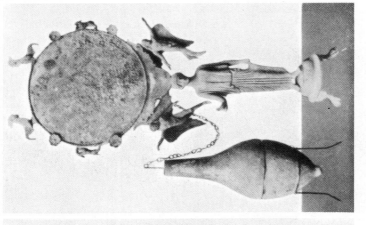

c. MIRROR AND SCENT-BOTTLE
IN THE LOUVRE

b. MIRROR
AT ATHENS

a. MIRROR
IN THE LOUVRE

PLATE LX

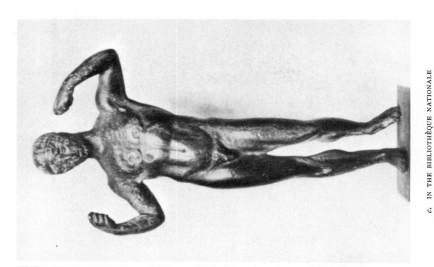

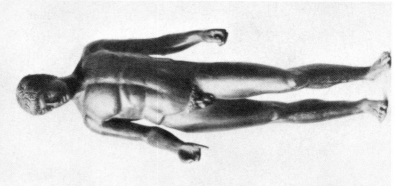

c. IN THE BIBLIOTHÈQUE NATIONALE

b. IN THE LOUVRE
BRONZES AFTER POLYKLEITOS

a. IN THE LOUVRE

PLATE LXII

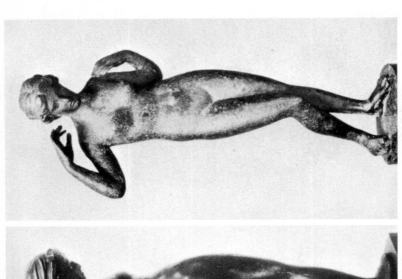

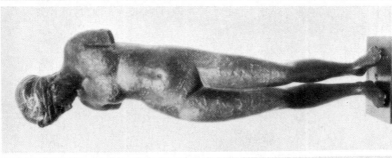

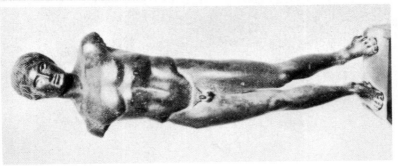

a. POLYKLEITAN ATHLETE
AT ATHENS

b. BATHING GIRL,
AT MUNICH

c. BATHING GIRL,
AT MUNICH

d. APHRODITE
IN THE BRITISH MUSEUM

PLATE LXIII

c. POSEIDON FROM DODONA
AT BERLIN

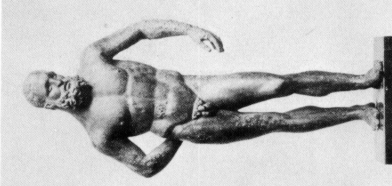

b. HERAKLES
AT BERLIN

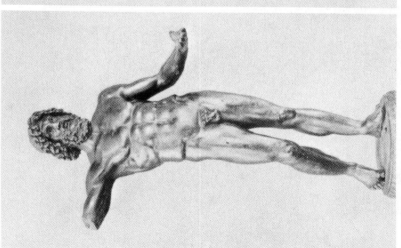

a. ZEUS FROM PARAMYTHIA
IN THE BRITISH MUSEUM

PLATE LXIV

a. RESTING MAENAD
AT BERLIN

b. RELIEF FROM LAKE BRACCIANO
IN THE BRITISH MUSEUM

PLATE LXV

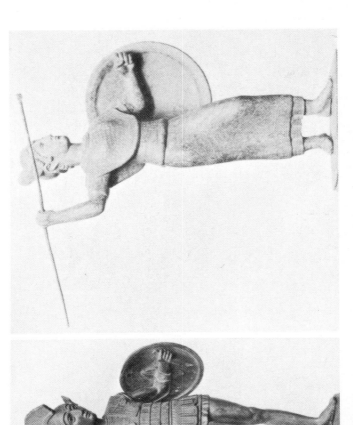

ETRUSCAN BRONZES

b. FIFTH CENTURY MARS AT FLORENCE

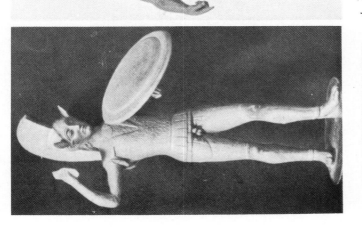

a. FOURTH CENTURY MARS IN THE BRITISH
MUSEUM

PLATE LXVI

a. FIGURES FROM LID OF FICORONI CISTA

b. ETRUSCAN WOMAN
IN THE BRITISH MUSEUM

PLATE LXVII

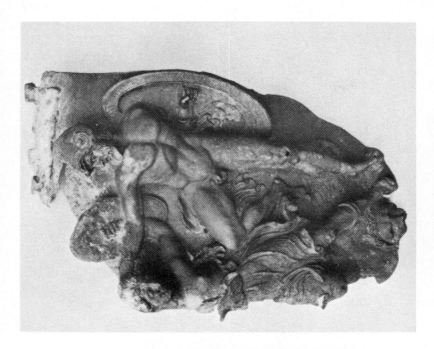

b. ONE OF THE SIRIS BRONZES
IN THE BRITISH MUSEUM

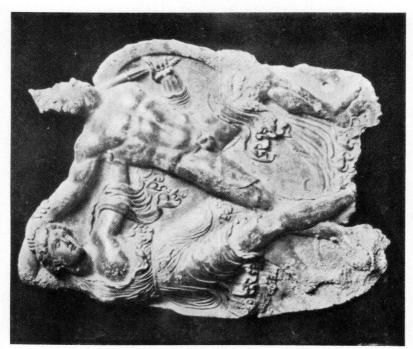

a. RELIEF FROM PALESTRINA
IN THE VILLA GUILIA

PLATE LXVIII

a

b

c

MIRRORS FROM VONITZA
AT NEW YORK

PLATE LXIX

a. MIRROR WITH PANS QUARRELLING
AT NEW YORK

b. ENGRAVED MIRROR-COVER
IN THE BRITISH MUSEUM

PLATE LXX

a. SOUTH ITALIAN MIRROR

b. MEDALLIONS FROM HARNESS

PLATE LXXI

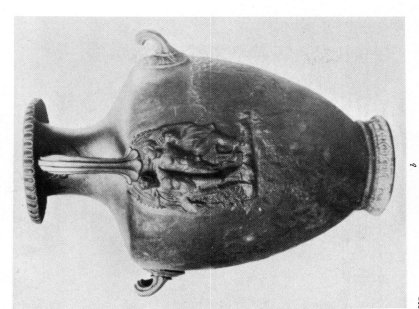

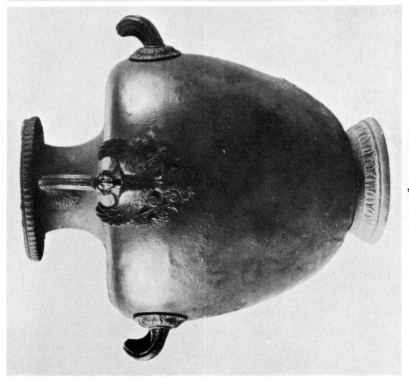

b

a

HYDRIAE AT ATHENS

PLATE LXXII

RELIEFS FROM THE PERSEUS PAIL, AT BERLIN

PLATE LXXIII

b. ITALIAN HYDRIA
AT NAPLES

a. PAIL
AT BERLIN

PLATE LXXIV

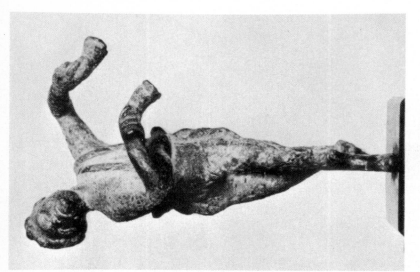

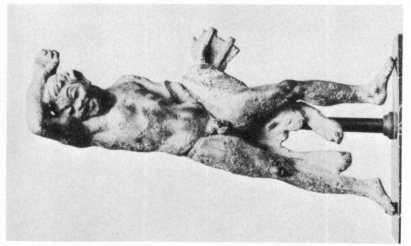

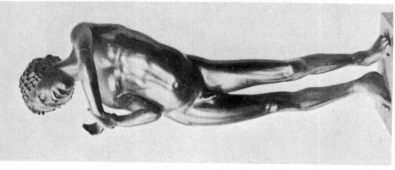

c. DANCER
AT MUNICH

b. SATYR FROM PERGAMON
AT BERLIN

a. NEGRO MINSTREL
IN THE BIBLIOTHÈQUE NATIONALE

PLATE LXXV

b. GAUL FROM TALAMONE
AT FLORENCE

a. GAULISH SLINGER
AT BERLIN

PLATE LXXVI

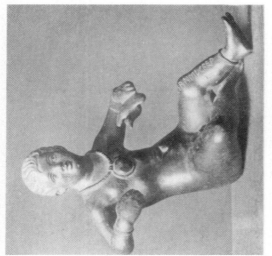

c. ETRUSCAN CHILD
IN THE VATICAN

b. BARBARIAN
IN THE LOUVRE

a. LITTLE GIRL WITH PUPPY
AT NEW YORK

PLATE LXXVII

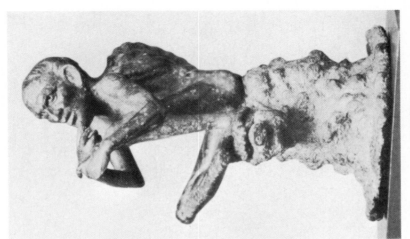

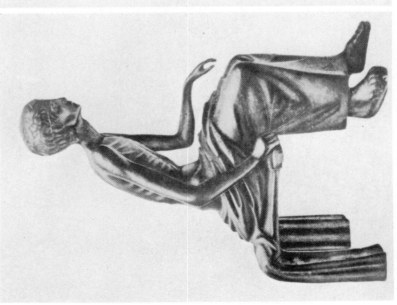

c. BEGGAR
AT BERLIN

b. GROTESQUE
AT NEW YORK

a. SICK MAN
FROM THE WYNDHAM COOK COLLECTION

PLATE LXXVIII

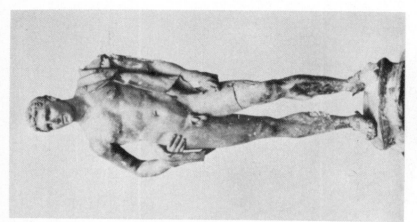

c. HELLENISTIC RULER
AT NAPLES

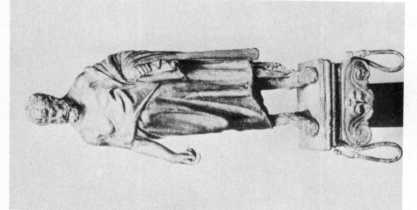

b. PHILOSOPHER
AT NEW YORK

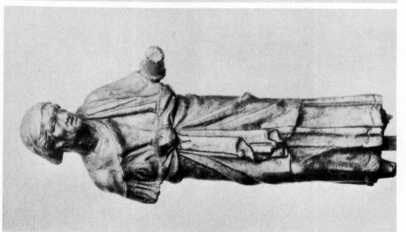

a. OLD WOMAN
AT VIENNA

PLATE LXXIX

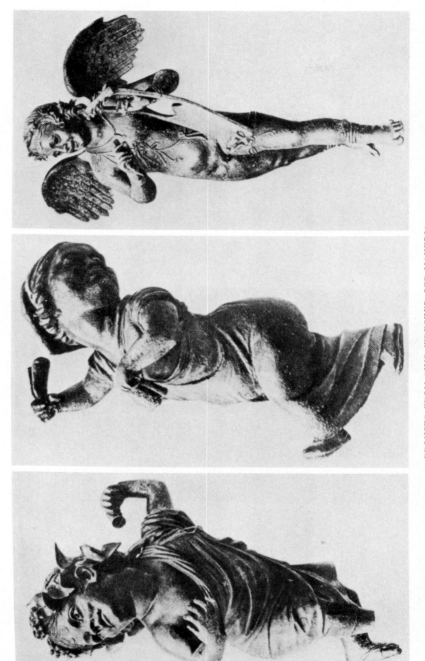

BRONZES FROM SHIP WRECKED OFF MAHEDIA

PLATE LXXX

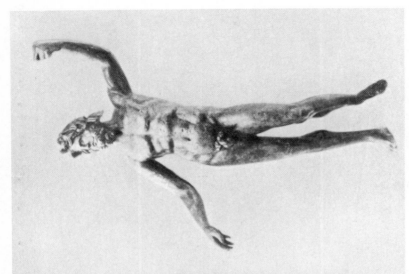

c. POSEIDON
IN LOEB COLLECTION

b. MINERVA FROM ORTE
IN THE VATICAN

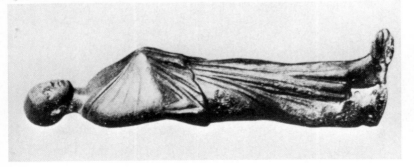

a. EGYPTIAN PRIEST

PLATE LXXXI

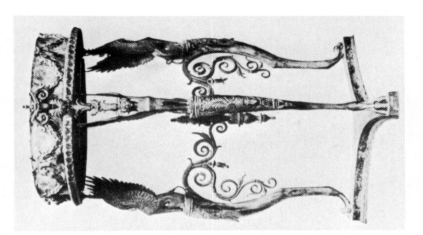

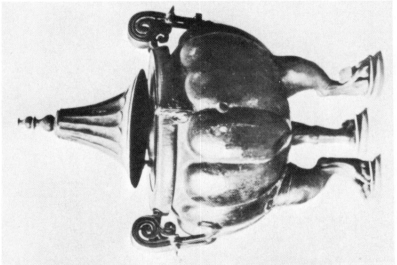

VESSELS AND TRIPOD FROM POMPEI

PLATE LXXXII

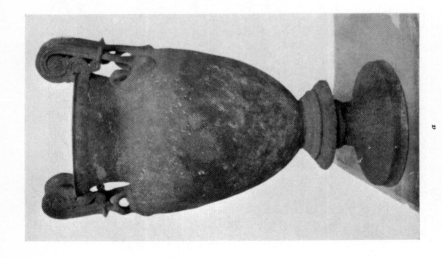

CRATERS AT NAPLES

b

a

PLATE LXXXII

a. IN THE BRITISH MUSEUM
b. AT FLORENCE

C. IN THE VATICAN

ETRUSCAN CANDELABRA

PLATE LXXXIV

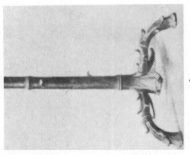

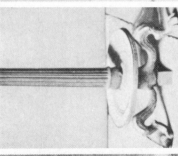

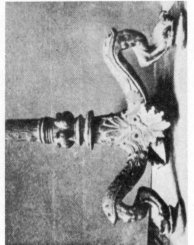

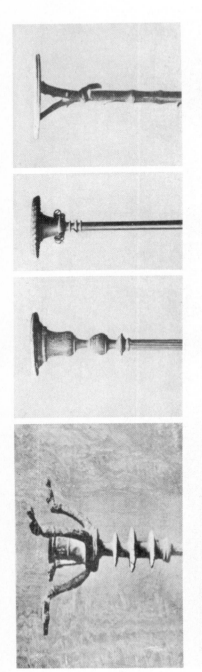

d

c

b

a

HELLENISTIC AND ROMAN CANDELABRA AT NAPLES

PLATE LXXXV

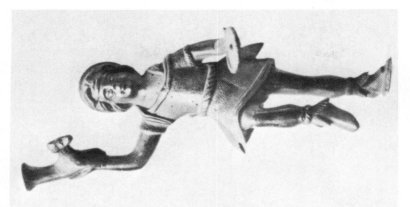

a. LAR, IN THE LOUVRE

b. ROMAN SACRIFICING, IN THE BRITISH MUSEUM

ROMAN BRONZES

c. LAR, IN THE LOUVRE

PLATE LXXXVI

c. ROMAN PRIESTESS IN THE BRITISH MUSEUM

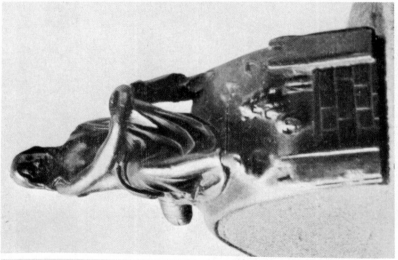

b. HANDLE WITH BARBARIAN WOMAN IN THE LOUVRE

ROMAN BRONZES

a. GAULISH PRISONER IN THE
BRITISH MUSEUM

PLATE LXXXVII

a. IN THE BRITISH MUSEUM   *b.* IN THE BIBLIOTHÈQUE NATIONALE

BRONZES AFTER POLYKLEITOS

PLATE LXXXVIII

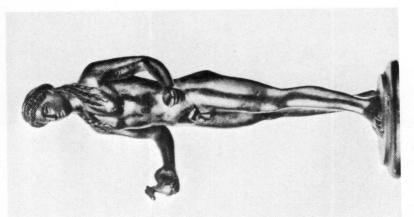

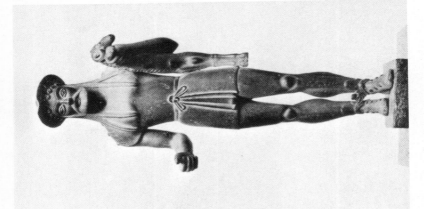

c. PAYNE KNIGHT APOLLO IN THE BRITISH MUSEUM

b. HERMES AT BOSTON

ARCHAISTIC BRONZES

a. KORE IN THE BRITISH MUSEUM

PLATE LXXXIX

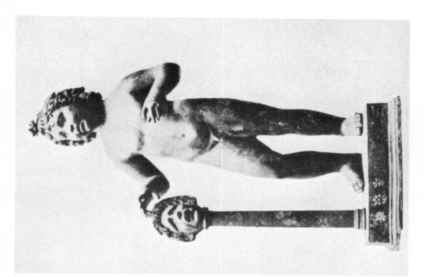

c. CUPID
FROM HERCULANEUM

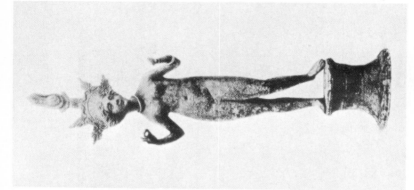

b. VENUS OF SYRIAN TYPE

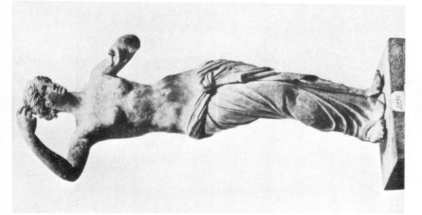

a. VENUS
FROM NOCERA

PLATE XC

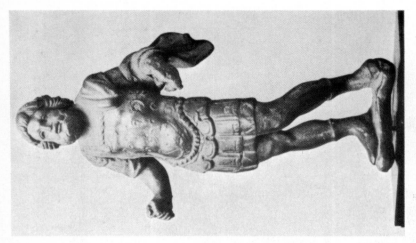

b. JUPITER DOLICHENUS FROM LICHTENBERG
AT BERLIN

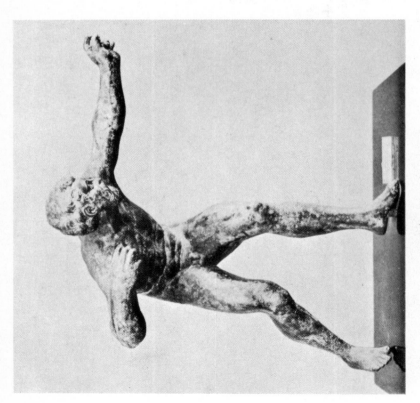

a. ARCHER FROM LONDON
IN THE BRITISH MUSEUM

PLATE XCI

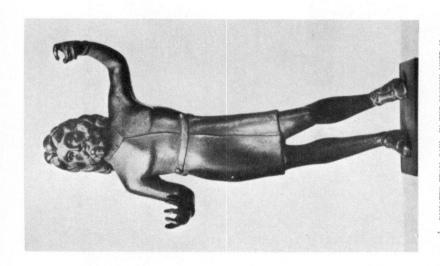

b. DISPATER FROM GAUL, IN THE BRITISH MUSEUM

a. DIANA FROM SCHEIBBS, AT VIENNA

PROVINCIAL BRONZES

PLATE XCII

THE GODDESS ARTIO AND BEAR
AT BERNE

PLATE XCIII

INLAID COUCH IN THE CONSERVATORI

PLATE XCIV

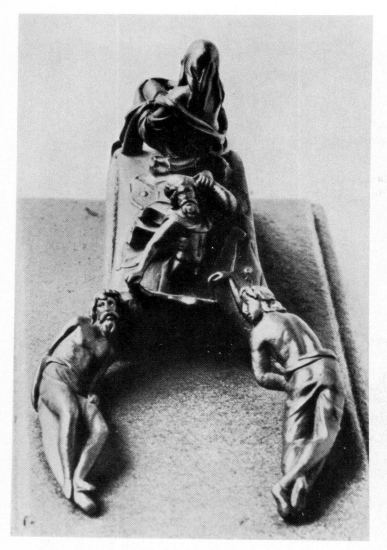

HANDLE WITH CAPTIVE BARBARIANS
IN THE LOUVRE

PLATE XCV

b. PAIL FROM POMPEI
AT NAPLES

a. CRATER FROM BOSCOREALE
AT BERLIN

PLATE XCVI

a. JUG FROM POMPEII   *b.* PAIL FROM GERMANY

c. CRATER FROM POMPEII   *a.* JUG
IN THE BIBLIOTHÈQUE NATIONALE